Shift + Function Keys	Use
Shift-F1	Display the Help index.
Shift-F2	Display the calculator.
Shift-F3	Enter historical data in customer, vendor, and product records.
Shift-F5	Enter alternative addresses for the company, customer, or vendor.
	Enter assembly components in a product record.
Shift-F6	Delete a transaction line item.
Shift-F7	Print a summary in check reconciliation.
Shift-F9	Sort records in the lookup window by code or name.

Keyboard Keys	Use
Alt	Select the Main menu item when the highlighted letter is pressed simultaneously.
Arrow-Left/Right (←/→)	Move the cursor horizontally without deleting characters.
Arrow-Up/Down (↑/↓)	Move the cursor vertically in a list or to the previous/next field on a screen without deleting characters.
Backspace	Delete the character to the left of the cursor and move the cursor and all remaining characters one position left.
End	Move the cursor to the last option on a menu or to the last field on a screen. Display the right side of a report or lookup window being viewed on screen.
Enter (↵)	Select the highlighted option on a lookup screen.
Esc	Exit the function without saving data just entered.
Home	Move the cursor to the first option on a menu or to the first field on a screen. Display the left side of a report or lookup window being viewed on screen.
Ins	Insert text between existing characters in a field.
NumLock	Toggle the 10-key pad keys between numeric entry and cursor movement.
Spacebar	Delete the character to the right of the cursor and move the cursor one position right. Insert blank spaces when Ins is on.

Computer users are not all alike.
Neither are SYBEX books.

We know our customers have a variety of needs. They've told us so. And because we've listened, we've developed several distinct types of books to meet the needs of each of our customers. What are you looking for in computer help?

If you're looking for the basics, try the **ABC's** series. You'll find short, unintimidating tutorials and helpful illustrations. For a more visual approach, select **Teach Yourself**, featuring screen-by-screen illustrations of how to use your latest software purchase.

Mastering and **Understanding** titles offer you a step-by-step introduction, plus an in-depth examination of intermediate-level features, to use as you progress.

Our **Up & Running** series is designed for computer-literate consumers who want a no-nonsense overview of new programs. Just 20 basic lessons, and you're on your way.

We also publish two types of reference books. Our **Instant References** provide quick access to each of a program's commands and functions. SYBEX **Encyclopedias** provide a *comprehensive reference* and explanation of all of the commands, features and functions of the subject software.

Sometimes a subject requires a special treatment that our standard series doesn't provide. So you'll find we have titles like **Advanced Techniques, Handbooks, Tips & Tricks**, and others that are specifically tailored to satisfy a unique need.

We carefully select our authors for their in-depth understanding of the software they're writing about, as well as their ability to write clearly and communicate effectively. Each manuscript is thoroughly reviewed by our technical staff to ensure its complete accuracy. Our production department makes sure it's easy to use. All of this adds up to the highest quality books available, consistently appearing on best-seller charts worldwide.

You'll find SYBEX publishes a variety of books on every popular software package. Looking for computer help? Help Yourself to SYBEX.

For a complete catalog of our publications:

SYBEX Inc.
2021 Challenger Drive, Alameda, CA 94501
Tel: (415) 523-8233/(800) 227-2346 Telex: 336311
SYBEX Fax: (415) 523-2373

SYBEX is committed to using natural resources wisely to preserve and improve our environment. As a leader in the computer book publishing industry, we are aware that over 40% of America's solid waste is paper. This is why we have been printing the text of books like this one on recycled paper since 1982.

This year our use of recycled paper will result in the saving of more than 15,300 trees. We will lower air pollution effluents by 54,000 pounds, save 6,300,000 gallons of water, and reduce landfill by 2,700 cubic yards.

In choosing a SYBEX book you are not only making a choice for the best in skills and information, you are also choosing to enhance the quality of life for all of us.

Mastering Dac Easy Accounting

Mastering DacEasy™ Accounting

Third Edition

Darleen Hartley Yourzek

San Francisco • Paris • Düsseldorf • London

Acquisitions Editor: Dianne King
Editors: Kathleen Lattinville, Marilyn Smith
Assistant Editor: Barbara Dahl
Technical Editor: Maryann Brown
Word Processors: Ann Dunn, Susan Trybull
Book Designer: Julie Bilski
Chapter Art and Layout: Charlotte Carter
Screen Graphics: Cuong Le
Typesetter: Stephanie Hollier
Proofreader: Lisa Haden
Indexer: Ruthanne Lowe
Cover Designer: Ingalls + Associates
Cover Photographer: Michael Lamotte
Screen reproductions produced by XenoFont.

Library of Congress Card Number: 91-65798
ISBN: 0-89588-876-9
Manufactured in the United States of America
10 9 8 7 6 5 4 3 2 1

To all who have motivated, taught, inspired, helped, and put up with me.

Acknowledgments

Thanks to SYBEX. It goes without saying that their team, listed on the back of the title page, contributes more time and effort to the production of a book than its author.

A special thanks, again, to the staff at Dac Software, Inc. for their help, enthusiasm, and friendliness.

Contents at a Glance

Table of Contents

Foreword

Since its introduction to the software market in 1985, DacEasy Accounting has become recognized as the value leader for small to medium-sized businesses. Combining power, flexibility, and ease of use, DacEasy Accounting, DacEasy Payroll, and DacEasy Graph+Mate provide solutions for management needs.

Mastering DacEasy Accounting, by Darleen Yourzek, is a hands-on guide for users of Dac programs. The book gives excellent, practical examples of accounting transactions and takes the user step by step through the processes.

I hope you enjoy *Mastering DacEasy Accounting*, and I especially want to thank you for placing your confidence in our software products!

Kevin Howe
President
Dac Software, Inc.

Introduction

THE FOCUS OF THIS BOOK IS DACEASY ACCOUNTING, a software product offered by Dac Software, Inc., to help you manage the financial data in your business. We also discuss DacEasy Payroll, another Dac Software program, which handles payroll data. Our purpose is to help you use these powerful products effectively.

ADVANTAGES OF DACEASY ACCOUNTING

DacEasy Accounting offers many advantages. Foremost, its price is outstanding, and the software is comprehensive and not difficult to use. Minimal accounting knowledge is required because DacEasy automates most of the bookkeeping procedures. The data-entry screen prompts are very clear, and on-line help is available. The program handles most of your mathematical tasks, such as extending amounts on invoices and calculating the discounts and taxes based on percentages in your files. After you set up your payroll data, the program calculates your employee's gross earnings, applicable taxes, and net pay.

The program stores three years of data, which facilitates in-depth, comparative reporting. In addition to the program's standard reports, you can create custom reports in both the accounting and payroll programs. By using passwords, you can restrict access to confidential financial information while allowing clerks to enter daily transactions.

You can record budgets for general ledger accounts. DacEasy forecasting uses historical data from your records to project activity and dollar amounts for the next year. You can make forecasts for accounts receivable, accounts payable, and inventory and services. Your forecast shows variances from the projection.

DacEasy Accounting is designed primarily for a product-oriented business, tracking products from the purchase-order stage to costing through sale and inventory maintenance. There are several features included in the package that a service-oriented company will not need, but they do not interfere with the operation of the product. A new feature in version 4.1 allows manufacturers to assemble products (finished goods) from components in their inventory.

WHO SHOULD READ THIS BOOK

Mastering DacEasy Accounting is for users who are venturing into automated accounting for the first time, as well as those who have used accounting programs. This book is written with the beginner in mind, but it also includes information about advanced features, such as customizing reports. A novice who has limited accounting experience or whose closest contact with a computer has been a typewriter keyboard will progress through the book and be ready when we discuss special features.

THE ACCOUNTANT'S ROLE

Often, people sneak out and buy a computer accounting package without telling their accountant. They mistakenly think an accountant will discourage them because he will "lose a customer." Nothing could be farther from the truth. When you start using an accounting package, it removes the burden of record keeping from your accountant's shoulders. The accountant becomes free to do what he does best—accounting!

So seek your accountant's advice when you make the transition to your own automated accounting system. From the start, an accountant can help you structure the chart of accounts to your specific business needs. Your accountant can suggest the best cost center and product-costing method for your purposes. Don't forget to ask about state and federal regulations. Finally, look to your accountant for income tax preparation and financial counseling based on the comprehensive and well-organized information you can bring from your DacEasy system.

SYSTEM REQUIREMENTS

Dac software recognized the growing sophistication of DacEasy users and released version 4.1 for hard disk users only.

You can run DacEasy Accounting version 4.1 on an IBM PC/AT, PC/XT, PS/2, or compatible computer, operating under PC-DOS or MS-DOS, version 3.0 or higher. Your system must have at least 640 kilobytes (K) of random-access memory (RAM), one 360K floppy disk drive, and a hard disk drive. Also many DacEasy functions send information directly to the printer, so you should have a printer capable of printing 132 columns in compressed mode.

The minimum requirements for version 3.1 are an IBM/PC, AT, XT, or PS/2 with 256K RAM and two 360K floppy disk drives, running under DOS version 2.0. You will need 512K RAM to run Graph+Mate.

USING THIS GUIDE

This book is written primarily for DacEasy Accounting version 4.1, but it includes notations and subsections about version 3.1. The chapter on DacEasy Payroll also focuses on version 4.1, with 3.1 notes and subsections.

Three different notes appear in the book margin:

3.1 Information pertaining to version 3.1 and the location of an option on the older menus are marked by this icon.

* Instructions for selecting a menu option in version 4.1 are marked by this icon.

Other noteworthy information appears in the margin next to this icon.

WHAT THIS BOOK COVERS

This guide covers preparing your data for conversion to DacEasy Accounting, installing the application on your computer, setting up your program, processing your work, and printing reports. The instructions in this book for setup and processing follow the sequence of logical operation. The last chapter introduces DacEasy Payroll.

The appendices should not be overlooked. In fact, you should read them before you set up your program. They contain helpful information and reference materials. Appendix A covers installing all the products discussed in this book. Appendix B contains instructions for upgrading your accounting program from an earlier version. The short refresher in accounting terms in Appendix C will help you understand the terminology and examples used throughout the book. Appendix D guides version 3.1 users through designing financial reports, and Appendix E covers the use of Graph+Mate with version 3.1.

DACEASY MODULES

DacEasy has seven modules that can be integrated to form a complete accounting system. You integrate data by telling DacEasy which accounts in the general ledger are to receive transactions from each module. These are designated in the general ledger interface table. The modules are as follows:

- The Purchase Order module tracks merchandise ordered, received, and returned. When merchandise is received, an invoice is created in the vendor's record.
- The Accounts Payable module pertains to the day-to-day debts you incur with your vendors and payments to them. It works in conjunction with the Purchase Order module.
- The Billing module in DacEasy actually refers to sales activities. You handle sales, customer invoicing, and sales returns through the Billing module. (Don't confuse this with the process of billing your customers after they have become an account receivable.)
- The Accounts Receivable module pertains to the amounts your customers owe you and payments you receive from them. It works in conjunction with the Billing module, which creates an invoice in the customer record when you record a sale. Cash sales create a paid invoice in your customer record.

- The Inventory module helps you maintain pricing on products, take a physical inventory of products on your shelves, and make resulting adjustments to your book inventory.
- The General Ledger module receives information from the other modules. You also make direct entries of transactions that do not pertain to activities in the other modules. The general ledger summarizes all activity and provides a picture of the financial state of your business.
- The new Cash module has been conceived by Dac Software as a means of entering cash receipts and generating checks. These functions are primarily a part of the accounts receivable and accounts payable process.

The book explains how to process your transactions in each module.

NOTES FROM THE AUTHOR

As an author, my responsibility is to the reader. However, a book of this nature cannot be well written without interaction between the author and the software developer. When I wrote the original *Mastering DacEasy Accounting*, and as this revision took shape, I found the staff at Dac Software to be helpful, responsive, and concerned.

Although DacEasy Accounting version 4.0 was a product released before its time, Dac Software quickly delivered a quality product to users in version 4.1.

If you purchased version 4.0 in late 1989 or early 1990 and sent in the registration card, you should have received a free upgrade from version 4.0 to version 4.1 from Dac Software. To receive the newsletter of software updates, you must be a registered user, so I recommend that you complete and mail your product registration card before you even install the software.

Upgrades from 4.0 to 4.1 have a new serial number. You must reregister with Dac Software to be eligible for customer support and future upgrades.

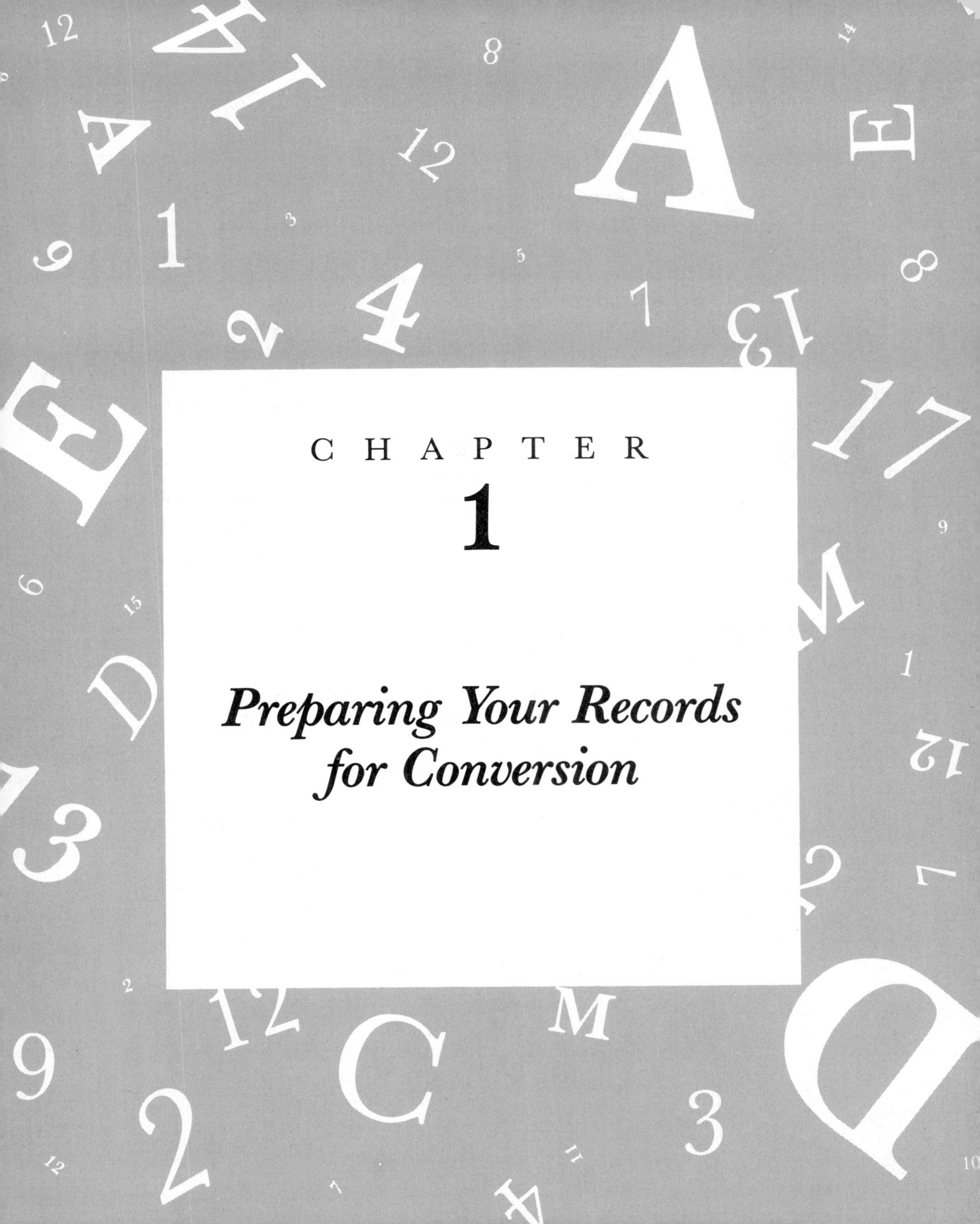

CHAPTER 1

Preparing Your Records for Conversion

THE HARDEST PART OF ANY NEW PROJECT IS STARTing it. Fortunately, DacEasy Accounting has half the work already done for you. It supplies the design, the file structure, and the record format for your information. All you have to do is enter basic information and historical data for each record, and then you're ready to go. You just have to fill in the blanks, so to speak.

Realistically, the development of any bookkeeping system takes time and effort. Whether you use a manual method known as a pegboard or one-write system, or the shoebox technique, in the final analysis, there has to be some rhyme and reason to the structure. If not, the result is chaos and, most likely, eventual bankruptcy. So, you're embarking on this adventure in automated record keeping to increase your chances for business success.

Those of you who have been using a structured method of keeping books up to this point have a running start, but everyone will catch up soon. So let's begin.

CONVERTING FROM YOUR OLD RECORD KEEPING SYSTEM

These instructions are for people who have not been using DacEasy. If you are converting from an earlier version of DacEasy Accounting, refer instead to Appendix B.

Before you convert to a new system, you must get your current accounting system in order. The summary below is provided to guide you in organizing your approach to the tasks at hand. It is an overview, and some of the points may not apply to your accounting system.

Generally, you must complete the following tasks to begin the transition to DacEasy:

1. Record all activity to date.
2. Total your customer accounts.
3. Total your vendor accounts.
4. Count and value your inventory.
5. List and value your assets.
6. Run a trial balance.

7. Adjust the appropriate general ledger accounts, for example inventory, depreciation, prepaid expenses, and accrued expenses.
8. Balance and close your present books.
9. Run or create an income statement and balance sheet.

After you create the appropriate records and enter the balances for your chart of accounts, customers, vendors, and products in DacEasy, you will run listings and financial statements to compare them to the figures your current system generates.

The following sections guide you through each task, whether or not you already have a formal set of books. If you are treading on unfamiliar territory or just need to refresh your memory, refer to Appendix C for basic accounting information.

RECORDING ALL ACTIVITY

Post all activity for the current accounting period. This step applies mostly to users of a standard bookkeeping method. It means completing all paperwork for the month.

For shoeboxers, it simply means making sure that you've opened all your mail, written down all your sales, deposited all your payments, written all the checks, and paid all the bills you are going to this month. In other words, bring all your activities up to date.

3.1 When preparing your records to convert from your old system, you will have to designate how many records you have so DacEasy can size your files. List and total your number of active and inactive customers, active and inactive vendors, and how many stockkeeping numbers you have.

TOTALING YOUR CUSTOMER ACCOUNTS

Balance each customer account and total the entire outstanding receivables amount. This means verifying that all the totals on your customer records add up to the total in your receivables account. If they don't, find the reason for the discrepancy and correct it.

Shoeboxers should sort the unpaid invoices into piles for each customer. Check each invoice to be sure it is correct. Add all the invoices together for each customer. Then add all the customer totals together to get a grand total for your accounts receivable amount.

TOTALING YOUR VENDOR ACCOUNTS

Balance each vendor account and total the entire outstanding payables amount. This means verifying that all the totals on your vendor records add up to the total in your payables account. If they don't, again, find the reason for the discrepancy and correct it.

Shoeboxers should sort the unpaid bills into piles for each vendor. Check each invoice for accuracy. Add all the invoices together for each vendor. Then add the vendor totals together to get the total of your accounts payable amount.

COUNTING AND VALUING YOUR INVENTORY

Take a physical inventory of your stock on hand. No matter how structured your record keeping has been, this procedure is the same. Make a list of everything you have available for sale, and then count how much you have of each item.

Valuing your inventory is fairly easy. Next to each inventory item, write down what you paid for it. If prices have fluctuated, use an average price. Multiply the purchase price times the number of items you have to arrive at a total for each item. Add all the totals together to place a value on your entire inventory.

LISTING AND VALUING YOUR ASSETS

Take a physical inventory of your fixed assets. Make a list of everything you own (or are buying on credit) and use in your business. This includes vehicles, machinery, office equipment, furniture, buildings, and property. If it is not immediately expendable in the course of business, like paper clips, it's a fixed asset.

If you have not been tracking values, you will have to establish a value for all your fixed assets. Take your list of fixed assets and assign a value to each item. A rule of thumb is to determine what you would pay for the item today if you bought it in its present condition. When valuing your assets, it's a good idea to consult an accountant about the various considerations involved in making these judgments.

List and value your *current assets,* which include the cash you have (on hand and in the bank), your accounts receivable, notes receivable, and inventory.

RUNNING A TRIAL BALANCE

Run a trial balance on your current system to determine the balance in each asset, liability, equity, expense, and income account. If you have been using a general ledger and preparing financial statements, this should be a familiar process.

If you don't already have a general ledger, you can make five major lists and break them down into categories and yet smaller subcategories, using the following procedure:

1. List your assets and group them into categories labeled Current Assets and Fixed Assets according to the definitions above. You can sort each category into subcategories, such as Cash, Receivables, Inventory, Equipment, and Vehicles.
2. List your liabilities and group them into categories labeled Short-Term Liabilities and Long-Term Liabilities. Short-term liabilities are accounts payable, some notes payable, and taxes you owe, such as sales tax, income tax, and payroll taxes. Long-term liabilities include mortgages and long-standing notes payable.
3. List your income and your expenses. The difference between income and expense amounts becomes the profit or loss that is posted to retained earnings at the end of a period.
4. List your equity, which is the difference between what you have (*assets*) and what you owe (*liabilities*). Basically, it is what the business owners have left for themselves. Equity can take the form of stock and retained earnings.

You can use the chart of accounts supplied with DacEasy to get a good idea of how detailed you want each list to be. Also, your accountant can help.

ADJUSTING GENERAL LEDGER ACCOUNTS

If you do not have a structured set of books, you can skip this step.

If you have a conventional system in place, make the necessary adjustments to your book inventory, assets, and expenses. A *book inventory* is your record of what you have in stock as opposed to the actual count of the items physically remaining on your shelves. The purpose of this step is to arrive at a true value in each of your accounts.

Bring each account up to date from a bookkeeping standpoint. Post depreciation, inventory losses, transfers from prepaid expenses, reserve for bad debts, accrued expenses, and so forth.

BALANCING AND CLOSING YOUR BOOKS

A *balance sheet* lists your assets, your liabilities, and the resulting equity. If you do not have an established set of books, create this report from data on hand. It will form the basis for the current balances in your general ledger accounts.

The listing of income, expense, and profit for the period is called an *income statement*. You might not have figures for individual income and expense accounts if you have not been using a conventional system.

Balancing your books in a conventional system means being sure your assets minus your liabilities equal your equity account.

Closing your books in a conventional system means making an entry in each income and expense account to bring the account balance to zero. The difference between the income and expense balances is your gross profit. This difference is posted to your retained earnings account as the offsetting entry to the ones that closed your income and expense accounts.

PREPARING WORKSHEETS FOR DACEASY

After your accounts are in order (you have accumulated the data discussed in the previous sections), you must define each record in detail. The process will go smoothly if you take one record type (such as customers, purchase orders, billing codes, and passwords) at a time.

Before you begin entering any data into DacEasy, you should prepare worksheets for each record. The rest of this chapter details the information you need for these worksheets. Follow the format outlined here, and just put each field name on a sheet of paper, leaving room to write in the information exactly as you will enter it in that field. Make copies of your original worksheets and fill out a worksheet for each record. When you finally sit in front of the computer, worksheets in hand, data entry will be a breeze.

The files that contain financial data are general ledger accounts, customers, vendors, products, and services. Each individual record in these files has three parts: the basic definition, the current balance, and historical information. Historical information, or statistical data, refers to summarized totals for various types of information, such as sales dollars and units sold, in specified time periods covering a three-year span. You can enter the definition, current balance, and historical information at the same time, or you can do it in stages.

You enter historical information only once during setup for activity that occurred before you converted to the DacEasy Accounting system. Thereafter, DacEasy updates this information automatically during routine processing.

If you have many records to convert and you want to get up and running on DacEasy as soon as possible, the most expedient method is to enter only the basic definition and the current balance. Then you can start processing your daily work. As time permits, you can go back and fill in the historical information. If you have only a few records, it is faster in the long run to eliminate the second pass and enter all the data at one time.

The other DacEasy files do not contain statistical data. They are designed to facilitate your operations and daily processing. Examples of such files are billing and purchase order codes, message codes, statement messages, sales tax rates, document numbers, and passwords.

As you can see, there are many files to set up to take full advantage of the features of DacEasy. The effort you put in to set everything up right in the beginning is worth the reward. You'll save time, avoid frustration, and gain the capability to make quality management decisions to ensure the good health of your business.

CODING AND SORTING CONSIDERATIONS

Because DacEasy allows both letters and numbers in codes, you can keep the coding system you now have for vendors, customers, products, and services. However, if you are creating a coding system for the first time, there are a couple of things you should consider. You want a code that you can remember and enter quickly. Because DacEasy, like most computerized accounting systems, requires you to identify all your vendors, customers, products, and services by code, this is an important matter.

In DacEasy, the code will always be converted to uppercase for consistency and ease of sorting. However, names of customers and vendors and descriptions of products and services can be in uppercase or initial capitals followed by lowercase. For example, a name could be entered as *EMMA SILVA* or *Emma Silva*.

When deciding which convention to use, consider that readability tests prove initial capital and lowercase combinations are easier to read. Whatever convention you select, the cardinal rule is: Be consistent.

Keep in mind that computers sort codes, names, and descriptions in a specific hierarchy. Blanks come first, numbers come before letters, and capital letters come before lowercase letters. For example, 456 comes before M123, and MURTON comes before Martin.

If you want to be able to sort names alphabetically, enter last names first, as in *Estes, Barbara*. The disadvantage to this is that the address on invoices, statements, and labels will print the last name first, which is not the most acceptable format for an address. Another way to be able to sort records alphabetically is to make the code alphabet characters and use it for sorting.

OTHER CODING CONSIDERATIONS IN VERSION 3.1 In version 3.1, there are only six characters possible for vendor and customer codes. You could use the first four letters of the customer or vendor name as its code. This system also creates codes that are easier to remember than numeric codes.

If more than one record begins with the same four letters, you can add a unique number at the end of the code. For example, you could enter *JONE* for Tom Jones, *JONE1* for Bill Jones, and *JONE2* for Pat Jones. This way, you can have 100 records that start with the same four letters: the original and 99 with numbers appended.

There is a problem, however, as you can see. Depending on the sequence in which you add the records, the sort by code won't be perfectly alphabetical. If you do not expect more than ten duplications of any five letters, you could use five alphabet characters and append only one number when duplicates arise. For example, you could enter *JOHAL* for Raj Johal, *JOHAN* for Eric Johansen, *JOHNS* for Tom Johnston, and *JOHNS1* for Ted Johnson. Still, you can run into a not-so-perfect alphabetical sort by code, as in this example, where Tom Johnston's record will come before Ted Johnson's.

CHOOSING A COST DISTRIBUTION CENTER

Many businesses track costs departmentally, which allows you to later analyze which department is most profitable or least productive. DacEasy is designed to track costs within departments by customer or by inventory. You can also decide not to break down your costs. However, you must choose a cost distribution method before you begin to structure your accounting system for DacEasy.

The sample chart of accounts (described below) has two departments. If you have three or more departments, you must add accounts to accommodate them. You need a sales account, a cost of goods sold account, and a sales return account for each department.

Other transactions are not broken down automatically into departments. You will have to add expense accounts for each department and manually enter those account numbers during data entry if you want to departmentalize expenses in addition to sales, cost of goods, and returns.

VALUING YOUR INVENTORY

The way that you value your inventory is important because it affects business profit calculations and taxes. There are three methods DacEasy accommodates. As with cost centers, you should decide on the method you will use before you set up your system (consult your accountant if you are unsure).

DacEasy provides three inventory cost system options:

- Last Purchase Price: Values the quantity on hand of each product at the last price you paid for it.
- Standard Cost: Values each item at an arbitrary cost you designate.

- Average Cost: Values the quantity on hand of each product at an average of the various prices you have paid over time for it.

ESTABLISHING ACCOUNTING PERIODS

Accounting periods divide your fiscal year into segments. Controlling your finances is easier when you review activity in these smaller segments rather than waiting until year-end to see the whole picture. Commonly, accounting periods coincide with the calendar year, and DacEasy defaults to those 12 periods. However, you can also define accounting periods according to a fiscal year. You can define up to 13 accounting periods in DacEasy Accounting. Your accountant can guide you in establishing accounting periods appropriate to your situation.

If you want to use different accounting periods, you must define them. Prepare a worksheet listing the number of periods, a description of each period, and each period's starting and ending dates.

CHART OF ACCOUNTS WORKSHEETS

The chart of accounts is the foundation of your accounting system. Everything that happens in your business should eventually find its way to a pigeonhole called a general ledger account. These accounts, which form your chart of accounts, summarize all your financial transactions. Your financial statements are based on the information stored in the general ledger accounts.

You can start with the full sample set of accounts supplied with the program and edit it to suit your needs, or you can create your own unique chart of accounts.

To convert your general ledger to DacEasy, you will need a hierarchical list of the accounts with their current balance. Categorize your accounts as assets, liabilities, capital, revenue, expense, other credits, or other debits. Determine the type of each account, either general or detail.

A general account in DacEasy is one that accumulates (rolls up) amounts from detail accounts or other, lower level general accounts. You cannot post directly to a general account. A detail account is one that is posted to directly during transaction processing. It is subordinate to a general account.

3.1 Version 3.1 has only five general ledger account levels instead of nine.

In your hierarchy, you must define the level of each account. Level 1 is the top level in the chart of accounts. It is reserved for general accounts and must be set up first. Levels 2 through 9 are subordinate to level 1 and to each other, in descending order. Accounts placed below the general account at level 1 are related to it.

Account numbers usually follow an outline format with the main account on top, supported by subaccounts. An example of this structure is shown below.

ACCOUNT NO.	*DESCRIPTION*	*ACCOUNT TYPE*	*LEVEL*
52	Administrative Expenses	General	1
5201	Payroll	General	2
52011	Salary, Administration	General	3
520111	Administration, Officers	Detail	4
520112	Administration, Managers	Detail	4
52012	Salary, Clerical	Detail	3
52013	Hourly	General	3
520131	Hourly, Secretarial	General	4
5201311	Secretarial, Corporate	Detail	5
5201312	Secretarial, Sales	Detail	5
520132	Hourly, Laborer	Detail	4
5202	Maintenance	General	2
52021	Autos and Trucks	Detail	3
52022	Computer Equipment	Detail	3

DacEasy allows you to bring together information from several companies through the use of a consolidated chart of accounts. The charts of accounts for the individual companies you want to consolidate do not have to be the same. We will discuss consolidation in Chapter 4. For now, leave the field titled Consolidation blank when you initially define your chart of accounts.

Your chart of accounts worksheet should include the fields and information shown in Table 1.1.

Table 1.1: Chart of Accounts Worksheet Information

Field	You Supply
Account	The general ledger account number (10 characters maximum).
Account Name	A description of the account (25 characters maximum).
Account Type	The type of account, general or detail.
Account Level	The level the account falls in: 1 through 9 possible.
General Account	The number of the general account that the account you are defining is subordinate to; for example, Cash in Bank, a detail account, is subordinate to Cash, a general account, which in turn is subordinate to another general account, Current Assets.
Account Group	Whether the account is an asset, liability, capital, revenue, expense, other debit, or other credit.
Consolidation	The account number into which this account is consolidated when adding data from two or more companies together. Only detail accounts can be consolidated.
Reconcile	Whether or not this account is to be used for a bank account in the Cash module.
Current	The balance to be used as a beginning balance when converting to DacEasy.
Account History Last Year	Account balance in each period from one year ago (12 numeric characters maximum).

Version 3.1: Only five account levels are available. The Account Group, Consolidation, and Reconcile fields do not exist. The Historical Information section includes four fields: Year Before Last, for the account balance from two years ago; Last Year, for the balance from one year ago; Current YTD, for the amount to date for this year; and Forecast at End Year, for your prediction for the current year.

BUDGET WORKSHEETS

DacEasy allows you to establish budgets for each period for each account. You can use this management tool to compare your planned expenses and income with what has actually taken place.

To prepare a budget worksheet, list your accounting periods down the side of the page, list the numbers of the accounts you want to budget across the top of the page, and enter an amount for each period. Only detail accounts can have budgets.

INTERFACE ACCOUNTS WORKSHEETS

Interface accounts tell DacEasy which accounts in the general ledger to post to for various transactions that take place in the program's subsidiary modules. This saves you from having to enter the appropriate account number for each transaction.

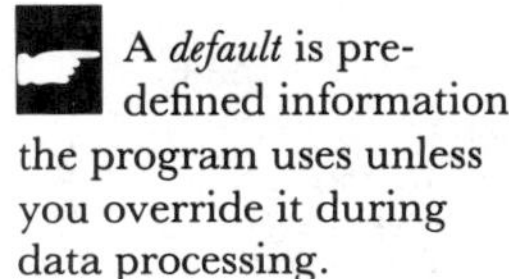

A *default* is predefined information the program uses unless you override it during data processing.

You set up these accounts in DacEasy's interface table. Enter the general ledger accounts that you want to be the default for the various account categories. Your worksheet should contain the fields and data shown in Table 1.2.

Table 1.2: Interface Accounts Worksheet Information

Field	You Supply
Distribution of Sales, Sales Returns and COGS	Select one from the following: *None*: All sales are reflected in one grand total, not by department. *Customer*: Each customer is assigned to a department. Sales figures reflect customer activity. *Inventory*: Each product and service is assigned to a department. Sales figures reflect inventory/services activity.
Banking	The general ledger cash account number for the bank used most often. This is an asset account, which becomes the default account when you write checks or receive payments. You can override it when you print checks or record customer payments. It should be a detail account.
Accounts Receivable	The account that will summarize all the transactions posted to your customer records. This is an asset account, which reflects the money that all your customers owe you. It should be a detail account.
Accounts Payable	The account that will summarize all the transactions posted to your vendor records. This is a liability account— you owe the amount of money reflected in the account to various creditors. It should be a detail account.
Inventory	The account that tracks the value of the items you have on hand to sell. This is typically an asset account. You own the inventory until it is sold. It should be a detail account.

Table 1.2: Interface Accounts Worksheet Information (continued)

Field	You Supply
Cost of Goods Sold	The account that summarizes the amount you pay for the products you resell. This is typically an expense account that is used to offset sales. The amount of your sales, less what you paid for the products you resold (the cost of goods sold) is the net profit on your sales. It must be a detail account if you do not track costs by department. It should be a general account if you departmentalize.
Sales	The account that will summarize the amount of products or services you have sold. This is typically an income account. You bring money into the business by selling your products or services. It should be a detail account if you do not track costs by department. It should be a general account if you departmentalize costs by customer or by inventory.
Sales Returns	The account that summarizes the amount of sales returns. This is typically the same account as your sales account. In practice, a return cancels the original sale. Some bookkeeping systems track sales returns in a separate expense account to analyze sales against the volume of returns. It must be a detail account if you do not track costs by department. It should be a general account if you departmentalize.
Finance Charge	The account that will summarize the finance charges you assess on past-due customer accounts. This is typically an income account. Finance charges are another way of bringing money into your business. It should be a detail account.
Sales Discounts	The account that summarizes all the discounts your customers take when they pay you early. This is treated as an expense account. In practice, it reduces the profit on a sale. Discounts vary and are tracked separately so you can analyze your sales based on the true selling price. It should be a detail account.
Purchase Discount	The account that will summarize all the discounts you take when paying vendors. This is treated as an income account. It reflects money you save by paying early. (Note that you still want to record the purchase at full price so you can track true inventory costs.)

Version 3.1: The Distribution field is called Cost Center. Two additional fields are Purchase Tax, for the detail account (typically an expense account) that will summarize all sales tax you pay on items you purchase; and Sales Tax, for the detail account (typically a liability account) that will summarize the sales tax you charge your customers.

SALES TAX RATE WORKSHEET

3.1 General ledger tax accounts are entered in the interface table instead of in the sales tax table.

The sales tax rate table can contain both the rates you charge your customers and the rates your vendors charge you. You will enter the related tax codes in your customer and vendor records, and DacEasy will know the percentage to charge on sales and purchases.

Your worksheet should contain the fields and data shown in Table 1.3.

Table 1.3: Sales Tax Rate Worksheet Information

Field	You Supply
Code	The code to identify the sales tax rate (5 alphanumeric characters maximum).
Tax Rate	The percentage to be used to calculate the tax for this code, entered in 99.999 format.
Sales Tax Account	The number of the general ledger account you use to track the sales tax collected from your customers. Typically, this is a liability account and it must be a detail account. You can use a different account per tax rate or the same account for all taxes collected.
Purchase Tax Account	The number of the general ledger account you use to track the sales tax you pay on purchases. Typically, this is an expense account, and it must be a detail account. You can use a different account per tax rate or the same account for all taxes paid.

CUSTOMER WORKSHEETS

Initially, you might want to enter only customers with an outstanding balance. You can add records for returning customers as they become active again. Basically, you will need a list of all your customers, the balance they still owe you, a list of each outstanding invoice's number and total amount, the sales tax percent you charge them, and the terms you allow them. If you don't have a record of each invoice, you can enter just the balance due.

If you sort your customer worksheets by city, you can reduce the amount of typing as you enter the information because the city, state, zip and area code, and credit limit from the previous entry remain in the respective input fields.

Table 1.4 shows the fields and data for your basic customer worksheets.

Table 1.4: Customer Worksheet Information

Field	You Supply
Code	A code that identifies this customer (10 characters maximum).
Name	The customer's name (30 characters maximum). Be consistent in the format— the placement of the last name and the case of the letters.
Contact	The name of the person responsible for this customer's account (30 characters maximum).
Address	The mailing address for invoices and statements (30 characters maximum).
City	The city where you mail invoices and statements (15 characters maximum).

Table 1.4: Customer Worksheet Information (continued)

Field	You Supply
State	The two-letter state abbreviation (3 characters maximum).
Zip	The postal zip code (9 numeric characters maximum).
Tax Id	The tax identification number for customers who have a resale license and do not pay sales tax on products you sell to them (13 characters maximum).
Phone	The customer's area code and phone number.
Fax	The customer's fax (facsimile machine) number.
Country	The country in which the customer is located.
Account Type	The customer type, either Open, Balance, or Cash. Open-item accounts keep detail on each transaction until it is offset by another entry. Balance-forward accounts remove detail after the end of the period in which the transaction occurs, leaving only a total amount due. Cash accounts do not track individual customer activity, only the sales dollars and quantities.
Price Group	The indicator of the discount this customer receives on merchandise, A, B, or C. Select None if the customer is charged full price. (Price groups are set up in the product file.)
Terms Code	The code which represents the number of discount days allowed and the number of days before the invoice is due.
Tax Code	The code from your tax table that represents the tax rate charged on sales to this customer.
Message Code	The code of any message defined in your message file that you want to display whenever there is activity on this account. (See the section about assigning message codes in this chapter.)
GL Department	The code of the general ledger department this customer's transactions are posted to (5 characters maximum). This is applicable only if you departmentalize by customer. If not, this field can be used for any purpose.
Billing Group	A user-defined code that allows invoices to be generated for all customers in the group.
Sales Person	The code for the salesperson who services this customer's account (4 characters maximum). There is no table for these codes—you must manually list any salesperson codes you create.
Finance Charge	The percent per month that you charge on past-due invoices for this customer (4 numeric characters, including 2 decimal places, maximum). For example, 1.50 is 1 percent per month, or 18 percent per year.
Credit Limit	The maximum amount you allow this customer to owe you (11 numeric characters, including 2 decimal places, maximum).

Version 3.1: The Fax, Country, Price Group, Terms Code, and Billing Group fields do not exist. The account type can be only open item or balance forward. Three additional fields are Discount %, for the percentage you allow this customer to take off the total invoice for early payment; Discount Days, for the number of days from the invoice date that the discount is available; and Due Days, for the number of days after the invoice date when payment is due. The Finance Charge field is called Monthly Interest Rate.

If you plan to enter historical information now, your worksheets should also include the following fields, with totals for two years ago, last year, and this year to date:

- Number of Invoices to Customer
- Total Dollars Billed to Customer
- Total Cost of Items Billed

Your list of outstanding invoices should include the following fields:

- Invoice Number
- Invoice Date
- Amount Balance

VENDOR WORKSHEETS

Vendors are entities who provide you with products for resale or use in your business or with services. You might want to only enter vendor accounts that have an outstanding balance at first. Basically, you will need a list of all your vendors, the balance you still owe them, a list of each outstanding invoice's number and total amount, the sales tax percent you are charged, and the terms each vendor offers you. If you don't have a record of each unpaid invoice, you can enter just the balance that you owe.

As with customer worksheets, sorting your vendor worksheets by city can make your data entry more efficient because DacEasy retains the previous entries. Table 1.5 shows the fields and data for your basic vendor worksheets.

Table 1.5: Vendor Worksheet Information

Field	**You Supply**
Code	A code that identifies this vendor (10 characters maximum).
Name	The vendor's name (30 characters maximum). Remember to be consistent in the form you use to enter vendor names, excluding or including articles such as *A* or *The*, and to use either all capital letters or initial capitals and lowercase.

Table 1.5: Vendor Worksheet Information (continued)

Field	You Supply
Contact	The name of the person in the vendor's office who handles your account (30 characters maximum).
Address	The mailing address for payments (30 characters maximum).
City	The city where you mail payments (15 characters maximum).
State	The two-letter state abbreviation (3 characters maximum).
Zip	The postal zip code (9 numeric characters maximum).
Tax Id	The vendor's federal tax identification number (13 characters maximum). This is used when you prepare 1099 forms to report payments made to this vendor.
Phone	The vendor's area code and phone number.
Fax	The vendor's fax number.
Country	The country in which the vendor is located.
Account Type	Vendor types are Open, Balance, or Cash. Open-item accounts keep detail on each transaction until it is offset by another entry (e.g., an invoice that is paid by a check), and are the best way to keep track of what you still have outstanding on your account. Balance-forward accounts remove detail after the end of the period in which the transaction occurs, leaving only a total amount due in your record. Cash accounts do not track an individual vendor's activity, only the purchase dollars and quantities.
Terms Code	The code from your terms table which represents the number of discount days allowed and the number of days before the invoice is due.
Tax Code	The code from your tax table that represents the tax rate charged on purchases from this vendor. You can override the calculated tax amount during transaction processing.
Message Code	The code of any message defined in your message file that you want to display whenever there is activity on this vendor. For example, a code for the message *Requires COD on purchases under $500.*
Territory	The code for the territory where this vendor is located (5 characters maximum). There is no table for these codes—you must manually list any territory codes that you create. Territory information can be useful if you are purchasing for several sites. You can reduce shipping time and charges by determining which vendor is closest to the location you are purchasing for.
Type	Enter 1099 if you must prepare a 1099 tax form for this vendor (5 characters maximum). This field is useful for sorting by 1099 vendors and printing 1099 reports.
Credit Limit	The maximum amount this vendor will allow you to owe him (12 numeric characters, including 2 decimal places, maximum).

Version 3.1: The Fax, Country, and Terms Code fields do not exist. The account type can be only open item or balance forward. Three additional fields are Discount %, for the percentage the vendor allows you to take off the invoice total for early payment; Discount Days, for the number of days from the invoice date that the discount is available; and Due Days, for the number of days after the invoice date when payment is due.

If you want to enter historical information now, your worksheets will need the following fields, with totals for two years ago, last year, and this year to date:

- Number of Invoices Received
- Total Dollars for Purchases

Your list of outstanding vendor invoices should include the following fields:

- Invoice Number
- Invoice Date
- Amount Balance

PRODUCT WORKSHEETS

Inventory is a combination of all the products you carry for sale. When you buy or sell a product, DacEasy adds or subtracts the quantity from your inventory count. To set up your inventory file, you need a list of all the products, their purchase and sales price, and how much stock you have on hand. You'll also need an understanding of how DacEasy defines a *product*.

Product code fields are 14 characters long, enough for a UPC (uniform product code) number or your own SKU (stockkeeping unit) number. For every sale, you will have to enter the product code, so keep your codes as simple as possible.

3.1 In the product record, *Measure* and *Fraction* both refer to the quantity in which you *sell* the product. There is no Purchase Measure or Purchase Fraction.

In your DacEasy product records, you will see the term *Measure*. This means the unit of measure for the product. The *Sales Measure* is the most common quantity in which you sell the product. The *Purchase Measure* is the quantity in which you buy it. Examples include a case of oil, a dozen eggs, a gallon of paint. If you order by the case, but sell the cans individually, enter Case in the Purchase Measure field and Each in the Sales Measure field.

Another term you need to understand is *Fraction*. This is the number of items that make up the unit of measure. The sales measure is the smallest quantity in which you sell the product. For example, it would be 4 per gallon and 12 per dozen. The sales fraction must be the same or smaller than the purchase fraction. How you intend to sell the product determines the number you enter in both the purchase and sales fraction fields.

To sell *only whole units,* enter 1 in both the purchase and sales fraction fields. To sell *portions of units,* enter the number of individual items that make up a whole unit (12 in a dozen) in both fields. To sell items *individually,* enter the number of individual items in a unit (12 for a dozen) in the purchase fraction field and enter 1 in the sales fraction field.

When you purchase an item, DacEasy multiples the number purchased by the purchase fraction and divides that total by the sales fraction to determine the quantity available for sale. The method you select to record the purchase and sales fraction determines the way you enter the quantity for a sale. If the purchase fraction is other than 1, you can sell a unit or part of a unit.

If you purchase and sell candy *only* by the pound, your inventory definition would be:

Purchase Measure:	POUND	Purchase Fraction:	1
Sales Measure:	POUND	Sales Fraction:	1

When you purchase 4 units (pound), the system computes the number of sales units as: 4 × (1/1) = 4 units (pounds) for sale. You cannot record the sale of less than one pound.

If you purchase and sell jelly beans by the pound but will sell a *portion* of a pound (ounce), your inventory definition would be:

Purchase Measure:	POUND	Purchase Fraction:	16
Sales Measure:	POUND	Sales Fraction:	16

When you purchase 4 units (pound), the system computes the number of sales units as: 4 × (16/16) = 4 units (pounds) for sale. You record the sale of one and one-half pounds as 1.8 units (.8 represents half of 16).

If you purchase and sell roses by the dozen but will sell less than a full dozen, your inventory definition would be:

Purchase Measure:	DOZEN	Purchase Fraction:	12
Sales Measure:	DOZEN	Sales Fraction:	12

When you purchase 4 units (dozen), the system computes the number of sales units as: 4 × (12/12) = 4 units (dozen) for sale. You record the sale of one and one-half dozen roses as 1.6 units (.6 represents half of 12).

If you purchase sodas in cartons of 12 bottles and will sell each bottle individually, your inventory definition would be:

Purchase Measure:	CARTON	Purchase Fraction:	12
Sales Measure:	BOTTLE	Sales Fraction:	1

If you purchase 4 units (carton), the system computes the number of sales units as: 4 × (12/1) = 48 units (bottles) for sale. You record the sale of one and one-half cartons as 18 (12 + 6).

If you purchase oil in cases that contain 24 cans and you sell each can individually, your inventory definition would be:

Purchase Measure:	CASE	Purchase Fraction:	24
Sales Measure:	CAN	Sales Fraction:	1

When you purchase 4 units (cases), the system computes the number of sales units as: 4 × (24/1) = 96 units (cans) for sale. You record the sale of one and one-half cases as 36 (24 + 12).

The purchase and sale prices you store in the product record are what you buy and sell a *unit of measure* for, not the price for a fraction of the whole unit. For example, the purchase unit for oil is one case, and the purchase fraction is 24. The purchase price would be $24 for a case of oil. On the other hand, the sale unit of measure for oil is can, the sale fraction is 1. The sale price would be what you charge for one can of oil. DacEasy performs the necessary calculations if you buy or sell a fraction of a unit.

CALCULATING HISTORICAL ENTRIES

Entering historical information for your products is not as straightforward as it is for other records. You must know how to value the inventory. The following is an example of how to determine the value of your inventory.

Let's begin with an item that was new to your product line last year. You have recorded the following parameters for that product:

Minimum stock = 3

Maximum stock = 7

Reorder recommendation = 7

The activity on this product has been:

Stock at end of last year = 2

Stock ordered this year = 5

Sold this year = 2

Current stock = 5

This provides an inventory with a value of 5 × $350 (on hand times last purchase price), which is $1,750. You can enter either the unit cost or total cost to record your current stock on hand.

The values for each time period for the sample product are calculated as follows:

Units Purchased = 15

10 @ $300 = $3,000

5 @ $350 = $1,750

$ Purchased = $4,750 (total purchase price)

Units Sold = 13

11 @ $749 = $8,239 (one out of oldest inventory; ten from previous shipment)

2 @ $789 = $1,596 (two from latest shipment)

$ Sales = $9,835 (total sales price)

Calculate Cost on 13 Units

9 @ $300 = $2,700 (sold units costed at previous purchase price)

4 @ $350 = $1,400 (units sold after arrival of latest shipment, costed at latest purchase price)

$ Cost = $4,100 (total calculated cost)

Now that you've got the basics, you can fill out your product worksheets. Table 1.6 shows the fields and information required for product records.

Table 1.6: Product Worksheet Information

Field	You Supply
Code	Your stockkeeping unit or UPC number (14 characters maximum).
Description	A description of the product (30 characters maximum). Remember to use a consistent format.
GL Department	The number of the department in the general ledger this product is posted to if you select to departmentalize by inventory. If you do not, you can use this field to further classify and sort the product in reports (5 characters maximum). For example, enter the product category, such as sport, or classify the products by season, such as fall.
Taxable	If this product is taxable when sold or purchased. Select Yes or No.
Bin	The location where you store the product (8 characters maximum).
Inventory Item	If this item is carried in your own inventory for resale. Select Yes or No.
Minimum	The minimum number of units you want to keep on hand (6 numeric characters maximum).
Reorder	The amount you want to reorder when the minimum is reached (6 numeric characters maximum). For example, if you get a price break when you order 100 of an item, enter 100.
Purchase Measure	The unit of measure—the most common quantity in which you buy the product (8 characters maximum).
Purchase Fraction	The number of items that make up the unit of measure; the smallest quantity in which you buy or sell the product (4 numeric characters, between 1 and 1000, maximum). You cannot change this number after the record is processed.
Purchase Vendor	The code of the vendor you usually buy this product from.
Purchase Number	The number the vendor uses for this item (14 characters maximum).
Standard Cost	If you select to use the standard cost method, enter the cost (11 numeric characters, including 3 decimal places, maximum).
Alternative Vendors	The codes of up to two other vendors from whom you can purchase this product.

Table 1.6: Product Worksheet Information (continued)

Field	You Supply
Alternative Vendor No	The number the alternative vendor uses for this item.
Sales Measure	The unit of measure—the most common quantity in which you sell the product (8 characters maximum).
Sales Fraction	The number of items that make up the unit of measure. usually the smallest quantity in which you sell the product (4 numeric characters, between 1 and 1000, maximum). You cannot change this number after the record is processed.
Sales Price	The price you sell a unit of measure for, not the price for a fraction of the unit (11 numeric characters, including 3 decimal places, maximum). For example, the unit of measure for carnations is one dozen, the fraction is 12, and the sales price is $28 for a dozen. When recording invoices, if you sell half a dozen, enter .6 for the quantity. The program calculates the sale as $14. (Note that the fraction is not in tenths, but in number of units making up a full unit.)
Price Group A, B, C	The code of the price group to use for each price level. (Codes are defined in the price table.)
Alternative Products	The code of up to two other products you can substitute for this one.

Version 3.1: The Inventory Item, Purchase Measure, Purchase Fraction, Purchase Number, Alternative Vendors, Alternative Vendor No, Sales Measure, Sales Fraction, Price Group, and Alternative Products fields do not exist. The Measure field is for the unit of measure in which you sell the product, and the Fraction field is for the number of items that make up the unit of measure in which you sell the product.

If you track services in a general ledger department separate from products, you must define a sales returns account and a cost of goods sold account for each service department you have established, even though they are redundant. This is one of DacEasy's idiosyncracies.

To enter historical information, you also need the following fields, with information for two years ago, last year, and this year to date:

- Units Purchased
- Total Cost of Items Purchased
- Units Sold
- Total Dollars in Sales
- Cost of Units Sold

SERVICES WORKSHEETS

Services are usually labor-related activities your customers pay you to perform. Basically, you need a list of the services you offer and the price you charge. Table 1.7 shows the fields and information required for your services worksheets.

Table 1.7: Services Worksheet Information

Field	You Supply
Code	The code that identifies this service (14 characters maximum).
Description	The description of this service (30 characters maximum). Remember to be consistent in the form you use to enter service descriptions.
GL Department	The number of the department in the general ledger this service is posted to, if you select to departmentalize by inventory. If not, you can use this field to categorize and sort the service in reports (5 character maximum). For example, enter the service type, such as prune.
Taxable	If this service is taxable. Select Yes or No. Some services that result in a product, such as photography, are taxable. Consult your state tax board.
Measure	The unit of measure—the most common quantity in which you sell the service, such as each or month (8 characters maximum).
Fraction	The number of items that make up a full unit, usually the smallest quantity in which you sell the product (4 numeric characters, between 1 and 1000, maximum). For example, 1 per each, 1 per month if your minimum charge is a full month, or 4 per month if your minimum charge is one week. Note that the fraction cannot be changed after the record is processed.
Price	The price you sell a unit of measure for, not the price for a fraction (11 numeric characters, including 3 decimal places, maximum). For example, the unit of measure for lawn and garden care is 1 month, the fraction is 4 for 4 weeks. You charge $120 for 1 month. When recording invoices, if you skip a week, you would enter .3 as the quantity to charge the customer for 3 weeks only. The program calculates the charge as $90. (Note the fraction is not in tenths, but in number of units making up a full measure.)

To enter historical information, you also need the following fields, with information for two years ago, last year, and this year to date:

- Units Sold
- Total Dollars in Sales

PRICE TABLE WORKSHEET

3.1 A price table does not exist. Only one price is possible.

You can automatically vary what you charge for a product by establishing price levels. Each product can have up to three different prices. For example, you might have a retail price, a wholesale price, and a quantity price.

After you set up a price table, you can assign one price level to a customer. When the customer purchases a product, DacEasy will automatically charge the amount established for the assigned price level.

Table 1.8 shows the fields and information for your price table worksheet.

Table 1.8: Pricing Worksheet Information

Field	You Supply
Code	A code to identify the price level (5 characters maximum).
Description	A description of the price level (30 characters maximum).
Rounding Method	Whether you want to round up the calculated price to the nearest penny, five cents, ten cents, or dollar.
Minimum	The minimum quantity the customer must buy before being eligible for the price break.
Discount %	The discount percentage used to calculate the price charged to the customer, entered in 99.999 format. For example, a 5¼ percent discount would be 5.250.

TERMS TABLE WORKSHEET

3.1 The terms table does not exist. Due days, discount percent, and days allowed are entered in the customer record instead.

Terms define when an invoice is due, when a discount can be taken, and the discount amount. In DacEasy Accounting, you can define these parameters by number of days from the invoice date or by exact day of the month. In other words, an invoice dated May 5 might be due in 30 days (June 4) or on the thirtieth day of the month (May 30).

Complete the fields described in Table 1.9 to prepare a terms table worksheet. After you define terms codes, you can assign the terms to customers and vendors.

DETERMINING DOCUMENT NUMBERS

Documents are pieces of paper on which you do business. They include invoices, purchase orders, checks, and so on. Usually, each set

Table 1.9: Terms Table Worksheet Information

Field	You Supply
Code	A code to identify the terms (5 characters maximum).
Type	The terms must be defined either by number of days from the invoice date or by day of the month.
Discount %	The percentage used to calculate the discount, entered in 99.999 format.
Discount Days	The number of days from the invoice date the discount can be taken.
Due Days	The number of days from the invoice date the invoice is due in full.
Discount %	The percentage used to calculate the discount for day of the month terms.
Discount Day	The day of the month the discount expires.
Due Day	The day of the month the invoice is due in full.

of documents has its own numbering scheme. DacEasy keeps track of some of those numbers for you and assigns the next number to the next document you use in the computerized accounting system.

You should determine the last number used in your old system, or the number preceding the one you want to begin your DacEasy program with, for the following documents. Alternatively, you can start at zero in the new system.

- Sales invoices
- Sales-return slips
- Purchase orders
- Purchase-return slips

ASSIGNING MESSAGE CODES

Message codes can be assigned to customer and vendor records. The related message is displayed when there is activity in that record. You can also print the messages on invoices and purchase orders.

Whenever a message appears on the screen during data entry, the credit limit, current balance, and credit available on the account also appear. To guarantee that the credit limit appears whenever a purchase order is entered for the vendor, you could create the message

Note Credit Limit and enter its code in the records of vendors who impose a credit limit.

PREPARING STATEMENT MESSAGES

In DacEasy, a statement message is one that you assign to the five standard, balance-due aging periods. The appropriate statement message prints on a customer's statement according to the aging status of the account's balance.

The statement message table contains five levels of messages. You should prepare the message text as follows:

- A First Message for customers whose account is inactive.
- A Second Message for customers whose account is current.
- A Third Message for customers whose account is 1 to 30 days past due.
- A Fourth Message for customers whose account is 31 to 60 days past due.
- A Fifth Message for customers whose account is over 60 days past due.

DEFINING PURCHASE ORDER AND BILLING CODES

Purchase order codes are used to order items that are typically not defined as a resale product in your files. You must identify the general ledger account you want the system to post to when you include that miscellaneous charge on a purchase order. DacEasy supplies 11 purchase order codes related to its chart of accounts, as listed in Table 1.10.

A billing code is used on invoices to charge a customer for items that are typically not defined as a product or service. You must identify the general ledger account you want the system to post to when you include that miscellaneous charge on an invoice. DacEasy supplies ten billing codes related to its chart of accounts, which are also listed in Table 1.10.

Table 1.10: DacEasy Billing Codes

Code	Description	P.O. Account	Billing Account
1	Freight	52081	4301
2	Insurance	52082	4302
3	Packaging	52083	4303
4	Ads-Radio/TV	52191	
4	Surcharge		4304
5	Ads-Print	52192	
6	Auto/Truck	12011	12011
7	Furniture/Fixture	12021	12021
8	Office Equip	12031	12031
9	Machinery	12041	12041
10	Other Fixed Assets	12061	12061

You can use these purchase order and billing codes, change the account number, delete them, or add others.

If you are adding purchase order or billing codes, prepare worksheets containing the information shown in Table 1.11.

ESTABLISHING PASSWORD PROTECTION LEVELS

Passwords protect the integrity of your files by restricting users to certain areas of your accounting system. They also keep unauthorized people out entirely. After passwords are defined, you must enter the password needed to gain entry to each level. Passwords are an option you can use to protect your financial data.

You should decide now which levels of access you want to apply to your files. Table 1.12 summarizes the password levels in version 4.1, and Table 1.13 lists those in version 3.1.

Table 1.11: Purchase Order and Billing Codes Worksheet Information

Field	You Supply
Code	A code for the noninventory billing or purchase order item (5 characters maximum).
Description	A description of the code that will print on the customer invoice or the purchase order for the vendor (40 characters maximum).
Account	The general ledger account number related to the item. For example, enter 52101 for Accounting Consulting Fees.
Taxable	If this item is taxable. Select Yes or No.
Discount	If this item can be discounted. Select Yes or No.
Amount	The amount typically charged for this item (12 characters, including 2 decimal places, maximum). If the amount varies frequently, you can leave the field blank. You can override the default amount during processing.
Version 3.1: In the Description field, only 20 characters are possible, but you can override the description during processing, using up to 40 characters. The Discount field does not exist.	

Table 1.12: Password Levels in Version 4.1

Password	Access
Level 1	Allows user to enter transactions in the subsidiary modules, print journals for those modules, and back up and restore DacEasy files.
Level 2	Allows user to enter general ledger transactions; process recurring transactions for all modules; print the cash register, the chart of accounts, and all customer, vendor, and product reports.
Level 3	Allows user to edit all data files, set program defaults, reconcile cash, assemble products, price inventory, adjust physical inventory, post all modules, print all financial reports, and access the report generator.
Level 4	Allows user to edit the interface table, run all periodic routines, and copy company data files.
Level 5	Allows user to process consolidations, edit the periods table and costing method, and open next year.
Controller	Allows user access to the entire DacEasy system, including the password table.

Table 1.13: Password Levels in Version 3.1

Password	Access
Level 1	Allows entry to certain functions in various modules, as follows: *Accounts Receivable*: Transaction entry, transaction journal, and cash receipts. *Accounts Payable*: Transaction entry, transaction journal, and payments journal. *Purchasing*: Purchase order entry. *Journals*: Billing, sales, purchase journal, purchase order status. No ability to add customers, vendors, products, or accounts during data processing.
Level 2	Allows users into level 1 and the following functions: *General Ledger*: Transaction entry. *Journals*: General ledger journal and activity report. *Reports*: Chart of accounts, accounts receivable, accounts payable, and inventory. Permits adding customers, vendors, products, and accounts during data processing. Also allows review of file status.
Level 3	Allows users into levels 1 and 2 and the following functions: *Maintenance*: General ledger accounts, customers, vendors, products, services, purchase order codes, statement text, and sales tax table. *Defaults*: Cost system, invoice/purchase order numbers, printer codes, monitor colors, and messages. *Posting*: All modules. *Inventory*: Price assignment and entry. Also allows file rehash and generation of financial statements.
Level 4	Allows users into levels 1, 2, 3 and the following functions: General ledger interface, company ID, and month-end and year-end closing for all modules.
Level 5	Allows users into all levels and functions, including passwords.

AN OVERVIEW OF THE CONVERSION TO DACEASY

Now that you have your accounts in order and your worksheets completed, you are ready to set up your system and transfer your data into DacEasy. To accomplish the conversion, you must take the following steps:

1. Install the software.
2. Set the printer and monitor parameters.
3. Define your accounting periods.

4. Enter your chart of accounts.
5. Add the current balance to your accounts.
6. Define the general ledger interface accounts.
7. Add active records to your customer file and enter outstanding invoices.
8. Add active records to your vendor file and enter outstanding invoices.
9. Add product records to your inventory file and enter stock on hand.
10. Enter service records.
11. Run reports in DacEasy and verify them against your data-input sheets.
12. Print a balance sheet in DacEasy and compare it with the one from your previous system.
13. Correct any errors you might have made during data entry and run a corrected set of reports to keep on file.

The following chapters will guide you through each step. In the next chapter, we will proceed through step 6 above to establish the framework of your DacEasy system.

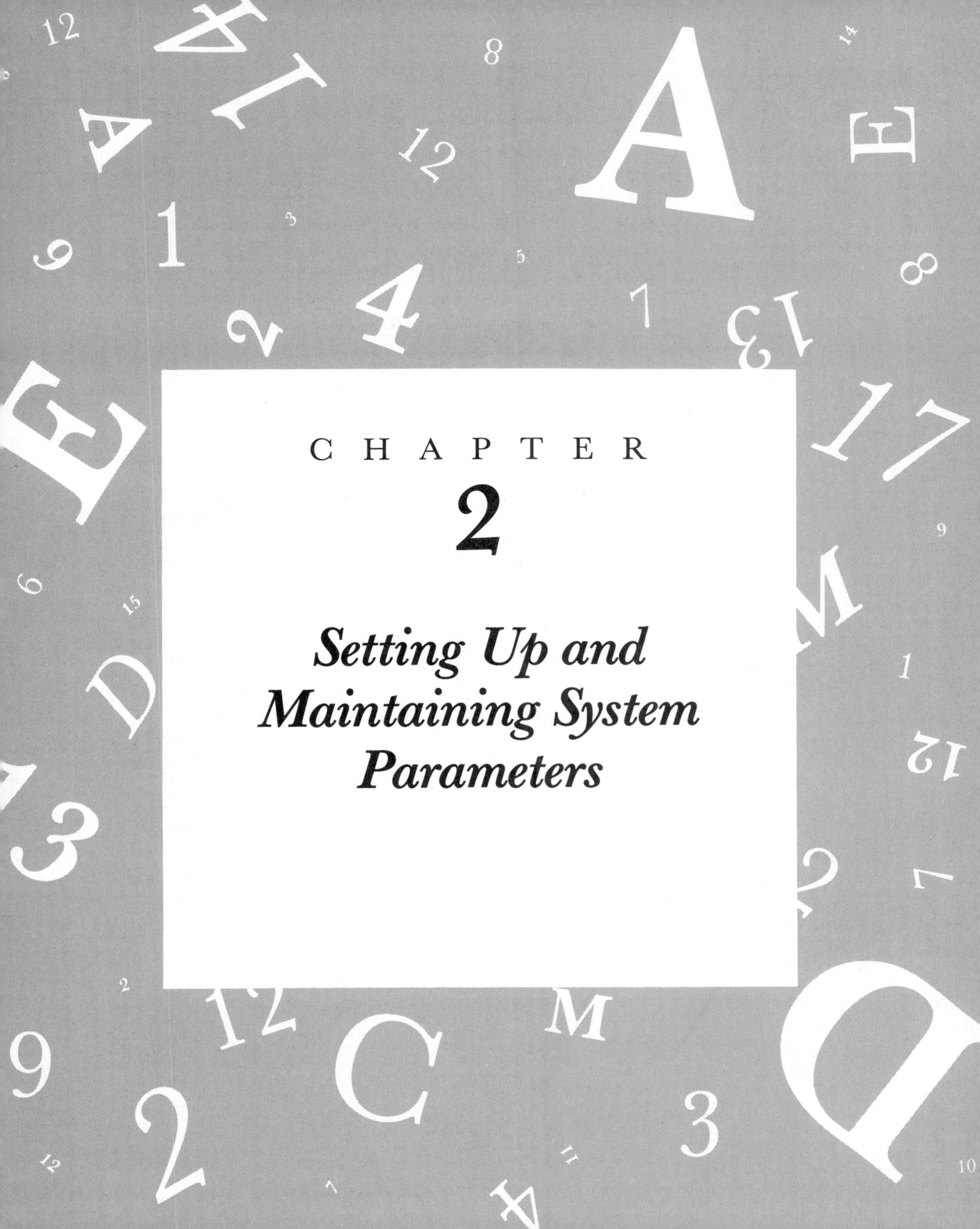

CHAPTER 2

Setting Up and Maintaining System Parameters

AFTER COMPILING ALL THE INFORMATION NECESsary for converting from your previous system, you should install your DacEasy Accounting software. The installation instructions are in Appendix A. Then you need to initialize the software program by defining the system parameters. System parameters include general ledger accounts, interface accounts, codes, methods of structuring your data, and the designation of where you want to store the data on the computer. These parameters rarely change after you define them.

INITIALIZING DACEASY ACCOUNTING

Now that your DacEasy Accounting software is installed, the next step is to initialize the program. To initialize the program, you will need 750,000 bytes of available disk space if you use the sample chart of accounts and 550,000 if you do not.

Follow these steps to initialize DacEasy:

3.1 In all cases, replace the **dea4** with a **dea3** for your version. You will be asked to define your monitor and name a data file subdirectory; if you want to use the sample chart of accounts; and to designate the number of accounts, customers, vendors, products, and invoices. Next, respond to the prompt to create files. Finally, enter your company name and address.

1. Type **cd\dea4** and press ↵ to change to the DacEasy directory. Then type **dea4** at the C: prompt and press ↵ to start the program. You will see a screen that asks if you are a new user or upgrading from an earlier version. If you are a new user, press ↵ to continue. If you are upgrading from DacEasy Accounting version 1.0, 2.0, 3.0, or 4.0, follow the instructions in Appendix B.
2. Next you will see a screen that asks for the name of your system and the subdirectory where you want to keep your data files. In the System Identification field, type the name of your company and press ↵. Then enter the subdirectory name in the Directory Name/Path field. The name FILES is suggested in the subdirectory DEA4.
3. If you do not plan to keep records for more than one company, the suggested name, FILES, is acceptable, and you do not need to change this default. If you plan to track one or more companies or facilities separately, you will want to put the information for each company in a different subdirectory. In this case, type

an easy-to-remember name designating the first company. Do not use spaces, symbols, or punctuation in the subdirectory name. If you do, the computer will display an error message.

4. Press F10. A screen appears asking whether you want to use the chart of accounts supplied with DacEasy.
5. If you want to start with this chart of accounts and then add or delete accounts to suit your needs, press ↵ to accept the default Yes. The file space requirements and available space are displayed. Press ↵. If there is sufficient space, the sample chart of accounts is moved into your DEA4\FILES subdirectory. If you do not have enough space, press Esc to exit the initialization. After making room on your disk, return to step 1 to begin the initialization process again.
6. If you have decided to create a completely different chart of accounts, use the left arrow key to move the cursor to No and press ↵. You must add your unique general ledger accounts individually, as explained in the section about setting up and maintaining your chart of accounts, later in this chapter.

3.1 When given a choice of predefined selections, instead of highlighting your choice to select it, you usually must enter a designating letter. For example, where the instructions say to select No, you must enter N instead.

After the program is initialized, the Main menu appears. In this book, we focus on the menu structure in version 4.1.

STARTING YOUR DACEASY PROGRAM

After you have the software successfully installed and initialized, you are ready to set up your company on DacEasy. Follow these steps:

3.1 Exit the program by pressing Esc. Version 3.1 selections may be made by pressing the first letter of the menu or option.

1. Exit the program by selecting Exit from the File menu. You can move the cursor across the Main menu by pressing the left and right arrow keys or by pressing Alt and the highlighted letter of the option you want. To select a menu option, press the up or down arrow key to move the cursor to it, then press ↵, or press the highlighted letter in the option

name (the X in EXit, for example). If you are using a mouse, place the pointer on your selection and press the left button.

2. After exiting DacEasy, press the following keys simultaneously: Ctrl-Alt-Del. This command restarts the computer and makes it acknowledge the changes you made to the buffers and files.

3.1 On a floppy system, load DOS, place Disk 1 in drive A, type **dea3**, and press ↵.

3. To begin the DacEasy Accounting program, type **dea4** at the C: prompt, then press ↵. The Main menu appears.

DEFINING YOUR COMPANY

* From the Edit menu, select Defaults. From the submenu, select Company Identification.

Your first step after completing initialization and starting the program is to define your company. Select Edit from the Main menu, Defaults from the Edit menu, and then Company Identification from the submenu. The screen shown in Figure 2.1 appears.

Type your own company name over the display. Use the spacebar to erase remaining characters, and then press ↵ to move the cursor to the address line. Type your street address on the next line, press ↵, and continue to replace the information with the rest of

3.1 Defining your company is part of initialization.

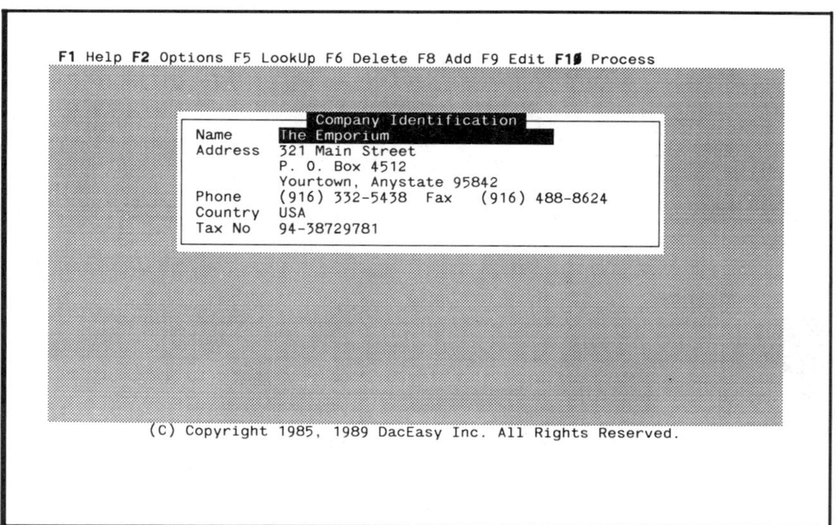

Figure 2.1: Entering your company information

your company address. The information you enter here will become the heading on your reports. Next, enter your business telephone and fax numbers, the country in which your company is located, and its federal tax identification number. Press F10 to record your company information. Then, press Esc to return to the Main menu.

SETUP SEQUENCE

The order in which you complete your setup is not the same as daily processing. Daily processing is discussed in Chapter 5.

Your next step is to define various files. You do this through the Edit menu.

You must set up your files in a prescribed order because several files use codes that must first be defined in other files. The sequence outlined in this chapter ensures that your setup procedure flows smoothly.

You should set up your files in the order listed in Table 2.1. The following sections guide you through the appropriate sequence.

Table 2.1: Setup Sequence

1. Accounting periods
2. Chart of accounts
3. Budgets
4. Company name
5. Department cost center
6. Interface general ledger accounts
7. Purchase order codes with general ledger defaults
8. Billing codes with general ledger defaults
9. Statement text
10. Inventory costing method
11. Last document number used on purchase order, purchase return, invoice, sales return
12. Tax rate table
13. Payment terms
14. Price table
15. Message codes for customers and vendors

Table 2.1: Setup Sequence (continued)

16. Default file lookups
17. Forms
18. Printer codes and monitor colors
19. Passwords
20. Customer files
21. Customer historical data
22. Outstanding customer invoices
23. Vendor files
24. Vendor historical data
25. Outstanding vendor invoices
26. Product files
27. Product historical data
28. Stock on hand
29. Service files
30. Service historical data
31. Custom reports

DEFINING ACCOUNTING PERIODS

* From the Edit menu, select Defaults. From the submenu, select Periods.

3.1 Version 3.1 does not include a periods table. You cannot change the 12 calendar-month accounting periods provided with the program.

DacEasy defaults to the 12 calendar accounting periods shown in Figure 2.2. You can accept the default periods or change the number of periods and the date ranges of those periods. For example, you could use a 12-month fiscal year instead of a calendar year. Note that you cannot change the accounting periods after you have entered transactions. You must establish your accounting periods before going further.

To change the periods, select Defaults from the Edit menu, and then select Periods from the submenu. You will see the periods table shown in Figure 2.2. Override the beginning date with the first day in your fiscal year. For example, to change to a fiscal year beginning May 1, 1990, enter 050190. The program supplies a name and

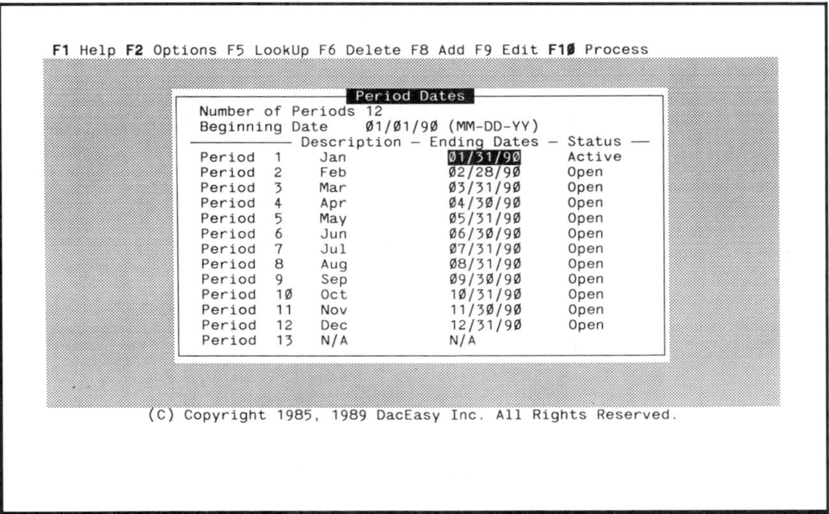

Figure 2.2: Defining accounting periods

calculates an ending date for each period using a standard, though revolving (May to April; October to September), calendar. You can edit the description and ending date of any period.

If you use 13 periods, DacEasy will divide the calendar into 13 periods, but you must supply the description and date of each one. If you use less than 12 periods, you must also complete both the Description and Ending Dates fields.

> If a portion of your screen is not visible, you will have to adjust the default colors. Refer to the section about setting monitor colors in Chapter 3.

By default, the Status field shows all periods as Open. If you want to restrict posting to only one period, make it the Active (current) period by positioning the cursor on it and pressing F3. Each time you close one period, you must return to the periods table and make the next period Active. You will be able to post to any period, but the program will warn you if it is not the current period. Press F10 to record your accounting periods.

SETTING UP AND MAINTAINING YOUR CHART OF ACCOUNTS

> * From the Edit menu, select Accounts.

If you selected to use the sample accounts supplied by DacEasy, you will probably need to add accounts and edit existing ones. You should also take the time to remove the accounts that you don't need

3.1 From the File menu, select Accounts. The sample chart of accounts differs slightly from the one provided with version 4.1, so some account numbers in the examples won't match.

from the sample list to conserve space on your disk. These procedures are described in the following sections.

If you want to use your own chart of accounts, you must add each general ledger account individually, as described below.

ADDING AND EDITING GENERAL LEDGER ACCOUNTS

To add an account, begin by selecting Accounts from the Edit menu. Enter the new account number and complete the fields on the Edit Account screen. You should have this information on the chart of accounts worksheet you prepared for converting your records to DacEasy. If you are adding a new account after conversion, see Chapter 1 for a description of the fields.

To edit an existing account, enter the account number in the first field in the Edit Account screen. When the record appears, make changes to the data already in the fields.

As an example, we'll add a new general ledger account to the sample chart of accounts. Let's add an account to Revenues, under Sales, called Sales Department 03, and give it the number 4103, as shown in Figure 2.3.

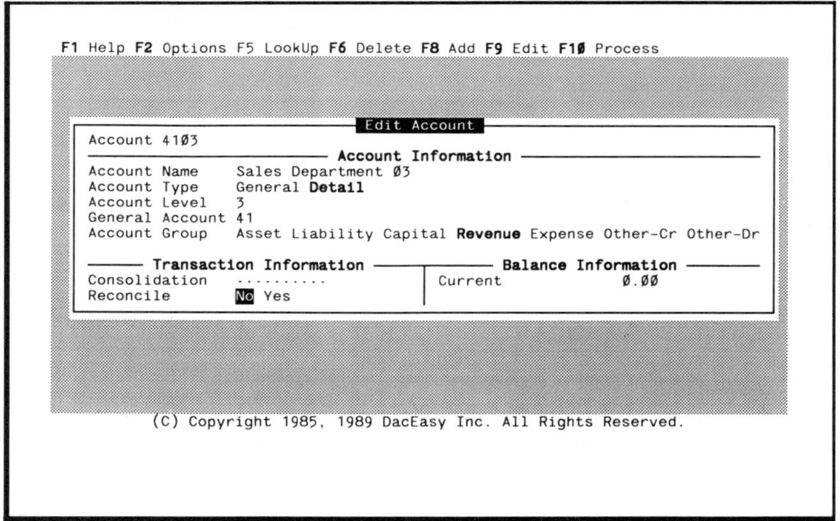

Figure 2.3: Adding a general ledger account

3.1 In the step-by-step examples, we use the field length available in version 4.1. When entering the sample data, occasionally you will have to shorten the description to accommodate the shorter field length in version 3.1. For example, instead of *Sales Department 03,* you must enter *Sales Dept. 03* for the description of the new general ledger account.

Follow the steps below to add the account. Note that in these steps and those throughout the rest of the book, rather than instructing you to type something and then press ↵, the term *enter* will be used. This means to type the information and enter it by pressing ↵.

1. Enter the account number **4103**.
2. Enter the account name **Sales Department 03**.
3. Select Detail as the account type because it is a subaccount of Sales.
4. Enter **3** to assign the account to level 3 because it falls under the primary account, Revenues, which is level 1 and under the secondary account, Sales, which is level 2.
5. Enter **41** to indicate the general account our example falls under, Sales. If you were adding a primary account (level 1), you would be asked to designate whether it was an Asset, Liability, Capital, Revenue, Expense, or Other type of account. All subordinate accounts default to the primary account type.
6. Press ↵ to skip the Consolidate field. You must set up a consolidated chart of accounts before you can enter the consolidation account number in your standard chart of accounts.
7. Accept the default No in the Reconcile field. If you were using this account in your Cash module transactions, you would select Yes to reconcile it.

3.1 Neither the Consolidation nor Reconcile fields are available when defining an account. The Type field must be completed for each detail account, and the account must be the same type as its primary account.

If you are departmentalizing by inventory, you will also need to add a Sales Return account (4203) and a Cost of Goods Sold account (5103) for transactions that occur in Department 03.

If you have more than one company, you might want to accumulate account balances from all of them into a set of consolidated figures. You would first create a separate chart of accounts that would be used for consolidation, as described in Chapter 4. Then you could enter the number of the consolidated account (from your consolidated chart of accounts) in the Consolidation Field of the account you want to include in the balance of that consolidated account.

The historical data you enter for each period is *not* the balance at the end of the period. It is the *total activity* for the period (the net result of all transactions posted that period).

ENTERING HISTORICAL INFORMATION When you are adding an established account to your general ledger, you will enter its historical information. As an example, suppose that you want to enter information for a machinery account (12041) you established in October of the previous fiscal year. To add historical information, press F2, and then press Shift-F3. Select Edit from the Options for Account History submenu. In the Last Year field, move the cursor to Oct, Period 10 and enter 3490.75. You must enter the decimal if the amount contains cents, but don't use a comma to separate hundreds from thousands. Because you did not purchase any machinery in November, press ↵ to reach Dec, the last period in your year. For this period, enter 2409.25, the amount you spent for a lathe that month. The system will total and display the balance that was in the account at the end of last year (5900.00), as shown in Figure 2.4.

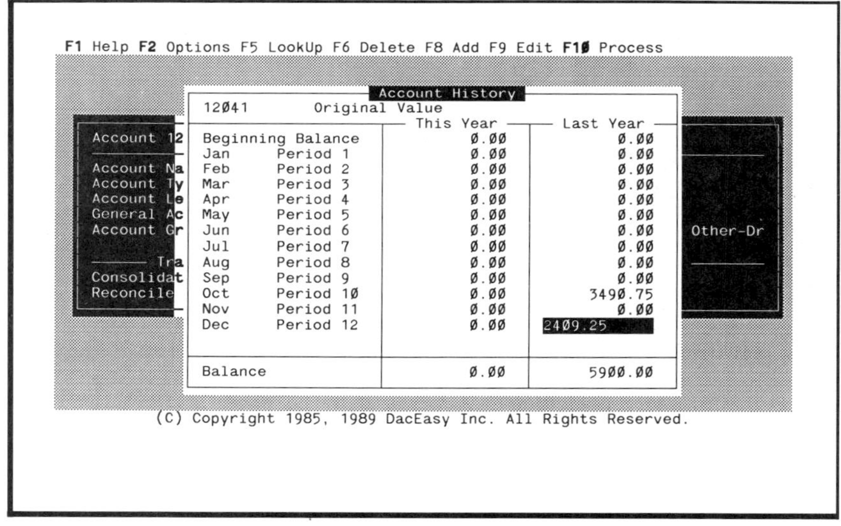

Figure 2.4: Entering historical information

At this point, the amount in the This Year field is zero. The program generates this figure when you enter the current balance during setup and updates it when you post activity throughout the year. Press F10 to save your entries, and then press ↵ to return to the Edit Account screen and enter the account's current balance.

ENTERING HISTORICAL INFORMATION IN VERSION 3.1

In version 3.1, the first historical data field is Year Before Last, where you enter the account balance from two years ago. You can press ↵ to skip this field if you do not have data for that year. In the Last Year field, enter the balance in the account at the end of last year. The program calculates the variance and percent of change for last year and the current year to date. Because you have not posted any entries for the current year yet, the variance from the amounts is a minus.

Next, the cursor moves to the Forecast at End Year field. In this field, enter your projection for the account balance at the end of the current year. The program calculates the variance between the forecast and current balance, and then the screen clears.

At this point, the Current YTD field is zero. The program generates this figure when you enter the current balance of this general ledger account, which is your next step, as explained in the following section.

ENTERING INITIAL GENERAL LEDGER ACCOUNT BALANCES

One reason for using DacEasy to track your accounting data is to have accurate, up-to-date information. For your balance sheet and income statements to reflect accurate data, you must enter the current balance for each general ledger account when you set up your system. Thereafter, DacEasy will update the balances automatically during routine processing.

DacEasy keeps a running balance for income and expense accounts until year-end, when they are cleared and the difference posted to retained earnings. If you do not have current year-to-date figures for your individual income and expense accounts, they can all be left at zero. DacEasy will begin to track them from your first transaction in the new system. Enter your current retained earnings amount. At year-end, the program will add its activity to your beginning balance.

Do not enter balances for your Accounts Receivable, Accounts Payable, or Inventory accounts in the general ledger.

As you enter the outstanding invoices for your customers and vendors and the stock you have on hand, the program accumulates the balance in the general ledger for your Accounts Receivable, Accounts Payable, and Inventory accounts.

All entries must be made to detail accounts. You cannot make an entry directly to an account classified as a general account.

During setup, DacEasy uses a unique account, called the Difference account, in the general ledger. This is the offsetting account the program uses when you enter outstanding invoices for customers and vendors, current inventory on hand, and general ledger account balances. It is closed at the end of the setup session.

You can enter current balances in your general ledger accounts as you define them. Simply press F7 from the Edit Account screen for the account to display an entry window, and then enter the balance for the account. You do not need to type a decimal and cents if the amount is whole dollars. Figure 2.5 shows a current balance of $5,900 entered for the machinery account we used as an example earlier. Even though the program calculates the ending balance from the historical data you entered, it does not carry that balance forward into the data for this year, so you must enter a current balance.

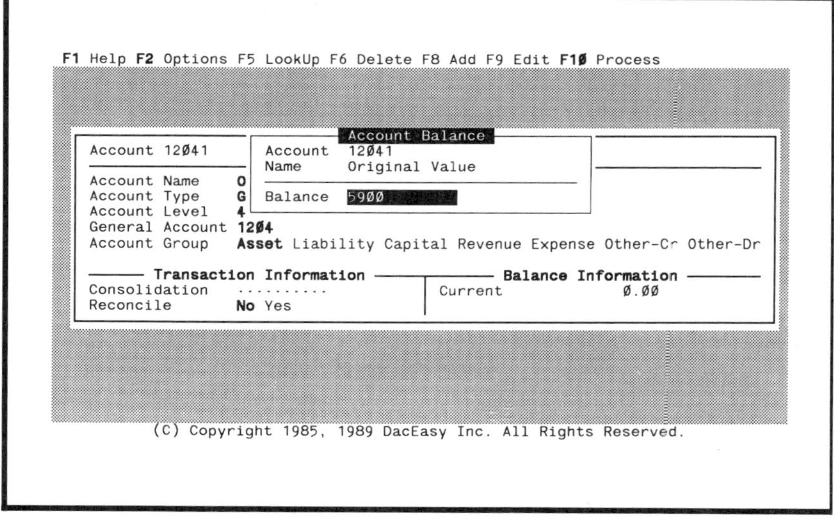

Figure 2.5: Entering general ledger account balances

The program date (which can be changed by pressing F4 from the Edit menu and entering a new date) determines which period of the current year the current balance is recorded in. If you are establishing your DacEasy program mid-year and want to show activity for the periods that have already passed, you must first enter the balance at the beginning of the year with a beginning year date. Then you enter and post the total activity for each period to bring the account balance up to the date you began using DacEasy. Chapter 5 provides an overview of these tasks, and Chapter 13 details how to enter a general ledger transaction.

Balances in contra accounts are preceded by a minus sign when you enter them during setup. A *contra account* is one whose balance is deducted from its related account to arrive at a true value. The most common contra asset account is Accumulated Depreciation, an asset account that is deducted from another asset account, such as Equipment. Assets normally carry a debit balance. The contra asset account carries a credit balance. The minus sign indicates the balance is abnormal for the account type. Another contra account is Sales Returns, a contra revenue account. It reduces the related revenue account, Sales. Revenue accounts normally carry a credit balance. The contra revenue account carries a debit balance.

During setup, a minus sign should precede any balance that is *abnormal* for the account type, even if the account is not a contra account. For example, Retained Earnings is a capital account, which normally carries a credit balance. If you posted a loss one year, the balance for that year would be a debit. You would precede the balance entry with a minus sign to indicate it is just the opposite of what you would expect for the account type.

DELETING GENERAL LEDGER ACCOUNTS

You cannot delete a general ledger account when a balance exists or if it is used in the interface accounts, billing codes, or purchase order codes table. You can delete an account in the sample chart of accounts or one that has a zero balance at the end of the year. To delete an account, enter its number in the Edit Account screen. When the account appears, press F6 to delete it. Select Yes when the program prompts you to verify the deletion.

For example, suppose that you want to delete account 21045, Foreign Tax. You would follow these steps:

1. Enter **21045** in the account number field. The description appears.

2. Press F6 to delete the account. The program asks

   Are you sure you want to delete this Account? Yes No

   The default is Yes.

3. Press ↵ to accept the default and delete the record.

ENTERING BUDGET AMOUNTS

From the Periodic menu, select General Ledger. From the submenu, select Budget.

3.1 Version 3.1 uses the word *Forecast* instead of *Budget*. You cannot budget by accounting period. A one-figure forecast for the entire year is the only budgeting tool available.

Any *detail* account in your chart of accounts can have a budget for each period you established. To set up a budget, select the General Ledger option from the Periodic menu, and then choose Budget. A list of general ledger accounts appears. As an example, let's budget the machinery account we have used in earlier examples.

1. Enter the machinery account number, **12041**, in the Search field at the bottom of the screen. The program will scroll through the list to display the account number you requested.
2. Place the cursor on the account number and press ↵. Select Edit. You will see the budget list, with the accounting periods and an Amount column.
3. For Jan, Period 1, press ↵ to accept zero because you did not budget any money for equipment purchases into that month.
4. In the Amount column for Feb, Period 2, enter **6200** for the heavy-duty sewing machine you expect to purchase for your tailoring shop that month.
5. Type **500** in the Amount column for Mar, Period 3.
6. Press F3 to duplicate the current entry (500) in the remaining periods. You do not have any specific expenditures planned, but you are setting aside $5,000 over the next 10 months for equipment, just in case something comes up. Figure 2.6 shows the completed budget.
7. Press F10 to save your entries, and then press ↵ to exit the budget list.

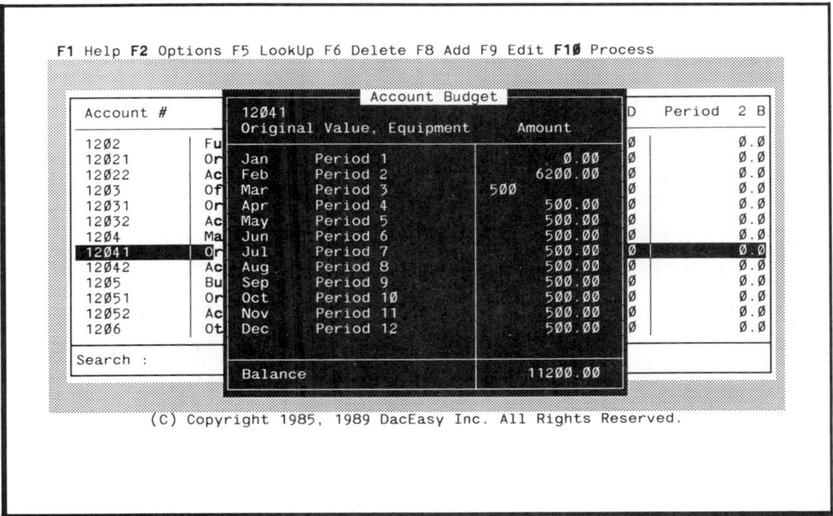

Figure 2.6: Entering budget amounts

SETTING UP YOUR INTERFACE TABLE AND DISTRIBUTION METHOD

* From the Edit menu, select Tables. From the submenu, select Interface.

3.1 From the Options menu, select Interface.

Select the Tables option from the Edit menu, and then choose Interface from the submenu to work with the general ledger interface table. If you chose to use the sample chart of accounts, the interface table has also been created for you. DacEasy displays the default cost center and interface accounts, as shown in Figure 2.7. It sets Inventory as your distribution method. If you don't want to base your cost centers on inventory, you can select a different method, as described in this section.

If you created your own chart of accounts, you must designate a cost center and which accounts will be used for the interface. Use the interface accounts worksheet you created in Chapter 1.

SELECTING YOUR COST DISTRIBUTION CENTER

If you prefer not to departmentalize your costs at all, or you prefer to track them by customer instead of inventory, you must edit the default interface table.

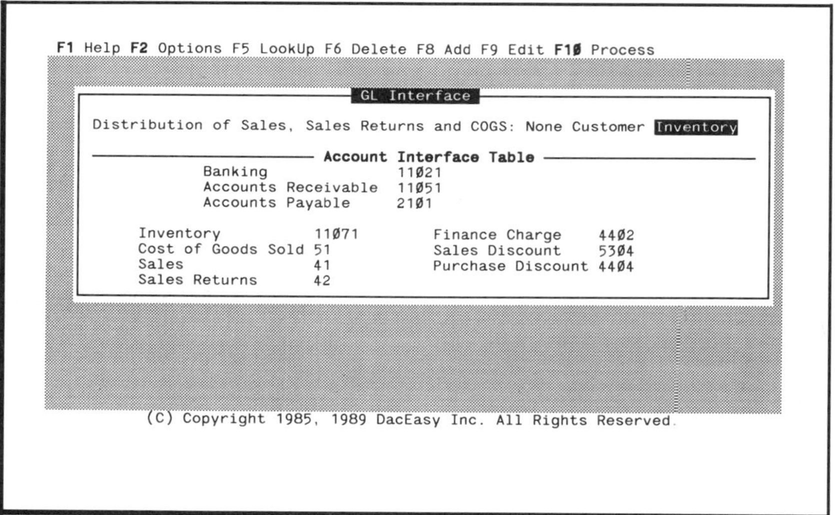

Figure 2.7: Default distribution method and interface accounts

Remember, the DacEasy program contains Help screens. You can learn more about what is expected in the field where the cursor rests by pressing F1. A window similar to the one shown in Figure 2.8 appears. Notice the arrows along the right side. Press PgUp and PgDn to scroll through all the help text for this field. Press Esc to exit the Help screen.

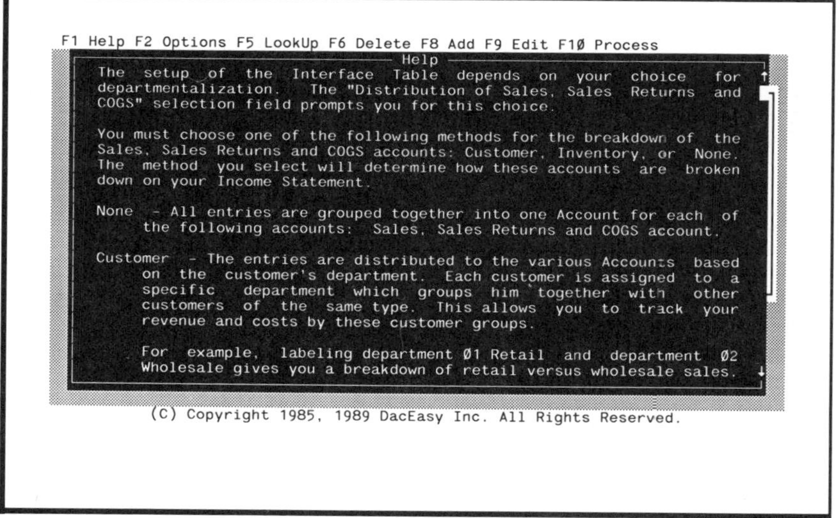

Figure 2.8: Distribution method Help screen

3.1 To change the cost distribution, press the spacebar until the method you prefer displays.

You change the cost distribution by moving the cursor until the distribution method you prefer (None, Customer, or Inventory) is selected. When you change the cost distribution from Inventory, you must also change the interface account for three accounts: Sales, Sales Returns, and Cost of Goods Sold, as explained below. Note that after you choose a cost distribution center and add customers or products, you cannot change it.

DESIGNATING INTERFACE ACCOUNTS

Interface accounts are those which DacEasy uses to post activity from the other modules to the general ledger. They form the path that connects the general ledger to its subsidiary ledgers.

In the sample chart of accounts, the Sales (41), Sales Returns (42), and Cost of Goods Sold (51) interface accounts are identified as general accounts for a cost center based on inventory or customer. When you use None as a cost center, you must change the designation of these three accounts to detail. Edit the supplied chart of accounts to change the interface account designations to Sales 4101, Sales Returns 4201, and Cost of Goods 5101, respectively.

If you choose None (not to departmentalize your sales activity), then all sales figures are accumulated in one general ledger account. In that case, there is also only one sales return account and one account for recording the cost of goods sold.

If you created your own chart of accounts or edited the sample chart of accounts, enter the number of the general ledger account that will serve as the interface for each category on your interface accounts worksheet. As explained in Chapter 1, whether you should set up the account as a general or a detail account depends on the cost center method you are using.

Use the interface accounts worksheet you prepared in Chapter 1 to complete the general ledger interface table.

DEFINING AND MAINTAINING PURCHASE ORDER CODES

* From the Edit menu, select Purchase Codes.

Purchase order codes are created for items that are neither a product nor a service, but are items the vendor will charge you for, such as freight or packaging. They are also used for items not purchased for

3.1 From the File menu, select Codes. From the submenu, select Purchase Order Codes.

resale, but for use in your business, such as computers or other fixed assets. You must assign a general ledger account to each purchase order code so the program knows where to store the expenditure.

ADDING AND EDITING PURCHASE ORDER CODES

To work with purchase order codes, select Purchase Codes from the Edit menu. All purchase order code accounts must be defined as detail accounts in the general ledger. Set up your purchase order codes table using the information on the worksheet you prepared for converting your records to DacEasy. If you are adding a new account after conversion, see Chapter 1 for a description of the fields on the Edit Purchase Order Codes screen.

3.1 You can define a maximum of 40 purchase and billing codes. To add a new code, simply enter a code, a description of up to 20 characters, an amount, and an account number, and designate whether or not it is taxable.

We'll enter the sample code shown in Figure 2.9 for practice.

1. In the Code field, enter **ACCTG**.
2. In the Description field, enter **Accounting Consulting Fee**.
3. In the Account field, enter **52101**, the number of the general ledger expense account related to the item. The account for this code cannot be a general account; it must be a detail account (you can only post to detail accounts).
4. In the Taxable field, select No because this item is not taxable. If the item is taxable when your vendor charges you for it, you would select Yes.
5. In the Discount Field, select No because this item is not discounted.

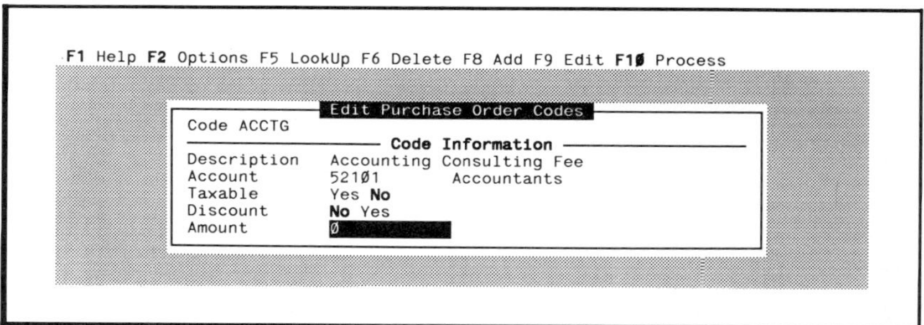

Figure 2.9: Entering a purchase order code

6. Leave the Amount field blank by pressing ↵ to move past it. In our example, the amount charged by the accountant varies. If you are usually charged the same amount, you would enter that amount here. You can enter an amount or override the default amount during processing.
7. Press F10 to exit and save your entries.

To edit an existing code, enter it in the Code field. When the code information appears, enter the new description, amount, or general ledger account number or change the Taxable or Discount field.

DELETING PURCHASE ORDER CODES

3.1 Use the arrow keys to move to the code you want to delete on the Purchase Order Code File Maintenance screen. Press Alt-D, and then press F10.

You can delete a purchase order code at any time. If you need it again later, you can reinstate it, with the same code or a different one.

To delete a purchase order code, enter its code in the Edit Purchase Order Codes screen. Press F6, and then respond to the prompt to verify that you want to delete the code.

DEFINING AND MAINTAINING BILLING CODES

* From the Edit menu, select Billing Codes.

3.1 From the File menu, select Codes. From the submenu, select Billing Codes.

You use billing codes for items you sell that are neither a product nor a service, but miscellaneous items you charge the customer for, such as shipping insurance. They are also used for items that are not sold from your inventory, such as used vehicles or other fixed assets.

ADDING AND EDITING BILLING CODES

To work with your billing codes, select the Billing Codes option from the Edit menu. The billing codes screen is similiar to the one for maintaining your purchase order codes.

All billing code accounts must be detail accounts. To set up a billing codes table, use the information on the worksheet you prepared in

Chapter 1. If you are adding a new account after conversion, see Chapter 1 for a description of the fields on the Edit Billing Codes screen.

As an example, here are the steps for entering a sample code:

1. In the Code field, enter **RENT**.
2. In the Description field, enter **Office Space Rental**.
3. In the Account field, enter **4504**, the general ledger account number for Rent under Other Revenue in our modified chart of accounts. Remember, the account must be a detail account.
4. In the Taxable field, select No because rent is not taxable. If this item is usually taxable when you charge a customer for it, you would select Yes.
5. In the Discount field, select No because rent is not discounted.
6. In the Amount field, enter **700**, the amount you charge for renting office space in your building (you can override this default during processing). If the amount varies frequently, you can leave the field blank.
7. Press F10 to exit and save your entries.

You can press F8 in the Account field to add a new account to your general ledger.

To edit an existing code, enter it in the Code field. When the code information appears, enter the new description, amount, or general ledger account number or change the taxable or discountable entries.

DELETING BILLING CODES

3.1 Use the arrow keys to move to the code you want to delete on the Billing Code File Maintenance screen. Press Alt-D, and then press F10.

You might create a billing code for one special circumstance, and then immediately delete it after it has served its purpose. As with purchase order codes, there are no restrictions on deleting billing codes.

To delete a billing code, enter the code in the Edit Billing Codes screen. Press F6, and then verify that you want to delete the code.

CREATING AND MAINTAINING CUSTOMER STATEMENT MESSAGES

As explained in Chapter 1, statement messages are printed on your customer statements depending on the aging of the account balance.

* From the Edit menu, select Defaults. From the submenu, select Statement Messages.

3.1 From the File menu, select Statement Messages.

You can define a message for inactive and 30-, 60-, and over 60-day accounts. DacEasy supplies these messages, but you can change them, as well as the aging periods. If you change the aging periods later, the messages defined here still apply to the most current through the most delinquent time frames. Figure 2.10 shows the Edit Statement Messages screen with the default messages and aging periods.

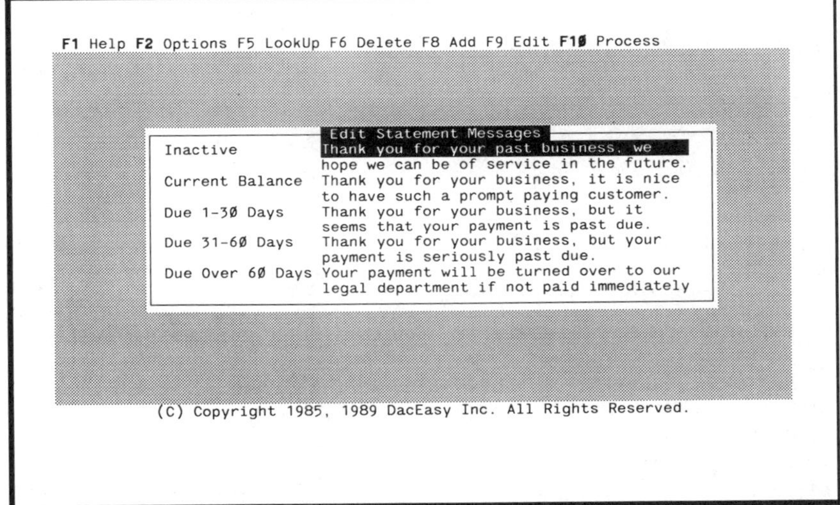

Figure 2.10: Default messages for customer statements

To work with customer statement messages, select the Defaults option from the Edit menu, and then choose Statement Messages from the submenu. You can change a message or aging period simply by typing over the default supplied by DacEasy. For example, you may want to entice your inactive accounts to start buying again by printing the message *Save 20% on your next purchase—use the enclosed coupon soon!* on their statements. To do this, you would type the text over the DacEasy default message for the inactive aging period.

As an example, we'll enter a new message for accounts that are 31 to 60 days old.

1. Use the arrow keys to move the cursor to Due 1–30 Days.
2. Type **Oops! Did you forget a payment?** over any existing message.

3. Press the spacebar to move over the characters remaining from the old message to erase them.
4. Press ↵ to move to the next line.
5. Press the spacebar to move through the entire second line and erase it.
6. Press F10 to exit and save your entries. You can press Esc to cancel any changes.

If you do not want to print a message on your statements, delete the message for that time period. As this example shows, deleting message lines is as simple as changing them. Just press the spacebar to delete each character.

SELECTING A METHOD TO VALUE YOUR INVENTORY

From the Edit menu, select Defaults. From the submenu, select Costing Method.

3.1 From the Options menu, select Defaults. From the submenu, select Cost System.

The costing system is the method by which you determine the cost and, therefore, the value of your inventory items. The DacEasy default is the average cost method, but you can change it. Select the Defaults option from the Edit menu, and then choose Costing Method from the submenu. You will see the screen shown in Figure 2.11.

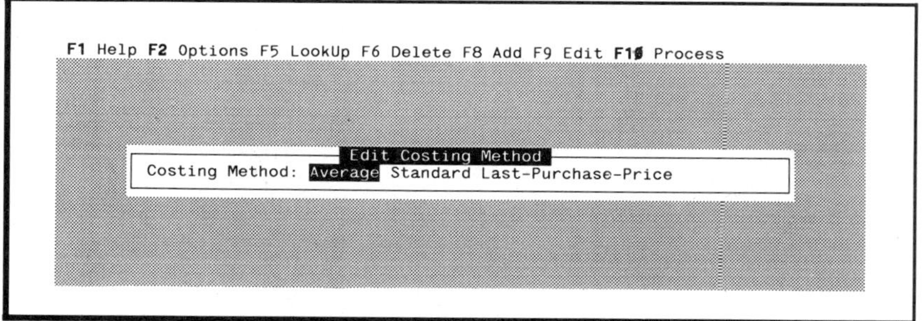

Figure 2.11: Selecting an inventory costing system

After you select a cost method, consult your tax accountant before changing it.

In retail, the last purchase price is commonly used as the costing system. It assumes that the first merchandise purchased is the first merchandise sold (FIFO, meaning first in, first out). Therefore, the cost of all the merchandise on hand is calculated using the most recent purchase price.

3.1 Press the spacebar until the method you want appears, press ↵, and then press ↵ again to verify the change.

If you want to change the cost method, move the cursor to the method you prefer. The program asks

Are you sure you want to change your Costing Method? Yes No

Press ↵ to accept the default, Yes.

ENTERING THE LAST DOCUMENT NUMBER USED

* From the Edit menu, select Defaults. From the submenu, select Last Numbers.

3.1 From the Options menu, select Defaults. From the submenu, select Invoice/ P.O. No. Document numbers are a maximum of five characters.

DacEasy generates document numbers for you. It automatically starts at 000001. You can enter the last number you actually used, and the program will assign numbers beginning with the next number. For example, if you enter the last number you used as 1537, the first invoice number generated by DacEasy will be 1538.

To enter last document numbers, select Defaults from the Edit menu, and then choose Last Numbers from the submenu. The example screen in Figure 2.12 shows a system that used purchase order and invoice numbers, but not purchase-return slip or sales-return slip numbers. Therefore, two document number fields are left at zero. The computer will begin to number the activity in these two areas at 000001. The numbers end at 999999, and then recycle beginning again at 000001.

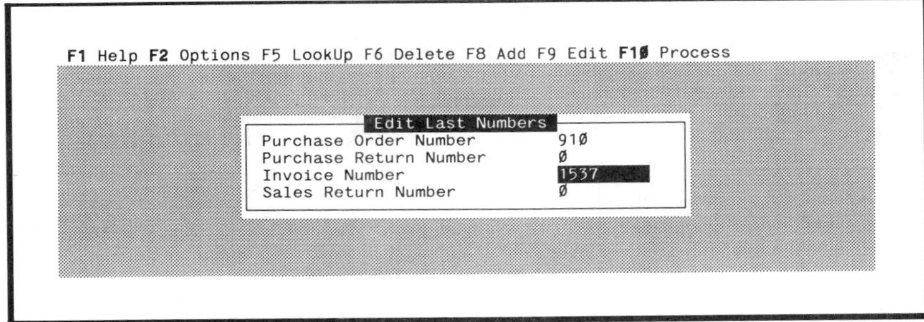

Figure 2.12: Entering the last document numbers used

Enter the last number you used in each category: purchase orders, purchase returns, customer invoices, and sales returns. As you process your work and DacEasy assigns numbers to your documents, these numbers will change.

SETTING UP AND MAINTAINING YOUR SALES TAX TABLE

* From the Edit menu, select Tables. From the submenu, select Tax.

3.1 From the Options menu, select Tax Table.

To set up sales tax codes, select the Tables option from the Edit menu, and then choose Tax from the submenu. After you define them, you can put sales tax codes in customer or vendor records. The program uses the related rate to calculate sales tax on the items being sold or purchased.

As an example, we'll set up the sales tax rate shown in Figure 2.13.

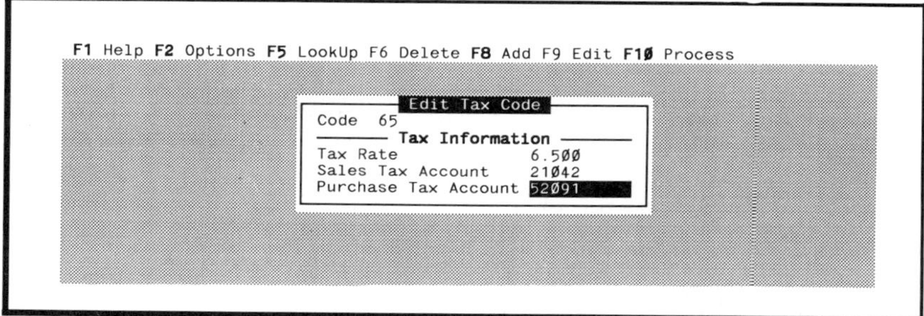

Figure 2.13: Entering sales tax rates

1. Enter **65** in the Code field. To help you remember the tax codes, whenever possible, make the code match the percentage. In this case, the sales tax rate is 6½ percent.
2. Enter **6.500** as the tax rate.
3. In the Sales Tax Account field, enter **21042**, the number of the general ledger liability account that tracks your liability to the state taxing agency.
4. In the Purchase Tax Account field, enter **52091**, the general ledger expense account where you track the amount of tax you pay to vendors.
5. Press F10 to process your entry.

3.1 In the tax table, there are only nine preassigned tax codes possible. Also, the default sales tax and purchase tax accounts are indicated in the interface table rather than in the tax table.

You can create a report to print a listing of the tax codes using the Report Generator option described in Chapter 15.

ESTABLISHING THE PRICE TABLE

* From the Edit menu, select Tables. From the submenu, select Price.

3.1 The price table does not exist. The only way you can discount the price you charge is by entering a percent in the Discount field on each line of the invoice.

As explained in Chapter 1, you can vary what you charge for a product. Each product can be assigned a maximum of three price levels.

To set up price levels, select Tables from the Edit menu, and then select Price from the submenu. To establish each price, enter a code and description. Select a rounding method and enter the percentage to be used when calculating the discount amount. Enter the minimum number of units that must be ordered to qualify the purchase for the price discount. A sample pricing is shown in Figure 2.14.

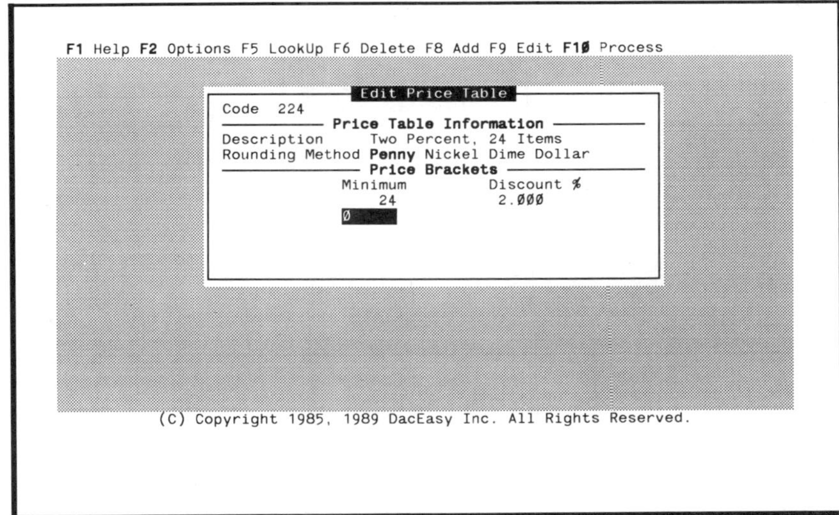

Figure 2.14: Making a price table entry

To print a listing of the price table codes, select Reports from the Main menu, and then select Inventory. Select Price Table from the submenu, enter a range of price codes if you wish, press F10, and choose Printer as the report disposition.

DEVELOPING A TERMS TABLE

A terms code defines the time in which an invoice is due, the discount percentage, if any, and the number of days the discount can be

* From the Edit menu, select Tables. From the submenu, select Terms.

3.1 The terms table does not exist. Discount percent, discount days, and due days are entered in the vendor or customer record instead of a terms code.

taken. The same terms code can be used in both vendor and customer records.

To define terms, select Tables from the Edit menu, and then choose Terms from the submenu. As an example, let's enter the typical terms definition shown in Figure 2.15: 2%, 10 days, net 30. This means that you can take a 2 percent discount if you pay within ten days after the invoice date; otherwise, the total invoice is due in thirty days.

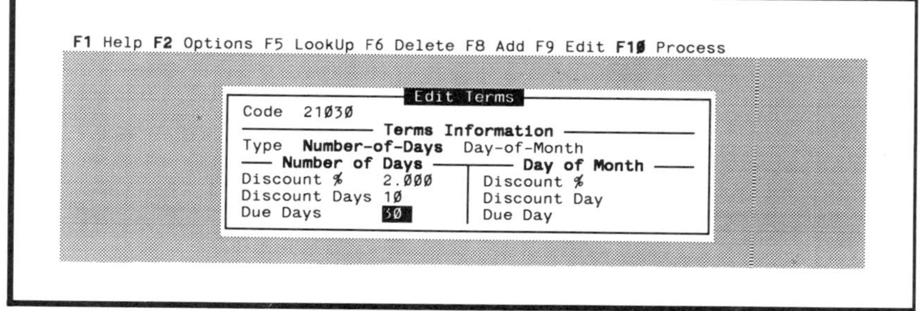

Figure 2.15: Entering a terms code

1. In the Code field, enter **21030**, a code that reflects the terms it represents.
2. Select Number-of-Days from the Type field to define the number of days from the invoice date that the discount is available and the invoice is due. If you select the other option, Day-of-Month, you would indicate the exact day of the month on which the discount expired and the invoice was due.
3. In the Discount % field, enter **2.000**, for 2 percent.
4. In the Discount Days field, enter **10**.
5. In the Due Days field, enter **30**.
6. Press F10 to save the definition.

You can create a report to print a listing of the terms codes by using the Report Generator option described in Chapter 15.

CREATING AND MAINTAINING DATA-ENTRY MESSAGES

✱ From the Edit menu, select Tables. From the submenu, select Messages.

3.1 From the Options menu, select Defaults. From the submenu, select Messages.

Data-entry messages appear when you process a transaction for a vendor or customer whose record contains a message code. They can also be printed on customer invoices or purchase orders to vendors. This is a neat way to include notations on your documents instead of handwriting them in.

To work with data-entry messages, select Tables from the Edit menu, and then choose Messages from the submenu. Press F5 to look up the messages that are supplied with the program. The screen shown in Figure 2.16 appears. You can use, change, or delete these messages.

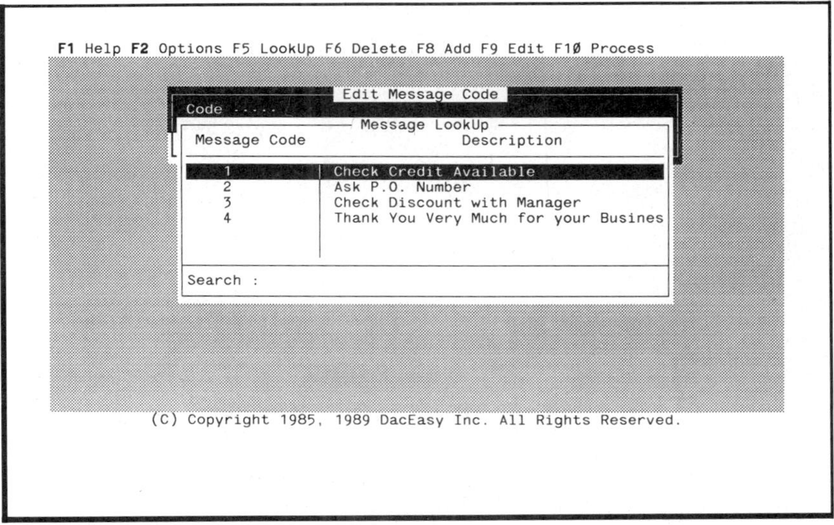

Figure 2.16: Data-entry messages supplied by DacEasy

3.1 You are limited to 40 data-entry messages. You can use the few that are supplied, type over them with your own messages, or add others. The codes, 1 through 40, are preassigned by the system.

To add a message, enter a code, for example, *PO*, then the related message, such as *Mr. Beimfohr must preapprove all POs*. Press F10 to save your entries or Esc to cancel any changes to the table. To use the sample message, you would enter the message code, PO, in each vendor record that the message applies to—the ones that require Mr. Beimfohr's approval before a purchase order is issued.

You can use any message in both customer and vendor files, as well as on purchase orders and invoices. Your messages can supply important information, such as *No charge for delivery* or *Becky can charge on Mrs. Kelly's account.*

DEFINING AND USING PASSWORDS

From the Edit menu, select Defaults. From the submenu, select Passwords.

3.1 From the Options menu, select Password.

If you use passwords, every level must be defined.

As explained in Chapter 1, you can restrict access to DacEasy by selectively allowing users into levels 1 through 6 by means of a password. Refer to Table 1.12 or 1.13 in Chapter 1 to review the access level for version 4.1 or 3.1, respectively.

To define passwords, select the Defaults option from the Edit menu, and then choose Passwords from the submenu. Figure 2.17 shows an example of a password definition screen. Remember, each level allows the user into all those below it. The highest level is Controller, allowing access to the entire program. In the example, THE BOSS is obviously the password for the business owner or manager, who can use the entire system without restriction.

To enter passwords, just move the cursor to each level in turn and enter a password for that level. The password can have up to eight characters. Use the password worksheet you completed in Chapter 1.

After passwords are established, DacEasy will require users to enter the correct password for any options they select. If an option is not accessible to their password level, they will not be able to use it.

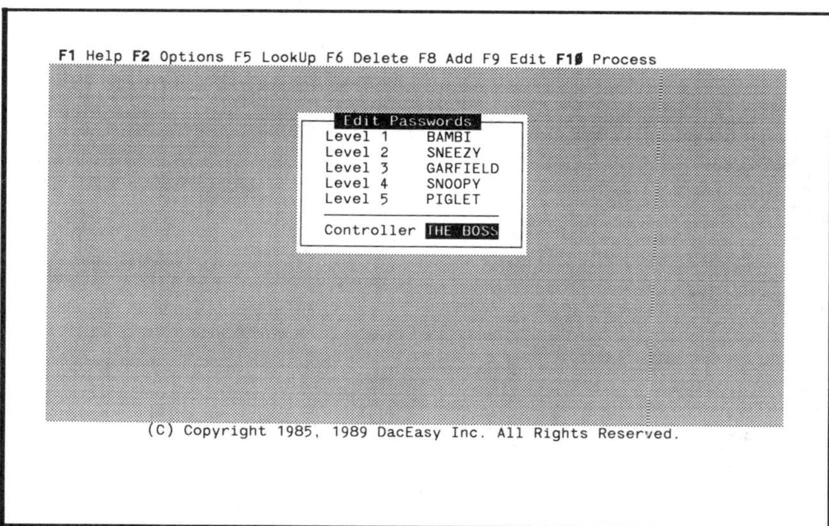

Figure 2.17: Defining passwords

When you exit DacEasy, restart the program (enter the command **dea4** at the drive prompt) and select a menu option, the program asks you to enter your password. Do so, then press F10. The password you type will not appear on the screen. This prevents people from leaning over your shoulder and learning the password. As you type, DacEasy blocks out the characters. You will only have access to the functions defined by the level you have been assigned.

DEFINING YOUR FINANCIAL STATEMENTS

3.1 A Changes in Financial Position report is provided. If you are using the sample chart of accounts, the report generator contains four report formats: balance sheet, income statement, and financial ratios #1 and #2 (RA1 and RA2).

DacEasy supplies you with three financial statements: balance sheet, trial balance, and income statement. The report generator contains formats for several other analyses, and you can also create your own report formats. Your chart of accounts should be in place before doing so. Refer to Chapter 15 for information about creating additional financial statements.

CHAPTER

3

Managing Your System

BEFORE YOU CAN ENTER THE INFORMATION YOU accumulated in Chapter 1, you must define the type of printer and monitor you are using so DacEasy Accounting can work with them. This chapter describes these procedures, as well as other system management tasks, such as making backup copies of your work and exporting and importing data.

If you are setting up your system, you only need to read the first two sections in this chapter now (if you are using a mouse, read the third section, too). Later, return and read the other important sections.

SETTING MONITOR COLORS

* From the Edit menu, select Defaults. From the submenu, select Monitor Colors.

3.1 From the Options menu, select Defaults. From the submenu, select Colors.

If you have a color monitor, you can set the colors you want to use for each section of the DacEasy screens. Monochrome monitor users also can choose from various tones for the screen sections and borders.

You will have to adjust the default colors if a portion of your screen is not visible. Perhaps the background and the prompts have similar settings, which result in little or no visible contrast.

To set monitor colors, select the Defaults option from the Edit menu, and then choose Monitor Colors. You will see the screen for setting colors, as shown in Figure 3.1 (of course, the reproduction is what you would see on a monochrome monitor). The window at the

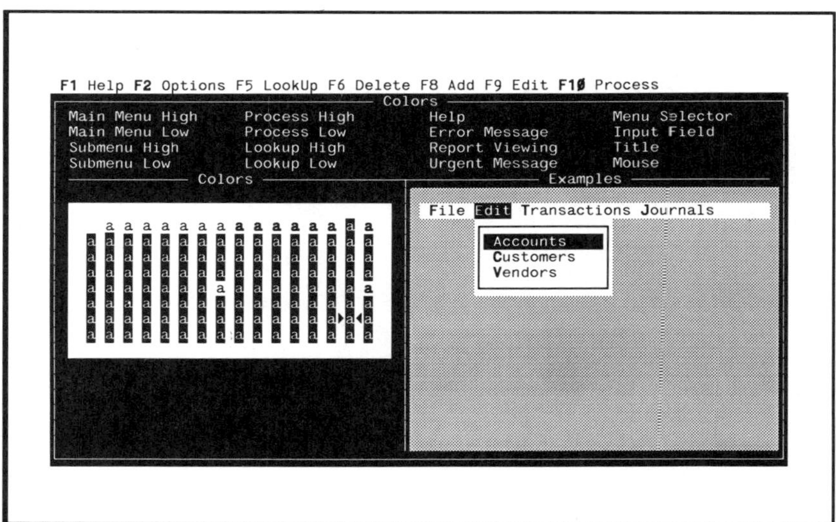

Figure 3.1: Setting colors for your monitor

top of the screen lists the areas for which you can select colors. The areas in version 4.1 are described in Table 3.1, and those in version 3.1 are described in Table 3.2.

Table 3.1: Monitor Color Definition Areas in Version 4.1

Color Definition Choice	Area of Screen
Main Menu High	Highlighted letter on horizontal menu.
Main Menu Low	Other characters on horizontal menu.
Submenu High	Highlighted letter on vertical menus.
Submenu Low	Other characters on vertical menus.
Process High	Text on process screens.
Process Low	Background on process screens.
Lookup High	Text in lookup windows.
Lookup Low	Background in lookup windows.
Help	The window containing help text that appears when you press F1.
Error Message	Prompts that let you know when there is an error.
Report Viewing	Reports viewed on screen.
Urgent Message	Prompts that let you know what the program is doing, such as printing.
Menu Selector	The indicator of where the cursor is placed on a menu item.
Input Field	The names of the input fields on the screen.
Title	Titles of screens and headers in windows.
Mouse	The marker indicating mouse position.

Table 3.2: Monitor Color Definition Areas in Version 3.1

Color Definition Choice	Area of Screen
Horizontal Menu	The Main menu across the top of the screen.
Vertical Menu	The submenu that appears beneath a Main menu option.
Menu Selector	The indicator of where the cursor is placed on a menu item.
Background	The background on the entire monitor.
Window	The boxes that appear with information in them.
Titles/Headers	Titles of screens and headers in windows.

Table 3.2: Monitor Color Definition Areas in Version 3.1 (continued)

Color Definition Choice	Area of Screen
Help Window	The window containing help text that appears when you press F1.
Prompt	The names of the input fields on the screen.
Active Field	The input field where the cursor is currently placed.
Inactive Field	Input fields that do not contain the cursor.
Line Status	The prompts at the bottom of the screen describing available function keys.
Urgent Status	Prompts that let you know what the program is doing, such as printing.

Each *a* in the window titled Colors represents one of the various color combinations. For example, choosing the *a* in the shaded box while Menu Selector is selected at the top of the screen would make the menu selector a shaded box. The bright letters are for high intensity; those on the left are the same color combinations in low intensity. The window titled Examples displays what each possibility looks like as you move the cursor, which appears as a double arrow, through the choices.

3.1 The cursor is on the Horizontal Menu area when you select Colors.

When you first select the Monitor Colors option, the cursor should rest on the area name Main Menu High. If you cannot see the cursor in the top window, just press ↵, and the currently selected area will be displayed (with the current color settings) in the Examples window.

To change the color settings, follow the instructions below.

1. Use the arrow keys to place the cursor on the name of the area of the screen you want to define, and then press ↵. A reproduction of the current choice will appear in the Examples window.
2. Use the arrow keys to move the cursor around the Colors window. As you do, the sample will change according to the selection the cursor is marking.
3. When you find the color setting you like, press ↵ to select it.
4. Repeat the first three steps for each area you want to change.
5. When you have selected all the settings, press F10 to process your choices. If you change your mind, you can press Esc to cancel all the changes you made.

You can return to the Color Definition screen and change the settings at any time.

If you have a monochrome monitor and you can't find a satisfactory setting, try starting the program with the command **dea4/bw**.

SETTING PRINTER CODES

* From the Edit menu, select Defaults. From the submenu, select Printers.

3.1 From the Options menu, select Defaults. From the submenu, select Printer Codes. You can only define one printer at a time and you must enter the codes. The default printer codes are for an IBM Proprinter or emulation.

Printer codes are electronic messages sent by DacEasy to your printer whenever a report is about to print. Most DacEasy reports are printed in condensed type, approximately 17 characters per inch. Some documents, such as checks, are printed using normal type, which is 10 characters per inch. The computer sends printer codes to the printer to tell it which type size to use for each document.

DacEasy allows up to three printer definitions at one time and supplies the codes for most popular printers. To define your printer settings, select the Defaults option from the Edit menu, and then choose Printers. You will see the Edit Printer Codes screen.

Select to define printer 1, 2, or 3. Press ↵. When the cursor is in the Printer Name field, press F5 to see a list of available printers, as shown in Figure 3.2. Press PgDn to scroll through the list.

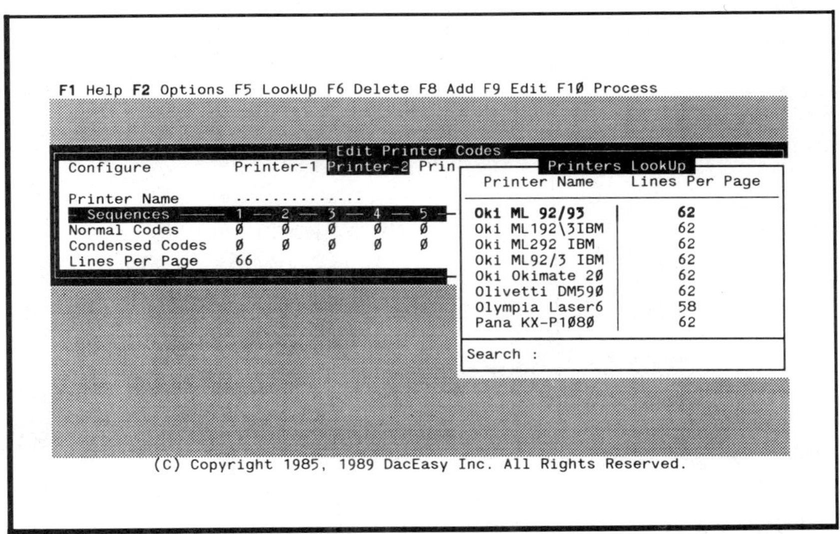

Figure 3.2: Selecting a printer

If your printer is not listed, you must enter the printer codes. Set the printer codes for normal and condensed type specified in your printer manual. Some printer manuals list the codes as ASCII characters. You must enter the decimal equivalents of the codes in the Edit Printer Codes screen. You'll also need to specify the number of lines you want printed on a sheet of paper. Standard paper is 11 inches long. On a printer set to print 6 lines per inch, 60 printed lines should give you ½-inch margins at both the top and bottom of the page. The default setting is 62. Laser printers need a larger margin; a typical setting is 58.

USING A MOUSE

3.1 You cannot use a mouse. Use the arrow keys to position the cursor on the option you want and press ↵, or enter the number of the option. Other functions listed across the bottom of the screen are accessible by pressing the indicated key, such as F1 for help.

If your system includes a mouse, you can use it to select items, access Help screens, exit the current function, process the current input, and delete characters within a field, as follows:

- To select a menu option, field entry, or record in a lookup window, position the mouse pointer on the item on which you want to take action and click the left button once.
- To display field-sensitive Help screens, click on F1.
- To display the Help index, click on F2, then on Help Index.
- To save your input, click on F10.
- To exit to the previous screen, click the right button once.
- To delete characters in an input field, position the pointer on the first character you want to delete, hold down the left button as you drag the pointer through all the characters to be erased, and release the button when all the characters are highlighted.

CHECKING FILE STATUS

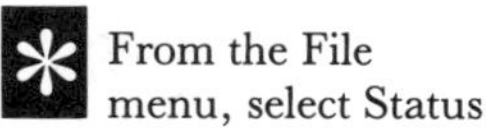
From the File menu, select Status.

Your file sizes increase and decrease as you enter transactions, post them, clear them, and remove them during end-of-period processing. The size of your chart of accounts, customer, vendor, and product files will not fluctuate as much as those that hold your transactions. To check the status of your files, select the Status option from the File menu. The File Status screen lists the total disk space available and how many records are in each file, as shown in Figure 3.3.

3.1 From the Options menu, select Status.

REVIEWING AND CHANGING FILE SIZES IN VERSION 3.1

With version 3.1, your files may grow beyond the space you originally designated for them. You may have to expand or reduce the number of records defined for a file to make better use of your disk space. You should periodically check on the amount of space remaining for each file and resize the file accordingly. When you choose the Status option from the Options menu, the program displays the number of records defined and the number of records actually used in each file of your program.

3.1 From the Options menu, select Rehash. But back up your files first to ensure that you won't loose data if a problem arises.

To change the space available for a file, select the Rehash option on the Options menu. The Rehash screen looks the same as the File

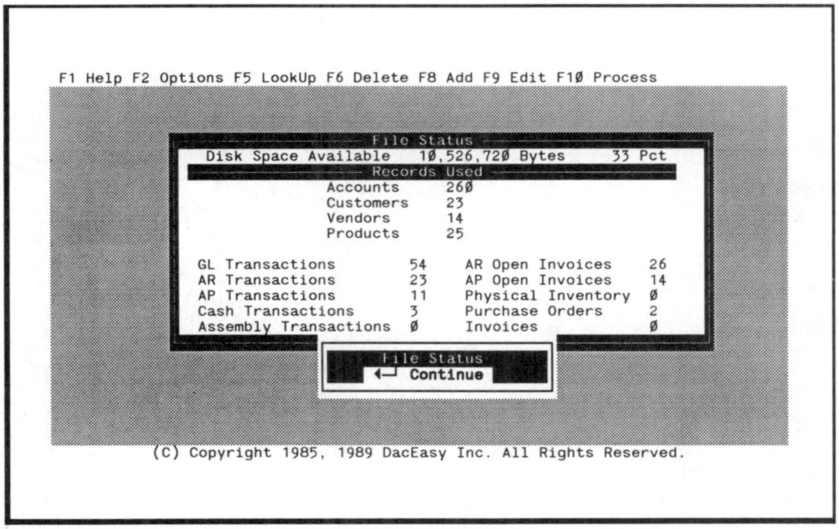

```
F1 Help F2 Options F5 LookUp F6 Delete F8 Add F9 Edit F10 Process

                         File Status
   Disk Space Available    10,526,720 Bytes        33 Pct
                         Records Used
                   Accounts      260
                   Customers     23
                   Vendors       14
                   Products      25

 GL Transactions          54     AR Open Invoices      26
 AR Transactions          23     AP Open Invoices      14
 AP Transactions          11     Physical Inventory    0
 Cash Transactions        3      Purchase Orders       2
 Assembly Transactions    0      Invoices              0

                         File Status
                         ↵ Continue

      (C) Copyright 1985, 1989 DacEasy Inc. All Rights Reserved.
```

Figure 3.3: Displaying file status in version 4.1

Status screen, but here you can change the numbers in the Defined column to make room for a growing database.

To rehash your files, press ↵ to move past any file that does not need attention. Change the number of records in files that are nearing capacity. Enter the number of records you now expect to need within the next two to six months. Press ↵ to move through the last file when you are finished adjusting the file sizes, and the rehash process will begin.

CHANGING THE PROGRAM DATE

When you return from a holiday or weekend, before entering transactions, you should change the program date to match the date of the transactions. You can even set the date back to the last day of the month you want to close.

You can change the program date from any menu by pressing F4 and entering the date you want to use to process your work. The prompt and a new date entry are shown in Figure 3.4.

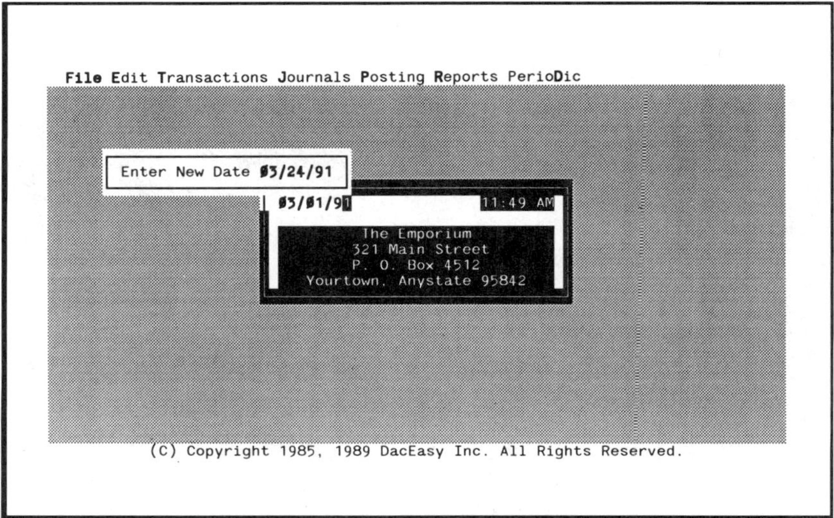

Figure 3.4: Changing the program date

PROTECTING YOUR FILES

Computers can be temperamental. They are sensitive to power fluctuations, cigarette smoke, magnets, and full moons. You should always take the precaution of backing up your files. This means making a duplicate copy of your work. If your files are damaged, you can use the backup files to restore your data. The amount of work that you will have to redo depends on how often you back up your files.

It is best to make backup copies of your work onto floppy disks and store the disks somewhere other than in your office. You can create a subdirectory on your hard disk (for example, one named BACKUP in the DEA4 directory) and back up your data files into it instead of using floppy disks. However, this is not recommended because if anything happens to your hard disk, both your original data and the backup data could be corrupted or lost.

BACKING UP YOUR FILES

* From the File menu, select Backup.

The procedure outlined here is for backing up all your data files. It is assumed that you have installed the program in a directory named DEA4 and placed your files in a subdirectory named FILES. If you substituted other names during installation, use them in your backup routine.

1. Format several blank disks. The number of blank disks you will need depends on the size of your data.
2. Select Backup from the File menu.
3. In the Data Directory field, press ↵ to accept the default C:\DEA4\FILES or enter the drive, directory, and subdirectory where your accounting data is located.
4. When backing up to a floppy disk, place a formatted disk in the drive you designated as the Backup Disk drive (usually drive A.). Any data on the disk in drive A (or in the subdirectory you entered in the Backup Disk field) will be erased.
5. In the Backup Disk field, press ↵ to accept the default A:\ or enter the drive, directory, and subdirectory to which you want the data copied. As the files are copied to the designated

location, they are listed on the screen. If your data exceeds the space available on the first disk, DacEasy prompts you to remove the disk and replace it with a fresh disk.

6. Label each disk as you remove it from drive A with the date and time of the backup routine and assign it a sequential number starting with 01. If you have to restore your data using backup disks, you must reenter the data in the order it was copied.

3.1 You can use Graph+Mate to create graphs and listings from your DacEasy Accounting files. Graph+Mate is covered in Appendix E.

BACKING UP YOUR FILES IN VERSION 3.1 With version 3.1, you can use either DOS (disk operating system) commands or an option provided with DacEasy Graph+Mate to back up your work. This section describes how to use DOS commands.

The procedure outlined here is for backing up all your data files. It is assumed that you have a hard-disk system and that you installed the program in a directory named DEA3 and placed your files in a subdirectory named FILES. If you substituted other names during installation, use them in your backup routine.

1. Format several blank disks. The number of blank disks you will need depends on the size of your data and how you issue the Backup command.

3.1 If you put DacEasy on a drive other than the one containing DOS, you must also include the drive designation immediately before the backslash that indicates the directory path. For example, if DacEasy is on drive D, you would type **backup d:\dea3\files a:**.

2. Turn the computer on. When the C: prompt appears, if you do not have DOS in the root directory (the one you access when you first turn on the computer), change to the directory where DOS was installed. The command is **cd** followed immediately by the name of the directory.
3. Place a formatted disk in drive A. Be aware that any data on the disk will be erased.
4. At the C: prompt, enter **backup \dea3\files a:**. This command will back up the data found in the subdirectory named FILES in the directory named DEA3 onto the disk in drive A.
5. As the files are copied onto the disk in drive A, they are listed on the screen. If your data exceeds the space available on the first disk, DOS prompts you to remove the disk and replace it with a second formatted disk, which DOS calls Backup Diskette 02.

6. Label each disk as you remove it from drive A with the date and time of the backup routine and assign it a sequential number starting with 01. If you have to restore your data using backup disks, you must reenter the data in the order it was copied.

RESTORING YOUR DATA FROM A BACKUP

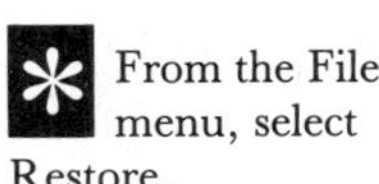

From the File menu, select Restore.

If you back up your files regularly, losing data will not be a catastrophe. Select the Restore option from the File menu, and then follow this procedure to restore the most recent copy of your work:

The data from the backup replaces the data currently in your files. Any entries since the last backup operation will be lost when you restore data.

1. Place the backup disk numbered 01 in drive A.
2. In the Data Directory field, press ↵ to accept the default of C:\DEA4\FILES or enter the drive, directory, and subdirectory where your DacEasy Accounting data is located.
3. In the Restore Disk field, press ↵ to accept the default of A:\ or enter the drive, directory, and subdirectory from which you are restoring the data. All the data found on the disk in drive A (or in the backup subdirectory) will be loaded into the subdirectory where your current DacEasy Accounting data is located.

If your data is contained on more than one disk, DacEasy prompts you to remove the first disk and replace it with the second backup disk. Be sure to restore the backup disks in the order you made them. As the files are copied back into the DacEasy subdirectory, their names are listed on the screen.

RESTORING YOUR DATA IN VERSION 3.1 With version 3.1, you can restore the most recent copy of your work from your backup disks using the following procedure:

1. Turn the computer on. When the C: prompt appears, if you do not have DOS in the root directory (the one you access when you first turn on the computer), change to the directory where DOS was installed.

2. Place the backup disk numbered 01 in drive A.
3. At the C: prompt, enter **restore a: \dea3\files*.***. This command will load all the data found on the disk in drive A into the subdirectory named FILES in the directory named DEA3.
4. If your data is contained on more than one disk, DOS prompts you to remove the first disk and replace it with the second backup disk, which DOS calls Backup Diskette 02. As the files are copied back into the DacEasy subdirectory, their names are listed on the screen.

3.1 If you put DacEasy on a drive other than the one containing DOS, you must also include the drive designation immediately before the backslash that indicates the directory path. For example, if DacEasy is on drive D, you would type **restore a: d:\dea3\files*.***.

All the data in your DacEasy files subdirectory will be overwritten by what is on the backup disk.

EXPORTING DACEASY DATA TO OTHER APPLICATIONS

3.1 If you want to export your DacEasy Accounting data, you must use Graph+Mate.

You can export (transfer) the data in DacEasy Accounting to a file, which can be imported (written into) another software application. You might want to transfer your account balances into a spreadsheet to do an analysis or put your customer's information into a database manager or word processor to use for form letters.

To create an export file, follow the steps below:

1. Choose a report that contains the information you want to transfer.
2. Select the report criteria and press F10 to process the report. The Report Disposition screen appears, as shown in Figure 3.5.
3. Select Export as the Report Disposition.
4. Press ↵ twice to skip the Printer Name and Lines Per Page fields. They are not applicable.
5. For Ascii File Name, enter a file name with an extension recognized by the application to receive the information or press ↵ to accept the default file name EXPORT.TXT if it is appropriate.

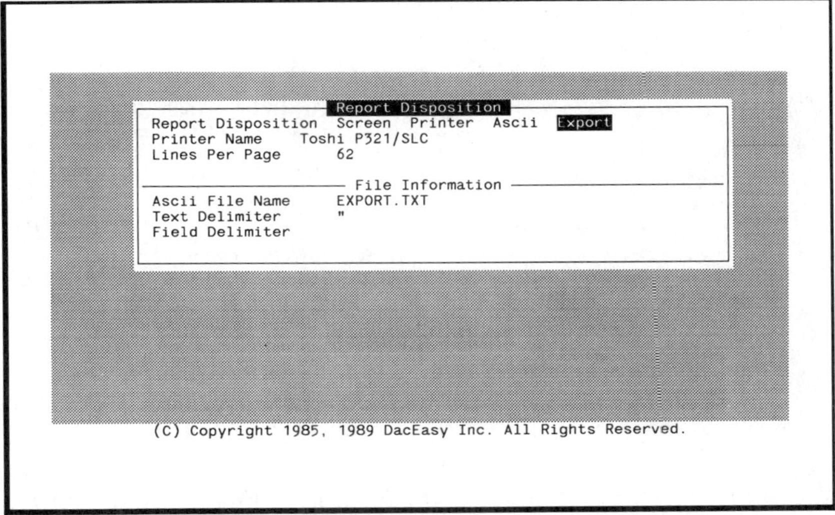

Figure 3.5: Creating an export file from DacEasy Accounting data

6. In the Text Delimiter field, enter the delimiter recognized by the application to receive the data or press ↵ to accept the default quotation marks if they are appropriate. A text delimiter tells the receiving application where a field starts and ends.
7. In the Field Delimiter field, enter the delimiter recognized by the application to receive the data or press ↵ to accept the default commas if they are appropriate. A field delimiter tells the receiving application what a field is within a string of characters.
8. Press F10 to process the transfer.

An export file will be created in the subdirectory with the name you designated. From there, you can move it into another application using features provided by the other software program.

IMPORTING DATA INTO THE DACEASY GENERAL LEDGER

* From the File menu, select Import.

DacEasy Accounting's Import option can be used to transfer financial data into your general ledger from another software application or, more commonly, to import data from one DacEasy company into a DacEasy consolidated company.

3.1 Version 3.1 does not include an Import option.

To create an ASCII file for importing data from another application, first enter a header line with the following information:

- A journal code (up to 6 alphanumeric characters)
- A reference to identify the transaction (up to 10 alphanumeric characters)
- The date of the transaction (entered in YYYYMMDD format, using the full year and two digits each for the month and the day)

Next create a detail line for each line item that contains the following:

- The general ledger account number for the company into which you are importing data (up to 10 alphanumeric characters)
- The account name (up to 25 alphanumeric characters)
- A flag indicating if the entry is a debit or a credit (D = debit, C = credit)
- The amount of the transaction for this line (up to 12 numeric characters, including the decimal point)

In the file, place a comma between fields. Do not use spaces between characters. For example, a detail line showing postage expense would be

```
5213,Postage,D,532.78
```

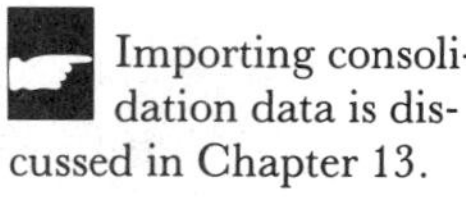

Importing consolidation data is discussed in Chapter 13.

After you create the file, save it under an ASCII file name.

To import the file, select Import from the File menu. At the prompt

```
Path/File Name:
```

enter the ASCII file name, drive, and subdirectory where the file can be found. The file will be copied into the DacEasy general ledger transaction file. You can review the data by selecting General Ledger from the Transactions menu and entering the journal code. Don't forget to post the data after it is imported.

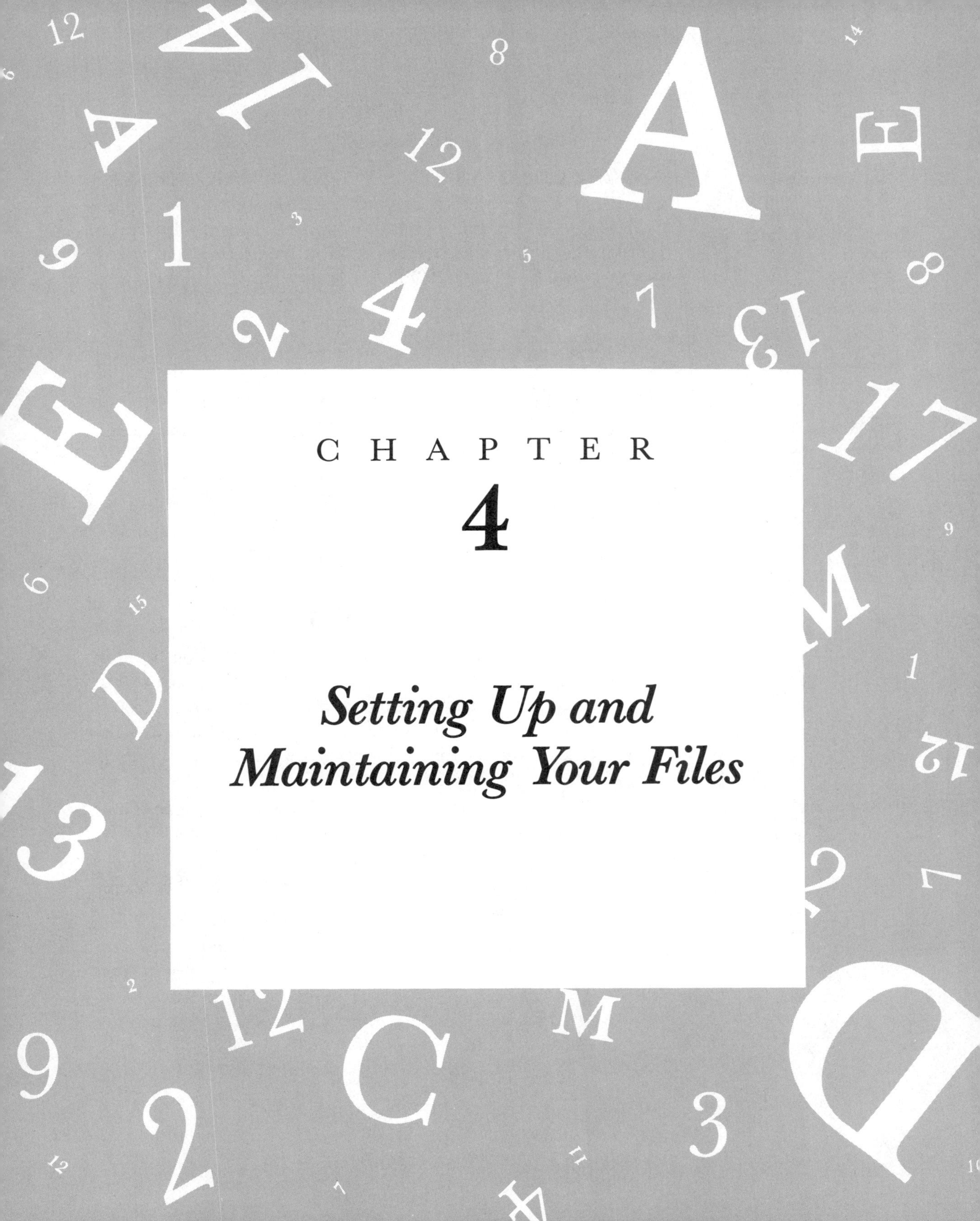

CHAPTER

4

Setting Up and Maintaining Your Files

3.1 As you create records, the order of the fields in which you enter data will be different than the steps in the examples.

IN CHAPTER 2, WE SET UP SYSTEM PARAMETERS, which form the foundation of your DacEasy system. Now you'll learn how to set up and maintain your files. You should create a record for each customer, vendor, product, and service you have in your business. You can add, edit, or delete records from these files.

MAINTAINING YOUR CUSTOMER FILE

* From the Edit menu, select Customers.

3.1 From the File menu, select Customers.

If you provide a product or service to customers and allow them to pay you a little each month, you need a method to track how much they still owe. When customers don't pay you immediately, the amounts they owe become your accounts receivable. You'll need to set up customer records to track their purchases and payments. DacEasy updates your inventory and sales files during daily processing.

ADDING CUSTOMER RECORDS

To add a customer record, select the Customers option from the Edit menu. You will see the Edit Customer screen, shown in Figure 4.1. Enter the information from your customer worksheets into the appropriate fields, which are described in Chapter 1. The fields that are not included on your worksheets are calculated by the program, as described in Table 4.1.

Figure 4.2 shows a sample customer record. As an example of how to set up an existing customer, we'll enter the sample record.

1. In the Code field, enter **MERC**, the code assigned to Mercy Hospital Guild.
2. In the Name field, enter **Mercy Hospital Guild**. If this customer were an individual, you would probably want to enter the first name followed by the last name, as in *Bertha Woodward*. This would be an appropriate format for customer invoices and statements.

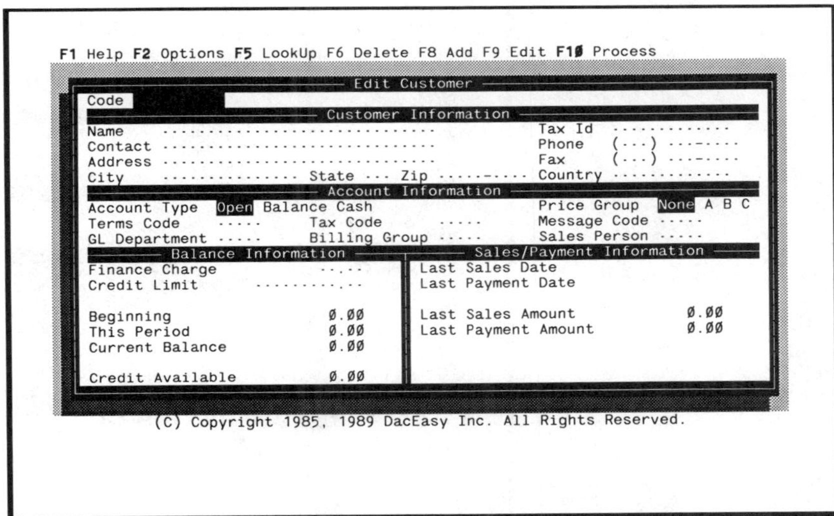

Figure 4.1: Edit Customer screen

Table 4.1: Program-Calculated Customer Record Fields

Field	Program Calculations
Beginning	The program generates the previous balance during period-end processing by adding the activity for the period being closed to the ongoing total balance of the account.
This Period	The program generates the balance for the activity posted this period from daily processing.
Current Balance	The program generates the ongoing balance of the account by adding the activity of the current period to the previous balance.
Credit Available	The program calculates the credit available by subtracting sales from the credit limit in the customer record. An amount preceded by a minus sign means the limit has been exceeded.
Last Sale Date	The program generates the last sale date from billing entries.
Last Payment Date	The program generates the last payment date from cash receipt entries.
Last Sales Amount	The program generates the last sales amount from customer billing entries, excluding sales tax.
Last Payment Amount	The program generates the last payment amount from cash receipts entries.

Version 3.1: The Last Sales Amount and Last Payment Amount fields do not exist.

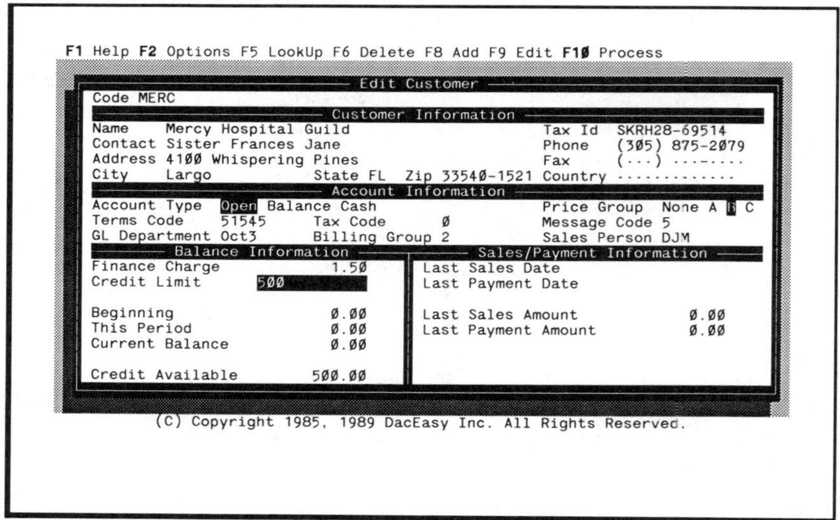

Figure 4.2: A completed customer record

3. Enter **Sister Frances Jane** as the Contact for this customer's account.
4. In the Address field, enter **4100 Whispering Pines**, the mailing address for invoices and statements.
5. Enter **Largo, FL, 33540 1521** (using the extended post office numbering) in the City, State, and Zip fields, respectively.
6. In the Tax Id field, enter **SKRH28-69514**. This is the customer's resale number. The guild purchases flowers from your florist department to sell in the hospital gift shop. You do not charge sales tax on purchases a customer makes for resale.
7. Enter **305 875 2079** in the Phone field.
8. Press ↵ to move through the Fax field. If the customer had a fax machine, you would enter its phone number here.

3.1 The Fax and Country fields do not exist.

9. Press ↵ to skip the Country field. All our customers are located in the same country, so there is no need to complete this field.

3.1 A Cash type customer does not exist. In addition to records for actual customers, you should set up customer records for a Cash account and for each credit card you accept so you can track all cash sales in one record. Keeping a separate record for each credit card allows you to analyze the value versus the cost of accepting the charge card, as well as verify the amount you should deposit to your account with the credit card institution.

3.1 The price and terms tables do not exist. You must enter the discount percent, discount days, and due days instead of the terms code in the customer and vendor records.

3.1 If sales tax does not apply to this customer, you do not have to make an entry in the Sales Tax Code field. When you do enter a code from your tax table, the actual tax rate appears in the Rate field.

10. For Account Type, select Open for an open-item customer account. Open-item accounts keep detail on each transaction until it is offset by another entry. For example, a credit memo will appear as an individual item until it is applied to an invoice. The other account types are Balance (balance-forward), which removes detail after the end of the period in which the transaction occurs and leaves only a total amount due; or Cash, for customers you don't want to record individually but whose purchases you want to track in inventory and sales.
11. In the Price Group field, select B, which represents the pricing we give to wholesale customers. When the customer purchases a product, the selling price in the inventory record will be discounted by the percentage defined in the price table.
12. In the Terms Code field, enter **51545**. During data entry, the code will be translated into the discount percent, discount days, and due days defined in the terms table. This code represents a 5 percent discount, which is the amount the customer is allowed off the total invoice for paying within the discount terms time frame; 15 discount days, which means that the customer can take the discount rate if payment is made within 15 days of the invoice date; and 45 due days, which gives the customer 45 days from the invoice date to pay the invoice in full.
13. Enter **0** in the Tax Code field because all this customer's purchases are for resale (you can't leave this field blank). If the customer ever does buy a taxable item, you can enter the tax amount when you create the invoice. If this customer usually did have tax charged on its purchases, you would enter the code from your sales tax table that represents the percent you must charge in sales tax.
14. Enter **5** for the Message Code. In the message code table, this code is defined as *No charge for delivery*. It will appear on the screen whenever there is activity—a sale, payment, or adjustment—on this customer's account.

15. In the GL Department field, enter **Oct3** (without any punctuation). Our sample company departmentalizes by inventory, not by customer, so the GL Department field is not applicable and can be used for another purpose. Here we record the birth date of the contact, Sister Frances Jane. At the end of each month, we sort the customers into a listing of those who have a birthday in the next month. Then, as a part of our public relations campaign, we send them all birthday cards.

3.1 The Billing Group table does not exist.

16. Enter **2** in the Billing Group field. This means an invoice will be created for this customer when recurring invoices are generated for billing group 2. Recurring invoices are discussed in Chapter 6.
17. In the Sales Person field, enter **DJM**, the initials of the salesperson who services this customer's account. DacEasy does not maintain a table for your salesperson codes, so you will have to keep a manual reference of who has what code.

3.1 Enter the monthly percentage in the Monthly Int. Rate field.

18. In the Finance Charge field, enter **1.50**. This is the monthly percentage that is charged on this customer's past-due invoices. One and one-half percent equals 18 percent per year.
19. In the Credit Limit field, enter **500**, the maximum this customer can owe at any time.
20. Press Shift-F5 after the record is defined to access the alternative address screen, then press F8 to add a new alternative address.
21. Enter Mercy Hospital Guild as the Name.

3.1 Alternative addresses for vendors and customers are not available. You can, however, override the address by entering a different one during data entry of invoices, purchase orders, and other documents.

22. Enter **4209 Whispering Pines, Largo, FL, 33540-1522**, the customer's shipping address, which is the location of the hospital gift shop.
23. Press ↵ to move through the Phone, Fax, and Country fields.
24. Enter **FTD** in the Ship Via field, and then press ↵ to skip the FOB field.
25. Select Yes for Default so that the alternative shipping address will be printed on all invoices. If you do not want this address printed on documents, choose No for Default.

26. Press F10 to save the address, and then press ↵ to return to the customer record. The completed alternative address is shown in Figure 4.3.

The program generates data for the Beginning, This Period, Current Balance, Credit Available, Last Sales Date, Last Payment Date, Last Sales Amount, and Last Payment Amount fields, as described in Table 4.1.

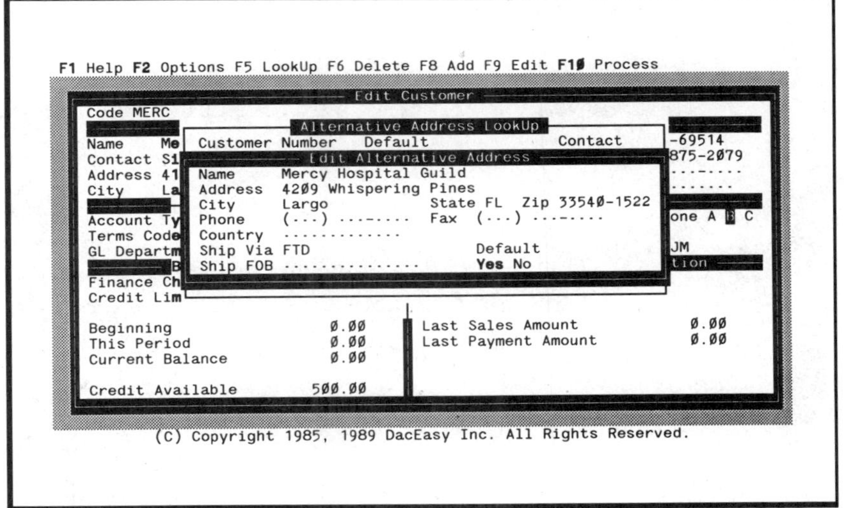

Figure 4.3: Entering an alternative address for a customer

If your system is already set up and you are simply adding a new customer, you are finished—a brand new customer has neither historical information nor outstanding invoices. However, if you are in the process of setting up your entire DacEasy Accounting system, you should continue to add information.

After you define each customer, you should enter the account's statistical data, as described below. If you are in a hurry to get up and going, you can come back and do it later, but don't forget. This historical information will help you analyze the growth of your business.

In the meantime, DacEasy will be tracking the current year's activity as you process your daily work. If you do not enter the information now, when you update the record, you will have to add the total to date from your previous system to the total DacEasy has been accumulating in the This Year field.

In any event, you need to continue with the record and enter outstanding invoices, as explained later in this section.

ENTERING STATISTICAL DATA FOR CUSTOMERS Adding initial statistical data to the files discussed in this chapter is done only once, during setup. Thereafter, the program updates the data from transaction processing and the year-end closing routine.

DacEasy retains three years of record history (for customer, vendor, product, and service records) in these time periods:

- Year Before Last: Amounts from two years ago.
- Last Year: Amounts from one year ago.
- This Year: Amounts from the current year.
- Budget: Your prediction for the current year.

3.1 *Forecast* is used instead of *Budget*.

The customer record accumulates statistical data in the following four categories. You can track statistics in each of them for every time period.

3.1 The row titled Returns does not exist.

- # Invoices: Number of invoices.
- # Returns: Number of returns from this customer.
- $ Sales: Sales in dollars.
- $ Costs: Costs in dollars.
- $ Profit: Profit in dollars.

3.1 You enter statistical data by category for each time period. For example, you indicate the # Invoices for the year before last, last year, this year, and forecast, then move on to $ Sales. As soon as you enter the forecast for the last row, the program records your entries and clears the screen for the next record. There is no need to press F10 to record your entries.

You enter the data in each category for the year before last, then all the data for last year, then the figures for this year to date, and finally, your budget for each category. Remember, the budget is for an entire year. The variance through the year is a gauge for how close you are to reaching your annual goal.

As you enter historical data in a record (again, this applies to vendor, product, and service records, as well as customer records), the program generates the information in the Variance and % fields for each category. The program calculates the variance by subtracting the budget from the current year's total. For the percentage, it calculates the percent of difference between the budget and the current year's total.

To demonstrate adding historical information, we will continue working with the sample customer record and add the data shown in Figure 4.4.

1. While the customer record is on the screen, press Shift-F3. The window for entering historical information appears.
2. The first entries in this window are data from the year before last (YBL). In the row titled Invoices, enter **1** to indicate the number of invoices you had for this customer two years ago. (Mercy became a customer in December two years ago, so its activity in this time period was minimal.)

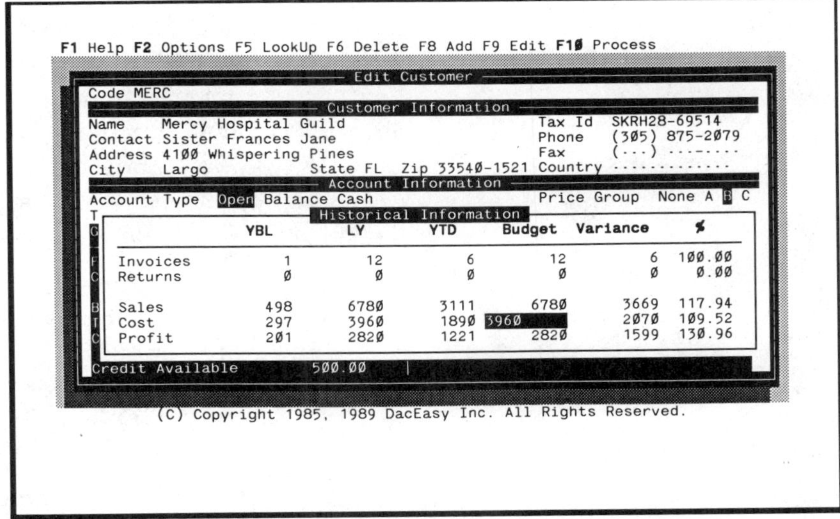

Figure 4.4: Entering historical information for a customer

3. The next row pertains to merchandise the customer has sent back. In this case, the customer has never returned any products, so press ⟵ to skip Returns.
4. In the next row, Sales, enter **498** to indicate the dollar amount sold to this customer two years ago.
5. In the fourth row, Cost, enter **297** to indicate the dollar amount you paid for the merchandise sold to this customer two years ago. If you have not kept accurate, detailed

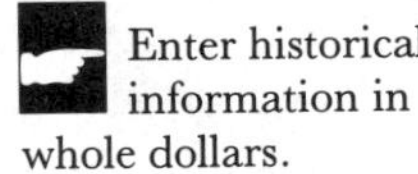
Enter historical information in whole dollars.

records, this figure may be difficult to reconstruct. If you must estimate, use a percentage of the sales dollars as a cost factor.

6. Under the column titled LY (last year), in the Invoices row, enter **12**, the number of invoices you had for this customer one year ago.
7. Press ↵ at Returns, and in the Sales row, enter **6780**, the dollar amount of sales made to this customer one year ago.
8. For Cost, enter **3960**, the amount you paid for items sold to this customer one year ago.
9. Under YTD (year to date), in the Invoices row, enter **6**, the number of invoices created for this customer so far this year. Be sure to count all the invoices that are still outstanding, too. When you enter this amount, the program calculates variance and percentage from the budget as a minus figure. You can then enter your budget, and the program will recalculate the actual variance and percentage. Notice that the year to date is compared to the expectations for the entire year.
10. Press ↵ at Returns, and for Sales, enter **3111**, the dollar amount of sales made to this customer so far this year. Be sure to include the amounts on invoices that are still not paid. When you enter the amount for this year, the program calculates variance and percentage.
11. For Cost under YTD, enter **1890**, the amount you paid for the items sold so far this year to the customer. Remember to include the cost for items on the outstanding invoices. Again, when you enter this data, the program calculates variance and percentage.
12. Under the column titled Budget, in the Invoices row, enter **12**, the total number of invoices you predict you will create this year for this customer.
13. Press ↵ at Returns, and for Sales, enter **6780**, the total sales dollars you predict you will sell this year to the customer (you expect business to remain the same as last year). The program updates the variance and percentage.

14. For Cost, enter **3960**, the total you predict it will cost you for merchandise you expect to sell to the customer this year. The program updates the variance and percentage for dollar costs.

As soon as you enter the budget for costs, the program calculates the profit in dollars, by subtracting costs from sales dollars.

15. Press F10 to save the historical data and return to the customer record.

ENTERING OPEN CUSTOMER INVOICES Entering open invoices in the customer record is done only once, during system setup. After you begin processing your daily work in DacEasy, customer invoices must be entered through the Billing module. That procedure is explained in Chapter 6.

We'll continue with our sample customer and add an outstanding invoice to this record. Figure 4.5 shows the information.

1. While the customer record is on the screen, press F7. The window for adding open invoices (those the customer has not yet paid in full) appears.

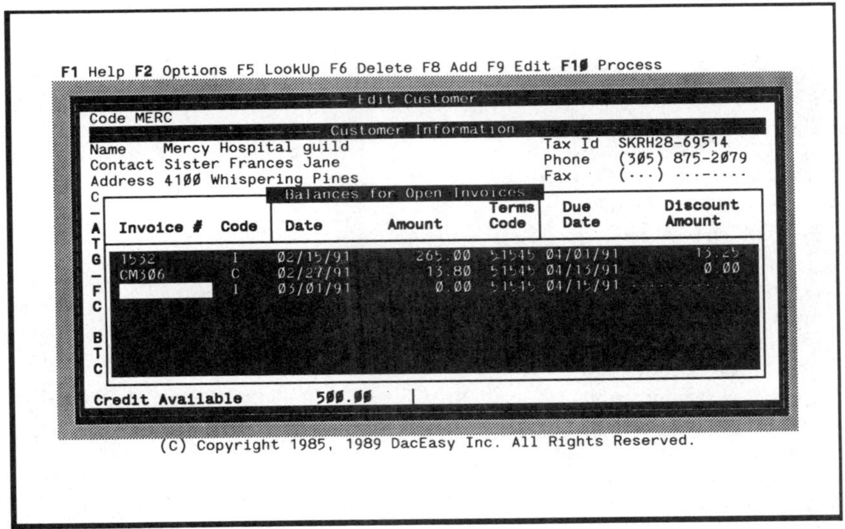

Figure 4.5: Entering open customer invoices

These entries are not added to the statistical information fields in the customer record. Be sure that you have included information from your outstanding invoices in your statistical figures.

2. In the Invoice # field, enter **1532**, the number of an existing unpaid invoice on this customer's account. If you cannot identify the individual invoices that make up what the customer owes you, you can make a single entry of the entire balance. Enter BALANCE (or whatever notation you prefer) in the Invoice # field and the total balance in the Amount field. As payments come in, apply them to the BALANCE invoice until it is paid in full.
3. In the Code field, enter **I** to indicate that this is an invoice. You can also enter miscellaneous debits or credits that have not yet been applied to an invoice on the customer's account. The transaction codes are I for invoice, D for miscellaneous debit, and C for miscellaneous credit.
4. Enter **021591** over the date in the Date field. The program inserts the system date in this field, but the original invoice has a different date, so we must override the default. Dates are entered in MMDDYY format (two digits for month, two for day, and two for year). The program supplies the slashes between month, day, and year.
5. Enter **265** as the Amount. When entering whole dollars, you do not have to type the cents. The program updates the This Period and Current Balance fields in the customer record as you enter each outstanding invoice. The Credit Available field, however, is only updated by entries during daily processing.
6. The program supplies the terms code from the customer record. Press ↵ to accept the default terms. You can override the terms code or the default in the Due Date and Discount Amount fields if you are using different terms for a particular invoice.

3.1 When entering outstanding invoices as you set up a customer or vendor record, there is also a Reference Number field, which is NONE by default. Press ↵ to accept the default, or enter the number on the purchase order you issued or received. Your entry appears in the reference number column on the statement. If you are entering an outstanding credit memo for a customer, enter the number of the paid invoice to which the credit relates.

If the customer has any open credits or miscellaneous debits, you should also enter them now, as described in the next section.

ENTERING OPEN CREDITS The window for open invoices is also used for recording outstanding credits. Our next entry for the sample customer is a credit memo issued for an invoice already paid in full. The customer discovered two broken bud vases in a case purchased last month. The memo has not yet been applied to an invoice, so it remains an open item and must be entered as such.

1. In the Invoice # field, enter **CM306**, the number of the credit memo issued to the customer.
2. In the Code field, enter **C** to indicate that this is a credit.
3. Enter **022791** over the date in the Date field. Remember, the program requires two digits for month, day, and year, without punctuation.
4. Enter **13.80** in the Amount field. When you enter cents, you must include the decimal point between them and the dollar amount. This amount is deducted from the This Period and Current Balance fields in the customer record.
5. Discounts do not apply to credits. DacEasy needlessly calculates the due date (DacEasy treats all credit memos as current). Press ↵ three times to bypass the Terms Code, Due Date, and Discount Amount fields.
6. You can continue entering as many outstanding invoices or open miscellaneous debits and credits as you have for this customer. When you are certain all your entries are correct, press F10 to save them and clear the screen for the next customer.

The credit amount you enter here will appear as an individual amount preceded by a minus sign when you view the open items for this customer on the Receipts or Adjustments screen.

Double-check your entries for accuracy and make any necessary corrections before pressing F10.

Transactions entered in this manner become entries in the Set Up Journal (identified as SU) and await posting to the general ledger in the General Journal. The entries to set up your customer's balance are posted to the Accounts Receivable account, with an offsetting posting to a unique account called Difference, which is used specifically for this purpose.

After you record the customer's invoices or balance, you cannot correct the entries using this method. If you discover an error, you must make an adjustment using the Accounts Receivable Transaction Entry screen, as described in Chapter 7.

PRINTING ACCOUNTS RECEIVABLE REPORTS

From the Reports menu, select Receivables. From the submenu, select Aging, then Directory.

When you have entered all your customers and their outstanding amounts, you should print accounts receivable aging and customer directory reports and compare them with the listings you prepared in Chapter 1 to be certain that you entered all your customer information accurately.

Be sure that your printer is connected to the computer, turned on, and filled with paper. Then follow these steps to print the reports:

1. From the Reports menu, select the Receivables option, and then select Aging from the submenu.
2. Press ↵ three times to select to sort by code, from first record to last record.
3. Press ↵ three times again to select to rank by code, from first record to last record.
4. Press ↵ to accept the default to run the report in detail rather than summary.
5. Press ↵ to accept the system date as the date of the report.
6. Press F10 to process the report.
7. Press ↵ to accept the default No, leaving the aging schedule intact for this first report.
8. At the Report Disposition screen, select Printer and press F10 to print the report. (Other report dispositions are discussed in Chapter 5.)
9. To print the customer directory, select Receivables from the Reports menu, and then choose Directory from the submenu.
10. Press ↵ to accept each default (as for the aging report).
11. Press F10 to process the report, select Printer as the Report Disposition, and press F10 again to print the report.

3.1 After you press ↵ to accept the last default, the report will print. There is no Report Disposition screen.

Make any necessary corrections and run the reports again. Your new accounting system is based on the information in the reports that you generate now, while you are setting up your customer, vendor, product, and service records. Keep the final copies for reference.

CHANGING AND DELETING CUSTOMER RECORDS

3.1 From the File menu, select Customers.

To have an accurate statistical picture of your business activity for the entire year, you should keep inactive customer, vendor, product, and service records on file until you run year-end reports.

To delete or edit an existing customer record, select the Customers option from the Edit menu. Enter the customer's code in the Edit Customer screen to recall the record. If you need to edit the record, just make the changes in the appropriate fields.

If you want to delete the record, you should first complete the following tasks:

- Complete and post all transactions for the customer so the customer balance is zero. You cannot delete a customer with an outstanding balance.
- Run a period-end closing routine for accounts receivable to remove all zero transactions from the open invoice file (see Chapter 8 for instructions).
- Run a customer statistical report for historical reference (Chapter 8 also describes this procedure).

Then, from the Edit Customer screen for the customer, press F6 to delete the record. The program displays the message

```
Are you sure you want to delete this Customer? Yes No
```

Press ↵ to accept the default Yes. If it is not the customer record that you want to delete, select No to cancel the request.

Until you end the period to clear paid invoices from the open invoice file, they continue to exist. Although the customer balance is zero, you cannot delete the customer record until the invoices are removed during period end processing.

MAINTAINING YOUR VENDOR FILE

* From the Edit menu, select Vendors.

Vendors provide you with merchandise for resale and services or items to use in your business operation. The bank you borrow money from becomes a vendor to whom you make monthly payments. The telephone company is also a vendor.

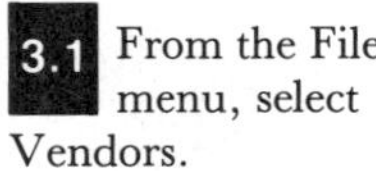
From the File menu, select Vendors.

If you do not pay for a product or service in full when you incur the obligation, the unpaid amount becomes an account payable. Even if you pay the vendor with a credit card, you still owe the credit card company. You should include your credit card accounts, such as Visa and American Express, as vendors in your files.

ADDING VENDOR RECORDS

To add a vendor record, select the Vendors option from the Edit menu. You will see the Edit Vendor screen, shown in Figure 4.6. Enter the information from your vendor worksheets into the appropriate fields, which are described in Chapter 1. The fields that are not included in your worksheets are calculated by the program, as described in Table 4.2.

Table 4.2: Program-Calculated Vendor Record Fields

Field	**Program Calculations**
Beginning	The program generates the previous balance during period-end processing by adding the activity for the period being closed to the ongoing total balance of the account.
This Period	The program generates the balance for the activity posted this period from daily processing.
Current Balance	The program generates the ongoing balance of the account by adding the activity of the current month to the previous balance.
Credit Available	The program calculates the credit available by subtracting your purchases from the credit limit in the vendor record. An amount preceded by a minus sign means you have exceeded your credit limit.
Last Purchase Date	The program generates the last purchase date from merchandise received entries.
Last Payment Date	The program generates the last payment date from check processing.
Last Purchase Amount	The program generates the last purchase amount from merchandise received entries.
Last Payment Amount	The program generates the last payment amount from check processing.

Version 3.1: The Last Purchase Amount and Last Payment Amount fields do not exist.

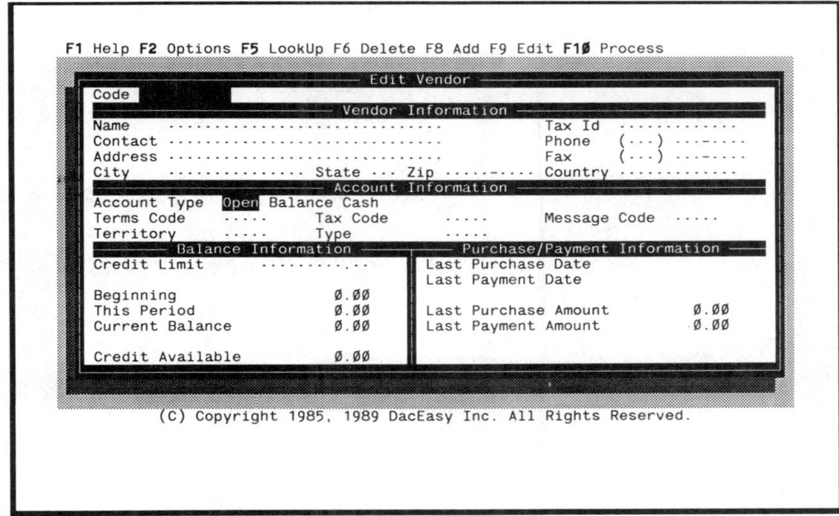

Figure 4.6: Edit Vendor screen

Figure 4.7 shows a sample vendor record. As an example, we'll create that record.

1. In the Code field, enter **PANI**, a code unique to this vendor.
2. In the Name field, enter **Paniolo Town Software**. Remember to be consistent in the form you use to enter vendor names, excluding or including articles such as *A* or *The*, and to use either all capital letters or initial capitals and lowercase letters.
3. As the Contact, enter **John Bear**, the person in the vendor's office who handles your account.
4. In the Address field, enter **56 Up Country Road**, the mailing address for payments.
5. Enter **Makawoa, Maui**; **HI**; **96768**; in the City, State, and Zip fields, respectively.
6. In the Tax Id field, enter **554-56-3593**, the vendor's federal tax identification number for 1099 reporting. This is used to identify the vendor when you prepare 1099 forms.
7. Enter **808 245 7788** in the Phone field.

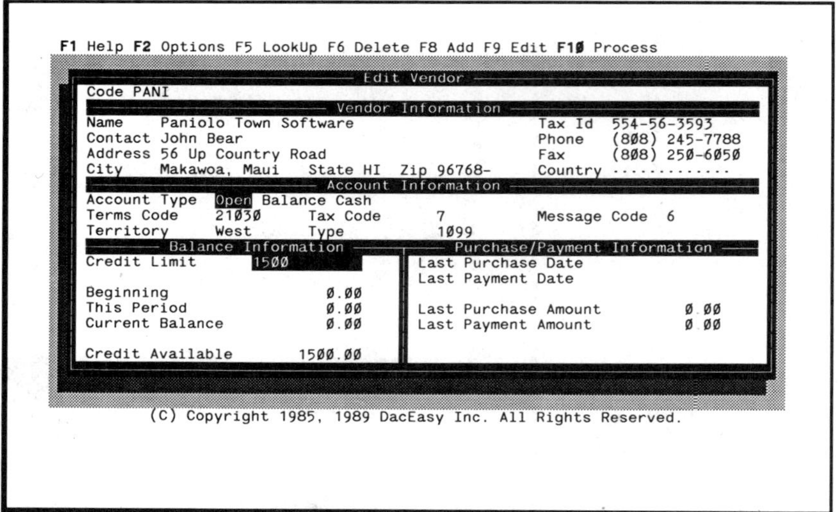

Figure 4.7: A completed vendor record

8. In the Fax field, enter **808 250 6050** for the vendor's fax number. Press ↵ to skip the Country field.
9. For Account Type, select Open. This specifies that the type should be open item, which is the best way to keep track of exactly what you still have outstanding on your account month to month.
10. In the Terms Code field, enter **21030**. Our code represents the discount rate, discount days, and due days in the terms table. This vendor gives a 2 percent discount that you can deduct from the total of your invoice if you pay within the number of days allowed, in this case within 10 days of the invoice date. Payment is due in full 30 days after the invoice date.
11. In the Tax Code field, enter **7**, the code from your tax table that represents the tax rate charged on purchases from this vendor. You can override the sales tax calculated from this percentage during purchase order entry. If you are purchasing merchandise for resale, you usually should not be charged sales tax.

12. Enter **6** as the Message Code. In the message code table for our sample company, the message code 6 is *Requires COD on purchases under $500*. This message will appear on screen whenever there is activity—for example, a purchase order or merchandise returned—on this vendor's account.
13. In the Territory field, enter **West**. DacEasy does not maintain a table for your territory codes, so you must keep a manual reference of the codes you create. If you do not want to record territories, you can use this field for other purposes, such as classifying vendors for reporting. For example, you could create a code to identify vendors who should be sent holiday greeting cards.
14. In the Type field, enter **1099**. This indicates that the vendor requires a 1099 tax form at the end of the year.

3.1 DacEasy totals *invoices* for the 1099 report, not *payments*! This assumes every invoice you enter for the vendor will be paid before the end of the year, and paid in full with no discount. If this is not your practice, beware. The 1099 report supplied by DacEasy will not present an accurate picture of the compensation the vendor received.

If you discover a vendor requires a 1099 and you did not have a notation on its account earlier in the year, you can change the vendor record before running the 1099 reports, and all the payments entered for that vendor throughout the year will be included. However, if a 1099 vendor changes tax status midyear, you must create a new vendor record with a new code that does not have the 1099 designation in the Type field. In this way, you can report on the payments that apply to the 1099 tax laws while excluding payments posted to the second record that do not. DacEasy does not classify individual transactions as applicable to 1099 reporting. It's all or nothing.

15. In the Credit Limit field, enter **1500**, the maximum amount this vendor will allow you to owe.

The program generates the data for the Beginning, This Period, Current Balance, Credit Available, Last Purchase Date, Last Payment Date, Last Purchase Amount, and Last Payment Amount fields, as described in Table 4.2.

You can also add an alternative address. For example, if the vendor has factored its receivable accounts and your payments are to be made to the institution who bought your account, you would need to

An amount preceded by a minus sign in the Credit Available field means that you have exceeded your credit limit. Although DacEasy allows this oversight, your vendor might not. That's why it's good practice to attach a message to the vendor record. Then you're reminded of your current credit status each time you enter a purchase order. The credit limit amount displays with any message you attach to the vendor record; the message need not pertain to the credit limit.

keep the other address on file. To add the address, press Shift-F5, then press F8 to add the alternative address. Complete the fields, as shown in the example in Figure 4.8. Notice that No is selected for the Default field, so the alternative address will not print on purchase orders or return slips.

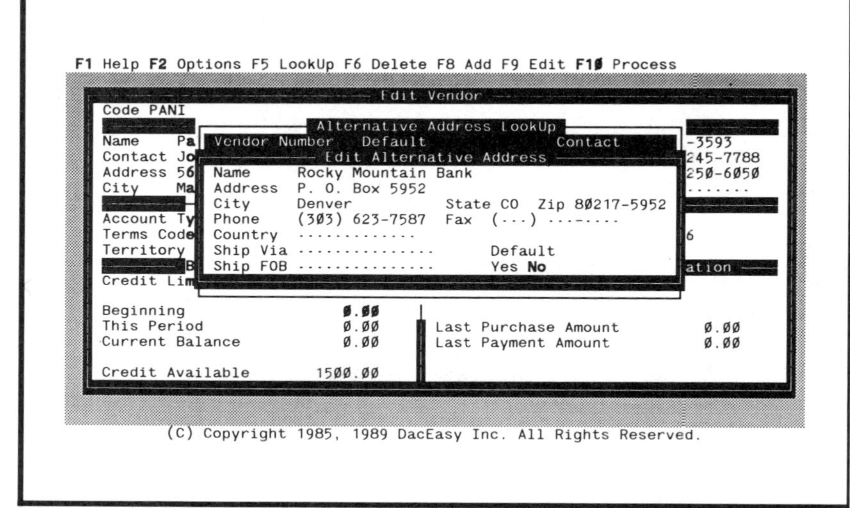

Figure 4.8: Entering an alternative address for a vendor

This would complete the record for a new vendor. However, if you are entering an existing vendor during setup, you should continue and enter statistical data, then outstanding invoices. Although you can put off entering the statistical data, you should enter any outstanding invoices and credits now.

ENTERING STATISTICAL DATA FOR VENDORS As with customer records, you can enter vendor statistical information data later, but it will require some calculations on your part to update information DacEasy has started to track for this year. Again, the historical information is valuable when analyzing your costs over a period of time. A statistical report showing three years' activity can also be good leverage when you negotiate pricing with a vendor.

The vendor record accumulates statistical data in the following four categories. You can track statistics in each of them for every time period.

- # Invoices: Number of invoices.
- # Returns: Number of returns.
- $ Purchases: Purchases in dollars.
- $ Payments: Payments in dollars.

To enter historical information, press Shift-F3. Figure 4.9 shows the statistical data for our sample vendor.

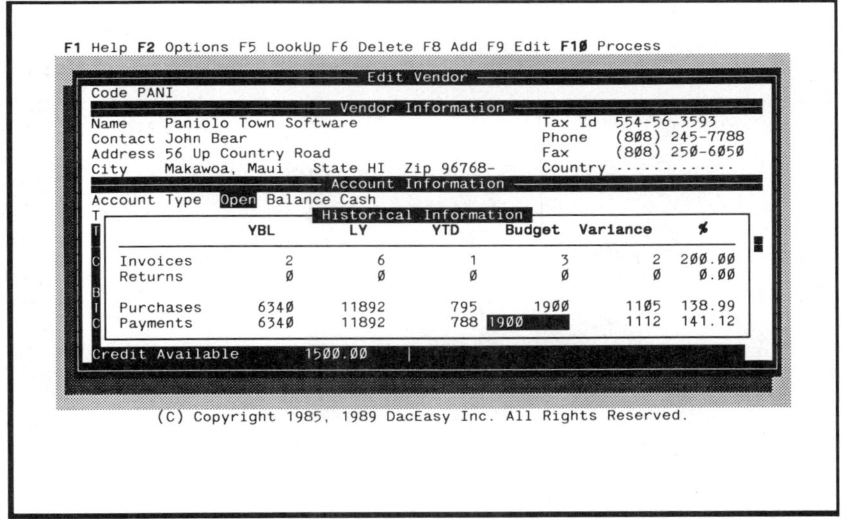

Figure 4.9: Entering historical information for a vendor

The first entries pertain to the category Invoices. In the example, two years ago (the year before last), the vendor provided consulting services and sent the company two invoices. Last year, the company bought products from this vendor to set up a new computer system, for a total of six invoices. Now that the computer system is established, the company will be buying less from this vendor; one invoice has been received for this year, and the budget for the year is three.

The second entries are in the Returns row, and they indicate how many times you returned merchandise to the vendor. The third and fourth entries are for the categories Purchases and Payments, and they indicate the dollar amounts purchased from this vendor and paid to the vendor in each time period and the budget for this year.

The business fluctuations reflected in this example are typical and are good reasons for calculating budgets on an individual-case basis rather than as simple global increases or decreases.

Press F10 to record the statistics.

ENTERING OPEN INVOICES AND CREDITS You use the same basic procedure to enter outstanding vendor invoices and credits as you did to record those for customers. While the vendor record is displayed on the screen, press F7 to open the window for adding outstanding invoices. Enter each item for this vendor (using the code I for Invoice, D for miscellaneous debit, or C for credit), check your entries carefully, and press F10 to save them.

As with customer records, outstanding invoices can only be added this way once, during setup. After you begin using the program, you must enter them as accounts payable transactions. Also, you cannot return to this window to correct any mistakes. You must make any adjustments through the Accounts Payable Transaction Entry screen. The procedures for processing accounts payable transactions are described in Chapter 10.

Figure 4.10 shows an example of a miscellaneous credit (code C) entered for the sample vendor record. This was a supplemental billing (the clerk forgot to charge sales tax) on a paid invoice. An account payable is a liability account. As such, a credit entry increases the balance. Therefore, this charge from the vendor must be entered as a credit. This is just the opposite of how you handle credit memos for accounts receivable customers.

PRINTING ACCOUNTS PAYABLE REPORTS

* From the Reports menu, select Payables. From the submenu, select Aging, then Directory.

Now that you have entered all your vendors and their outstanding amounts, it is time to print accounts payable aging and vendor directory reports and compare them with the listings you prepared for the conversion.

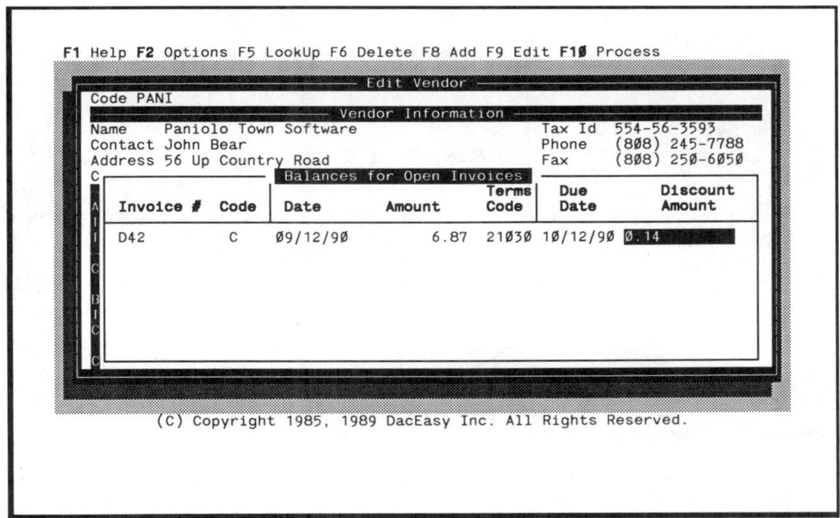

Figure 4.10: Entering open vendor invoices

3.1 From the Reports menu, select Accounts Payable. From the submenu, select Aging, then Directory.

Prepare your printer and follow the same steps that you used to produce the accounts receivable reports for customers, except select the Payables option from the Reports menu.

If necessary, correct the reports and print them again. Keep this important information for reference.

CHANGING AND DELETING VENDOR RECORDS

3.1 From the File menu, select Vendors.

To delete or change an existing vendor record, select the Vendors option from the Edit menu. Enter the vendor's code in the Code field of the Edit Vendor screen to recall the record. Make any changes in the appropriate fields.

Before deleting a vendor record, you should do the following:

- Complete and post all transactions for the vendor so the vendor balance is zero. You cannot delete a vendor with an outstanding balance.
- Run a period-end closing routine for accounts payable to remove all zero transactions from the open invoice file (see Chapter 11 for instructions).

- Run a vendor statistical report for historical reference (Chapter 11 also describes this procedure).

To delete the vendor record displayed on the Edit Vendor screen, press F6. You will see the message

Are you sure you want to delete this Vendor? Yes No

Press ↵ to accept the default Yes. If it is not the vendor record that you want to delete, select No.

MAINTAINING YOUR PRODUCT FILE

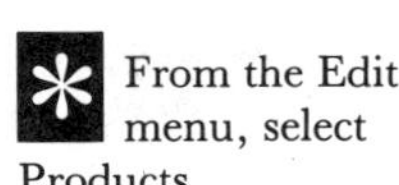
From the Edit menu, select Products.

3.1 From the File menu, select Products.

The product file contains a record of every item in your inventory. You might also want to add a product record titled Special Orders (in the Description field) to use whenever you buy and sell an item that you do not intend to stock. The purchase price of the last item received will be retained in the record. When you create a purchase order for a different product, you can simply override the default purchase price.

Instead of storing a sales price in the record, you would need to enter the selling price of each special order when you create the customer invoice. The inventory for the product, Special Orders, will revert to zero after the transaction is complete.

ADDING PRODUCT RECORDS

To add a product record, select the Products option from the Edit menu. You will see the Edit Product screen, shown in Figure 4.11. Enter the information from your product worksheets in the appropriate fields, which are described in Chapter 1. The fields that are calculated by the program are described in Table 4.3.

As an example, we'll add the product record shown in Figure 4.12.

1. In the Code field, enter **A1040** as your stockkeeping unit number.

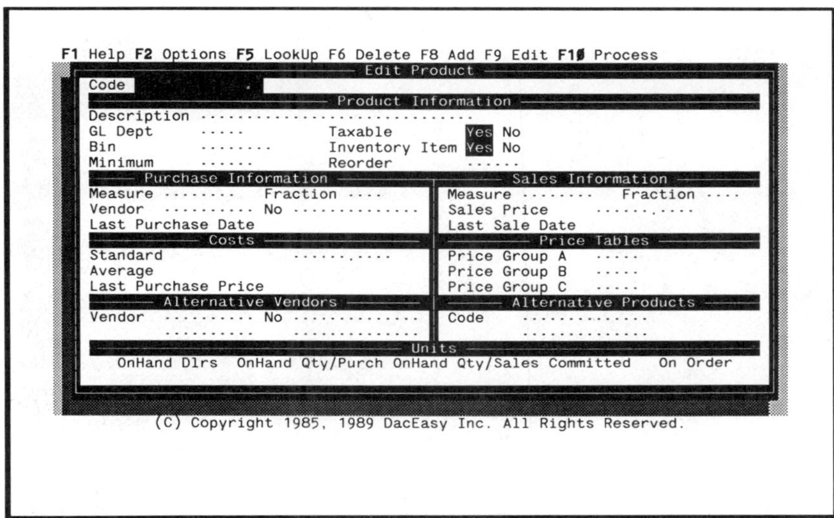

Figure 4.11: Edit Product screen

Table 4.3: Program-Calculated Product Record Fields

Field	**Program Calculations**
Last Purchase Date	The program generates the last purchase date from merchandise received entries.
Average Cost	The program calculates the average cost from units purchased and purchase price. This amount will be used if you selected the Average Cost method.
Last Purchase Price	The program calculates the last purchase price from the price paid on the last merchandise received entry for this product. The program will use this amount to value your inventory if you selected Last Purchase Price as your inventory costing method.
Last Sale Date	The program calculates the last sales date from billing entries.
On Hand Dlrs	The program calculates the value of the on-hand units.
On Hand Quantity/Sell	The program calculates the on-hand units as the difference between merchandise received entries and customer billing entries using the selling fraction.
On Hand Quantity/Buy	The program calculates the on-hand units using the buying fraction.
Committed Units	The program calculates the committed units from customer invoice entries. When the invoices are posted, the committed units are released, and the on-hand units are reduced.
On Order	The program calculates on-order units from purchase order entry. When merchandise is received for the purchase order, the on-order units are released and the on-hand units are increased.

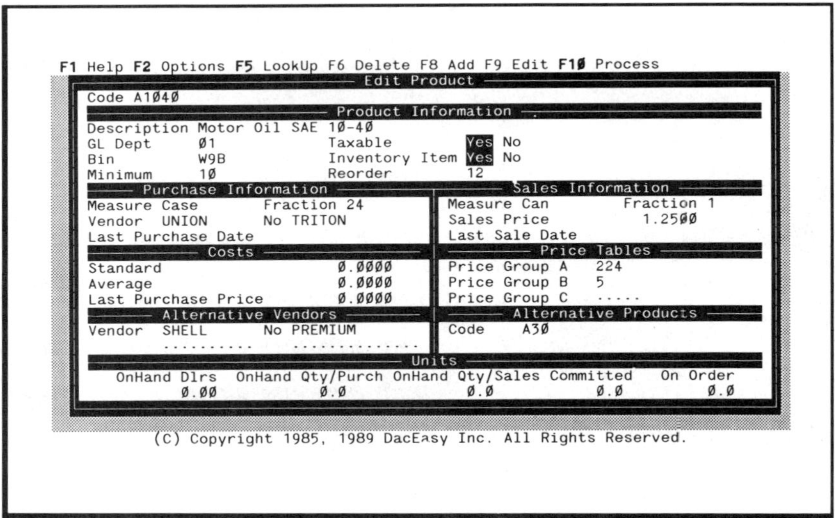

Figure 4.12: A completed product record

2. For Description, enter **Motor Oil SAE 10-40** to describe the product.
3. Enter **01** in the GL Dept field. It is the number of the department in the general ledger this product is posted to; this company departmentalizes by inventory. If you do not departmentalize by inventory, you can use this field to further classify and sort the product in reports.
4. Select Yes in the Taxable field because you usually charge sales tax on the products you sell. If this is a product you carry and sell solely to customers who then resell it, you would select No.
5. This product is stored in the warehouse, aisle 9, shelf B. Enter the code for this, **W9B**, in the Bin field.
6. Select Yes for Inventory Item, indicating this is an item you stock and sell from your own inventory.
7. The Minimum field indicates the minimum number of units you want to keep on hand. Enter **10**, meaning ten cases.

3.1 The Purchase Measure and Purchase Fraction fields do not exist.

8. In the Reorder field, you place the amount you want to reorder when the minimum number is reached. Enter **12** (the company gets a special price when ordering a dozen cases).
9. In the Purchase Measure field, enter **Case**. This is the most common quantity (unit of measure) in which you buy the product.
10. Enter **24** in the Purchase Fraction field. This is the number of items that make up the unit of measure. In this instance, a case contains 24 cans, which we sell individually.
11. For Purchase Vendor, enter **UNION**, the code for the vendor you usually buy this product from.
12. In the No field, enter **TRITON**, the identifier used by the vendor for this item. This could also be a model number that you would use when ordering the item. DacEasy generates the information for the Last Purchase Date, as described in Table 4.3.
13. Press ↵ to bypass the Standard field under Costs. We will leave this field blank because the company costs its inventory by last purchase price. If you use the standard cost method, you would enter your value for this item. The program calculates both the Average and Last Purchase Price field entries, as described in Table 4.3. These amounts will be used to value your inventory if you selected the average cost or last purchase price method.
14. For an alternative vendor, enter **SHELL**, the vendor we will order from if the Union vendor cannot fill our order.
15. Enter **PREMIUM**, the alternative vendor's stockkeeping number, in the No field. Press ↵ to skip the second alternative vendor fields.
16. Enter **Can** for Sales Measure, the quantity in which you sell the product.
17. In the Sales Fraction field, enter **1**, the number of individually saleable units that make up the sales measure. Thus, you can sell 1, 2, 3, up to 24 cans (a full case) of oil, even though you only purchase it by the case.

You cannot change the purchase or sales fraction after the stock on hand has been recorded.

18. Enter **1.25** in the Sales Price field. It is the price you sell a sales measure for, not the price for the sales fraction of the unit. If, however, the sale measure were case and the sale fraction 24, you would enter $30 as the sales price of an entire case, not the price for one can of oil (although each piece can still be sold separately). If you sell six cans of oil, the system will calculate the total price as $7.25 ($30 ÷ 24 cans = $1.25 × 6 cans = $7.25). The program calculates the Last Sale Date field from invoice processing.

3.1 The Price Group fields do not exist.

19. In the Price Group A field, our retail group, enter **224**, the code from the price table that represents a 2 percent discount when the customer purchases 24 cans or a full case.
20. For Price Group B, our wholesale group, enter **5**, the code that represents a 5 percent discount for wholesale customers who usually buy only by the case. Press ↵ to skip Price Group C.
21. As an alternative product, enter **A30**, which represents 30-weight motor oil that can be substituted on an order if SAE 10-40 is out of stock. Press ↵ to move through the second alternative product field.

After you input the product information, you can continue and add statistical data or return to it later. Regardless, you must enter your stock on hand for DacEasy to keep accurate track of your inventory, as described later in this section.

ENTERING STATISTICAL DATA FOR PRODUCTS As with customer and vendor records, historical data for products is retained for three years in the same time periods described for those records. DacEasy also calculates the variance and percentage for each category in the same manner.

The product record accumulates statistical data in several categories. To demonstrate how to enter product statistical data, we'll make the entries shown in Figure 4.13.

Suppose that this is a new product line that was just added this year, so there is no data for last year or the year before last. In each

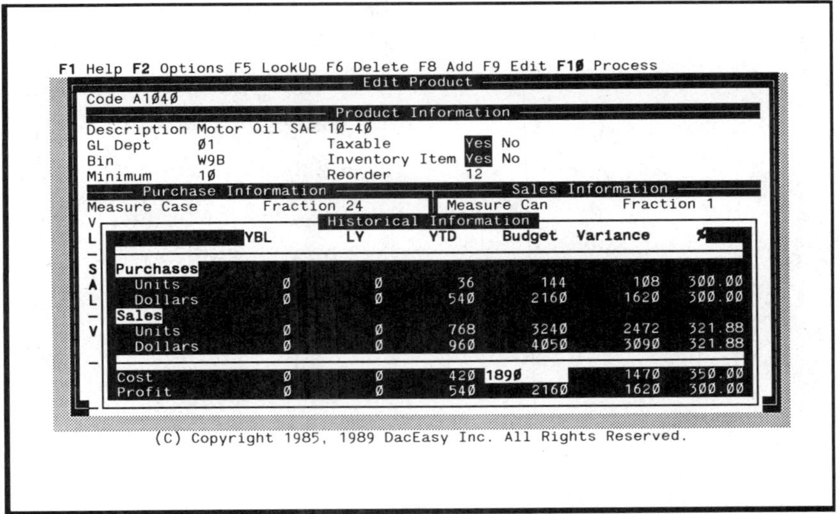

Figure 4.13: Entering historical information for a product

category, we will skip the YBL (year before last) and LY (last year) fields.

1. Press Shift-F3 to display the statistical data window.
2. Press ↵ to bypass the YBL and LY columns. Our entries begin in the YTD column.
3. In the Purchases, Units category, enter **36**, the number of cases bought so far this year. The program calculates variance and percentage from budget as a minus figure.
4. Enter **540** for Purchases, Dollars. This is the dollar amount paid for the oil. Again, the program recalculates the variance and percentage after you enter the budget.
5. In the Sales, Units category, enter **768**. This is the number of cans sold so far this year.
6. In the Sales, Dollars field, enter **960**, the total dollar amount sold. If you have not kept accurate, detailed records, you might not know how much of your sales dollars were generated by this particular item. If you must estimate, use the average sale price times the number of units you sold.

7. For Cost, enter **420**. This represents the total dollar amount it cost this year to purchase the units sold.
8. In the Budget column, enter **144** as the budget for the units that will be purchased this year.
9. Enter **2160** as the budget for dollars purchased.
10. Enter **3240** as the budget for the number of cans that you predict you will sell this year.
11. The budget for the dollar amount generated by sales of this product is **4050**.
12. Enter **1890** as the budget for Cost.
13. Press F10 to save the historical information and return to the product record.

3.1 DacEasy also calculates the data for the Times Turn and Gross Return fields. The times turn data, which is the times this item turned over, is derived by dividing the units sold by the on-hand units. DacEasy calculates the gross return by multiplying the on-hand units by the dollar profit, and then dividing the result by the times turn rate.

The program generates the data for the last three categories. It calculates the figure that is probably of most interest to you, profit, by subtracting costs from sales dollars.

ENTERING STOCK ON HAND When you have defined the product, you should continue and enter the stock you have on hand to sell. Refer to the inventory worksheet you prepared in Chapter 1.

You can only enter stock on hand this way once, during setup. All later additions or deletions must be made through purchases or inventory-closing entries.

As an example of entering current inventory, we'll continue with the same record and enter the data shown in Figure 4.14.

1. Press F7. The window for entering stock on hand appears.
2. Enter **4**, the number of purchase units currently on hand, in the Units field. Notice the program multiplies the purchase unit times the purchase fraction divided by the sales fraction (4 × 24/1 = 96) to determine the sales quantity on hand. To record cost, enter a number in either of the next fields, as described below, and the program will calculate the other value for you.

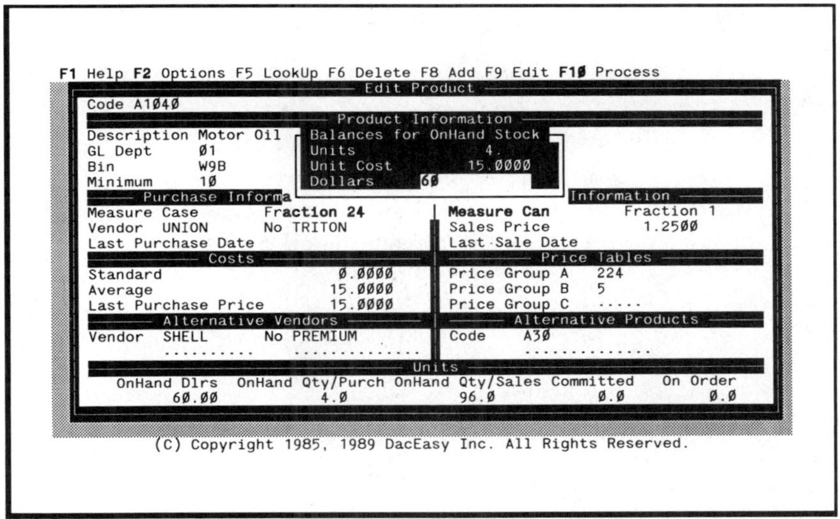

Figure 4.14: Entering stock on hand

3. For Unit Cost, enter **15** as the purchase cost of one unit, in this example one case. Use the latest purchase price, standard cost, or average cost, according to the method of costing you selected. This is the cost for the full unit of measure, not the fraction. For example, the cost of a product whose unit of measure is dozen and whose fraction of a unit is 12 boxes would be $12, not $1, which is the cost of a single box.

If you do not enter the unit cost, you must enter the total value of stock at cost in the Dollars field. You would enter 60 for this example. DacEasy calculates the on-hand units and dollars and average cost and displays them in the product record on the screen. The committed units and on-order units are only updated by entries during daily processing.

Double-check your entries for accuracy and make any necessary corrections before saving them.

4. Check the amounts, and then press F10 to record the stock on hand. Press F10 to save the new product record. Unlike errors in the customer and vendor open invoice window, mistakes in the stock-on-hand entries can be corrected in this window.

When all your products are entered, you should run product reports, as described below. If you find an error in the stock on hand or the unit cost, you must reverse the units, and the dollar amounts will follow suit. For example, to correct the data for our sample product, follow these steps:

1. Enter the product number, **A1040**, in the Edit Product screen to access the record.
2. Press F7 to enter stock-on-hand figures.
3. To reverse the original entry, type – 4 (*minus* 4) in the Units field.
4. Type **15** in the Unit Cost field. The on-hand dollars and quantity fields displayed in the product record should both change to zero.
5. Press F10 to process the correction.
6. Press F7 from the product record and enter the correct stock-on-hand data in the usual manner.

PRINTING PRODUCT REPORTS

* From the Reports menu, select Inventory. From the submenu, select Price List, then Activity Report.

3.1 From the Reports menu, select Inventory. From the submenu, select Product Price List, then Product Activity Report.

To ensure that you entered all your products accurately, print product price list and product activity reports and compare them with the information you collected for your current system. Follow these steps:

1. Select the Inventory option from the Reports menu, and then select Price List from the submenu.
2. Press ↵ six times to accept the default parameters for sorting, ranking, and the Cost Code field.
3. Press F10, select Printer as the Report Disposition, and press F10 to print the report.
4. Select Activity Report from the submenu.
5. Repeat steps 2 and 3.

CHANGING AND DELETING PRODUCT RECORDS

3.1 From the File menu, select Products.

To edit or delete a product record, select the Products option from the Edit menu. Enter the product code in the Edit Product screen. When the record appears, you can edit it by making changes in the appropriate fields.

Note that you cannot delete a product that has units on hand. To delete the product record displayed on the screen, press F6. When you are asked if you are sure that you want to delete this record, press ↵ to accept the default Yes, or select No if it is not the product record that you want to delete.

DEFINING COMPONENTS AND PRODUCTS TO ASSEMBLE

3.1 Product assembly does not exist. You must list every product and component individually on an invoice.

In your business, you may combine existing individual products to make a new product. The original products are called components, and the new product is called finished goods. In DacEasy, the components can be still be sold individually as well as combined to form finished goods. This feature is useful if you are manufacturing or bundling items for a package deal.

Creating an assembled product is a five-step process:

- Define the components.
- Define the product to be assembled.
- List the components needed for the assembly.
- Enter an assembly transaction to create a quantity of the new product.
- Post the assembly transaction.

As an example, suppose that you sell a souvenir to tourists and sell the pieces that make up the souvenir individually to other craftspeople. Follow these steps to define the product to be assembled:

1. Set up a separate product record for each component: a pyrite specimen, gold panning figurines, and a redwood block.

2. Create another product record for the finished goods, a gold panning souvenir.
3. When you complete the finished goods definition, press Shift-F5 to display the window for listing the product assembly components.
4. Enter the code of the component, **M65**. The description, Pyrite Specimen, appears.
5. Enter **1**, the number of units of the component that go into the creation of the new product.
6. Enter **GP3**, the code for lost wax gold panning figurines.
7. Enter **2**, the number of units needed in the new product.
8. Enter **RB6**, for the redwood block, and enter **1** for the number of units.
9. Press F10 when all components and required quantities have been listed. The completed window is shown in Figure 4.15.

Remember, you have only *defined* the product to be assembled. You must still enter an assembly transaction to actually create the finished goods in your files, as discussed in Chapter 12.

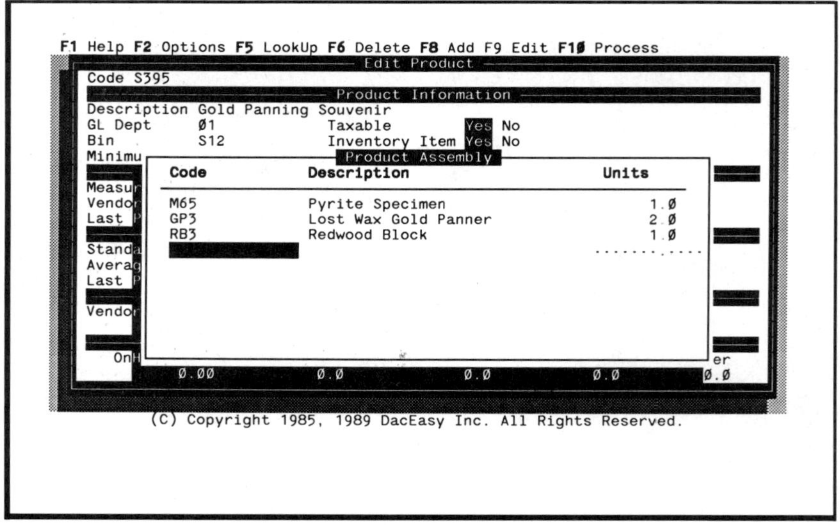

Figure 4.15: Defining a product to be assembled

MAINTAINING YOUR SERVICE FILE

* From the Edit menu, select Services.

3.1 From the File menu, select Services.

A service is some form of labor you sell to your customers. It differs from, but is usually related to, a product. Gardening is a service. The tree you plant is a product. Repairing a flat tire is a service, but the rubber patch you put on the leak is a product. The service file contains a record of all the services you sell.

You cannot create finished goods for a service. However, you can include the cost of an item in your service price and still track the item. For example, you could include the patch in the tire-repair service, and still keep track of the number of patches in inventory. Set up a product record for Patches and leave the sales price at zero. When you do a tire repair, enter the product code for the patch on the customer invoice. There will be no charge for the patch, but DacEasy will reduce the number of units on hand in the product record.

ADDING SERVICE RECORDS

To add a service record, select the Services option from the Edit menu. You will see the Edit Service screen. Enter the information from your service worksheets in the fields, which are described in Chapter 1.

Let's duplicate the entries shown in Figure 4.16 to demonstrate adding a service record.

Don't forget, if you track services in a general ledger department separate from products, you must define a sales returns account and a cost of goods sold account for each service department you have established.

1. In the Code field, enter **GCARE**, the code that identifies this service.
2. In the Description field, enter **Landscaping/Lawn Care** to describe this service.
3. For GL Dept, enter **03**. The company departmentalizes by inventory and wants to total income from services in a separate department. If you do not departmentalize by inventory, you can use this field to categorize and sort the service for reports.
4. In the Measure field, enter **Month**, the unit of measure you sell this service in most often.

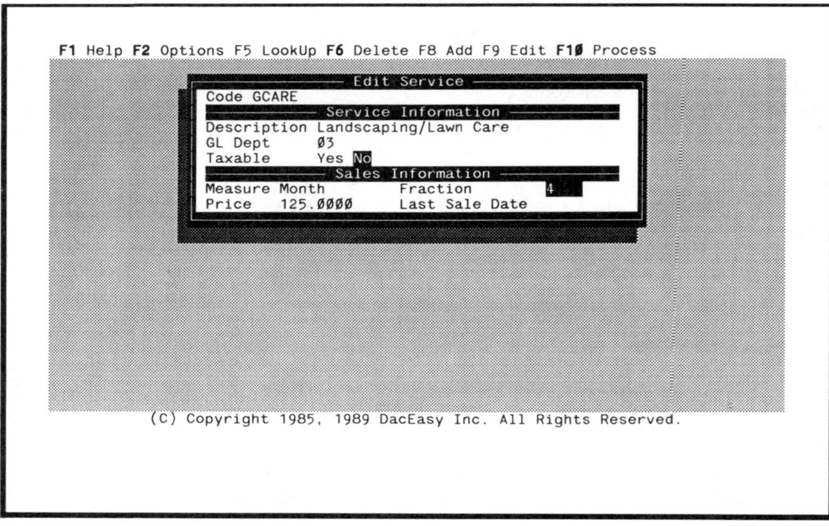

Figure 4.16: A completed service record

The fraction cannot be changed after the record is processed.

5. Enter **4** in the Fraction field. This represents four weeks in a month. The minimum charge is for one week.
6. Enter **125**, for $125, in the Price field. This is the sales price for a unit of measure, not for a fraction. When you charge a customer for just one week, or a fraction of the unit of measure, you would enter .1 as the quantity. The program would calculate the price as 31.25 for one week.
7. Select No in the Taxable field because this service is not taxable. If it were, you would select Yes. The program calculates the Last Sale Date entry from customer invoices.

Now you are ready to finish setting up the service by entering the statistical data.

ENTERING STATISTICAL DATA FOR SERVICES After you input the service information, you can continue and add statistical data or return to add it later. Service records, like other DacEasy records, retain three years of historical information.

Service records accumulate data in the following two categories. You can track statistics in each of them for every time period.

- Sales Units: Number of units sold
- Sales Dollars: Dollar amount of sales

You can continue with the example and enter the statistical information shown in Figure 4.17. While in the service record, press Shift-F3.

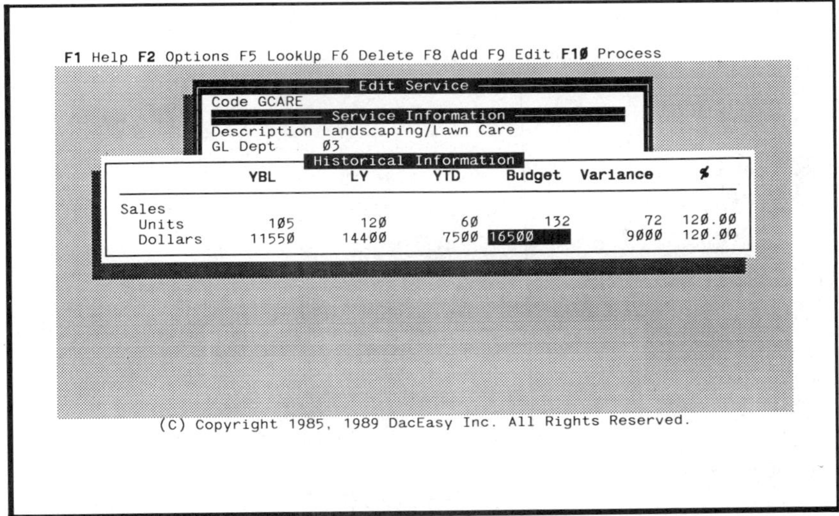

Figure 4.17: Entering historical information for a service

The first category is Sales Units. The company sold 105 units of this service two years ago, 120 units last year, and 60 so far this year. Landscaping and lawn care are more popular each year, so the budget for the total number of units expected to sell this year is 132.

If you have not kept accurate, detailed records, you might not know how many units you sold of this service. If you must estimate, divide the total sales dollars by an average price for one unit of this service.

The second category is Sales Dollars. The figures indicate the dollar amount sold of this service for the time periods and the budget for this year. Because of the popularity of the gardening service, monthly rates have been raised each year. Thus, the sales dollars reflect an incremental growth due to the increase in fees and customers.

PRINTING A SERVICE REPORT

* From the Reports menu, select Inventory. From the submenu, select Service Listing.

3.1 From the Reports menu, select Inventory. From the submenu, select Service Report.

After you define all your services, you should print a service report and compare it with the information you collected for your current system. Select the Inventory option from the Reports menu, and then choose Service Listing from the submenu. Press ↵ six times to accept the sorting, ranking, and sales information defaults. Press F10, select Printer as the Report Disposition, and press F10 again to print the report.

CHANGING AND DELETING SERVICE RECORDS

3.1 From the File menu, select Services.

To change or delete a service record, select the Services option from the Edit menu and enter the code for the service in the Edit Service screen. You can edit it by making changes in the appropriate fields.

If you want to delete this service, press F6, and then press ↵ at the prompt to verify that the record should be deleted.

CREATING MULTIPLE COMPANIES OR DIVISIONS

3.1 Defining a second company is discussed at the end of the chapter.

You can keep a separate set of books for each division of your organization or for entirely different companies. If the companies or divisions are related, you can accumulate data from each company into consolidated account totals, which represent the activity of the entire organization.

You can add a new company from scratch or copy an existing company. Both procedures are described in the following sections.

ADDING A NEW COMPANY

* From the File menu, select Open.

Follow these steps to add a company to your system:

1. Select Open from the File menu.
2. When the list of existing companies appears, press F8 to add a new set of files.

3. In the Identification Name field, enter the name of the company or division you want to track separately.
4. In the Directory Name/Path field, enter the drive, directory, and subdirectory where you want to store the data for the new company or division. Use a subdirectory name that will indicate what data is stored in it. Although it is not necessary, placing the subdirectory beneath the DacEasy Accounting directory is recommended.
5. Press F10, and you will see the prompt

   Do you wish to use the sample Chart of Accounts? Yes No

   as shown in Figure 4.18.
6. Select Yes if you want to use the sample chart of accounts that comes with the DacEasy Accounting package. Select No if you want to create your own chart of accounts for the new company. You can also use an existing chart of accounts that you created, as explained in the following section.
7. The program displays the File Space Requirements. Press F10 to create the new company.

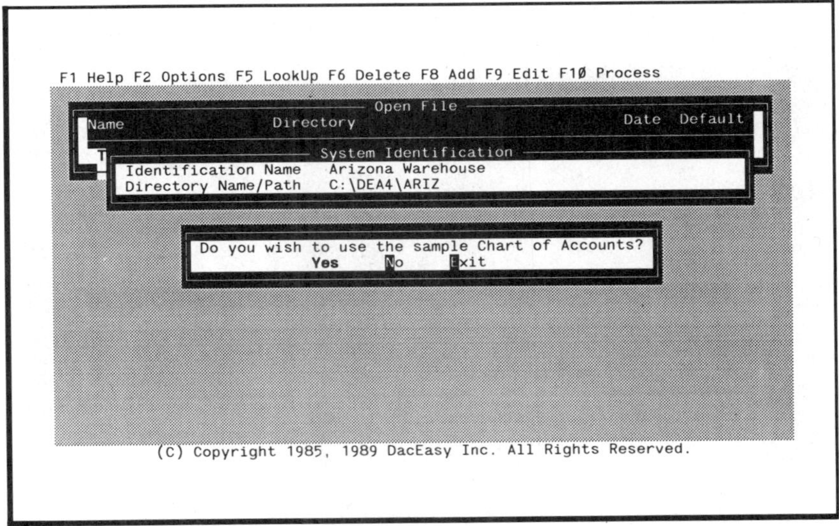

Figure 4.18: Adding a new company

COPYING AN EXISTING COMPANY

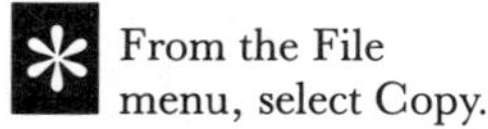
From the File menu, select Copy.

You can create a new company by copying all or part of the structure of an existing company. This includes the chart of accounts, customer, vendor, product, and service records. Although you probably would want to eliminate the balances and statistical data from all the records, you can copy the company with data intact.

To copy an existing company, follow these steps:

1. Select Copy from the File menu. A list of existing companies appears.
2. Place the cursor on the company you want to copy, and then press ↵.
3. Enter the name of the new company in the Identification Name field.
4. In the Directory Name/Path field, enter the drive, directory, and subdirectory where you want to store the files for the new company.
5. Press F10, and then select which account balances you want to *exclude*. You can choose All, to zero the amounts in the general ledger accounts, customers, vendors, products, and services files, copying only the record definition. Your other choices are Accounts, to copy only the accounts in the general ledger excluding balances, and excluding customer, vendor, product, and service files; or None, to copy the records and balances in all your files into the new company. After your selection, DacEasy displays the space required to create the new company and the available space.
6. If there is sufficient space, press ↵ to create new data files. Otherwise, cancel the process.

You must establish tables, defaults, and a company identification for every new company or division.

CHANGING COMPANIES

The company you created when you initialized DacEasy for the first time is the default, the company that is accessed when you start the program. All entries, printing, and posting will take place in the company that is open. You can change the default to the company where you do your most frequent work or simply choose to work with a company other than the default for the current session.

In the sample shown in Figure 4.19, the program and company data files have been loaded onto drive D. If you accepted the default drive during installation, your program and files will be on drive C.

To change the default or work with another company, first select Open from the File menu. A list of defined companies appears, similar to the one shown in Figure 4.19.

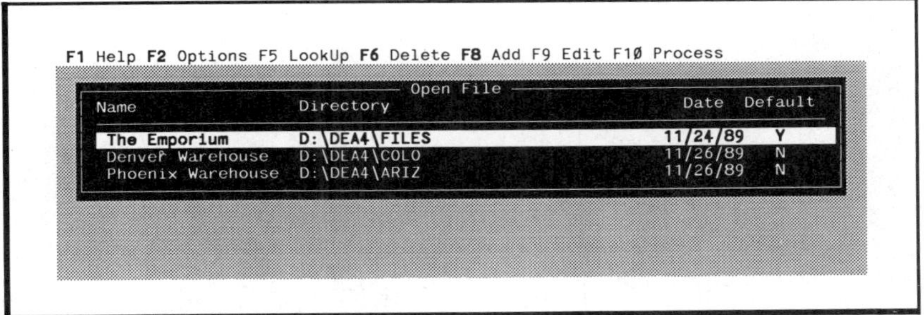

Figure 4.19: The list of defined companies

The Default field contains a Y next to the company that is accessed automatically when you start DacEasy. If you want to change the default, place the cursor on the company you want to use and press Shift-F8. If you just want to switch to another company for this session, place the cursor on that company and press ↵.

CREATING A CONSOLIDATED CHART OF ACCOUNTS

When you have multiple companies, even though you track their transactions separately, you might want to consolidate the account balances to enable you to print a balance sheet or income statement that gives you the whole picture.

To do so, just create a special company with a unique chart of accounts, as described in the section about adding a new company. Then, in the charts of accounts of all the companies you want to total together, enter the number of the consolidated account where you want the consolidation to take place.

It is not necessary to make a third company to consolidate data. You can consolidate the balances from Company 2 into Company 1 if you want; however, you will no longer be able to view the activity for Company 1 by itself.

Here is an example of the consolidated chart of accounts under Corporation:

Corporation		*Company 1*		*Company 2*	
Acct#	*Name*	*Acct#*	*Name*	*Acct#*	*Name*
1C	Total Assets	1102	Cash	110	Cash
		11051	Accts Rec.	1105	Accts Rec.
		11071	Inventory	12041	Machinery
2C	Total Liability	2101	Accts Pay.	2102	Notes Pay.
		21042	Taxes Pay.		

The accounts in Company 1 and Company 2 that are accumulated into the consolidated account are listed across from it. For Company 1, in the account records 1102, 11051, and 11071, you would enter 1C in the Consolidation field. Notice the account numbers and the types of accounts for Company 1 do not have to be the same as those for Company 2.

DEFINING A SECOND COMPANY IN VERSION 3.1

With version 3.1, all the definitions you entered for the first company apply to the second company as well. All you do is create a second subdirectory for the files or data for the second company and work in that subdirectory when you are processing data for that company. However, if you are using a hard disk and want to set up your second company with different definitions or a different chart of accounts, you must completely install the program in a totally separate directory (one other than DEA3).

To create a second subdirectory for another company, at the C:\DEA3 prompt, type DEA3, press the spacebar once, and type DATA (substitute the name of the second company's data file). DacEasy will create a second subdirectory and then proceed through the installation routine automatically so you can define the second company.

To process transactions for either company, you must type DEA3, press the spacebar once, and then type DATA (substituting the name of the data files for the company you are processing). If you only type DEA3 without designating the company's subdirectory, DacEasy will bring up the last company defined.

On a floppy disk system, create a second data disk and label it with the name of the second company. Insert that data disk when processing work for that company.

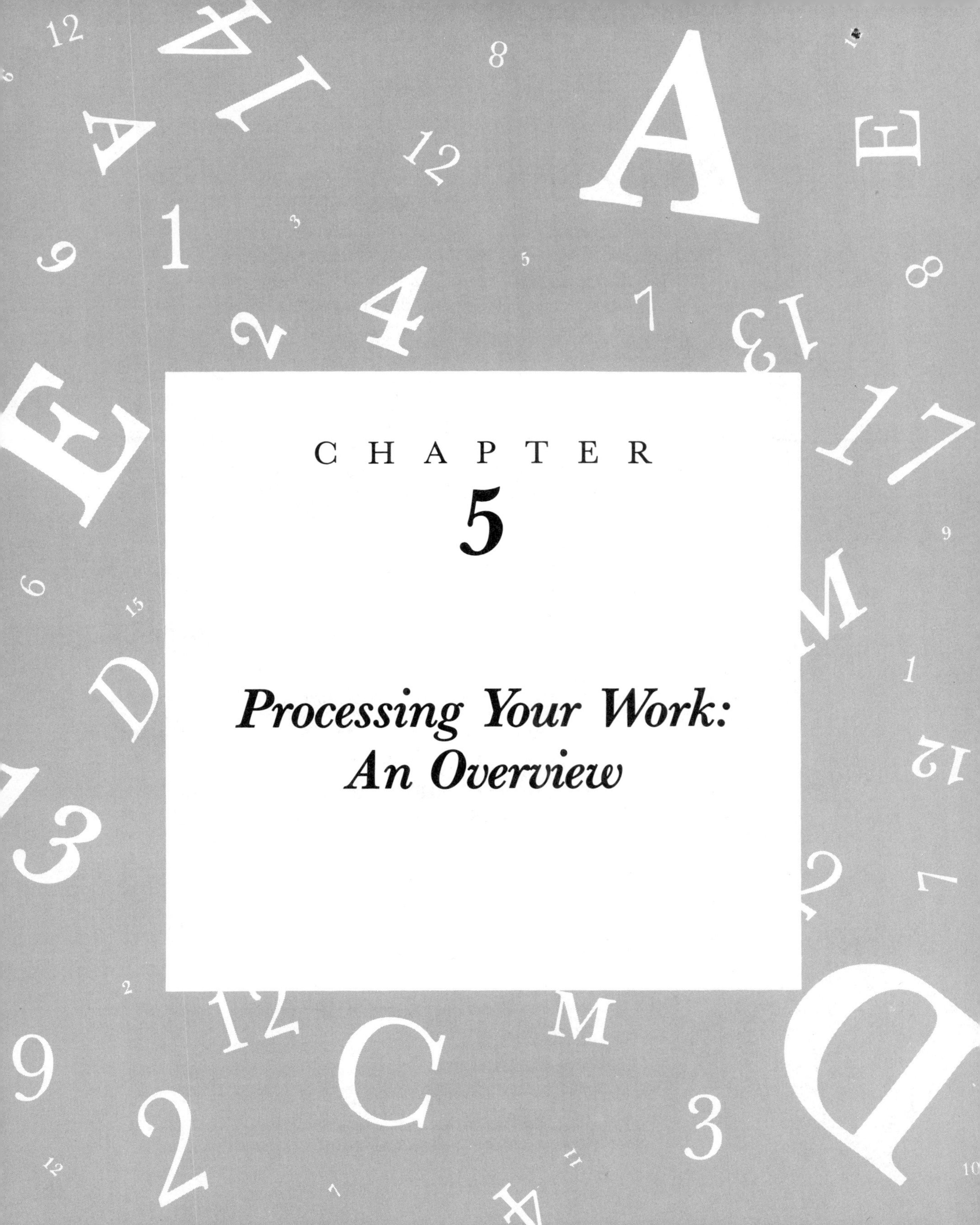

CHAPTER 5

Processing Your Work: An Overview

THIS CHAPTER PRESENTS AN OVERVIEW OF THE processing procedures and gives instructions for performing common functions, such as adding records while entering data, correcting entries, printing documents, posting, and closing periods. Any specific details that relate to an individual module are covered in the following chapters. However, the general procedures for these tasks are the same, and you will find many references to this chapter throughout the book.

SEQUENCING YOUR TASKS

Some bookkeeping functions should be done daily, while others are performed less frequently. The frequency of each process is determined by the volume of your work and how closely you want to monitor your business.

The sequence in which you perform each task is important. For example, the following sequencing is necessary:

- Print a journal before posting so you have a copy of the transaction detail.
- Generate finance charges before printing customer statements.
- Print statistical year-to-date reports before you close a period so you have a record of the period's activity.
- Close the period before printing an aging report to clear transactions with no amount due from the file.

Table 5.1 lists the daily functions and their proper sequence, and Table 5.2 summarizes the periodic functions and the order in which they should be performed.

Table 5.1: Daily Accounting Functions and Their Sequences

Billing Functions
1. Enter sales (customer invoices)
2. Enter payments
3. Print packing slips and invoices

Table 5.1: Daily Accounting Functions and Their Sequences (continued)

Billing Functions (continued)
4. Enter sales returns
5. Print sales-return slips
6. Print the Billing (Sales) journal
7. Post to Billing
Accounts Receivable Functions
1. Enter miscellaneous invoices
2. Enter debit and credit memos
3. Enter payments received
4. Print the Accounts Receivable Transactions journal
5. Print the Accounts Receivable Cash Receipts journal
6. Post to Accounts Receivable
7. Post the Cash Receipts
Purchase Order Functions
1. Create purchase orders
2. Enter merchandise received (vendor invoices)
3. List merchandise received
4. Enter purchase returns
5. Print purchase orders
6. Print merchandise-received slips
7. Print returns and packing slips
8. Print the Purchase journal
9. Post to Purchase Order
Accounts Payable Functions
1. Enter miscellaneous invoices
2. Enter debit and credit memos

Table 5.1: Daily Accounting Functions and Their Sequences (continued)

Accounts Payable Functions (continued)
3. Print the Accounts Payable Transaction journal 4. Post to Accounts Payable
Inventory Functions
1. Print the product alert report
General Ledger Functions
1. Enter miscellaneous transactions 2. Print the General Ledger journal 3. Post to the general ledger

Table 5.2: Periodic Accounting Functions and Their Sequences

Accounts Receivable Functions
End of Period 1. Generate finance charges 2. Print customer statements 3. Print the statistical year-to-date report 4. Close the period 5. Print the Accounts Receivable aging report **Yearly** 1. Calculate next year's forecast 2. Print the forecast 3. Close the year **As Needed** 1. Print the customer directory 2. Print customer labels

Table 5.2: Periodic Accounting Functions and Their Sequences (continued)

Accounts Payable Functions
Weekly 1. Print the Accounts Payable aging report 2. Print the payments report 3. Enter manual payments to vendors 4. Enter payments to make to vendors 5. Print the Accounts Payable Checks to Print journal 6. Print computer-generated checks 7. Print the Cash Payments journal 8. Post the Cash Payments **End of Period** 1. Reconcile bank account 2. Print vendor statements 3. Print the statistical year-to-date report 4. Close the period **Yearly** 1. Print 1099 forms 2. Calculate the forecast 3. Print the forecast 4. Close the year **As Needed** 1. Print the vendor directory 2. Print vendor labels
Purchase Order Functions
Weekly 1. Print the purchase order status report

Table 5.2: Periodic Accounting Functions and Their Sequences (continued)

General Ledger Functions
End of Period 1. Print the general ledger account activity detail report 2. Print the trial balance 3. Enter closing adjustments 4. Print financial statements 5. Print financial ratios and custom reports 6. Print the statistical year-to-date report 7. Close the period **Yearly** 1. Calculate the budget 2. Print the budget 3. Close the year 4. Open next year **As Needed** 1. Print the chart of accounts list 2. Consolidate multiple companies
Inventory/Service Functions
End of Period 1. Print the service listing 2. Print the product activity report 3. Print count sheets 4. Take an inventory count 5. Enter the physical inventory 6. Print the Inventory journal 7. Post inventory adjustments 8. Print the statistical year-to-date report

Table 5.2: Periodic Accounting Functions and Their Sequences (continued)

Inventory/Service Functions (continued)
Yearly
1. Calculate the forecast
2. Print the forecast
3. Close the year
As Needed
1. Print a product listing
2. Print the product price list
3. Enter price changes
4. Assemble products

ADDING AND EDITING RECORDS DURING DATA ENTRY

You can add records, such as those for new vendors, terms, and products, during data entry. To do so, press F8 when the cursor is in the field where you would normally enter the code for the type of record you want to add. The Edit screen for that record type will appear. Fill in the information and press F10 to save your entry. The program inserts the code in the field where the cursor was when you pressed F8 to add a record. Figure 5.1 shows a sample Edit Customer screen completed while entering an accounts receivable transaction.

To edit an existing code, press F5 in the field where you would enter the code. A list of the records in the file appears. Place the cursor on the record you want to edit and press F9. Change the fields, then press F10 to save your changes.

ADDING RECORDS DURING DATA ENTRY IN VERSION 3.1

With version 3.1, you can add a skeletal record for a detail account beneath an existing general account during data entry. Enter the new account number, and then respond Y when DacEasy asks if you

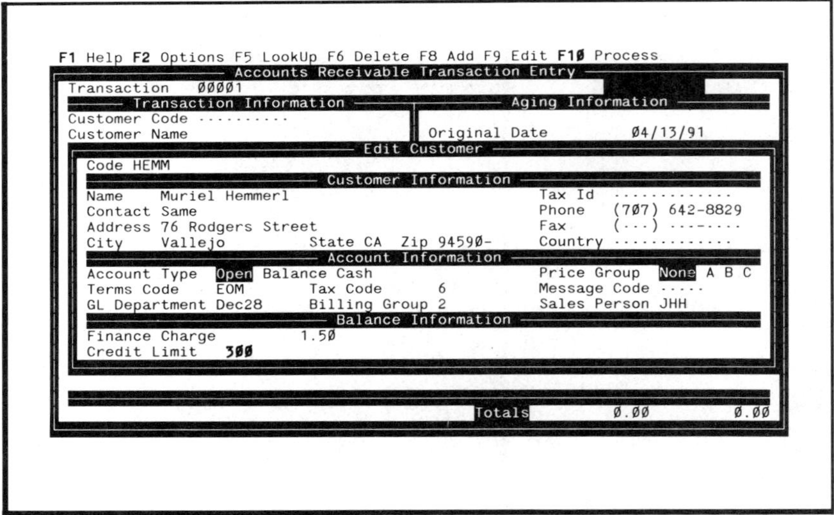

Figure 5.1: Adding a new customer record during data entry

want to add it. When you add an account this way, it is important that you recall the record later and indicate the account level for the new account.

To add a new customer or vendor record during data entry, enter the new code, and then respond Y to the prompt

Account number is Invalid...Do you want to Add one N

Complete the fields displayed by the program. While adding a customer or vendor, you can also add a new tax code and rate by pressing F2.

It is important for you to recall the new, but incomplete, customer record later and enter the monthly interest rate if you assess finance charges. For a new vendor entry, remember to return to the record later and enter the tax identification number for 1099 vendors, along with any other information you did not enter earlier.

To add a new product or service record or billing or purchase order code, enter the new code, and then respond Y to the prompt asking if you want to create an inventory item. Select the record type: 1 for products, 2 for services, or 3 for codes. Finally, complete the fields that display. Remember to recall the new, but incomplete, product record later and enter its location, vendor, and reorder information.

DEFINING AND PERFORMING LOOKUPS

* From the Edit menu, select Defaults. From the submenu select Default Lookups.

3.1 You must use Graph+Mate to perform record lookups.

You can view the codes and names or descriptions of your customers, vendors, products, and services during data entry. You can also see a list of customer or vendor invoices with their due and discount dates.

The default lookup sorting for customers, vendors, products, and services is by code, or you can select, instead, to sort by name or description. For invoices, sorting is by invoice number. To change the default sorting method for these lists, select the Defaults option from the Edit menu, and then choose Default Lookups from the submenu. On the Default Lookups screen, highlight your sorting preference for Customers/Vendors and Products/Services, and then press F10. Other files, such as the terms table, general ledger, and messages table, also allow lookups, but they are only sorted by code.

To look up a file during data entry, place the cursor in the field where you would normally enter the code for that type of record and press F5. During a lookup, you can temporarily change the sorting method of the file types for which you set defaults by pressing Shift-F9. The vendor, customer, product, or service file will be resorted by name.

Use the PgUp or PgDn key to scroll through the lookup screen. If you enter all or a portion of the code (or name, depending on the sorting method) in the Search field of the lookup screen, the program will scroll to the record that most closely matches your criteria. Highlight the record you want and press ↵ or click on it with the mouse. DacEasy will insert the code in the data-entry screen.

USING THE CALCULATOR

3.1 Press Alt-C to access the calculator functions using Graph+Mate.

You can use the calculator included with DacEasy Accounting to do simple mathematics and insert the results in the field where the cursor is located. To display the calculator, press Shift-F2.

The calculator works much like a regular pocket calculator. If you toggle the computer keyboard Num Lock key on, the keypad can be used to enter numbers (and + and −). You can also enter numbers from the top row of the keyboard. You must enter the appropriate symbol to let the program know whether to add (+), subtract (−), multiply (*), or divide (/) a figure, or to total the calculation (=).

You use the letter keys to request the square root of a number (S), to clear an entry (C), toggle from fixed decimal point to floating decimal (F), recall the amount in memory (M), or to paste the result of a calculation into a field (P).

The example in Figure 5.2 calculates the amount of loss on the sale of a fixed asset during entry of the general ledger transaction. To perform this calculation, you would enter the depreciated value of the asset (1250 in the example), type − (minus), enter the amount for which the asset was sold (700), and type = (equals) to see the result (550.00). Press P to paste the answer into the amount field in the transaction screen.

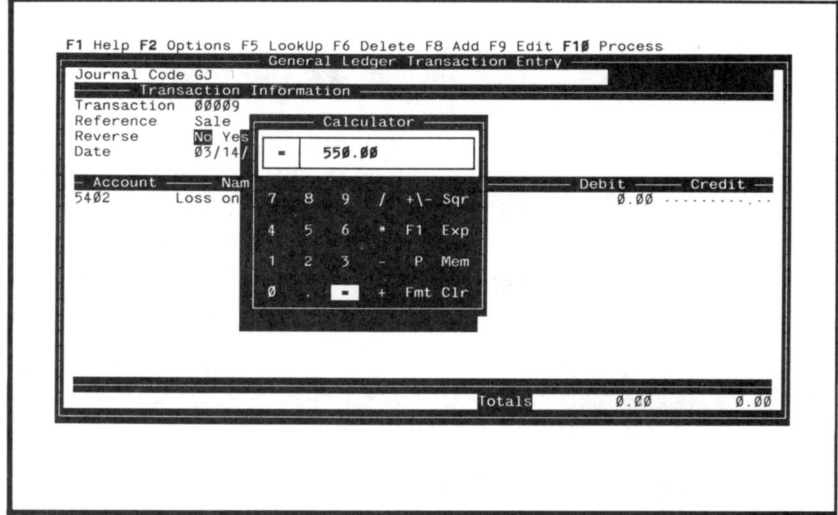

Figure 5.2: Using the calculator

PRINTING BUSINESS FORMS, REPORTS, AND FINANCIAL STATEMENTS

Printing DacEasy documents will be one of your most common tasks. You can print purchasing and sales documents, journals, and reports.

CHOOSING FORMS FOR PRINTING DOCUMENTS

* From the Edit menu, select Defaults. From the submenu, select Forms Setup.

3.1 You cannot predefine a format for each form. Instead, you choose the form type each time you print a document.

DacEasy allows you to select from three types of forms for your printed documents. The default setting is plain, 11-inch forms, with codes and item numbers printed. You can change the default format for purchase orders, merchandise-received slips, purchase-return forms, invoices, sales-return slips, and customer statements.

To set up form types, select the Defaults option from the Edit menu, choose Forms Setup, and then select the type of form you want to define. You will see the Forms Setup menu, as shown in Figure 5.3.

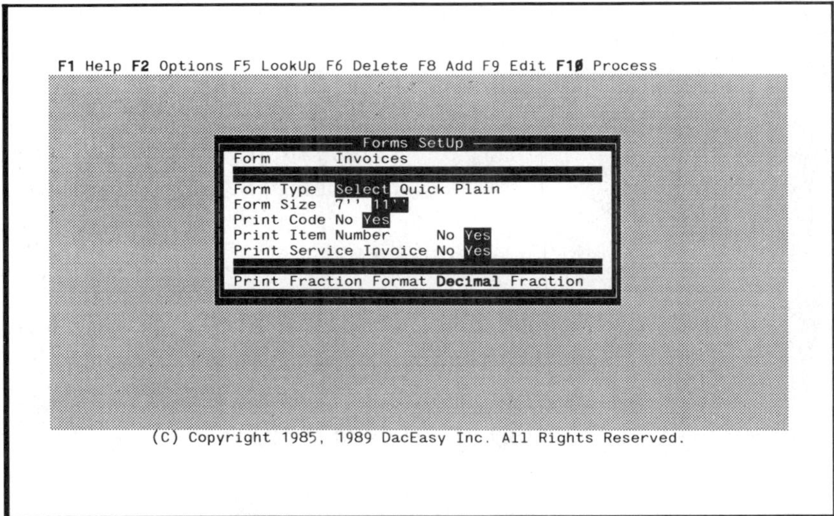

Figure 5.3: Choosing formats for invoices

3.1 Forms that have your company information already printed on them are called *Preprinted* instead of *Select*.

Your form type choices are as follows:

- *Select forms* are preprinted with your company name and logo already imprinted on them. They also have headings pertinent to the document you are printing, such as Invoice Number, Terms, Reference Number, Item Number, Quantity Shipped, Backordered, Unit Price, Tax, and Total. (You can order preprinted forms from Dac Software, Inc.)
- *Quick forms* are stock forms with preprinted column headings, but no company information. The program prints your company information from the name and address you set up for your company identification. The information is printed in

the proper format to fit the form. Quick forms are less expensive than select forms.

- *Plain forms* are simply blank computer paper. In addition to your company name and address, the program will print column headings above the itemized information in the document.

There are two form size choices. You must select 11″ for plain forms, but you can choose either 7″ or 11″ for preprinted forms. If only a few lines will appear on a document, you can use 7-inch paper. Use 11-inch paper for printing documents that list many items.

The Print Code option allows you to print the customer code, as well as the name and address, on invoices. The Print Item Number option prints the product number on the invoice, thus using two lines per entry. Another option, Print Service Invoice, prints invoices that do not include Shipped and Back Ordered fields. The last option, Print Fraction Format, allows you to print units in decimal format (3/4 of 12 would print .75) or in product fraction format (3/4 of 12 would print 9).

When you print a document, the program will use the format you defined. Don't forget you can also define three different printers. This means you can leave invoice forms in one printer, purchase-order forms in the second, and merchandise-received forms in the third. At print time, you designate which printer the information should go to.

SELECTING REPORT DISPOSITION

3.1 Journals and reports are automatically printed on the one printer you can define. You do not have the option of printing them on screen, nor of exporting data. However, you can use Graph+Mate to create reports that can be printed or displayed and to export the contents of a DacEasy file.

Journals, reports, and documents can be printed, displayed on the screen, or exported (exporting is discussed in Chapter 3). After you define the report you want to print, the Report Disposition screen appears (see Figure 3.6).

To print on paper, press the left arrow key to highlight Printer in the Report Disposition field. The printers you have defined are displayed in the Printer Name field. Highlight the printer you want to use, and the lines per page from the printer definition will appear in the next field. The File Information portion of the screen is only necessary when you are creating an ASCII or export file. Press F10 to print the report.

To display the report on screen, select Screen as the Report Disposition and press F10. You must print journals before you can post. If you do not want to keep paper copies of your transactions, you can display them on the screen to satisfy this requirement. Ignore the Printer Name field (and the alignment prompts). The report will be processed and displayed on the monitor. Use the PgUp and PgDn keys to scroll through the report. Use the Home and End keys to move from side to side. The arrow keys move one line or one space at a time. Press Esc to exit the report. The Report Redirection screen displays. You can send the report to a printer after viewing it on screen.

PRINTING PURCHASING AND SALES DOCUMENTS

If you want to change the form type for a particular document, use the Forms Setup option on the Edit Defaults submenu before printing.

During data entry in the Purchase Order and Billing modules, you can print purchase orders, merchandise-received slips, purchase-return forms, invoices, and sales-return slips individually. After you enter the data for the transaction, press F7 to record the entries and print the document.

If your volume of paperwork is heavy, however, you might want to wait until the entire day's work has been entered, and then print all documents of the same type at the same time. For example, you could print all the purchase orders in one run, all the sales returns in another run, and so on. This way, you won't have to change the printer forms so often if you have only one printer.

The Packing List option is not offered when you are printing purchase orders.

Figure 5.4 shows the Print Invoices screen. When you print documents through a print option, you can also choose to print a packing slip for each document or reprint documents you printed earlier.

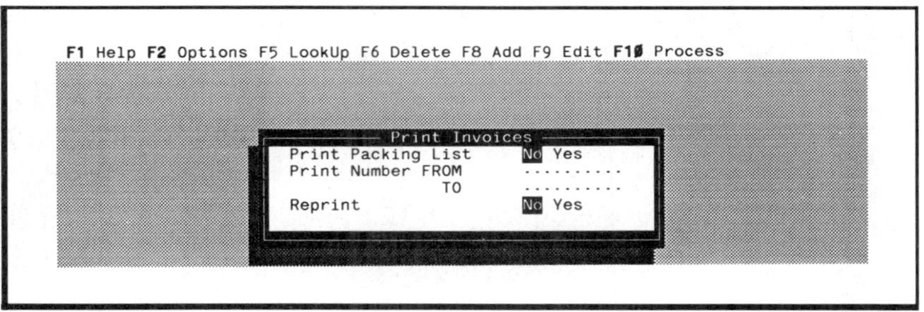

Figure 5.4: Print Invoices screen

A packing slip looks like the original document, except it does not include the costs or totals.

As an example, here are the steps for printing a group of invoices, beginning with number 1562:

1. In the Print Packing List field, select No.
2. In the Print Number From field, enter **1562**, the number of the first invoice you want to print. You can press ↵ to have the program supply the first record available in the sales-entry file.
3. Press ↵ in the Print Number To field to insert the last record available in the sales-entry file.
4. In the Reprint field, select No because this is the first printing of invoices today. If the printer mangles the forms, or if you already printed them during data entry, you can return to this screen to reprint them.
5. Press F10 to proceed. The Report Disposition screen appears.
6. Select Printer, and then press F10. The following prompt appears:

    Place the forms in the printer and press any key when ready to align. Press F7 to skip alignment.

Before responding to the alignment prompt, you can change the form's setup. To do so, press F3, select the form type, and alter the format. Press F10 to record the new setup, and then press Esc to return to the alignment prompt.

7. If you are an old pro at loading DacEasy forms into the printer, you can press F7 to skip the alignment, and the documents will begin to print immediately. To check the alignment before printing, put the proper forms in the printer, align them, and then press ↵. The program will print a line of characters on the page. This alignment test should print

3.1 Enter the number corresponding to the type of form to be printed in the Forms Type field and then press ↵ to accept the system date as the date to print on the documents, or type another date in this field. Press F6 (instead of F7) to skip the alignment.

across the perforation of the form. After the test, the program displays the prompt

Are the forms aligned?
A 'N' will repeat the print test

8. If the line printed on the perforation, press ↵ to accept the default Yes. If the forms are not aligned, move them into position, and then enter N for No to repeat the test. When the forms are correctly aligned, respond to this prompt with Yes.

Invoice 1562 through the last invoice created that day will print.

PRINTING JOURNALS

All the entries you make in the Billing, Accounts Receivable, Purchase Order, Accounts Payable, Cash, and Inventory modules go into a journal to await posting. The detail of each transaction is listed in the journal.

First, you post the transactions to the records in the subsidiary module, and later you post them to the accounts in the general ledger. When you post to the subsidiary modules, the transactions are summarized into account totals in preparation for posting to the general ledger. This means that the detail of each individual transaction is lost after it is posted. For this reason, it is crucial that you print the subsidiary journal *before* posting to the module. The transactions entered directly into the general ledger go into whatever general ledger journal you designate. These journals can also be printed.

3.1 When you request to print a journal, DacEasy will prompt you for the first (Transaction # From:) and last (To:) transaction numbers. Enter the numbers of the first and last transactions you want to include in the journal. You can press ↵ in the From field to begin with the first transaction in the file and in the To field to end with the last transaction in the file.

You can print a *journal* for a specific period showing the transactions awaiting posting in that period or a *listing* of all the transactions in the file (posted and unposted). You can review summarized transactions from the subsidiary modules in the general ledger listing. To print a journal or listing, select the module from the Journals menu. Complete the fields on the left side of the screen to print a journal or the fields on the right side of the screen to print a listing. Figure 5.5 shows examples of the completed fields for printing a general ledger journal and listing.

Printing subsidiary journals or listings is similar to printing ones for the general ledger. The fields you will encounter when printing journals and listings are described in Table 5.3.

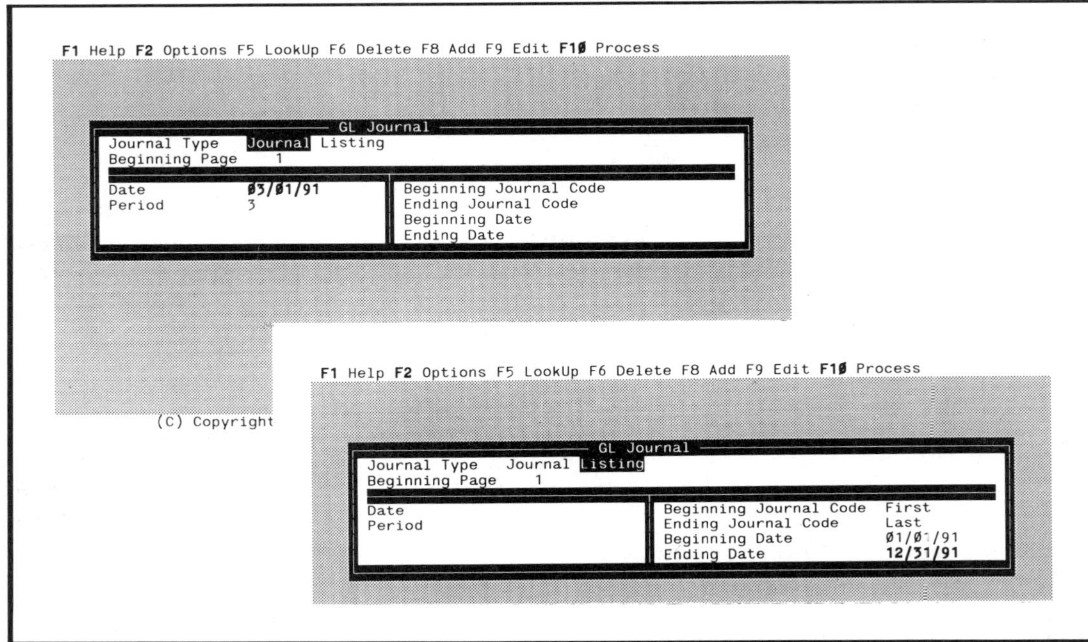

Figure 5.5: Printing a general ledger journal or listing

Table 5.3: Fields for Printing Journals and Listings

Field	You Supply
Journal Type	Select Journal to print all unposted transactions or Listing to print all transactions in the file.
Beginning Page	Enter the number you wanted printed on the first page of the general ledger report.
Date	Enter a date within the period you want to print.
Period	The program supplies the period in which the date you entered falls.
Beginning Journal Code	The code of the first journal in the general ledger you want on the report. Press ↵ to start with the first journal in the file.
Ending Journal Code	The code of the last journal you want on the report. Press ↵ to end with the last journal in the file.
Beginning Date	The first date in the journals requested that you want on the report. Press ↵ to start with the first date in the file.
Ending Date	The last date in the journals requested that you want on the report. Press ↵ to end with the last date in the file.

Table 5.3: Fields for Printing Journals and Listings (continued)

Field	You Supply
Beginning Transaction Number	The first transaction you want included in the subsidiary journal. Press ↵ to start with the first unposted transaction in the file.
Ending Transaction Number	The last transaction you want included in the subsidiary journal. Press ↵ to end with the last unposted transaction in the file.

You should review every journal for errors and make corrections prior to posting. You can reprint a journal until you post transactions to the corresponding module.

SORTING AND RANKING STANDARD REPORTS

DacEasy generates numerous reports, in the form of listings, which draw detail from your entire database. These reports include aged invoices, customer labels, product listings, and customer and vendor directories.

When you print reports of this type, you can sort and rank the information in many ways. The program will organize information on the report according to the criteria you designate. By alternating the sorting and ranking criteria, you can obtain subtotals for various categories. Each module lists its own sorting and ranking criteria choices, which are summarized in Table 5.4.

Here are some examples of sorting criteria selection:

- In the Accounts Receivable module, sort the customer directory by salesperson to provide each member of your sales staff with a listing of his or her accounts.
- In the Accounts Payable module, sort labels by vendor type, selecting 1099 vendors for a mailing requesting verification of their tax identification number.
- In the Inventory module, sort by vendor and rank by sales units to determine which slow-moving items should be purged from your inventory.
- Sort service reports by department to compare the total sales revenue for each area.

3.1 You can also rank customers by credit available and profit; billing group is not available. You can sort vendors by credit available. You can sort inventory by on-hand units and dollars, profit, turns, and gross profit.

Table 5.4: Criteria Selections for Report Sorting and Ranking

Sort by Selections	Rank by Selections
Accounts Receivable	
Code	Code
Name	Name
Department	Credit Limit
Sales Person	Current Balance
Zip Code	Last Sales Date Last Payment Date Invoice Count (Sales Units) Sales Dollars Billing Group
Accounts Payable	
Code	Code
Name	Name
Territory	Credit Limit
Type	Current Balance
Zip Code	Last Purchase Date Last Payment Date Invoice Count (Purchase Units) Purchase Dollars
Inventory	
Inventory Number	Inventory Number
Description	Description
Department	Sales Units
Bin	Sales Dollars
Vendor	Last Sales Date Purchase Units Purchase Dollars Last Purchase Date
Service Reports	
Service Code	Service Code
Description	Description
Department	Sales Units Sales Dollars Last Sales Date

When you request to print one of these standard reports, you will be prompted to select sorting criteria from those displayed. The program will subtotal the data by the sorting group you choose. You also specify the first and last records you want included in the report in the From and To fields. As usual, you can press ↵ to start with the first record or end with the last record in the file. Records excluded from the sorting range will not be printed or included in the totals.

Next, you must choose the ranking criteria from those displayed. This is a ranking within each sorting group. Again, enter the first and last records to be included in the report in the From and To fields. Records excluded from the ranking range will not be printed, even though they match the sorting criteria.

PRINTING FINANCIAL STATEMENTS

DacEasy prints financial reports that deal solely with the balances in your general ledger. These include a list of the chart of accounts, an account activity listing, a trial balance, a balance sheet, and an income statement. You can include all your accounts in these reports or select a range of accounts.

When you select to print a financial report (select General Ledger from the Reports menu and the report you want from the submenu), DacEasy will display the fields described in Table 5.5.

Table 5.5: Fields for Printing Financial Reports

Field	You Supply
Print Accounts From	The first account you want on the trial balance or account activity report. Press ↵ to start with the first account in the file.
To	The last account you want on the report. Press ↵ to end with the last account.
Print Dates From	The first date you want included on the trial balance or account activity report. Press ↵ to start with the first date in the file.
To	The last date you want included. Press ↵ to end with the last date in the period.
Period	The number of the period for which you want to print a balance sheet.
Print Accounts to Level	The account level in the general ledger account definition. Enter the lowest level you want on the trial balance, balance sheet, or chart of accounts report. Level 9 gives you the most detail, and level 1 is a complete summary.

Table 5.5: Fields for Printing Financial Reports (continued)

Field	You Supply
Include General Accounts	General accounts accumulate data from lower level general accounts and detail accounts. Select Yes to include general accounts on the trial balance or balance sheet report or No to exclude them, thereby printing only detail accounts.
Include Inactive Accounts	Select Yes if you want accounts with a zero balance included in the report. Select No if you only want to print accounts with activity or a balance in the period you are printing.
Initial Page	Select the starting page number for the trial balance, account activity, or chart of accounts report. Press ↵ to begin your listing with page 1. If you are keeping a consecutively numbered series of financial statements, enter the next number in the sequence.
Print by Page	Select Yes if you want to print one account per page on the account activity report. Select No if you want several accounts on a page.
Ranking	Select Date to print the account activity in date order or select Journal to print by journal code.

CORRECTING TRANSACTIONS PRIOR TO POSTING

You can correct or delete a transaction during data entry or before you post it, even if you have recorded the transaction (by pressing F10) and printed the journal. If an unposted transaction appears in a printed journal and you go back to correct it, then reprint a second journal, the corrected transaction will appear in the reprint. When you post, only the latest version of the transaction will be posted and summarized for transfer to the general ledger.

The steps to correct an unposted transaction are outlined below.

1. Recall the transaction by entering the document or transaction number. The transaction record appears for verification.
2. Press F10 to move the cursor to the line item section of the screen.
3. Move the cursor to the line containing the mistake.

3.1 Delete the entire line by pressing Alt-D (instead of Shift-F6).

4. Replace incorrect data with new information or delete the entire line by moving the cursor to the Account field and pressing Shift-F6.
5. Add a new line item if necessary.
6. Press F10 to process the corrected transaction.

If you want to delete the transaction entirely, after the transaction record appears, move the cursor to the Account field and press F6. DacEasy will display a window asking you to verify the deletion. Press ↵ to accept the default Yes or select No to cancel the request to delete the transaction.

POSTING TRANSACTIONS

After you print and review the journals and make any corrections, you are ready to post the transactions. When you post, the transactions become a permanent entry in your records and cannot be changed. Instead, you must make a reversing entry. Reversing entries for each module are explained in the chapter about the particular module.

Each module—Purchase Order, Accounts Payable, Billing, Accounts Receivable, Cash, and Inventory—is posted separately. The transactions are summarized into journals, which are posted to the general ledger along with miscellaneous general ledger transactions.

Before posting any transactions, complete the following steps:

3.1 The program will display the system date in the Posting Date field, which is the date the entries in the subsidiary modules will be effective in your general ledger. If the posting date is correct, press ↵ to accept the Y and continue. If it is not the date you want to use, enter N to cancel the process and return to the Posting menu. Press F4, enter the date you want to use, and then reselect the posting option. Press ↵ at the next prompts (or enter N to cancel) and respond to the final prompt.

1. As the program warns, enter all invoice, sales-return, cash-receipt, merchandise-received, and purchase-return transactions for the day.
2. Print all the invoices, computer-generated checks, return slips, and other documents.
3. Print the related journals.
4. Back up your files.

When you request to post subsidiary modules, you can enter a reference to identify the summarized transactions in the general ledger. Enter the date in the Date to Post field, and the program displays the period in which that date falls. After entering a reference, press F10. All the transactions in the period indicated will be posted in the subsidiary module. When posting to the general ledger, enter the date you want the entries from the subsidiary modules to be effective in your general ledger, regardless of their individual transaction dates. Only miscellaneous transactions entered directly in the general ledger retain their original transaction date.

CLOSING THE PERIOD

The purpose of closing a period is to clear your files of unnecessary baggage. You have the option of removing all transactions from the file in the module you are closing. In the Accounts Payable and Accounts Receivable modules, invoices that have been paid are removed, along with the related payments. The current and previous period balances in the records you select to close are also updated during period-end processing.

To close the period, select the module you want to close from the Periodic menu, and then select Period End from the submenu. You will see the prompt

Date to Close

Press ⟵ to accept the system date or enter a date in the period you want to close. The program displays the period for the date you entered.

You are asked

Delete Transactions No Yes

If you delete the period's transactions in the general ledger, your on-line audit trail will be truncated, and the general ledger listing will no longer contain the transactions in the period you are closing.

Select Yes to delete all the transactions in the period you are closing. Press ⟵ to accept the default No. It is recommended that you do not delete transactions if you have sufficient disk space. Press F10 to close the period.

CLOSING THE MONTH IN VERSION 3.1

With version 3.1, the program automatically removes all posted transactions from the general ledger transaction file instead of giving you a choice.

When you request to close the month (through the Periodic menu), you are asked if you want to continue, respond Y to continue with the month-end close or N to cancel the process. In the Enter the Closing Date field, press ↵ to accept the system date or enter a different date. The program uses this closing date instead of a period indicator to determine which items in the open file to process. Items that are dated prior to and including this date are affected by the close; those with a later date are not. For example, if an invoice has been paid in full, but the invoice date is after the closing date, it should not be processed. If you print customer statements, the paid invoice should still be listed.

In the From and To fields, enter the code of the first and last records you want to process (or press ↵ for the first or last record). Records not included in the range will not be affected. At the last prompt

```
Start closing now (Y/N)? Y:
```

Press ↵ to begin the closing process, or enter N to cancel.

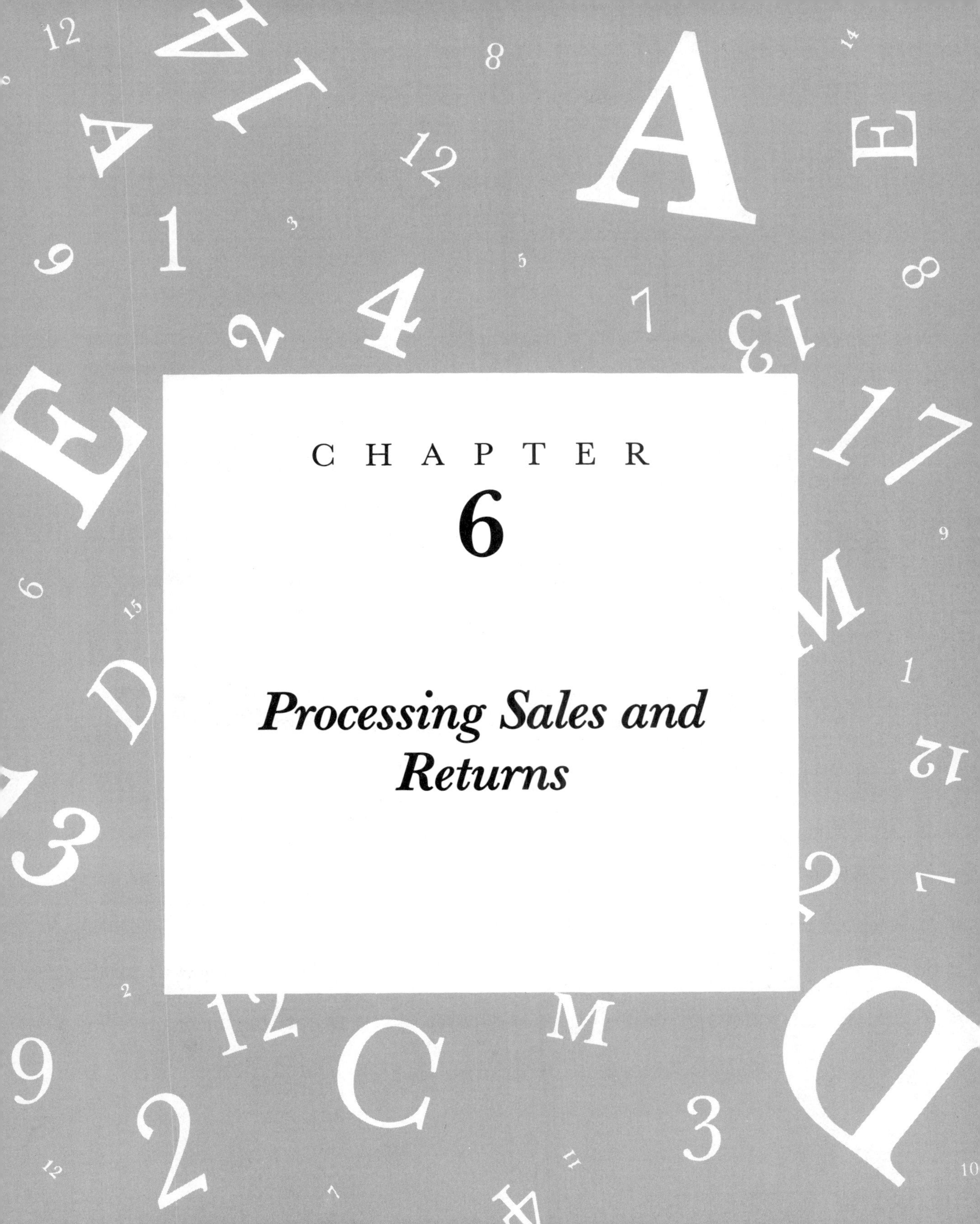

CHAPTER 6

Processing Sales and Returns

SALES ARE THE LIFEBLOOD OF YOUR COMPANY. YOU will want to track what is sold, at what price, and if any items are returned for a refund or credit. You will also want to print invoices, packing slips, and sales-return slips. DacEasy handles sales through its Billing module.

RECORDING SALES

* From the Transactions menu, select Billing. From the Entry submenu, select select Invoices.

3.1 From the Transaction menu, select Billing. From the submenu, select Enter Invoices.

Whenever you sell a product or a service, you need to record the transaction. To enter the sale, select the Billing option from the Transactions menu, and then choose Invoices from the Entry submenu. You will see the Invoices screen, as shown in Figure 6.1. The fields on this screen are described in Table 6.1.

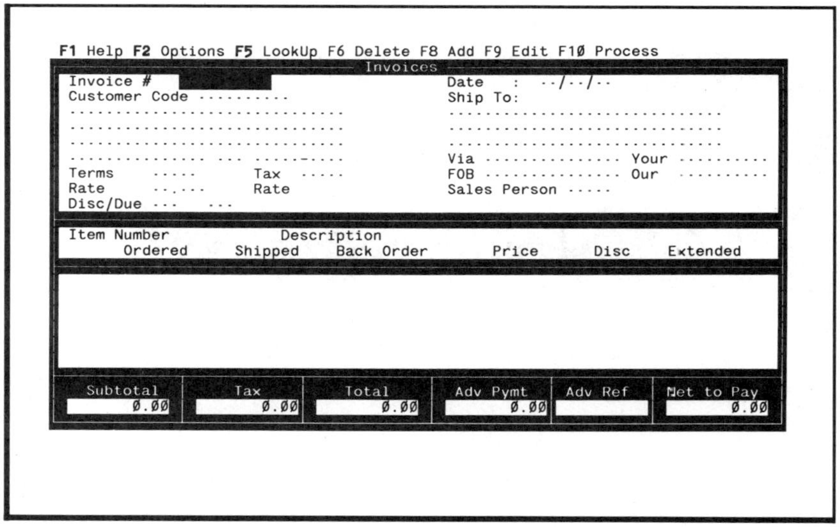

```
F1 Help F2 Options F5 LookUp F6 Delete F8 Add F9 Edit F10 Process
                              Invoices
Invoice #                                 Date    :   --/--/--
Customer Code ..........                  Ship To:
Terms      .....     Tax   .....          Via ............... Your ..........
Rate       ..,...    Rate                 FOB ............... Our  ..........
Disc/Due ...    ...                       Sales Person .....

Item Number              Description
      Ordered     Shipped    Back Order        Price       Disc    Extended

  Subtotal       Tax        Total      Adv Pymt    Adv Ref    Net to Pay
      0.00       0.00        0.00          0.00                     0.00
```

Figure 6.1: Invoices screen

To record a sale, press ↵, and the program assigns an invoice number to the sales entry. After you enter the customer's code, DacEasy supplies default information from the customer record. You can accept these defaults and just enter the data specific to this sale, or override the defaults if you want to handle the sale differently.

Table 6.1: Fields on the Invoices Screen

Field	Description
Invoice #	The program assigns a number to a new invoice. To edit an existing invoice, enter its number here.
Date	The program supplies the system date.
Customer Code	The code of the customer making the purchase.
Customer Name	The program supplies the name in the customer record. You can enter an override for the current transaction.
Contact	The program supplies the contact person in the customer record. You can enter an override for the current transaction.
Address	The program supplies the address in the customer record. You can enter an override for the current transaction.
Terms	The program supplies the terms code in the customer record. You can enter an override for this transaction.
Rate	The program supplies the discount rate from the terms table. This is the percent the customer can deduct from the total invoice when making an early payment; for example, 1.5 is one and one-half percent. You can enter an override for this transaction.
Disc/Due	The program supplies the number of days after the invoice date that the customer can take a discount for early payment. It also supplies the number of days after the invoice date the customer must pay the invoice in full or the day of the month when the invoice is due, depending on the definition of the terms code in the terms table. You can enter an override for the current transaction.
Tax/Rate	The program supplies the tax code from the customer record and the tax rate from the tax table. This is the percent that will be charged on every item defined as taxable in the product, service, and billing code records. You can override the tax rate code during sales entry.
Ship To	Any notation or instructions pertaining to this invoice, for example, the customer's shipping address.
Via	How the purchase is to be shipped, for example, DHL.
FOB	The name of the city where the freight charges to the customer originate (freight on board).
Your	The reference notation to appear under Reference # on the customer statement.
Our	Your own reference notation, if any. This appears on the customer invoice after Our #.
Sales Person	The code for the salesperson who sold the items on this invoice.

Table 6.1: Fields on the Invoices Screen (continued)

Field	Description
Item Number	The inventory number of the product or service being purchased. You can also enter a billing code, free text, or a message code. Enter a *C* followed by a space and a billing code for a nonproduct or nonservice item, *D* followed by a space and up to 40 characters of free text, or *M* followed by a space and a message code to print the associated message on the invoice.
Description	The program supplies the item description from the product record.
Ordered	The quantity ordered by the customer using the sales unit and fraction of measure; for example, one and one-half gallons is 1.2 using four quarts in a gallon.
Shipped	The program calculates the number of items that are in stock, available for shipment.
Back Order	The program determines the quantity of ordered items that are out of stock and unavailable for sale on this invoice.
Price	The program supplies the sale price in the product or service file. You can enter an override for this transaction.
Disc	The percent by which you want to reduce the price normally charged for this item; for example, 10 is ten percent.
Extended	The program calculates the amount due for this item (shipped × price – calculated discount amount).
Subtotal	The program calculates the subtotal after the completion of each item.
Tax	The program calculates the sales tax according to the tax percentage in the customer record after the completion of each item that's defined as taxable.
Total	The program calculates the total after the completion of each item (subtotal + tax).
Adv Pymt	The amount of any advance payment made with the order.
Adv Ref	The check number or reference to any payment made with the order.
Net to Pay	If payment is entered with the invoice, the summarized net amount is all that appears on the customer statement and the aging report. The original total of the invoice and the amount of the payment do not appear separately.

Version 3.1: The Date, Ship To, Terms, and Disc/Due fields do not exist. Additional fields are Remark, for your notations; and Disc. Days, Disc. %, and Due Days, which are supplied from the customer record.

When you have completed the fields on the screen, press F7 to record the sale and print the invoice, or press F10 to simply record it and clear the screen for entering another sale. DacEasy will create an invoice and update the customer, product, accounts receivable, and inventory records.

As an example, suppose that you own a camera shop and sometimes take trade-ins on camera sales. One out-of-town customer collects old cameras for display in its store. This customer just purchased one of the trade-ins, an old press photographer's 4 × 5 camera. The completed sales entry for this transaction is shown in Figure 6.2. The following procedure is used to record the sale.

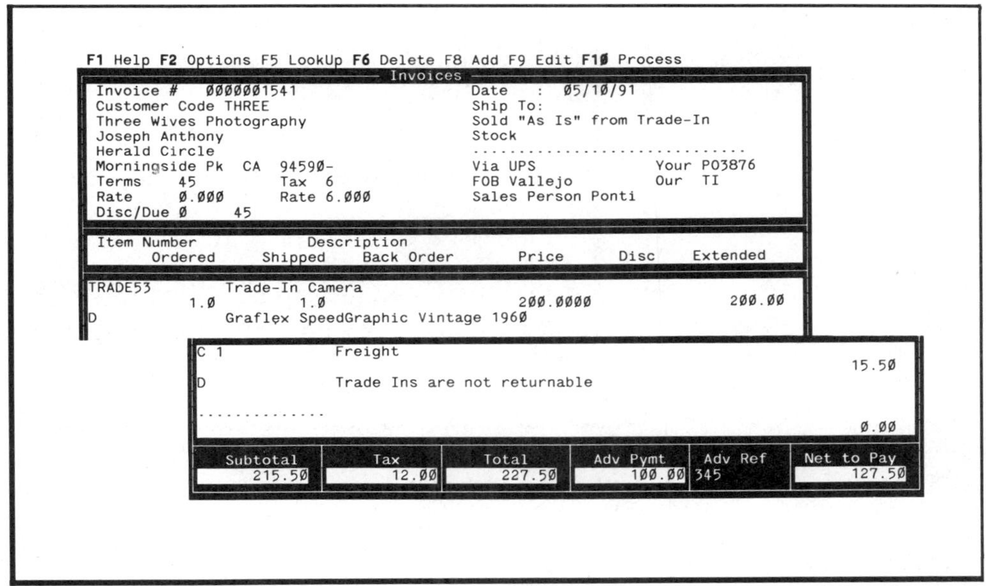

Figure 6.2: Completed sales entry

1. In the Invoice # field, press ↵ to assign a new invoice number. The program inserts the system date in the Date field.

3.1 The Date field does not exist.

2. Press ↵ to accept the date. You can enter an override to change the date of the invoice. You cannot use F4 to change the date for the current transaction. If you used F4 now, the *next* transaction would have the new system date.

3. In the Customer Code field, enter **THREE**, the code for the customer making the purchase, Three Wives Photography. Using the first letters of the customer's name for the code makes it easier to remember the codes. It also produces an alphabetical listing when you run reports sorted by customer code.

Because this code is for a customer who has a message attached to its record, a window appears. This window displays the message, the customer's credit limit, current balance, and credit available, as shown in Figure 6.3.

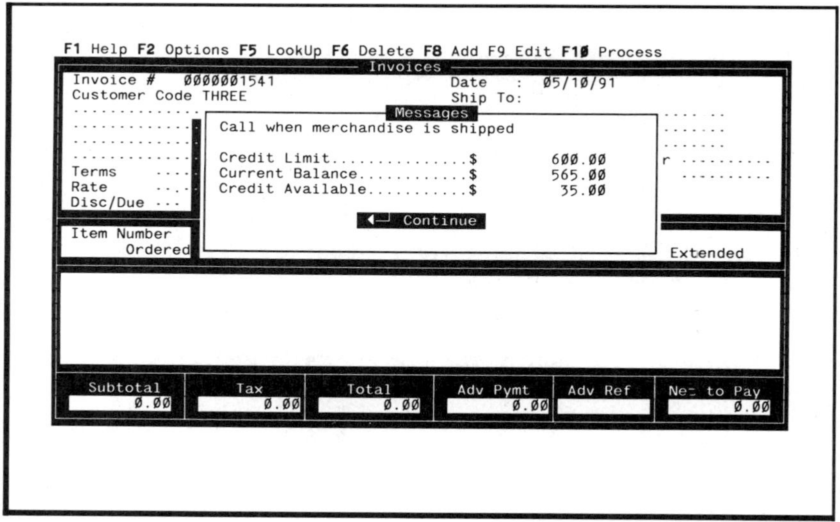

Figure 6.3: Message display

Don't be misled; the message code is completely independent of the customer's credit status. The display of the current status is just a side benefit of displaying a message. If this invoice exceeds the customer's credit limit, that, in and of itself, will not cause a warning to display. In fact, the credit limit is not updated until the invoices are posted to Billing. Therefore, you might not notice that a customer has made several purchases that exceed its credit limit until you post your daily work.

To monitor customer accounts with a credit limit, create a message, such as *Note Credit Limit*, and include its code in their records. When you enter an invoice for one of these customers, you will see the Messages window showing the account's current status. Check that the total of the current sale and the current balance do not exceed the credit limit.

4. Press any key to continue recording the sale.

Overrides during data entry do not change what is in the customer record. They only change the terms for the current invoice.

3.1 You must override the discount percent and the discount and due days directly.

5. The program displays the name in the customer record for verification. Press ↵ to accept it, and then press ↵ to accept the contact and address. You can enter different information in any of these fields if you want to override the defaults for a particular sale.

The program supplies the default terms code from the customer record and the discount rate from the terms table. It calculates the amount of discount the customer is allowed to take when paying within the discount days and how many days from the invoice date the invoice is due in full, based on the terms code. This example uses different terms for this particular invoice. If you just override the Rate or Disc/Due field entry, the program will revert back to the terms defined by the terms code. You must change the Terms field entry.

6. Press the Del key to erase the number in the Terms field. Then enter **45**, the terms code for zero discount, due in 45 days. No discounts are allowed on trade-in sales, but this gives the customer longer than usual to pay the invoice to compensate for the lack of an early payment discount.
7. Press ↵ to accept the tax code supplied from the customer record. You can change this during data entry. The program displays the related tax rate. Each item on this invoice that is defined as taxable in the product and service files is multiplied times this percent to determine the sales tax. When you post the entries to your general ledger, your sales tax liability account will be credited to indicate how much you owe the government taxing agency.

3.1 The Ship To field is called Remark.

8. In the Ship To field, enter **Sold "As Is" from Trade-In Stock.** The Ship To field is for any notation or instructions pertaining to the invoice. Typically, you would enter the customer's shipping address if it is different from the billing address.
9. In the Via field, enter **UPS**, which is the freight company that will deliver the purchase to the customer.
10. In the Your field, enter **PO3876**, the customer's purchase order number.

11. Enter **Vallejo** in the FOB (freight on board) field. The merchandise will be shipped from the overstock warehouse, and the customer pays the freight charges.
12. For Our, enter **TI** to indicate it is a sale of trade-in merchandise. This field is for your own reference for this sale.
13. Press ↵ to accept the default salesperson. You can enter an override if the salesperson who regularly services this account did not make the sale.

You cannot return to the header by pressing Esc after the cursor moves to the Item Number field. You must record the transaction and then edit it.

14. In the Item Number field, enter **TRADE53**, the inventory number of the traded-in camera the customer is buying. DacEasy provides the description from the product record.

3.1 The field for inventory numbers is called Inv. #.

15. In the Ordered field, enter **1**. If the customer is not buying a whole unit, enter the unit and fraction of the item ordered. For example, if you are selling one and one-half dozen roses, the unit and fraction would be 1.6 (12 fractions to a unit of roses; 6 fractions equals six roses, or one-half dozen). The quantity will be added to the committed field in the product record when you process the invoice. When the invoice is posted to Accounts Receivable, the committed units are released, and the quantity in the stock-on-hand field is reduced.

If you do not have enough items in stock and the customer's invoice creates a back order, remember to print a packing slip later to help you track it. Tracking back orders is discussed later in the chapter.

The program calculates how many items are in stock, available for shipment, and places this figure in the Shipped field. It then determines the quantity of out-of-stock items on the invoice and places this figure in the Back Order field. In our example, one camera is in trade-in stock, and only one camera is being sold. There is no back-ordered amount.

16. The program displays the sales price in the product record. Press ↵ to accept the default. Even if you want to give the customer a break on the price, it is good accounting practice to charge full price for the item, then give the customer a discount (in the next field) to reduce the actual cost.
17. Press ↵ to skip the Disc field. You could enter the percent by which you want to reduce the price normally charged for this item. This percent is taken off the extended amount and

the invoice total. Don't confuse this price discount with the discount allowed for early payment. The discount allowed for early payment is in addition to the discount you give on the price.

The program calculates the Extended field, which is the amount due for this item (shipped × price – calculated discount amount). The cursor moves back to the Item Number field so you can add items to the invoice.

In the Item Number field, you can enter a billing code rather than an inventory number to identify an item that is not in your inventory. You can also enter free text, which will be printed on the invoice, or a message code, which will print the associated message on the invoice. Just type the letter corresponding to the entry, press the spacebar, and enter the code. If you are entering free text, press ↵ after typing the letter, and then type the text in the window DacEasy displays. Precede a billing code with a C, free text with a D, and a message code with an M.

18. In the Item Number field, type **D**, press the spacebar, and then press ↵ to open a window where you can type free text.
19. Enter **Graflex SpeedGraphic Vintage 1960** in the text window to describe the specific camera the customer bought. There is no general ledger account or amount related to free text. The text you type here will print on the invoice.
20. In the Item Number field, type **C**, then press the spacebar to indicate you are entering a billing code.
21. Enter **1**, the billing code that represents freight. The description from the billing code table appears. Because the amount of freight fluctuates from delivery to delivery, there isn't an amount defined in the billing code table for this code. If the table did contain an amount for the code, it would also appear.
22. Press ↵ to accept the description and enter **15.50** in the Extended field as the freight charge on this invoice. The account numbers are defined in the billing codes table, so the

program knows which general ledger account to credit for this sale when you post.

23. In the Item Number field, type **M**, and then press the spacebar to indicate that you are entering a message code.
24. Enter **12** for the message code. The related message, *Trade Ins are not returnable*, appears on the screen and will print on the invoice. The M12 in the Item Number field is replaced by a D for Description.
25. Press F10 to process all the entries.

The program calculates the subtotal of the extended amounts, the sales tax (according to the tax percentage in the customer record), and the total (subtotal plus tax) after it processes each item. When this invoice is posted to the general ledger, the sales tax liability account in the general ledger will be credited, increasing the sales tax you owe to the government taxing agency.

3.1 Enter the check number in the Pmt. Ref. field, and then enter the advance payment amount in the Payment $ field.

26. The customer made a $100 down payment. The balance will be paid later in accordance with the terms on the invoice. Enter **100** in the Adv Pymt field. In the Adv Ref field, enter **345**, the number of the check given with the order.

If an advance payment has been posted to the customer's account through the Accounts Receivable module on a special order that was not in inventory at the time of the order, enter ADV in the Adv Ref field, but do not enter the payment amount; it is already on the customer's account. Only enter here the cash, check, or credit card amount you receive and can deposit today. It will be posted to the general ledger cash account defined in the general ledger interface table. If this money is not being deposited into that general ledger account, you will have to transfer funds between cash accounts, as described later in the chapter.

27. The program calculates the Net to Pay field (total minus payment). The amount is debited to your customer's account, increasing what is owed on the account. To record the invoice and print it, press F7. You can also press F10 to simply record it and clear the screen for the next invoice.

Processed invoices, even before you post them to Billing, are listed for payment on the Accounts Receivable open invoices lookup screen. However, neither an invoice nor a payment affects the customer's balance until it has been posted to the appropriate module.

SETTING UP AND PROCESSING RECURRING INVOICES

3.1 You cannot set up recurring invoices.

You cannot enter sales tax on a recurring invoice.

From the Transactions menu, select Recurring. From the Entry submenu, select Invoices.

Recurring invoices are billings that are repeated regularly. For example, a gardening service that you perform weekly can be set up as a recurring invoice. When you generate the invoice for billing, you can create an invoice for just one customer or for all the customers in a billing group, as long as the appropriate billing group code is entered in the record of every customer who is to be billed automatically.

To set up a recurring invoice, select the Recurring option from the Transactions menu, and then choose Invoices from the Entry submenu. You will see the Recurring Invoices screen. At the Tran # field, press ↵ to assign the next recurring transaction number. The Via field is for the carrier you use if this invoice is for a product you are delivering. FOB is for the city where shipping charges originate. You can use the Your field for the number of an open purchase order issued by an individual customer or a generic notation of what a group of customers order. Use the Our field as an internal reference or further description of the invoice.

Complete the remaining fields as you would a normal invoice, and then press F10 to save your work. Figure 6.4 shows an example of a completed Recurring Invoices screen.

From the Transactions menu, select Recurring. Select Generation, then Invoices from the submenu.

To generate a recurring invoice, select Recurring from the Transactions menu, select Generation, and then choose Invoices from the submenu. Enter the transaction number of the recurring invoice you want to generate and the date you want on the invoice. To create an invoice for a single customer, enter the customer code in the Customer field. To create invoices for all customers in a billing group, enter the code for the group in the Customer Group field. Press F10 to generate the invoice. Figure 6.5 shows an example of generating recurring invoices for a group of customers.

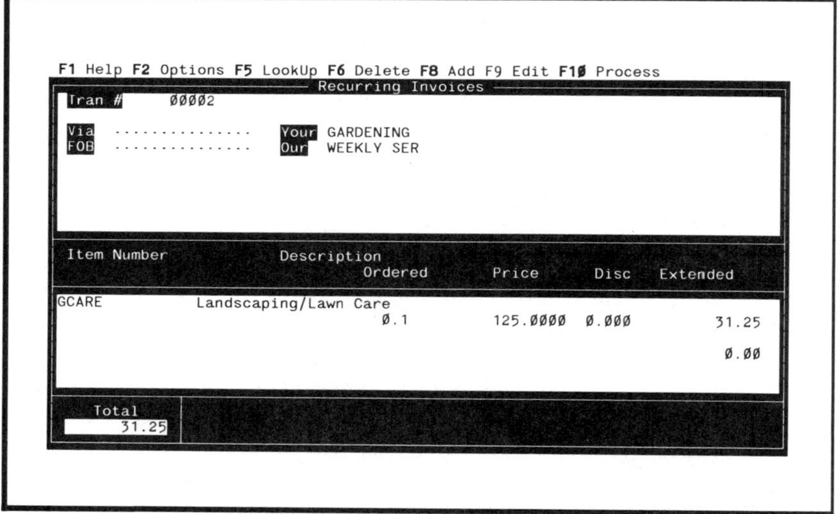

Figure 6.4: Setting up a recurring invoice

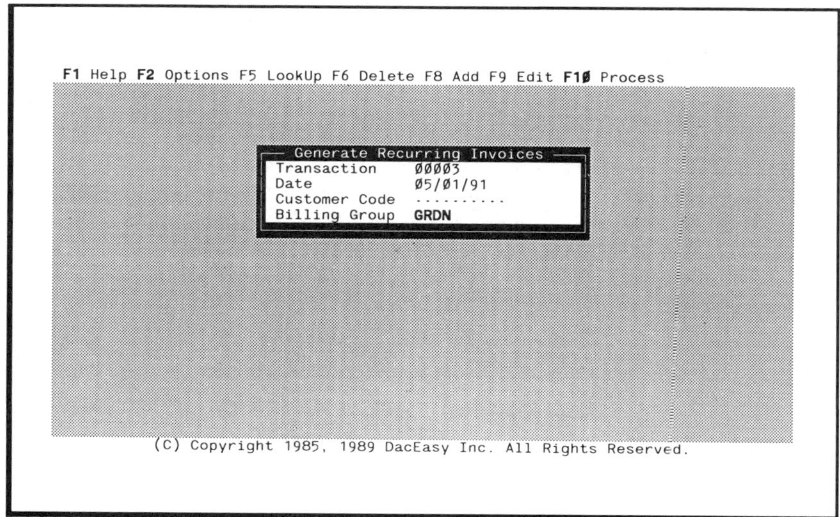

Figure 6.5: Generating recurring invoices

Each invoice generated is assigned the next available invoice number and is placed in the Billing transaction file.

To review or alter a recurring invoice that has been generated, select Billing from the Transactions menu, and then choose Invoices from the Entry submenu. Press F5 to look up the recurring invoice, highlight the invoice you want to edit, and press ↵. When the invoice is displayed, you can add information, such as the name of the salesperson who handles the account, or sales tax if necessary, as shown in Figure 6.6.

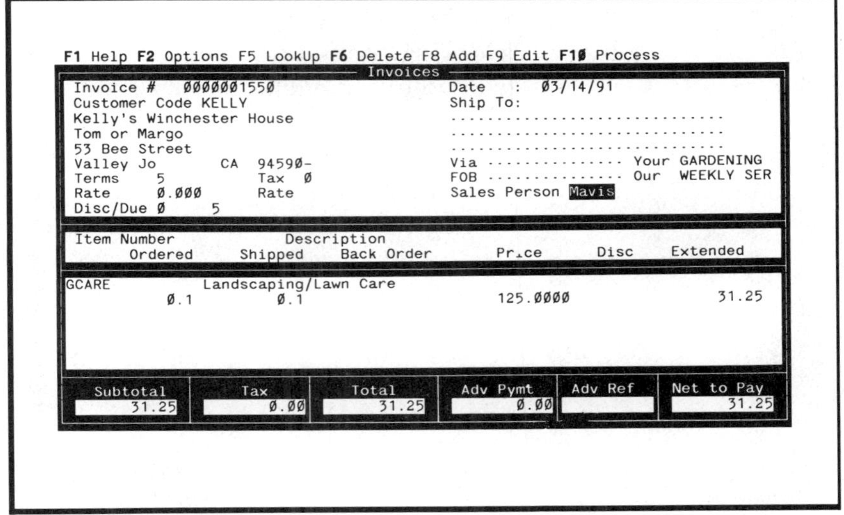

Figure 6.6: Editing a generated recurring invoice

RECORDING CASH SALES

> A good accounting control is to balance the amount you deposit into your bank account each day with the amount of cash and credit card payments posted to your customer accounts. To do so, print the Billing (Sales) journal (as described later in this chapter) and the Cash journal (as described in Chapter 7). Sum the payment totals from both modules and compare the result to your bank deposit. They should agree; if they don't, locate the error and correct it.

The procedure for entering a cash sale or one paid for by credit card is the same as the one for entering customer sales. The difference is that you may want to record these types of sales using a special account rather than a customer account.

It was suggested that, during setup, you create a customer record with the title Cash Sales and either a summary customer record with the title Credit Card Sales or one record for each credit card you accept. Use those special accounts each time a customer pays in cash or with a credit card.

To record a point-of-sale transaction, select the Billing option from the Transactions menu, choose Entry, and then Invoices. Type the customer code assigned to the cash or credit card record, and type in the name and address of the customer making the purchase. Enter the payment along with the transaction to record the sale, leaving the account with a zero balance.

If an established customer pays in cash occasionally, you should enter the transaction on the customer's account rather than on the Cash Sales account. This gives you an accurate historical record of the customer's activity with your company. The invoice will appear on the customer's statement as a zero transaction—no charge, no payment amount shown.

The amount you enter in the Adv Pymt field is debited to the checking account defined in the general ledger interface table when you post your Billing transactions to the general ledger.

Herein lies one of DacEasy's shortcomings: You cannot post activity in the Billing module to more than one general ledger cash account. This means that DacEasy assumes that you deposit all your billing receipts and credit card vouchers into the same checking account. To remedy this misconception, follow the instructions in the section below.

TRANSFERRING FUNDS BETWEEN CASH ACCOUNTS

✻ From the Transactions menu, select General Ledger.

3.1 From the Transaction menu, select General Ledger.

To transfer funds on your books from the cash account defined in your general ledger interface account to another general ledger cash account, so the accounts reflect the actual amounts in the bank account they represent, you must make a direct entry to the general ledger. Select the General Ledger option from the Transactions menu to display the General Ledger Transaction Entry screen.

As an example, suppose that you have two stores, but not enough business to warrant keeping two sets of books. You just keep the cash in separate accounts and identify sales and costs in two departments: 01 for the activity in one store and 02 for the activity in the second store. You do the posting for store 2 after the fact, using handwritten documents turned in at the end of the day.

When you enter money received on invoices from store 2, due to DacEasy's design, it is arbitrarily posted to the one account defined for cash in your general ledger interface account, 11021. The money from store 2 is actually deposited into an account at another bank. That bank account is represented in the general ledger by account 11023. You have to make an adjustment to your general ledger each day to correct the cash accounts. This transfer is illustrated in Figure 6.7.

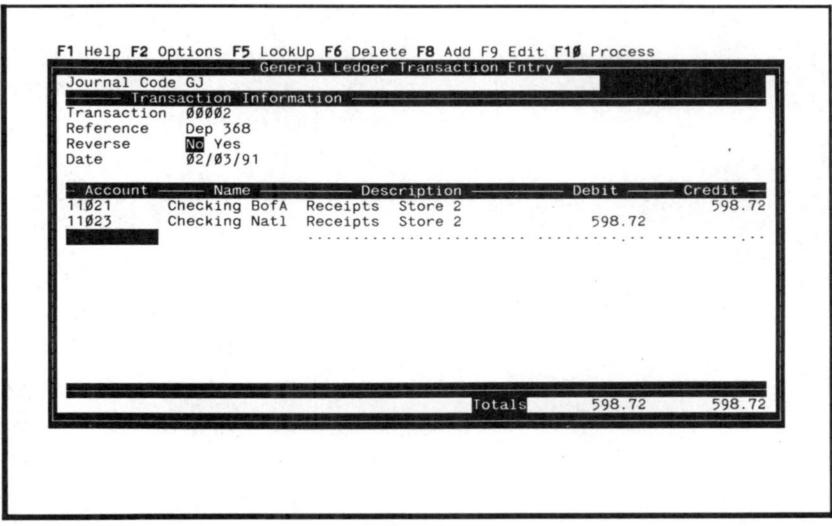

Figure 6.7: Transfer between general ledger cash accounts

Here is the procedure used to enter the data shown in Figure 6.7:

1. Enter **GJ** for General journal in the Journal Code field.

3.1 You must enter a transaction number.

2. Press ↵ to assign the next transaction number. It is good practice to keep a sequential numbering system for each day. The journal entry can then be easily identified by journal type, transaction number, and date.

3.1 The Reference and Reverse fields do not exist.

3. Enter **Dep 368** in the Reference field, indicating the number of the deposit slip used by store 2.
4. In the Reverse field, press ↵ to accept No because you do not want to reverse these transactions.
5. Press ↵ to accept the system date as the date you want this transaction to be effective in the general ledger.
6. In the Account field, enter **11021**, the general ledger account for the Bank of America checking account. The account name from the general ledger account record appears.
7. Enter **Receipts Store 2** in the Description field to describe the transaction.

8. Press ↵ to move past the Debit field. Usually, in formal accounting practices, the debit entry is listed before the credit entry. Yet it is easier to enter the part of the transaction that you think of as coming first. In this case, we are taking money out of one account and putting it into another. The logical first step is to credit the cash account from which you are transferring the funds.
9. Enter **598.72** in the Credit field to reduce the amount of money reflected in the general ledger account for the Bank of America account.
10. In the Account field, enter **11023**, the number of the general ledger account in which the money is really deposited at National Bank. The account name appears, and the transaction description from the previous entry is duplicated.
11. Press ↵ to move the cursor to the Debit field and enter **598.72** to increase the balance in cash account 11023, which represents the money in the National Bank account.
12. When your transaction balances (debits equal credits), press F10 to record it.

The transaction is placed in the General Ledger journal to await posting to the general ledger.

ADJUSTING THE CASH ACCOUNT FOR A CREDIT CARD DISCOUNT

You must also make a direct entry into your general ledger to reduce the account in which you deposit your credit card income. You need to subtract the fee for the discount the bank charges on your credit card deposits. An example of this type of entry is illustrated in Figure 6.8.

Choose the General Ledger option from the Transactions menu to display the General Ledger Transaction Entry screen. Enter GJ in the Journal Code field and press ↵ to assign a transaction number in the Transaction field. Press ↵ through the Reference and Reverse fields. In the Account field, enter the number of the general

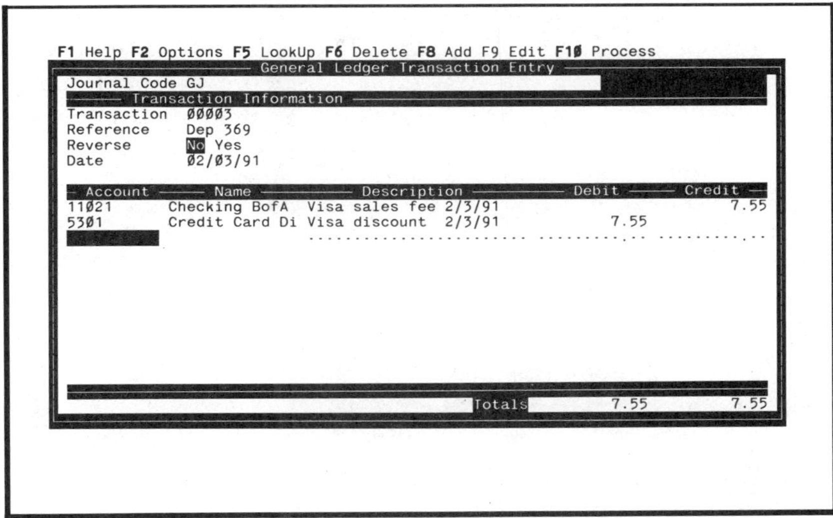

Figure 6.8: Entering a credit card discount fee

ledger account you use to track credit card deposits and the transaction description. In the Credit field, enter the discount fee. Then type the number of the general ledger account you use to track credit card discount expenses and enter the discount fee in the Debit field. Press F10 to process the entry.

ENTERING SALES OF FIXED ASSETS

The format for entering the sale of a fixed asset is basically the same as that for recording other sales. However, there are some other considerations.

To record a fixed asset sale, select the Billing option from the Transactions menu, and then choose Invoices from the Entry submenu. Enter the customer code and change the fields pertaining to the customer account as appropriate. To identify the item, use the code that you defined in your billing codes table for fixed assets. In the Item Number field, type C, press the spacebar, and enter the billing code for the fixed-asset account for the item. Type the description of the item sold over the one that appears from the billing codes table. DacEasy will post the transaction to the fixed-asset account in your general ledger. The rest of the sales-entry procedure is the same, except that you may need to make an adjustment to the general ledger if you did not break even on the sale of the asset.

Typically, when you buy an item you classify as a fixed asset, you will record the original value of the asset, and then enter depreciation as the book value of the asset declines. When you sell the asset, you must determine its current book value by subtracting the depreciation from the original value. If there is a difference between the current book value and what you sold the asset for, you must post a gain or loss to your general ledger.

As an example, suppose that you are replacing an old pickup truck with a brand new delivery truck. You have sold the old truck for cash to a teenager who answered the ad. Figure 6.9 shows the sales-entry data for this transaction.

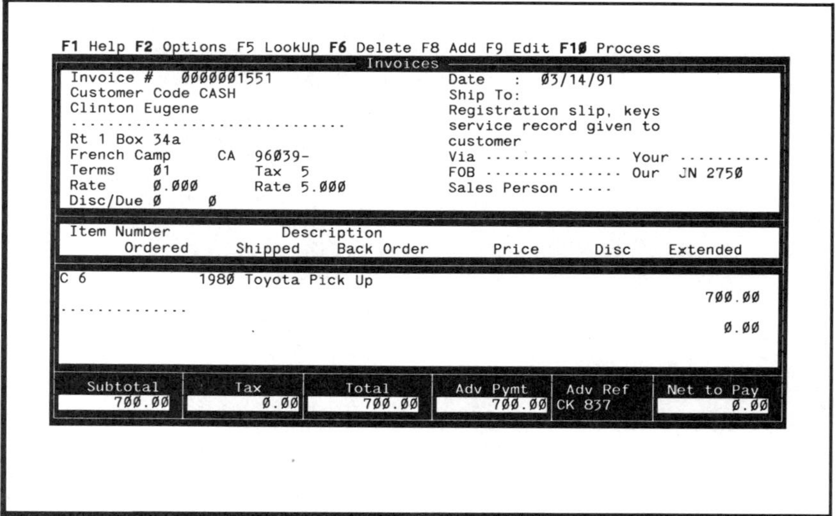

Figure 6.9: Selling a fixed asset

The following procedure is used to record the sale of the fixed asset in the example.

1. Press ↵ to assign a number to the invoice and enter **CASH** for the customer code. The cursor moves to the Terms field.
2. Move the cursor back to the field under Customer Code.

3. Enter **Clinton Eugene, Rt 1, Box 34A, French Camp, CA 96039** for the customer name and address.
4. Press ↵ to accept the default terms and tax rate from the customer record. In this case, the terms are no discount, due today, and the tax code represents the local rate.
5. In the Ship To field, enter **Registration slip, keys, service record given to customer**.
6. Press ↵ to pass through the next three fields: Via, FOB, and Your. None of these shipment or reference fields pertain to this cash sale.
7. In the Our field, enter **JN 2750**, the license plate of the truck.
8. Press ↵ through the Sales Person field.
9. In the Item Number field, type **C**, and press the spacebar.
10. Enter **6**, the billing code for the fixed-asset account for autos and trucks. In the billing codes table, this item does not have an amount defined; it is charged against account 12011 and is not taxable.
11. Type **1980 Toyota Pick Up** over the description that appears from the billing codes table.
12. In the Extended field, enter **700**, the amount you are charging for the truck. This entry reduces the total fixed assets on the books by posting a $700 credit to account 12011 as defined in the billing codes table. The offsetting debit will be automatically posted to Accounts Receivable.
13. Enter **700** in the Adv Pymt field. The customer paid for the truck in full. This amount will be credited to Accounts Receivable, balancing the entry for the item you sold and returning the total Accounts Receivable to what it was before you entered the transaction. The automatic offsetting entry is a debit to Cash, increasing the money in the cash account defined in your general ledger interface table. The net to pay is zero.

When you sell a vehicle, you usually don't charge tax. The Department of Motor Vehicles takes care of collecting the sales tax on cars and trucks.

14. Press F10 to process the item. Then enter **CK 837** in the Adv Ref field as the number of the check the customer gave you.
15. Press F7 to record and print the sale.

The final step is to adjust your general ledger if you sold the asset for a gain or loss. When you sell the asset for a profit, you must remove the remaining amount of the original value, reverse the total depreciation, and post the gain. In the example, the truck was originally purchased for $1,500. It has depreciated $1,250, so its book value is $250. You sold it for $700, resulting in a profit of $450. The general ledger adjustment for this is shown in Figure 6.10.

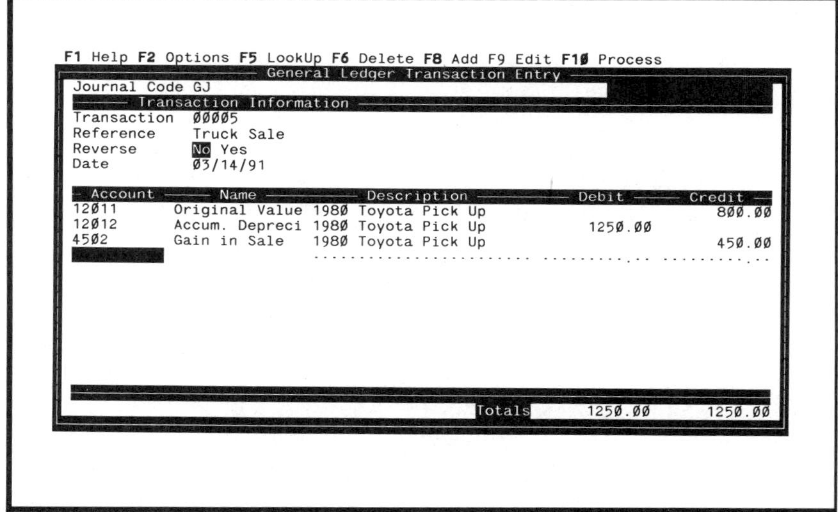

Figure 6.10: Recording a gain on the sale of a fixed asset

TRACKING BACK ORDERS

You must post the Billing invoices before backorder information is available.

When you record a sale and create an invoice, DacEasy determines how many ordered items cannot be shipped due to an on-hand stock shortage. It places this quantity in the Back Order field of the sales-entry screen as a notation of how much of the customer's order you cannot presently fill. Backorders are also included in the Committed Units field of the product record. You can print sales analysis and back-order status reports to keep track of back orders. When the

3.1 The program does not track customer back orders after noting them on the invoice. One method you can use to track them is to print a packing slip at the time you create the original invoice. Place the slip in a manually maintained back-orders file. Regularly check that file against the merchandise you receive. When the stock arrives, prepare a new invoice for the quantity you are now shipping.

product is again in stock, you can bill the customer for the back-ordered merchandise.

USING THE SALES ANALYSIS FILE

***** From the Transactions menu, select Billing; from the Entry submenu, select Sales Analysis.

DacEasy maintains a Sales Analysis file that allows you to track back orders and create sales analysis reports using the report generator. Although this information is useful, it can take up significant disk space. If you do not want to retain this file, select the Billing option from the Transactions menu, and then choose Sales Analysis from the Entry submenu. Select No, meaning you do not want the file created each time you post invoices in the Billing module.

You can keep the file and still conserve disk space by purging the invoices in it periodically. To do so, select the Billing option from the Transactions menu, and then choose Purge Sales Analysis from the Entry submenu. At the prompt

```
Purge all sales analysis records prior to: MMDDYY
```

enter the last date for which you want to retain sales analysis records and press F10.

PRINTING THE BACKORDER STATUS REPORT

***** From the Transactions menu, select Billing. From the submenu, select Print, and then select Backorder Status.

To remind yourself of items that customers ordered but you couldn't deliver, print the back-order status report. Select Billing from the Transactions menu, then Print, and then Backorder Status.

To print the report by product, enter P; to print the report by customer, enter C. Press F10 and select the report disposition.

GENERATING INVOICES FOR BACK ORDERS

***** From the Transactions menu, select Billing. From the Entry submenu, select Backorders.

When you receive backordered merchandise, you can then bill your customer. Do not enter another invoice. Instead, select the Billing option from the Transactions menu, and then choose Backorders from the Entry submenu. The program will generate invoices for back orders. Complete the information on the screen, as follows:

1. Enter the customer code, and the customer name displays for verification.

2. Press ↵ to accept the system date, or enter a different date for the invoice. All back-ordered items for the customer appear.
3. Move the cursor to the Quantity Shipped field for the product that is now in stock, and enter the number of items you are delivering to the customer.

Each line is processed immediately when you enter the quantity shipped.

4. Repeat step 3 for each back-ordered item.
5. Press F10 to exit the function.

You cannot print invoices for back orders during data entry. Instead, select Billing from the Transactions menu, then Print, and then Invoices. Any back order that still could not be filled will remain in the back-order file. The invoices generated from back orders are assigned the next available invoice number and become part of the Billing transaction file. The new invoice has BACK ORDER in the Your reference field and the year, month, and day in the Our reference field.

CORRECTING SALES ENTRIES

From the Transactions menu, select Billing. From the Entry submenu, select Invoices.

3.1 From the Transaction menu, select Billing. From the submenu, select Enter Invoices.

You can correct or delete an entire invoice after it has been processed and printed, but you must reverse the transaction if it has been posted, as explained later in the chapter. To recall the invoice, select Billing from the Transactions menu, and then choose Invoices from the Entry submenu. Follow the procedure described in Chapter 5 for correcting or deleting a transaction before it has been posted.

Note that when you complete the heading on a sales entry, the invoice number is used by the program. If you later delete the invoice, DacEasy keeps the number for auditing purposes. The number of the deleted invoice is included on listings with the notation VOID.

PROCESSING SALES RETURNS

It's a fact of life: customers return items you sold them for one reason or another. When you enter a sales return, DacEasy does four

* From the Transactions menu, select Billing. From the Entry submenu, select Sales Returns.

3.1 From the Transaction menu, select Billing. From the submenu, select Enter Sales Returns.

things for you:

- Credit the customer's account.
- Return the product to inventory.
- Subtract the amount from your total sales.
- Subtract the sales tax from your sales tax liability.

When a customer returns merchandise, select the Billing option from the Transactions menu, and then choose Sales Returns from the Entry submenu. You will see the Sales Return screen, as shown in Figure 6.11. Enter the quantity and dollar amount to create a credit memo against the original invoice, and DacEasy will do the rest. The fields on this screen are described in Table 6.2.

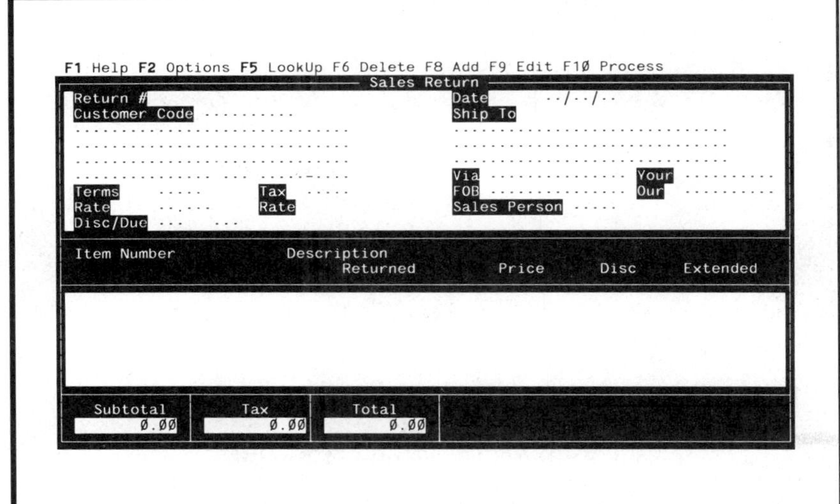

Figure 6.11: Sales Return screen

Table 6.2: Fields on the Sales Return Screen

Field	Description
Return #	The program assigns a number to the return. To edit an existing return, enter its number here.
Date	The program supplies the system date.

Table 6.2: Fields on the Sales Return Screen (continued)

Field	Description
Customer Code	The code of the customer returning the merchandise.
Customer Name	The program supplies the name in the customer record. Enter the name shown on the original invoice.
Contact	The program supplies the contact person in the customer record. Enter the name of the person presenting this return.
Address	The program supplies the address in the customer record. Enter the current address where the credit is to be sent.
Terms	The program supplies the terms code in the customer record.
Rate	The program supplies the discount rate from the terms table.
Disc/Due	The program supplies the terms from the terms table.
Tax/Rate	The program supplies the sales tax code from the customer record and the tax rate from the tax table.
Ship To	Any notation or instructions pertaining to this return, for example, wrong color or size.
Via	How the merchandise was returned. For example, OTC could mean the merchandise was returned over the counter, or perhaps it was shipped back via DHL.
Your	The customer's reference, for example, the original purchase order number or merchandise return number.
FOB	The name of the city where the freight charges originate. This is not usually applicable to sales returns.
Our	The exact number of the original invoice, including leading zeros.
Sales Person	The code of the salesperson to be charged with this sales return.
Item Number	The inventory number of the product being returned. You can also enter a billing code, free text, or a message code. Enter a *C* followed by a space and a billing code for a nonproduct or nonservice item, *D* followed by a space plus up to 40 characters of free text, or *M* followed by a space and a message code to print the associated message on the sales-return slip.
Description	The program supplies the item description from the product record.
Received	The quantity returned using the unit and fraction of measure.
Price	The program supplies the sale price in the product or service file. Enter the price charged on the original invoice.
Disc	The program supplies the discount percent given for this specific item on the original invoice.

Table 6.2: Fields on the Sales Return Screen (continued)

Field	Description
Extended	The program calculates the credit due for this item (received × price + calculated price discount amount).
Subtotal	The program calculates the subtotal after the completion of each item.
Tax	The program calculates the sales tax according to the tax percentage code after the completion of each item.
Total	The program calculates the total after the completion of each item (subtotal + tax).

Version 3.1: The Date, Ship To, Terms, and Disc/Due fields do not exist. Additional fields are Remark, for your notations; and Disc. Days, Disc. %, and Due Days, which are supplied from the customer record.

On the customer statement, a credit to an unpaid invoice appears below the invoice without an identifying number, and it reduces the balance due on the invoice. A credit for a paid invoice appears as an unapplied credit referencing the original invoice number.

As an example, suppose that a customer bought some chocolate truffles as a gift for her mother. When they opened the box, the candy was stale. The customer is returning the merchandise and does not want an exchange. The completed sales return for this transaction is shown in Figure 6.12.

Here is the procedure for recording the sample merchandise return:

1. In the Return # field, press ↵ to assign a new sales-return number.
2. Press ↵ to accept the system date or override the date and continue.
3. Enter **WING** for the customer code. The program displays the customer name in the customer record. If the name on the original invoice is different, verify that you have the correct account. If you do, change the name in this field to the one on the original invoice.
4. Press ↵ to accept the default contact and address from the customer record. If the person presenting this return is

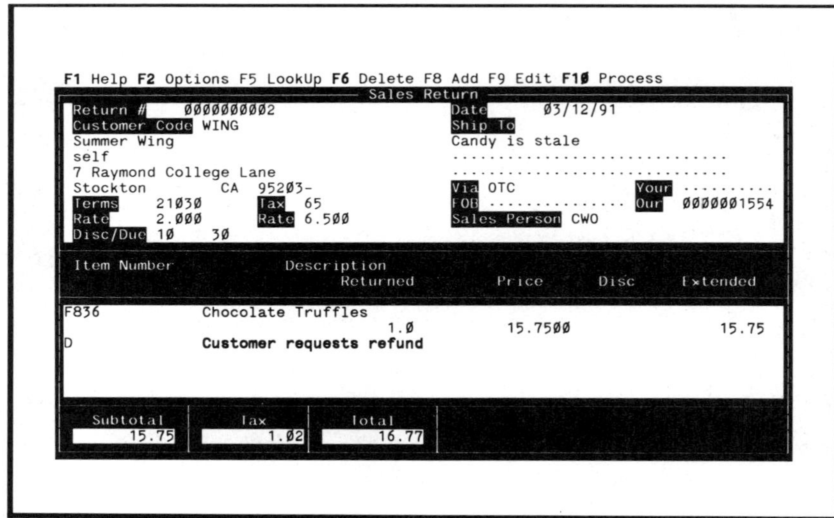

Figure 6.12: Completed sales return

different from the sale contact, or the credit is to be sent to another address, you could override the program-supplied information.

5. Press ↵ to accept the defaults in the next five fields pertaining to terms and tax rate.

Although the program calculates the discount available on a sales return and displays it on the Receipts screen, it really is not applicable to a sales return.

Sales returns that are applied against an invoice take on the due date of that invoice if the invoice has not been paid and cleared from the open-invoice file during period-end closing. Sales returns that are not applied to an open invoice are, like miscellaneous credits, always listed as current on the aging report.

The program supplies the tax code and the related sales tax rate from the customer record. Each item on this return that is defined as taxable in the product or service file is multiplied times this percent to determine the applicable sales tax credit.

3.1 The Ship To field is called Remark.

6. In the Ship To field, enter **Candy is stale** to explain the reason for the sales return.

7. To indicate how the merchandise was returned, enter **OTC** (as an abbreviation for over the counter) in the field labeled Via. In another situation, the merchandise might be returned via a freight carrier, such as P.I.E.
8. Press ↵ to move past the Your field. If this return were from a company rather than from an individual, you would enter the original purchase order number or merchandise return number.
9. Also press ↵ to move past the FOB field. If the merchandise were being returned from a large company across the country and you had agreed to pay freight from a particular city, you would enter the name of the city where your freight charges originate.
10. Enter **0000001554** in the Our field. This is the exact number of the original invoice, including the leading zeros. DacEasy uses this information to apply the credit to an existing invoice. Otherwise, you will have a credit on the customer account that you must later apply to the related invoice to clear both open items from the record.
11. Press ↵ to accept the salesperson in the customer record.
12. In the Item Number field, enter **F836**, the inventory number of the product being returned. The description appears.
13. Enter **1** in the Returned field to indicate the quantity returned. In the example, the customer returned a full unit. You should enter the fraction of measure if the return is only part of a unit. The quantity will be subtracted from the committed field in the product record as soon as the return is processed. When the return is posted, the committed quantity is reversed and the quantity is added to units on hand.

In this case, the candy won't be returned to stock, but the company's inventory will look like it was. This is one reason why the actual versus book inventory can show a variance when you take a physical inventory. Print and keep a copy of the return in a special inventory adjustments file to help you reconcile your physical count with your ongoing bookkeeping total.

14. The program displays the sale price from the product or service file. In the example, the price of truffles has gone up since the customer purchased her box. You don't want to credit her more than she paid, so override the current price and enter the price from the original invoice, **15.75**.
15. There was no price discount given on the original invoice, so press ↵ to move past the Disc field. The program calculates

the credit due for this item and places it in the Extended field (received × price + calculated price discount amount).

16. When the cursor returns to the Item Number field, enter **D** to add free text to the body of the return slip. Then enter the note **Customer requests refund**. This instructs the office staff how to handle the credit—whether to issue a check or leave the credit on the customer's account to be applied to a future purchase. You could also print a message from the messages table by entering M and the number of the message. However, you should be aware that this information will appear on the customer's copy of the sales-return slip.
17. Press F10 to record the items.
18. The program calculates the subtotal, sales tax, and total (subtotal + tax) after the completion of each item. When you have completed the sales return, press F7 to record and print it. You can also press F10 to record and clear the screen for entering another sales return.

The program calculates the sales tax according to the tax percentage in the customer record. When the return is posted to the general ledger, this amount will be debited to the sales tax liability account, reducing what you owe the government taxing agency. Be sure that you are returning the same amount of tax you originally collected on the item. If you are not, there are two possibilities:

- The quantity received, the price, or the price discount entered on the sales return is wrong and should be corrected.
- The sales tax rate in the customer record has been changed since the purchase. You should use the previous tax rate for this transaction and enter the original tax amount in the Tax field.

3.1 Checks are written in the Accounts Payable module.

The total amount calculated by the program is credited to the customer account when you post sales returns, reducing what the customer owes you. If the customer already paid for the returned item, the account will have a credit balance. The credit can be applied against future purchases, or you can refund the customer's money. To refund money, you must write a check in the Cash module and create a miscellaneous debit in the Accounts Receivable module to offset the credit balance. These procedures are explained in Chapters 9 and 7, respectively.

A sales return will appear as an open item in the customer record or be applied to the related invoice immediately, but the customer balance won't be updated until the return is posted to Billing.

PRINTING INVOICES, PACKING SLIPS, AND SALES RETURNS

* From the Transactions menu, select Billing. From the submenu, select Print, and then select Invoices or Sales Returns.

3.1 From the Transaction menu, select Billing. From the submenu, select Print Invoices or Print Sales Returns.

You can print each invoice individually as you enter it (by pressing F7 from the Invoices screen), or you can print all the invoices for the day at one time. To print all the day's invoices, select the Billing option from the Transactions menu, choose Print, and then select Invoices. You will see the Print Invoices screen (see Figure 5.4). Chapter 5 describes how to print documents. We will review the procedure briefly here.

To print or reprint invoices, enter the number of the first one to print in the Print Number From field and the number of the last one to print in the To field. You can also press ↵ in the From and To fields, and DacEasy will enter the first and last invoice numbers in the sales-entry file, respectively.

DacEasy lets you reprint invoices you printed during invoice entry. If you print invoices for customers throughout the day, you could print duplicate copies at the end of the day for reference. Select Yes in the Reprint field after you specify the numbers of the invoices to reprint them.

From this screen, you can also choose to print packing slips, which exclude costs and totals. Customers can compare the packing slip with their orders. Packing slips should accompany the merchandise to the customer's shipping address, while invoices should always be sent to the billing address.

After you enter the range of the documents to print, select Printer as the report disposition. At the printer alignment prompt, you can press F3 to redefine the document format before printing.

The procedure for printing and reprinting sales returns and packing slips to accompany the merchandise to the warehouse (to help the staff return the item to inventory) is basically the same as that for printing invoices. Select the Billing option from the Transactions menu, then Print, and then Sales Returns. Complete the fields as described earlier in this section.

PRINTING THE SALES JOURNAL

* From the Journals menu, select Billing.

3.1 From the Journals menu, select Sales Journal.

After you have made all your sales and sales-return entries for the day, you should print a Sales journal as a permanent record of the day's transactions. You must print all invoices and sales-return slips before you can print the journal.

To print the summary of merchandise sold or returned, select the Billing option from the Journals menu. Press ↵ to print the report, and then select the report disposition, or press Esc to cancel the request. Press F10 to process the report.

There are two parts to the Sales journal: a detail of the invoices and sales returns you entered and a departmentalized summary of the products and services affected. Review the entries on the printout and make any corrections before posting the invoices and sales returns.

POSTING INVOICES AND SALES RETURNS

* From the Posting menu, select Billing.

After printing a journal of the day's transactions, you should post them to Billing. You cannot post before you print the invoices, sales returns, and Sales journal.

To post your billing transactions, select the Billing option from the Posting menu and respond to the prompts. For a full description of the posting procedure, refer to Chapter 5.

The entries in the Sales journal are posted to the appropriate customer and product files. The entries are also placed in the BI journal to be posted to the general ledger. DacEasy updates the statistical history in the product, service, customer, and general ledger files.

REVERSING A POSTED INVOICE

After an invoice is posted, you must make a reversing entry in order to void it. The best method for reversing a posted invoice is to create a credit memo by entering a sales return, as described earlier in the chapter. This ensures that the inventory and cost of goods sold figures are corrected.

CHAPTER 7

Processing Daily Accounts Receivable

3.1 The Cash module does not exist. Payments from customers and adjustments are recorded through the Accounts Receivable module.

YOU HANDLE MISCELLANEOUS TRANSACTIONS THAT do not involve products or services through DacEasy's Accounts Receivable module. You record customer payments on posted invoices, enter advance payments, and apply credits through the Cash module.

RECORDING MISCELLANEOUS TRANSACTIONS

* From the Transactions menu, select Receivables.

3.1 From the Transaction menu, select Accounts Receivable. From the submenu, select A/R Transaction Entry.

If your company is making full use of DacEasy, do not enter your invoices or sales returns directly into the Accounts Receivable module.

Because most invoices are created through the Billing module, you will enter very few invoice-related transactions directly into Accounts Receivable. Routine sales and returns should be entered through the Billing module, which creates printable invoices, adjusts inventory, and posts costs. The Accounts Receivable module does none of this. Its transaction-entry option is designed to be used primarily for miscellaneous entries, such as those discussed in this chapter.

If you create invoices by hand or on another system, you can enter the data from those invoices directly into the Accounts Receivable module. You can then record payments and print reports through DacEasy. However, a better method of recording invoices created elsewhere is to enter a summary of the transactions in the Billing module, which also updates your cost of sales and inventory.

To enter miscellaneous Accounts Receivable transactions, select the Receivables option from the Transactions menu. You will see the Accounts Receivable Transaction Entry screen, shown in Figure 7.1. The fields on this screen are described in Table 7.1.

Table 7.1: Fields on the Accounts Receivable Transaction Entry Screen

Field	Description
Transaction	The program assigns a transaction number. To edit an existing unposted transaction, enter its number here.
Customer Code	The customer code.
Customer Name	The program supplies the name from the customer record.
Type	Select Invoice, Debit, or Credit.

Table 7.1: Fields on the Accounts Receivable Transaction Entry Screen (continued)

Field	Description
Invoice	A new invoice number or the number of the original invoice the miscellaneous debit or credit relates to. This number appears on the aging report and the customer statement as the invoice number.
Reference	The origin of the transaction (the debit or credit memo number or number of a returned check). This appears under Reference # on the customer statement.
Date	The program supplies the system date. You can enter an override. This is the data entry date.
Original Date	The program supplies the system date. You can enter an override to use the date from the invoice. This date appears in the Accounts Receivable journal and on the customer statement and is used for aging the invoice.
Due Date	The program calculates the due date from the terms in the customer record. You can enter an override for this transaction. This date is used to determine if an item is listed as past due in the aging report (except for unapplied credit memos, which always appear as current). Applied credit memos take on the terms of the related invoice or debit memo. The due date also appears for each item on the customer statement.

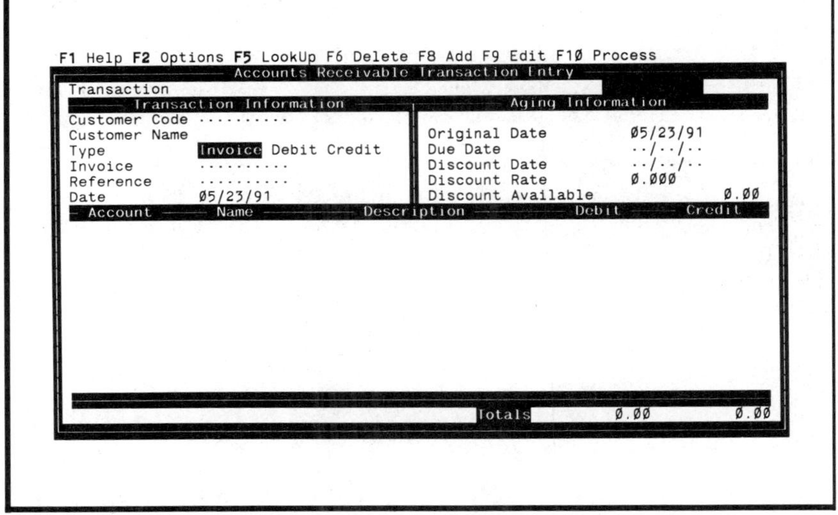

Figure 7.1: The Accounts Receivable Transaction Entry screen

Table 7.1: Fields on the Accounts Receivable Transaction Entry Screen (continued)

Field	Description
Discount Date	The program calculates the discount date from the terms code in the customer record. You can enter an override for this transaction. Although the program calculates a discount date for all entries, it is only applicable to invoices.
Discount Rate	The program calculates the discount amount on invoices only. It does not calculate discounts on debit or credit memos.
Discount Available	The program calculates the discount available from the terms code code in the customer record after the Accounts Receivable amount is entered.
Account	For the first entry, the program supplies the Accounts Receivable account number in your general ledger interface table.
Name	The program supplies the name for the account number entered.
Description	A description of the transaction. This prints with the transaction in the Accounts Receivable journal.
Debit	The amount of the debit side of the transaction.
Account	The account number of the offsetting general ledger account for the transaction.
Name	The program supplies the name for the account number entered.
Description	The program inserts the description you entered for the previous line. You can enter an override.
Credit	The amount of the credit to be charged to the general ledger account.

Version 3.1: The Type field is called Trans. Code. Enter I for invoice, D for miscellaneous debit, or C for miscellaneous credit. The Discount Rate field does not exist.

You cannot enter transactions for customers classified as cash in the customer record.

You cannot print copies of debit memos, invoices, or credit memos entered through the Accounts Receivable Transaction Entry screen. The debit or credit will appear on the customer's statement beneath the invoice you relate it to, and it will be applied against the balance due on that invoice. Your record of the transaction will appear in the Accounts Receivable journal.

ENTERING MISCELLANEOUS DEBITS

A miscellaneous debit is a charge against the customer's account that normally would not appear on a sales invoice. A miscellaneous debit increases both what a customer owes you and the total Accounts Receivable, an asset account in the general ledger. Offsetting entries are credits, typically to sales accounts. You enter a miscellaneous debit when refunding money to a customer for returned merchandise. It reflects the money you give back to the customer and offsets the credit resulting from the sales-return entry.

Another reason to enter a miscellaneous debit is to add charges to an invoice that has already been posted, rather than creating an entirely separate invoice for the additions. For example, suppose that a customer ordered a large shipment of ceramic vases yesterday, and you already posted the invoice. This morning, the customer called to tell you to have the carrier insure it against damage. Now you need to add a charge for the shipping insurance. The completed Accounts Receivable Transaction Entry screen for this miscellaneous debit is shown in Figure 7.2.

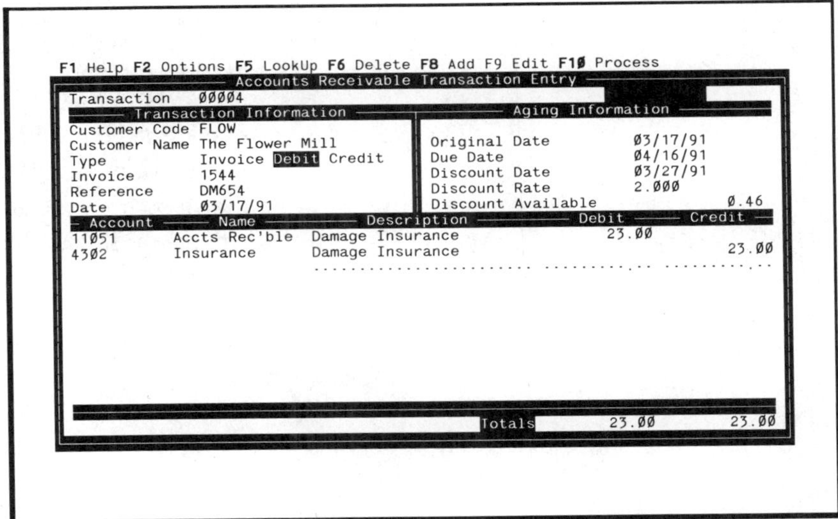

Figure 7.2: Entering a miscellaneous debit

The following procedure is used to enter the sample debit memo:

1. Press ↵ in the Transaction field to assign a transaction number and enter **FLOW** for the Customer Code. The customer name, The Flower Mill, appears. (Notice that the customer code is made up of the first letters of the name excluding the article *The*.)

3.1 Instead of selecting from the options displayed for the Type field, enter I for Invoice, D for Debit, or C for credit in the Trans. Code field.

2. In the Type field, select Debit to enter a miscellaneous debit.
3. Enter **1544** in the Invoice field. This is the number of the original invoice. If you do not enter the original invoice number, the debit memo will appear on the customer's statement and account as an unrelated open item. (Remember, for an open-item customer account, each debit transaction—invoice or debit memo—must have a payment or credit applied to it reducing the amount due to zero before it can be removed during period-end processing.)
4. For Reference, enter **DM654**, the number of this debit memo. You should identify the reference with some short abbreviation to make it more understandable on the customer statement. Here the DM stands for debit memo.
5. The program supplies the system date in the Transaction Date field. Enter **031791** (remember to enter two digits each for the month, day, and year) to replace it with the date the memo was actually issued.

The program calculates the due date from the terms in the customer record and the transaction date. Because this debit is applied to an existing invoice, the debit memo takes on the due date of that invoice. However, the date you see on this screen appears on the customer statement for this item.

6. For consistency, override the date in the Due Date field by entering **041691**, the same due date as the original invoice.

The program calculates the discount date from the terms in the customer record. This is both confusing and redundant. In DacEasy, the debit memo takes on the discount date of the invoice to which it applies. Discounts are not calculated on unapplied debit memos. The program calculates the next field, Discount Available, only for invoice entries.

You cannot cancel an entry after the cursor has moved to the detail line portion of the screen. You must record the transaction, and then delete it.

7. For the first entry in the Account field, the program supplies the Accounts Receivable account number in your general ledger interface table. The name Accts Rec'ble appears.

8. The cursor waits at the beginning of the Description field. Enter **Damage Insurance**. This will print in the Accounts Receivable journal to help you identify the transaction.
9. In the Debit field, enter **23** as the $23 premium for insurance on the shipment. The cursor moves to the next Account field so you can enter the account number for the offsetting account.
10. For the offsetting Account, enter **4302**, the number of the revenue account, Insurance, and its name will appear in the Name field.
11. The program inserts the description you entered for the previous line. Press ↵ to accept it.
12. In the Credit field, press F7 to insert the same amount you entered in the Debit field. Press ↵, and then press F10 to process the transaction. If the debit is to be charged to several other accounts, you would have to enter the amount for this specific account. Then you would continue, entering other accounts and the amounts to be charged to them.

In Accounts Receivable transaction entries, you cannot use a billing code, as you can in the Billing module. You must enter the general ledger account number directly.

3.1 Use F9 to insert the same amount.

The 23.00 in the Credit field indicates the $23 revenue generated by charging the customer for insurance on the shipment. Of course, an expense for the same amount will be incurred when the freight carrier is paid for the coverage, but that is a separate transaction in Accounts Payable when the shipping company's invoice arrives.

ADJUSTING FOR A RETURNED CHECK When a customer's check is returned to you by a bank, you must adjust your records. To debit the customer and credit your cash account, enter the returned check as a miscellaneous debit through the Accounts Receivable Transaction Entry screen.

In the Account field, enter the offsetting general ledger account number representing the bank account that was charged for the check. When entering a returned check, you want to reduce the account for the bank account it was originally deposited to; if you do not, your general ledger balance and your bank account balance will not reconcile.

Figure 7.3 illustrates an example of the entries for a returned check. In the Invoice field, BAD CHK is entered instead of an invoice number because the transaction does not relate to a specific invoice. The debit memo will appear as an unpaid item on the customer statement with the reference CK, which will help identify the transaction. Don't be misled by the appearance of a discount date during data entry. Remember, debit memos are not discounted.

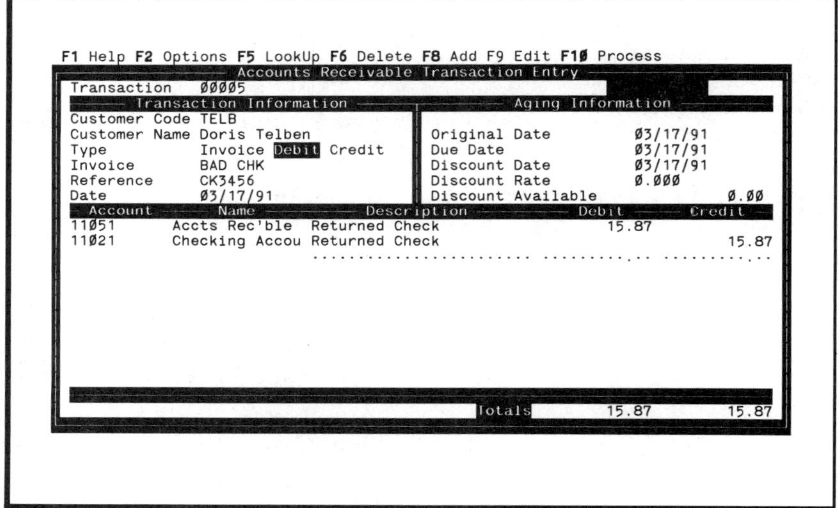

Figure 7.3: Adjusting your records for a returned check

ENTERING INVOICES CREATED ELSEWHERE

The optimum use of DacEasy is to enter your sales and sales returns through the Billing module. However, if you have elected to create your customer invoices elsewhere, you can enter the information directly into Accounts Receivable. This allows you to track your customer balances and update your general ledger with sales and accounts receivable data. Remember, DacEasy does not record the cost of the sale or the change in inventory, and you cannot print the invoices when you enter sales transactions through the Accounts Receivable module.

An example of an invoice entry in Accounts Receivable is shown in Figure 7.4. The following procedure is used to enter this sale:

1. In the Transaction field, press ↵ to assign a transaction number and enter **WADE** for the Customer Code. The name in the customer record appears. If a message is attached to the customer record, a window will open, displaying the message, the credit limit, and current balance.
2. In the Type field, select Invoice.
3. In the Invoice field, enter **A826**, the number of the original invoice. DacEasy does not automatically assign invoice numbers when you enter invoices through Accounts Receivable as it does when you create an invoice in the Billing module. The program assumes that you have a numbering method external to DacEasy and are entering invoices after the fact.
4. In the Reference field, enter **PO4937**, the customer's reference.
5. Press ↵ twice to accept the transaction date and the original date (the sale is being entered into DacEasy the same day that

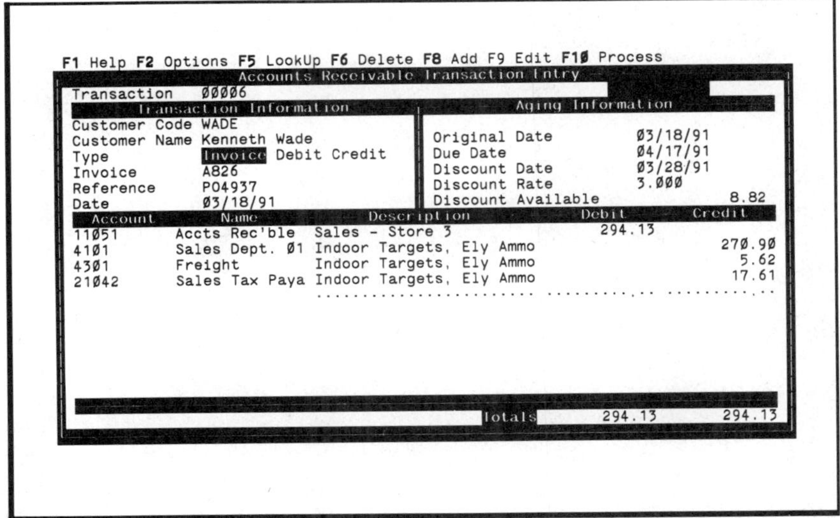

Figure 7.4: Entering invoices directly into Accounts Receivable

the invoice was issued elsewhere). The program calculates the due date from the terms in the customer record, based on the date in the Original Date field.

6. Press ↵ three times to accept the due date and the discount date calculated by the program and the discount rate from the customer record. If you did not use the terms in the customer record for this invoice, override the due date with the one you assigned on the original invoice so your aging report will agree with the terms noted on the customer's invoice. You can also override the discount date or rate if it differs from the one you assigned on the original invoice.

The program calculates the discount available from the terms and the debit amount you enter for the Accounts Receivable account. DacEasy assumes that you are discounting the total invoice, including any freight or sales tax you might charge the customer. You cannot override this field during invoice entry, but you can ignore it later when you enter the customer's payment.

7. The program supplies the Accounts Receivable account number and name in the first Account and Name fields. Enter **Sales-Store 3** in the Description field to identify the source of this transaction.
8. Enter **294.13** in the Debit field. This is the total amount of the invoice to be charged to the customer and to Accounts Receivable. The cursor moves back to the Account field. Typically, you will credit one or more sales accounts in turn. If you charged sales tax, you will also credit your sales tax liability account. If you charged the customer for shipping, you may credit a freight and shipping insurance account.
9. In the Account field, enter **4101**, the general ledger account number for Sales Department 01, where you track the revenue from product sales.
10. Enter **Indoor Targets,Eley Ammo** to override the default description. This is a general description of the sharpshooting products sold.

11. In the Credit field, enter **270.90**, the total amount of the products sold.
12. In the Account field, enter **4301**, the account number for freight.
13. Press ↵ to accept the description and enter **5.62** in the Credit field. This is the revenue generated by charging freight on this invoice.
14. For Account, enter **21042**, the number of the Sales Tax Payable account, and press ↵ to accept the description.
15. In the Credit field, enter **17.61**, the amount you charged for sales tax on this invoice, and then press F10 to process the invoice. Sales tax is entered as a credit because it is a liability. You are only acting as a temporary custodian for the funds, collecting them for a government agency.

You cannot use billing codes, message codes, or type free text on an invoice entered through the Accounts Receivable module.

In this example, the customer is to be billed for the purchase. The payments on the posted invoice are entered through the Cash option, as described later in the chapter. If the customer paid at the time of purchase, you would credit the Accounts Receivable account and debit the Cash account.

ENTERING MISCELLANEOUS CREDITS

A miscellaneous credit is one that does not result from a sales return. Anything that decreases what is owed to you is a credit to your Accounts Receivable account in the general ledger. The offsetting entries are typically debits to sales accounts, which reduce the total revenue reported, or debits to expense accounts, which increase the total expenses.

For example, suppose that an existing customer referred a new customer to you, and you issue a $10 coupon to your old customer to thank her for the referral. The entries for this miscellaneous credit are illustrated in Figure 7.5.

The following procedure is used to enter the sample credit:

A miscellaneous credit in Accounts Receivable decreases what is owed to you. Offsetting entries are debits.

1. Press ↵ to assign a transaction number and enter **ELLI** for the Customer Code. The customer name from the customer record appears for verification.

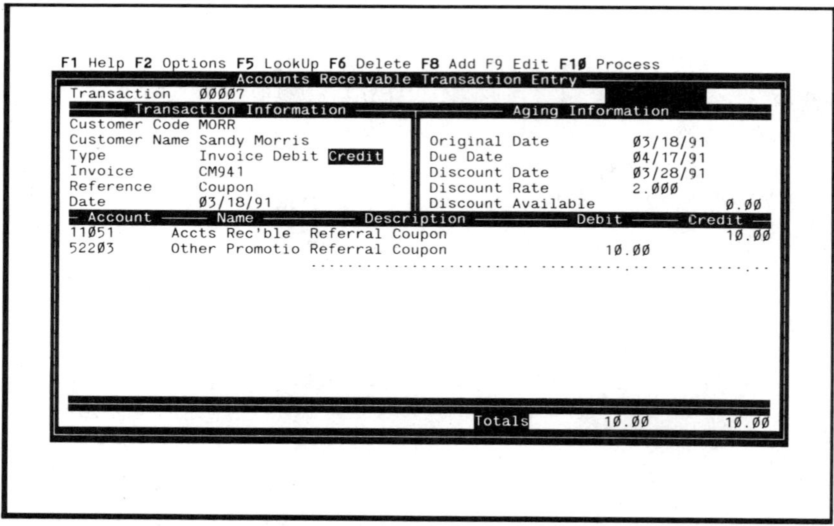

Figure 7.5: Entering a miscellaneous credit

2. Select Credit in the Type field.
3. For Invoice, enter **CM941**, the credit memo number. In the example, the credit does not apply to a specific invoice. The customer can use it at any time. It will appear on the customer's statement and account as a stand-alone open item. You should enter the invoice number here if the credit applies to an unpaid invoice.
4. The customer's reference goes in the Reference field. Enter **Coupon** to identify the origin of this transaction.
5. Press ↵ three times to accept the transaction, invoice, and the default due dates. (DacEasy will still treat the unapplied memo as current.)

Remember, on an open-item customer account, each credit transaction (cash receipt, credit memo, etc.) must be applied to a charge on the customer's account so that there is no amount available before it can be removed during period-end processing. You can recall the customer record later and apply the credit to future invoices.

Although the program supplies Discount Date and Discount Rate entries, they are irrelevant because it does not calculate a discount available on miscellaneous debit or credit entries.

6. In the Description field for the first account entry, type **Referral Coupon**. The cursor moves to the Credit field because you identified the transaction as a miscellaneous credit.

7. Enter **10** as the amount in the Credit field. This reduces both the customer balance and your Accounts Receivable by $10.
8. In the second Account field, enter **52203**, for Other Promotions (the expense account for coupon giveaways), and press ↵ to accept the default description.
9. Enter **10** in the Debit field to record the expense (or press F7 to have the program insert the same amount you entered in the Credit field), and then press F10 to process the transaction. If the credit is to be charged to several other accounts, you have to enter each amount individually.

The credit memo will appear immediately as an open item on the customer record, identified by the invoice number you entered for it on the Accounts Receivable Transaction Entry screen. However, the customer balance will not be updated until you post your transactions to Accounts Receivable.

Note that when you apply a credit memo to an existing invoice, DacEasy does not reduce the discount available on the invoice. It does, accurately, reduce the amount the customer owes you on that invoice. For example, if you have an invoice for $1,000 with an early payment discount of 5 percent, or $50.00, and you issue a $500 credit against that invoice, the discount available on the Receipts screen will remain at 50.00, even though it should be reduced to 25.00. Fortunately, the customer does not see this figure. The correct discount is calculated by subtracting the credit from the invoice, then multiplying the remainder by the discount percent.

WRITING OFF A BAD DEBT Like it or not, some accounts are uncollectable. When you finally give up and decide it is costing you more to try to collect than the account is worth, it's time to remove the balance from Accounts Receivable. This is also handled as a miscellaneous credit to Accounts Receivable. Figure 7.6 shows an example of the entries to write off a bad debt. This transaction closes a customer's account and transfers the balance to a bad debt expense account.

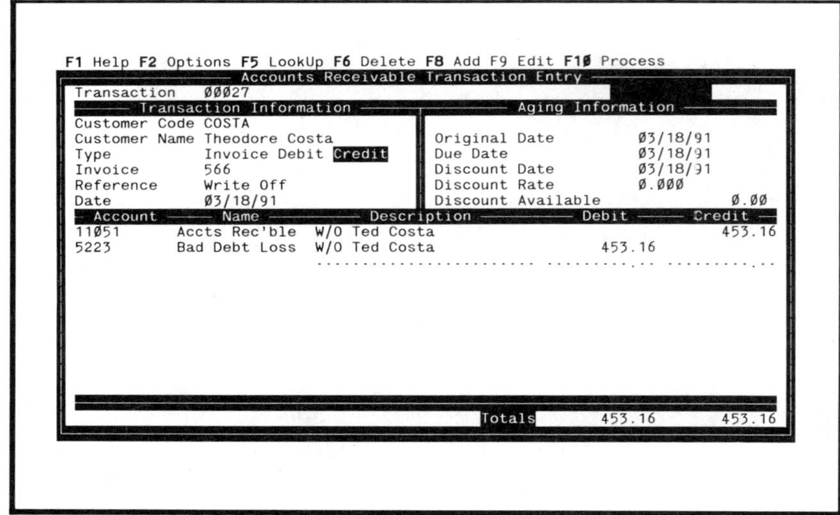

Figure 7.6: Writing off a bad debt

If several invoices make up the bad debt, you might enter the word *Balance*. Remember, you will have to apply this credit individually if more than one invoice is involved. Refer to the discussion of applying an unapplied credit, later in the chapter.

RECORDING CUSTOMER PAYMENTS

> * From the Transaction menu, select Cash. From the Entry submenu, select Receipts.

> 3.1 See the following section for a description of entering customer payments through the Accounts Receivable module.

Payments made at the time an invoice is created in the Billing module can be entered along with the invoice, as discussed in Chapter 6. When a customer makes a payment on a posted invoice, you enter it as a cash receipt in the Cash module. Payments on invoices created in the Accounts Receivable module are also recorded this way.

To enter a customer payment, select Cash from the Transactions menu, and then choose Receipts from the Entry submenu. You will see the Receipts screen, shown in Figure 7.7. The fields on this screen are described in Table 7.2.

Table 7.2: Fields on the Receipts screen

Field	Description
Transaction	The program assigns a transaction number. To edit an existing unposted transaction, enter its number here.
Date	The date of the transaction. This date is printed in the Cash journal and on the customer statement.
Bank	The program supplies the account number of the cash account in the general ledger interface table. This is the general ledger account that represents the bank account where the payment is deposited. You can enter an override.
Deposit	The number of the bank deposit slip for this cash receipt.
Paid From	The origin of the cash: Customer, GL (general ledger), or Vendor. Select GL for miscellaneous cash that does not affect a customer or vendor account.
Code	If payment is from a customer or vendor, the customer or vendor code.
Name	The program supplies the name and address from the customer or vendor record.
Reference	The number of the check, money order, or cash receipt related to this payment.
Amount	The amount of the payment.
Applied	The program calculates the applied amount as payments are applied to open items.
To Apply	The program calculates the remainder of the amount as you apply it to various open items.
Invoice	The program displays the identification number of each selected open item: invoices, debit memos, and credit memos.
Reference	The program displays the reference on the original item. You can override it.
Amount	The program displays the amount of the item that has not been paid.
Discount Available	The program displays the amount the customer can take for paying early according to the terms in the customer record or on the original invoice.
Applied	The amount of the payment you want to apply to each item.
Discount Taken	The discount amount the customer took when paying for an item.
New Balance	The program calculates the balance remaining on the invoice, debit or credit memo, or advance.

Version 3.1: The screen is called Cash Receipts and Adjustments, the Bank field is called Account #, and the Reference field is called Check #. The transaction date in the Date field appears in the Accounts Receivable Cash Receipts journal. The Paid From, Deposit, Reference (in transaction portion), and New Balance fields do not exist. An additional field is Transaction Type. Enter P for payment or A for adjustment. Also, in the transaction portion, the program displays the transaction date of the open item in the Date field and the date the item is to be paid in the Due field.

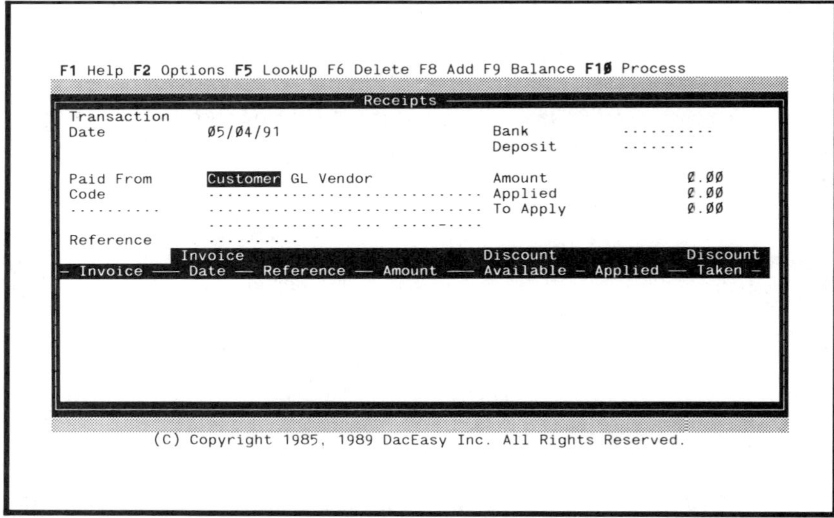

Figure 7.7: Receipts screen

Figure 7.8 shows a completed Receipts screen for a sample payment. The following procedure is used to enter the example:

1. Press ↵ to assign a transaction number.
2. The program inserts the system date in the Date field. Press ↵ to accept the date if the payment was received the same day it will be posted. You can override the date and enter the actual date of the payment. The date entered here appears in the Cash journal and on the customer statement. However, the date you use when posting to Cash is the date that will appear in the general ledger.
3. In the Bank field, the program supplies the account number in the general ledger interface table for your checking account. Press ↵ to accept the default account number. If this payment is to be deposited to another bank account, enter the corresponding general ledger account number.
4. Enter **03250002**, a user-defined number that identifies the deposit slip on which this payment will be recorded. In this example, 0325 is for March 25, and 0002 is for receipts from store 2 (you must use all eight characters).

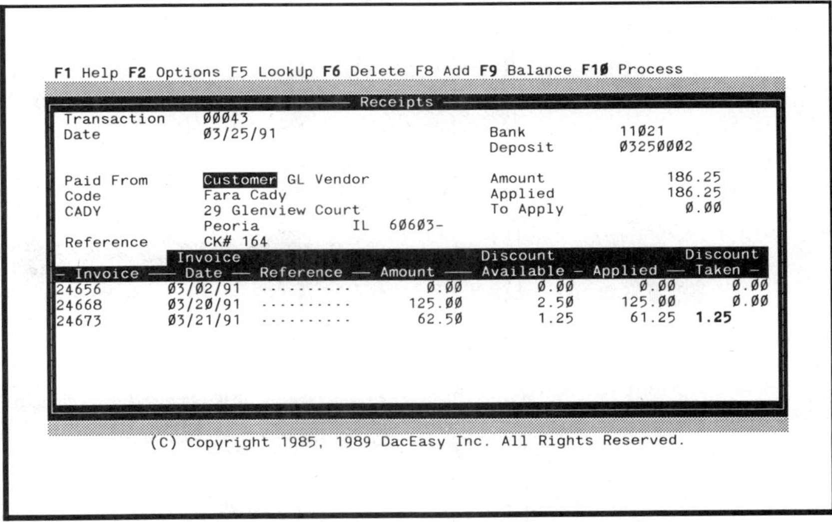

Figure 7.8: Entering payments against open invoices

5. Select Customer in the Paid From field.
6. Enter the customer code **CADY**. The program displays the name in the customer record. Verify that you are applying the payment to the correct account.
7. In the Amount field, enter **186.25**, the amount of the check.
8. Enter **CK# 164**, the number on the check received from the customer, in the Reference field. This reference will appear on reports to help identify the transaction. The open invoices appear in the line item detail window of the screen, as shown in Figure 7.9.

DacEasy defines open invoices as all invoices that have not been paid in full, as well as those that have been paid but not yet removed from the open-invoice file. Invoices, such as number 24656 in Figure 7.9, are left in the open file until period-end processing, when the program removes all items with no amount due.

In this list, the Invoice field shows the identifier from the open Accounts Receivables file, which can be the original invoice number, the information you entered in the Our field on the sales return, or the invoice number on a miscellaneous debit or credit memo. If you entered an invoice number in the Your field on a sales return, the sales return will not appear as an individual item here. Instead, the amount of the return will be deducted from the amount of the related invoice. The program-assigned number for a sales-return slip could also appear here if you left both the Our and Your fields blank when you entered the sales

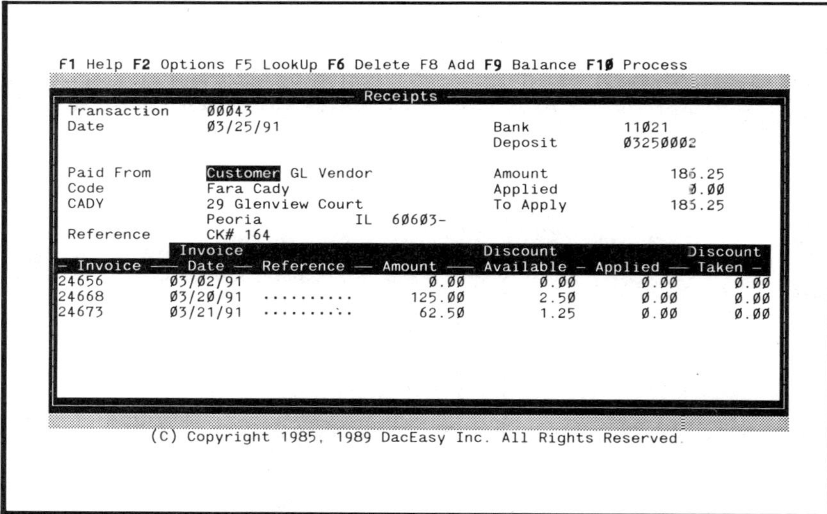

Figure 7.9: Open items in a customer record

return. Finance charges do not appear separately; they are added to the balance of the invoice to which they relate.

The Invoice Amount is the amount still unpaid on the invoice or unused on a credit. An unapplied credit memo, sales-return credit, or advance payment will appear with a minus sign preceding the amount, indicating a reduction in the customer balance. The Invoice Date is the date on the original transaction.

9. In the Applied field on the line for invoice 24668, enter **125**, the amount of the payment to be applied to this invoice.
10. Enter **0** (zero) in the Discount Taken field because the customer did not take the available discount.

The Discount Available is the discount for the total invoice. An amount appears here only if terms that allowed an early payment discount were entered on the original invoice *and* the system date is not beyond the number of days allowed for the discount in the invoice's terms.

One of DacEasy's quirks is to calculate the early payment discount on the *total* invoice. This means the discount has been applied not only to the items you sold, but to the sales tax as well. Most companies do not discount sales tax; therefore, the amount displayed in the Discount Available field may not be the discount you really want to give the customer.

Fortunately, the invoice your customer receives only notes the discount *percent* allowed, it does not print the discount *amount* to be taken for early payment. Be aware, also, that if a credit has been applied to the invoice, DacEasy does not reduce the discount amount accordingly.

If the customer took only a partial discount or none at all, an amount remains in the Discount Available field, as shown in the example in Figure 7.8. Don't worry. This will be cleared when the paid invoice is removed from the open-invoice file during period-end processing or when the current date exceeds the discount days allowed.

If the customer takes more than the allowed discount, you can enter the actual amount in the Discount Taken field. The Discount Available amount will be preceded by a minus sign. (This information is also removed with the item when you close the period.) If you don't want to give the extra discount, enter only what you allow in the Discount Taken field, leaving a balance due on the invoice.

11. In the Reference field for invoice 24673, press F7 to apply the amount remaining on the check (61.25) to this invoice.
12. In the Discount Taken field, press ↵ to accept **1.25**, the amount of the discount taken by the customer on the second invoice.
13. Press F10 to process the payment.

The payment will not appear in the customer record nor be included on the customer statement until you post the Cash module.

A failing of DacEasy is that it does not allow you to print a cash-receipt slip as proof of payment for a customer who pays cash in person. If the customer paid at the time the invoice was created, and you process sales through the Billing module, you can enter the payment and print a copy of the invoice, which includes the payment, for the customer. After the invoice is posted, however, you must enter payments through the Cash module, and DacEasy does not generate a copy of the receipt.

RECORDING CUSTOMER PAYMENTS IN VERSION 3.1

3.1 From the Transaction menu, select Accounts Receivable. From the submenu, select A/R Cash Receipts.

In version 3.1, you enter payments made by a customer on a posted invoice through the A/R Cash Receipts option in the Accounts Receivable module. When you select this option, the Cash Receipts and

Adjustments screen appears (see Table 7.2 for a description of the fields).

In the Transaction # field of the Cash Receipts and Adjustments screen, press ↵ to assign a transaction number. Enter the customer code, and DacEasy will display information about all the open invoices on the account. If an invoice has been paid in full, but the available discount was not taken, that information will appear. This information is removed with the item when you close the period.

For Transac. Type, enter P for payment. In the Account # field, accept the default, or if this payment is to be deposited to another bank account, enter the corresponding general ledger account number. Press ↵ to accept the system date in the Date field or enter an override. Enter the number on the check received from the customer in the Check # field. If the customer paid cash, you might enter the word *Cash*. In the Amount field, enter the amount of the check.

In the Amt. Applied field, enter the amount of the payment to be applied to the invoice on that line. In the Disc. taken field, enter the amount of the discount actually taken by the customer. If the customer takes more or less than the allowed discount, DacEasy lets you enter the actual amount. Press F10 to process the payment.

ENTERING AN ADVANCE PAYMENT

There are at least two reasons for entering an advance payment on a customer's account: if a customer places a special order and makes a down payment on that order, or in the unlikely event a customer sends a check for more than is owed on the account.

If the customer is paying on a special order and you know how much the charges are going to be, you can create an invoice in the Billing module and enter the down payment along with the invoice. But if the customer places a special order and you do not know exactly what the amount will be, you enter the down payment as an advance payment through the Cash module.

To record an advance payment, select Cash from the Transactions menu, and then choose Receipts from the Entry submenu. Enter the customer code for the account and the payment information. If there are no open invoices on the customer's account, you are prompted

No invoices exist for this customer/vendor.
Do you want to create an advance?

Press ↵ to enter an advance payment.

If invoices exist, in the Reference field, press F3 to enter an advance payment. The program places the amount of the advance in the Applied field, as shown in Figure 7.10. If the customer makes an overpayment, apply payments to the appropriate invoices, then press F3 to enter the remaining amount of the check as an advance payment.

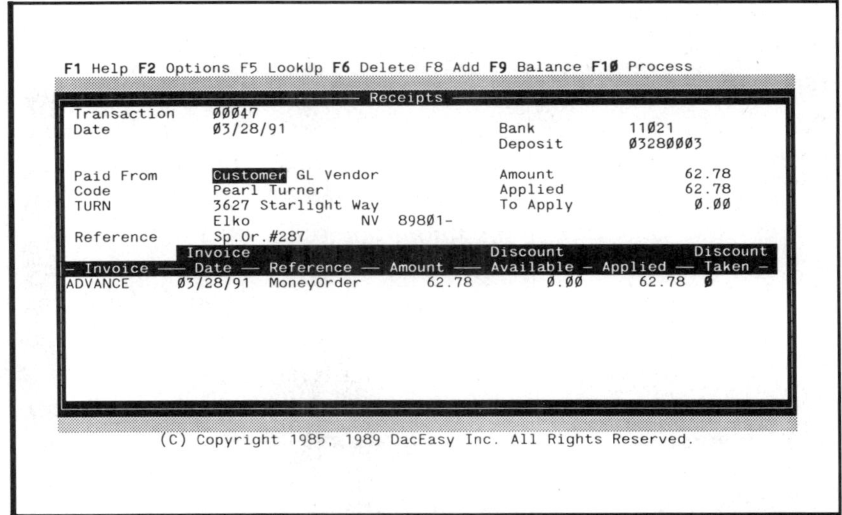

Figure 7.10: Entering advance payments

3.1 Payments do not appear on the customer statement until Accounts Receivable transactions are posted.

The advance will appear on the open invoice lookup screen if you recall the entry, but the payment will not appear in the customer record until the Cash transactions are posted.

ENTERING AN ADVANCE PAYMENT IN VERSION 3.1 With version 3.1, you enter advance payments through the Cash Receipts and Adjustments screen. To record an advance payment, select Accounts Receivable from the Transaction menu, and then select A/R Cash Receipts. Enter the customer code for the account and complete the fields on the screen, as described earlier.

When there are no invoices on the account, the program asks

```
No Open invoices exist, Do you want to create an advance N
```

Enter Y for yes to enter the amount as an advance on the account. The program enters the payment in the Amt. Applied field and identifies it with the invoice number *Advance*. If open invoices exist, press F2 to enter the check as an advance payment.

APPLYING AN ADVANCE PAYMENT OR AN UNAPPLIED CREDIT

* From the Transactions menu, select Cash. From the Entry submenu, select Customer Adjustment.

When you enter a sales return, it reduces the amount the customer owes you. However, if you did not enter the invoice number as the customer's reference, the sales return becomes an unapplied credit. It appears on the Accounts Receivable open invoice lookup screen as an amount preceded by a minus sign.

Sometimes you will issue a miscellaneous credit that is not related to a specific invoice through the Accounts Receivable Transaction Entry screen, as in the earlier example of a promotional coupon for a new customer referral. When an invoice is posted in the future, you can apply the open credit memo to it.

You cannot adjust items that have not been posted.

An advance payment and an unapplied credit result in the same circumstance: there is an open credit on the customer's account that must be applied to an invoice or debit memo. To apply either an advance payment or an unapplied credit, you record it as an adjustment. The cash account is not affected by this entry. You are merely transferring a previously received payment or a credit memo to an invoice; no money is coming in or going out.

To transfer amounts from one transaction to another, select Cash from the Transactions menu, then select Customer Adjustment from the submenu. Figure 7.11 shows a completed Customer Adjustments screen. The following steps are used to enter the example:

1. Enter **TURN** in the Code field.
2. In the Invoice field, press F5 to display the open items on the customer's account. Figure 7.12 shows an advance and an

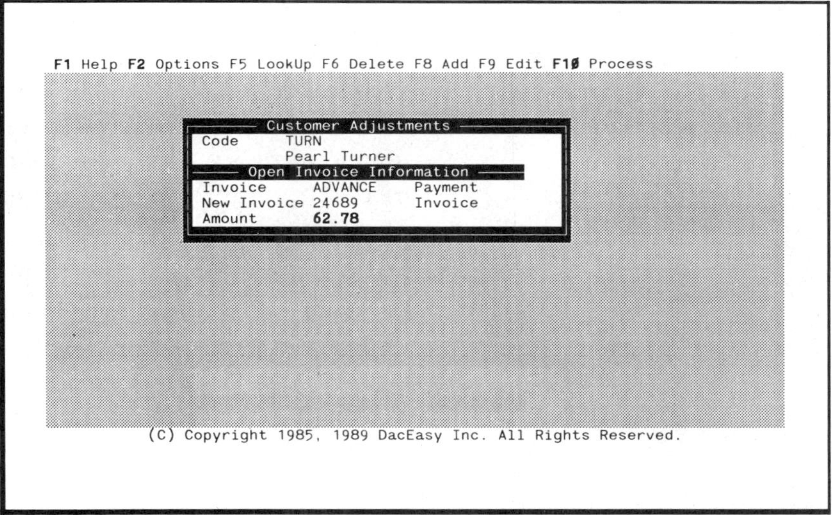

Figure 7.11: Applying an advance payment to an open invoice

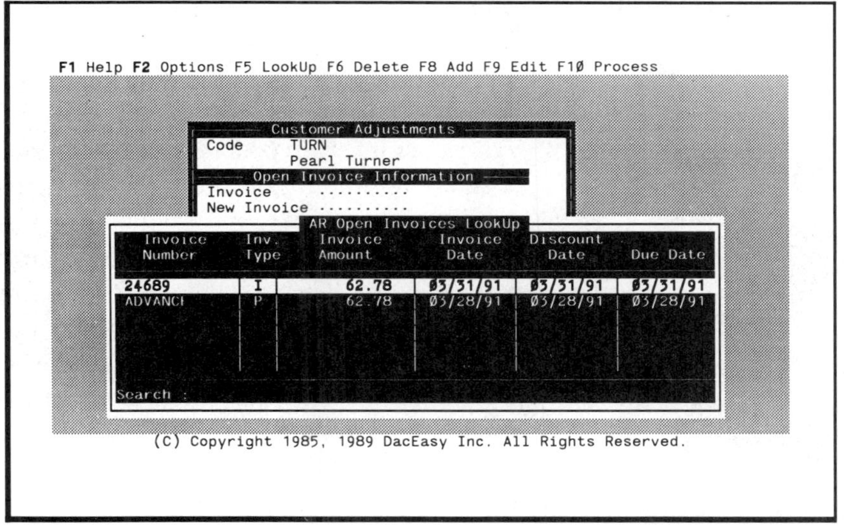

Figure 7.12: An advance payment and an unpaid invoice on a customer's account

unpaid invoice on the lookup screen. Instead of using the lookup screen, you could enter the identifier of the advance payment (or the number of the credit memo) you want to apply to an open invoice.

3. Highlight the advance or credit you want to apply and press ↵ to select it.
4. In the New Invoice field, enter **24689**, the number of the recent invoice to which you want to apply the advance payment (or credit). The full amount of the advance (or credit memo) from the Invoice field appears in the Amount field.
5. Press ↵ to apply the full amount of the advance to the invoice. If you want to use less than the full amount of the advance or credit memo, enter an override in the Amount field. If you want to pay several invoices, enter the amount to be applied to this invoice and save the transaction. Then repeat the steps, selecting another invoice as the New Invoice to which a portion of the advance is to be applied.

APPLYING ADVANCES OR CREDITS IN VERSION 3.1 To apply either an advance payment or an unapplied credit in version 3.1, you record it as an adjustment on the Cash Receipts and Adjustments screen. Press ↵ to assign a transaction number, and then enter the customer code. Enter A in the Transac. Type field to indicate this is an adjustment. Although the program supplies the cash account in the general ledger interface table, the cash account is not affected by this entry. You are merely transferring a previously received payment or a credit memo to an invoice.

Press ↵ twice to move past the Account # field and accept the system date. For Check #, enter the word *Adjust* to identify the transaction as an adjustment to a previous entry. The information you enter here appears in the Reference column of the customer statement. You could enter the number of the original check, but that might give the impression the check was posted to the account twice.

The Amount field is not applicable to this transaction, and the program skips it. The program also skips the Applied and To Apply fields.

The open items on the customer's account appear, showing the advance and the recent invoice. Move the cursor to the line for the advance or unapplied credit. Advance payments and credit memos are preceded by a minus sign, indicating that they are a deduction from the balance. Enter the amount of the advance you want to use, preceded by a minus sign. You do not have to use the full amount of the advance or credit memo for the transaction.

The Applied and the To Apply fields at the top of the screen reflect the amount now available. You cannot process the transaction until there is nothing left to apply from the credits you selected to use. Press ↵ to move past the Disc. taken field, and then use the arrow keys to move the cursor to the Amt. Applied field on the line containing the invoice to which the advance or credit should be applied. Enter the amount to apply to this invoice (as a positive figure) and press F10 to process the adjustment. You do not have to apply the advance solely to one invoice; you can apply it in part to several invoices.

VERIFYING CASH RECEIPTS AGAINST DEPOSIT SLIPS

* From the Journals menu, select Cash. From the submenu, select Receipts Report.

* From the Journals menu, select Cash. From the submenu, select Cash Journal.

3.1 The cash receipts report does not exist.

You must indicate a deposit-slip number for every cash receipt you enter through the Cash Receipts option. You might deposit cash and checks on one deposit slip and payments made by credit card on a separate slip. All receipts recorded with the same deposit number appear together in the cash receipts report. You can use this report in combination with the Billing journal to verify that every item on the deposit slips you make up for the bank is entered in your DacEasy records. Refer to the Recording Cash Sales section in Chapter 6.

To print the cash receipts report, select Cash from the Journals menu, and then select Receipts Report.

CORRECTING AND DELETING ACCOUNTS RECEIVABLE ENTRIES

3.1 You can correct and delete unposted adjustments as well.

3.1 The deleted transaction number will not appear on any listings.

You can correct or delete a miscellaneous transaction or cash receipt after it has been processed, even if the Accounts Receivable or Cash journal has printed. However, you must create adjusting entries after you have posted the original transaction, as explained at the end of the chapter. The procedure for correcting transaction entries is explained in Chapter 5.

If you delete an entire transaction or cash receipt, the program removes it and its related number from the file. The number appears on reports with the notation DELETED.

PRINTING THE ACCOUNTS RECEIVABLE JOURNALS

* From the Journals menu, select Receivables.

3.1 From the Journals menu, select A/R Transactions and A/R Cash Receipts.

3.1 Enter the numbers of the first and last transaction you want to include in the journal.

The miscellaneous transactions and invoices you enter directly into Accounts Receivable are contained in the Accounts Receivable journal. The customer payment and adjustment entries are kept in the Cash journal. You should print both of these journals, review the entries, make any corrections, and reprint them, before posting the transactions to Accounts Receivable or to Cash.

To print the Accounts Receivable journal, select the Receivables option from the Journals menu. To print the Cash journal, select Cash from the Journals menu, and then select Cash Journal from the submenu. Enter a date within the period you want to print. For a full description of the procedure for printing journals, refer to Chapter 5.

POSTING TO ACCOUNTS RECEIVABLE AND CASH

* From the Posting menu, select Receivables or Cash.

3.1 From the Posting menu, select Accounts Receivable.

Before you post, remember to print the Accounts Receivable and Cash journals. Otherwise, you will not have a record of the individual transactions you are about to post because the detail is removed once posting is complete.

The entries in the Accounts Receivable and Cash journals are posted to the appropriate customer records and placed in journals labeled AR and CH, respectively, to be posted to the general ledger.

To post your Accounts Receivable or Cash transactions, select the Receivables or Cash option from the Posting menu and respond to the prompts. Chapter 5 describes the procedure for posting.

When the transactions have been posted, DacEasy displays the total debits and total credits. You must still post the Accounts Receivable and Cash journals to the general ledger by selecting the General Ledger option from the Posting menu, as discussed in Chapter 13.

REVERSING A POSTED TRANSACTION

To reverse a posted transaction, you must enter another transaction that is the opposite of the original. In other words, if you entered

3.1 Instead of a screen display, DacEasy prints a report titled Posted to G/L. However, the heading is misleading. The transactions were posted to Accounts Receivable, not to the general ledger.

an invoice, you must enter a credit memo using the same accounts you entered on the invoice. You have to put the exact amount in the credit column where the original amount went in the debit column. If the original entry was in the credit column, you enter the amount in the debit column.

For example, suppose that the sample invoice shown in Figure 7.4 was entered with the wrong customer code and then posted. The credit memo entries to reverse the amounts posted are shown in Figure 7.13. After making the correction, you can reenter the invoice using the correct customer code.

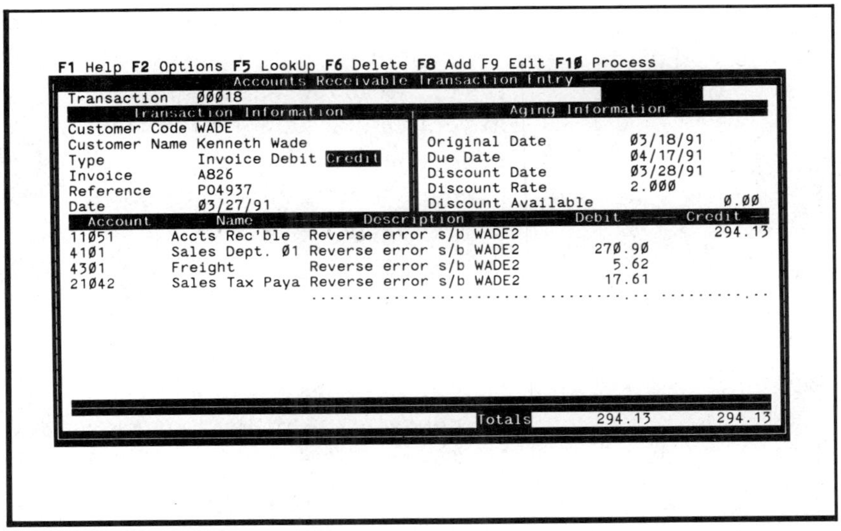

```
F1 Help F2 Options F5 LookUp F6 Delete F8 Add F9 Edit F10 Process
              Accounts Receivable Transaction Entry
Transaction    00018
      Transaction Information              Aging Information
Customer Code WADE
Customer Name Kenneth Wade            Original Date        03/18/91
Type          Invoice Debit Credit    Due Date             04/17/91
Invoice       A826                    Discount Date        03/28/91
Reference     P04937                  Discount Rate        2.000
Date          03/27/91                Discount Available                0.00
Account     Name            Description                Debit      Credit
11051       Accts Rec'ble   Reverse error s/b WADE2                294.13
4101        Sales Dept. 01  Reverse error s/b WADE2    270.90
4301        Freight         Reverse error s/b WADE2      5.62
21042       Sales Tax Paya  Reverse error s/b WADE2     17.61

                                           Totals      294.13      294.13
```

Figure 7.13: The credit memo to reverse a posted invoice

Be sure to reverse each individual line item, or the amounts in your general ledger accounts will be wrong. Use a copy of the Accounts Receivable journal and mark off each line item as you reverse it. Notice the document is dated as of the original invoice date, which differs from the transaction date.

If you post an invoice, and then enter a credit reversing the entries to each account, the amount due for the invoice becomes zero. The invoice and credit both appear on the Accounts Receivable Open Invoice Lookup screen with duplicate amounts. The original invoice and the credit appear as offsetting entries in the customer statement with no balance owing.

If you want to correct a posted credit memo, enter a miscellaneous debit reversing the entries to each account. The amount due on the credit memo appears on the Receipts screen as zero. Both the credit memo and the debit memo appear as offsetting entries on the customer statement, with no amount due.

REVERSING A POSTED CASH RECEIPT

In reality, you cannot reverse a posted cash receipt. You must create adjusting entries to offset the original posting. For example, suppose that when you are verifying your posted receipts against your bank slips, you discover that you entered a larger payment on the customer's account than was actually made. He paid $25; the clerk misread the figure as $35. You must reduce the amount posted to your cash account by $10 and correct the customer's balance. A miscellaneous debit handles both entries nicely. You would debit Accounts Receivable to increase the total owed to you by your customer, and you would credit your cash account to reduce the balance in the general ledger account. An example of this entry is shown in Figure 7.14.

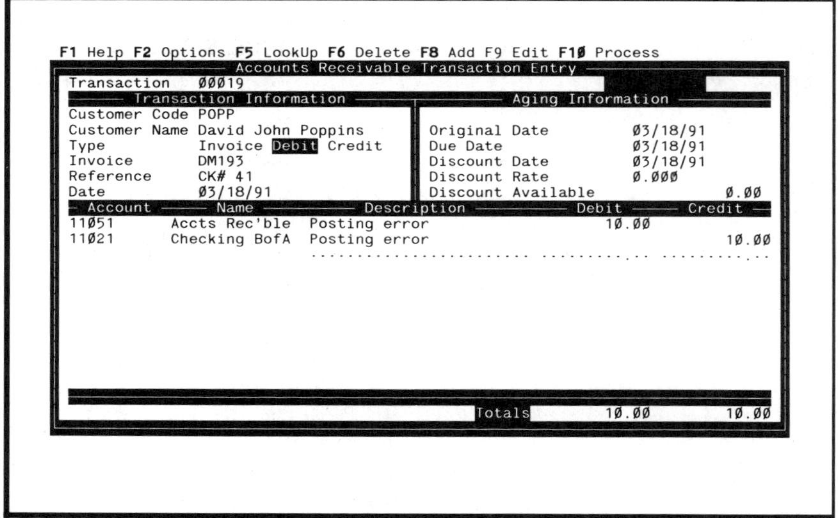

Figure 7.14: Correcting a posted receipt

To correct a payment posted to the wrong customer, you must enter a debit for one customer and a credit for the other through the Accounts Receivable Transaction Entry screen. This is accomplished in two separate transactions, as shown in Figure 7.15.

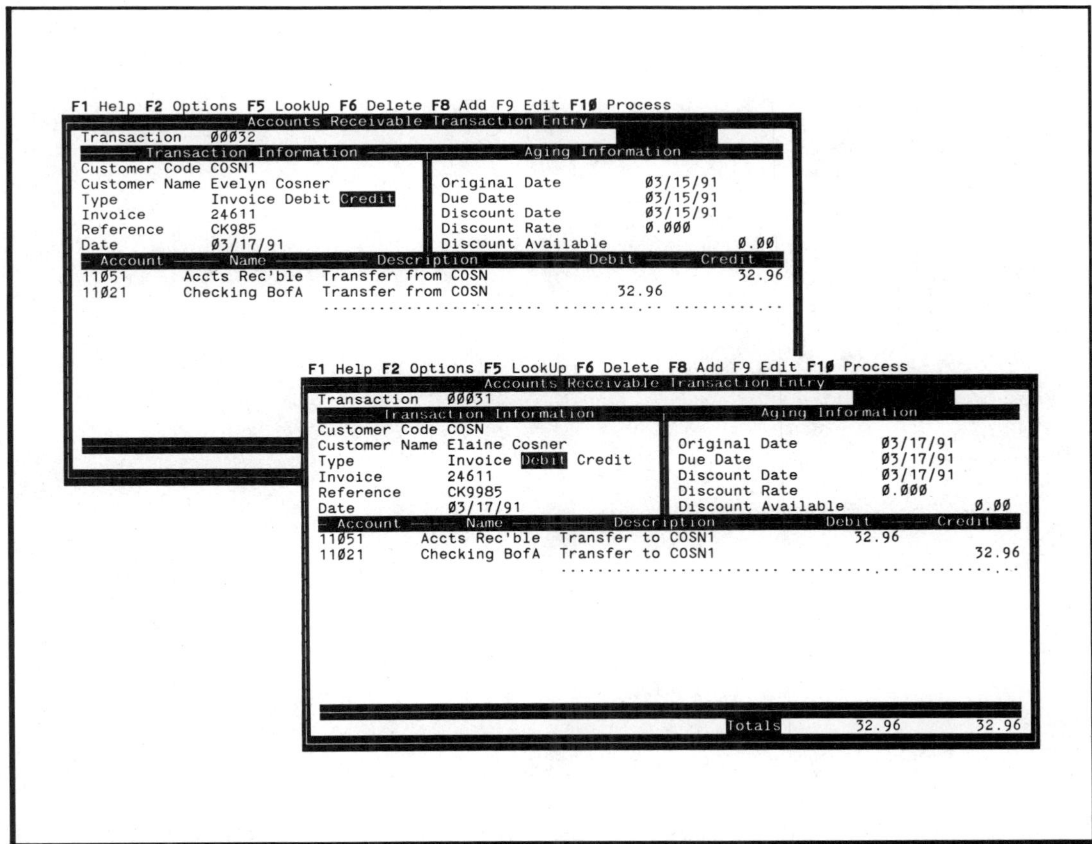

Figure 7.15: Transferring a payment from one customer to another

When you transfer a payment from one customer to another, your cash account is not actually affected. The money remains in the bank account, and the credit for that payment is transferred from one customer's account to another.

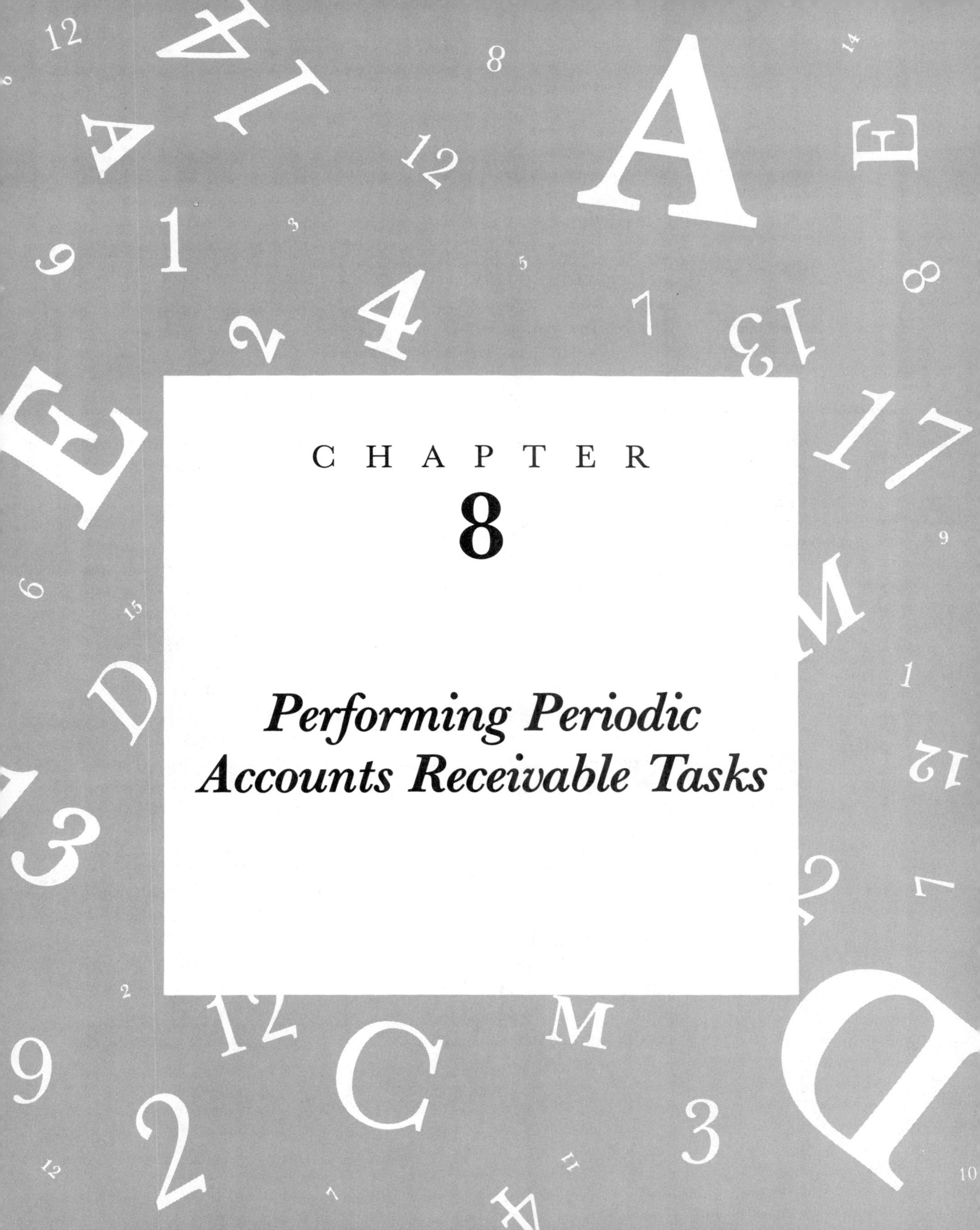

CHAPTER

8

Performing Periodic Accounts Receivable Tasks

PERIODIC ACCOUNTS RECEIVABLE TASKS INCLUDE monthly routines, such as assessing finance charges, printing statements, and closing periods; and other tasks that you will perform as necessary, such as printing aging reports, customer labels, and statistical reports. This chapter describes how to perform these functions. The Accounts Receivable forecasting and year-end functions are covered in Chapter 14.

GENERATING FINANCE CHARGES

* From the Periodic menu, select Receivables. From the submenu, select Generate Finance Charges.

3.1 From the Periodic menu, select Accounts Receivable. From the submenu, select Generate Fin. Chgs.

You can generate finance charges more than once in any period. Be careful because DacEasy will charge the customer each time without warning you.

You cannot select a range of eligible customers to be assessed late charges—it's everyone or no one.

Finance charges are amounts added to past-due customer accounts. DacEasy automatically calculates and posts these charges to each customer according to the interest rate in the customer's record. Before you have DacEasy generate finance charges, you should print the Accounts Receivable journals and post all billings and payments.

A separate finance charge is assessed for each past-due invoice and debit memo in the customer account. On the customer statement and aging report, these charges appear as a separate entry beneath the related item. They are accumulated into the balance for that item, which is then aged according to the item's original due date.

Finance charges are prorated on a daily basis for items 1 to 30 days past due. Items more than 30 days past due are assessed the full charge. For example, a customer who has a $100 item that is more than 30 days past due with a 5 percent late penalty would be charged $5. If the item were 15 days past due, the prorated finance charge would be $2.55.

To assess finance charges, select the Receivables option from the Periodic menu, and then choose Generate Finance Charges. The program displays the system date as the closing date. This date is used to calculate whether an item is past due; items that were due one day or more before this date are assessed a late charge. If you do not want to use the system date, press Esc to exit, then press F4. Change the date and reselect Generate Finance Changes. Enter a reference to accompany the summary posting to the General Ledger. Press F10 to generate the charges, and then select Printer as the report disposition. As the charges are posted to Accounts Receivable, the Accounts Receivable Finance Charges journal is printed, and the changes are placed in the AR journal to await posting to the general ledger.

PRINTING CUSTOMER STATEMENTS

* From the Reports menu, select Receivables. From the submenu, select Statements.

3.1 From the Reports menu, select Accounts Receivable. From the submenu, select Statements.

You might want to break your customer list down into four sections. You can print statements for one section of customers each week during the month. If you mail statements every week to one-fourth of your customers, you will generate a steady cash flow. Mailing statements at the same time to everyone results in hills and valleys of money coming into the company.

In addition to the individual invoices that you print through the Billing module, you can print customer statements, which show all outstanding transactions. On the statement, each invoice is listed by number with any related payments, finance charges, and debit and credit memos listed beneath it. Unapplied debit and credit memos are also listed individually by number with related transactions beneath them. The remaining balance on each item is noted. Any amount past due and the number of days it is delinquent appear in separate columns.

The program also prints messages on the statements depending on the age of the account. Refer to the discussion of statement messages in Chapter 1 for instructions on how to define messages for each aging period.

To print customer statements, select the Receivables option from the Reports menu, and then choose Statements. Load the preprinted forms or the plain computer paper in your printer. Next, choose the sorting and ranking criteria from those displayed in the Sort by and Rank by fields. Enter the first and last records for which you want to print statements in the From and To fields, or press ↵ to specify the first and last record in the file.

At the prompt

```
Include Customers with Zero Balance No Yes
```

select Yes if you want to print statements for customers whose accounts are paid in full. If you do, you could include a statement message to encourage them to do further business with you. Select No if you do not want to send statements to customers who do not owe you anything.

Figure 8.1 shows an example of an Accounts Receivable Statements screen for sorting statements by zip code. DacEasy will print statements for all zip codes in zip code order, but only for customers in the G through L section. In the example, ranking is used to restrict the range of statements that will print. Refer to Chapter 5 for more information about ranking and sorting reports.

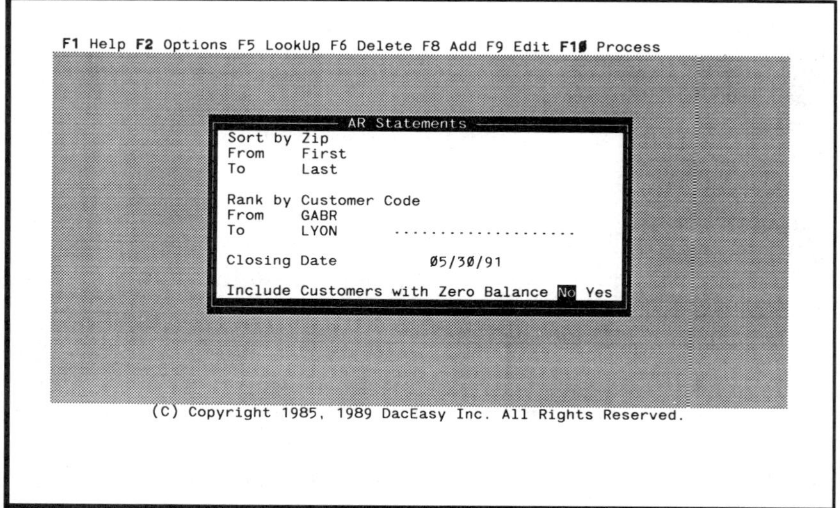

Figure 8.1: Defining criteria for printing statements

Next, press ↵ to accept the system date as the Closing Date, or enter a different date. Only transactions dated prior to and including the closing date will be printed on the statement and included in the balance, even if transactions have occurred since.

You cannot change the statement format at the alignment prompt. You must use the option on the Edit Defaults menu.

Press F10 to process the statements. Select Printer as the Report Disposition. Press ↵ when you are ready to test the alignment on preprinted forms, or press F7 to skip the test. The alignment test prints at the perforation line on the forms.

If there are more items than will fit on one form, the program rolls to the next form, prints another heading, and continues printing the items in the appropriate area. You can reprint the statements if the printer does not print them properly.

PERIOD-END PROCESSING

* From the Periodic menu, select Receivables. From the submenu, select Period End.

3.1 From the Periodic menu, select Accounts Receivable. From the submenu, select End Month.

You must end, or close, each period in Accounts Receivable. Figure 8.2 shows an example of an Accounts Receivable Open Invoice Lookup screen listing two invoices that have no balance due. These are being held in the open-item file until period-end.

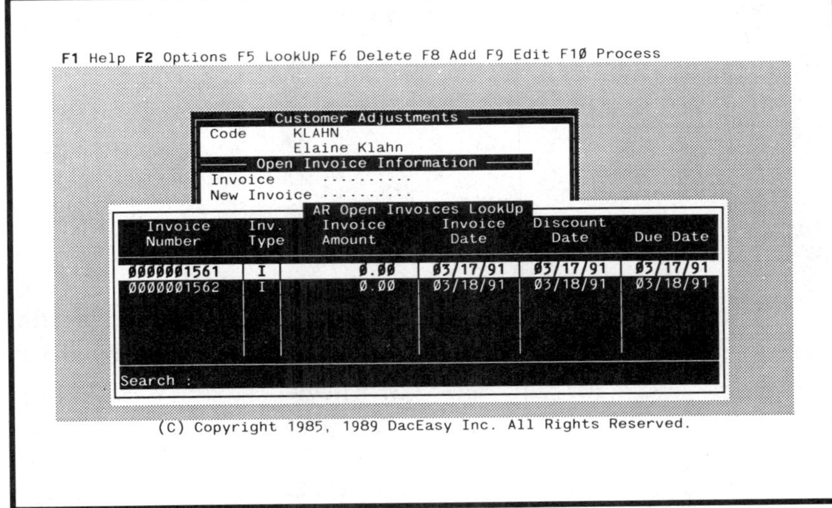

Figure 8.2: Cleared invoices before period-end

When you close the period, all transactions with no amount remaining will be removed from your open-item accounts, leaving only items that are not cleared in the file. For balance-forward accounts, all transactions will be totaled into the ending balance, and then removed from the open-receivables file. The detail of these transactions will be lost; that is why it is critical to maintain a printed record of all activity.

Before you close the period, remember to print your Accounts Receivable and Cash journals and post all your Accounts Receivable and Cash activity. You will also want to print the Accounts Receivable statistical year-to-date report if you are tracking monthly progress, as discussed later in the chapter. Also, you should always back up your files before closing a period, as described in Chapter 3.

To close the period in Accounts Receivable, select the Receivables option from the Periodic menu, and then choose Period End. Respond to the prompts displayed by the program. Chapter 5 describes the period-end routine in more detail.

PRINTING THE ACCOUNTS RECEIVABLE AGING REPORT

* From the Reports menu, select Receivables. From the submenu, select Aging.

3.1 From the Reports menu, select Accounts Receivable. From the submenu, select Aging.

You'll want to keep on top of past-due accounts. Studies and experience prove the longer an account sits on your books, the less chance you have of ever getting your money.

The Accounts Receivable aging report separates your customers' balances into the time periods you designate. This helps you determine which accounts are past due and the number of days they are delinquent. Typically, your aging periods parallel your billing periods. You can select to print just totals per period (a summary) or to print every transaction. The summary provides a shorter report, which management could review for the overall picture. The detailed listing is a comprehensive report, which the collection department can use when talking to customers with past-due accounts.

Before you print the aging report, close the period to remove transactions with no balance due from the detail. To print the report, select the Receivables option from the Reports menu, and then choose Aging. Select the sorting and ranking criteria from those displayed, and enter the From and To records.

The program displays the system date as the closing date. You can enter a different date. All activity prior to and including the closing date will be listed on the report. The program uses the closing date to determine the age of each item.

For the Report Type, select Detail if you want to print a detailed report, with every item listed individually in its appropriate aging category. Otherwise, select Summary, for a report that only lists totals for each aging period. Then press F10.

The next prompt asks

```
Do you want to edit the aging schedule?  No  Yes
```

If you respond Yes, you will see the screen shown in Figure 8.3. Note that this aging schedule is supplied only if you use the sample chart of accounts. If you do not use the sample accounts, you must define your own aging periods.

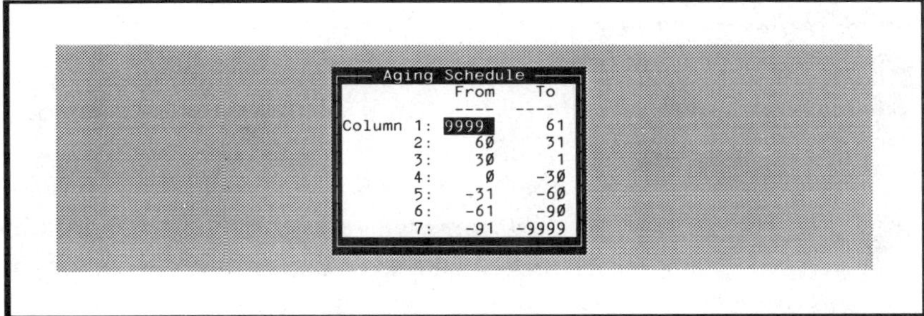

Figure 8.3: An Accounts Receivable aging schedule

The screen lists seven unique aging ranges in columns 1 through 7. DacEasy starts at the closing date and counts forward or backward to the due date on each open item to determine if it is current or past due. Positive figures in a column indicate a past-due time period. For example, 1 to 30 would include items that are from 1 to 30 days past due, and 61 to 90 would include items from 61 to 90 days past due. Figures preceded by a minus sign indicate a time period that is current or future. For example, 0 to −30 would include items that are current or not due for 30 days, and −31 to −60 would include items that are not due for 31 to 60 days.

The program calculates the beginning of each period depending on the ending date of the previous period and places the figure next to the column number in the From field. The To field contains the last day of the aging period. A minus sign preceding a figure indicates future days. For example, −30 means invoices will be due in one month from the closing date of the report.

To define or change the aging periods, enter the last day of each aging period in the To field for the appropriate column. You can change the periods in a column or press ↵ to accept them and move to the next column, but you must press ↵ at each column up to the last one.

When the aging periods are set, press F10 and select Printer as the Report Disposition. The program calculates and prints the aging report according to the criteria you entered. Advance payments and unapplied miscellaneous credits always appear on this report as current, regardless of when they were entered. Unapplied miscellaneous debits are aged by the due date entered when they were created, although the due date doesn't appear on the report.

PRINTING A CUSTOMER DIRECTORY

* From the Reports menu, select Receivables. From the submenu, select Statements.

3.1 From the Reports menu, select Accounts Receivable. From the submenu, select Directory.

3.1 The customer directory can help the data-entry clerk locate the customer code if you don't use DacEasy Graph+Mate.

The customer directory is a listing of your customers, including terms, credit limit, balance, salesperson, contact, address, and telephone number. Salespeople can use the directory to identify and call their customers. The credit department can use it to keep an eye on customers who exceed their credit limit. Management finds this document helpful in determining if customers are underusing or overusing their credit privileges.

To print the directory, select the Receivables option from the Reports menu, and then choose Directory from the submenu. Select the sorting and ranking criteria, press F10, and choose Printer as the Report Disposition. DacEasy will print the directory.

PRINTING CUSTOMER LABELS

* From the Reports menu, select Receivables. From the submenu, Labels.

3.1 From the Reports menu, select Accounts Receivable. From the submenu, select Labels.

DacEasy will print customer labels, which you can use for mailings. Each label includes the customer code, customer name, contact, address, city, state, zip code, and telephone number. You can eliminate the customer code and telephone number. The information fits on a 1-inch deep label, although you can print on larger labels.

To print labels, select the Receivables option from the Reports menu, and then choose Labels. Next, specify the sorting and ranking criteria. You might want to sort by zip code to divide your customer labels into groups for bulk mailing.

The prompt

```
Lines per label...6:
```

shows that, by default, DacEasy will print on 1-inch labels. Most printers print six lines per inch, which is the minimum number of lines DacEasy will assign for a label. Therefore, your labels must be at least 1-inch high. Press ↵ to accept six lines per label for 1-inch labels. If your labels are 2 inches high, you would enter 12 here.

At the prompt

```
Include Customer Code  No Yes
```

choose Yes if you want the customer code on the label; otherwise, select No. To print the telephone number, respond to the prompt

Include Phone Number No Yes

by selecting Yes. If you don't want the number on the label, select No.

Load the labels in your printer, press F10, and select Printer as the Report Disposition. Press ↵ to test the alignment, or press F7 to skip the test. The alignment test prints above the perforation.

PRINTING ACCOUNTS RECEIVABLE YEAR-TO-DATE STATISTICS

* From the Periodic menu, select Receivables. From the submenu, select Print Statistical YTD.

3.1 From the Periodic menu, select Accounts Receivable. From the submenu, select Forecasting, then select Print Statistical YTD.

3.1 The program will display a prompt asking if you want to include cost of merchandise sold and profit on sales per customer.

The Accounts Receivable statistical year-to-date report compares your actual activity throughout the year with the forecast for number of invoices, sales dollars, costs, and profit for each customer and calculates the variance. From this information, you can gauge if you are under or over your projections.

To print a statistical report, select the Receivables option from the Periodic menu, and then choose Print Statistical YTD. Next, select to sort by code, department, or salesperson. If you have not set up your revenue centers by customer, you can use the department field in the customer record to further categorize customers, and then sort the statistical report by that field. DacEasy prints totals of all the customers in the category you chose to sort by. For example, you might want a total for each salesperson so you can determine which ones should receive yearly bonuses.

In the From and To fields, enter the first and last record you want included in your report (or press ↵ to print from the first and last records in the file). Press F10 and select Printer as the Report Disposition.

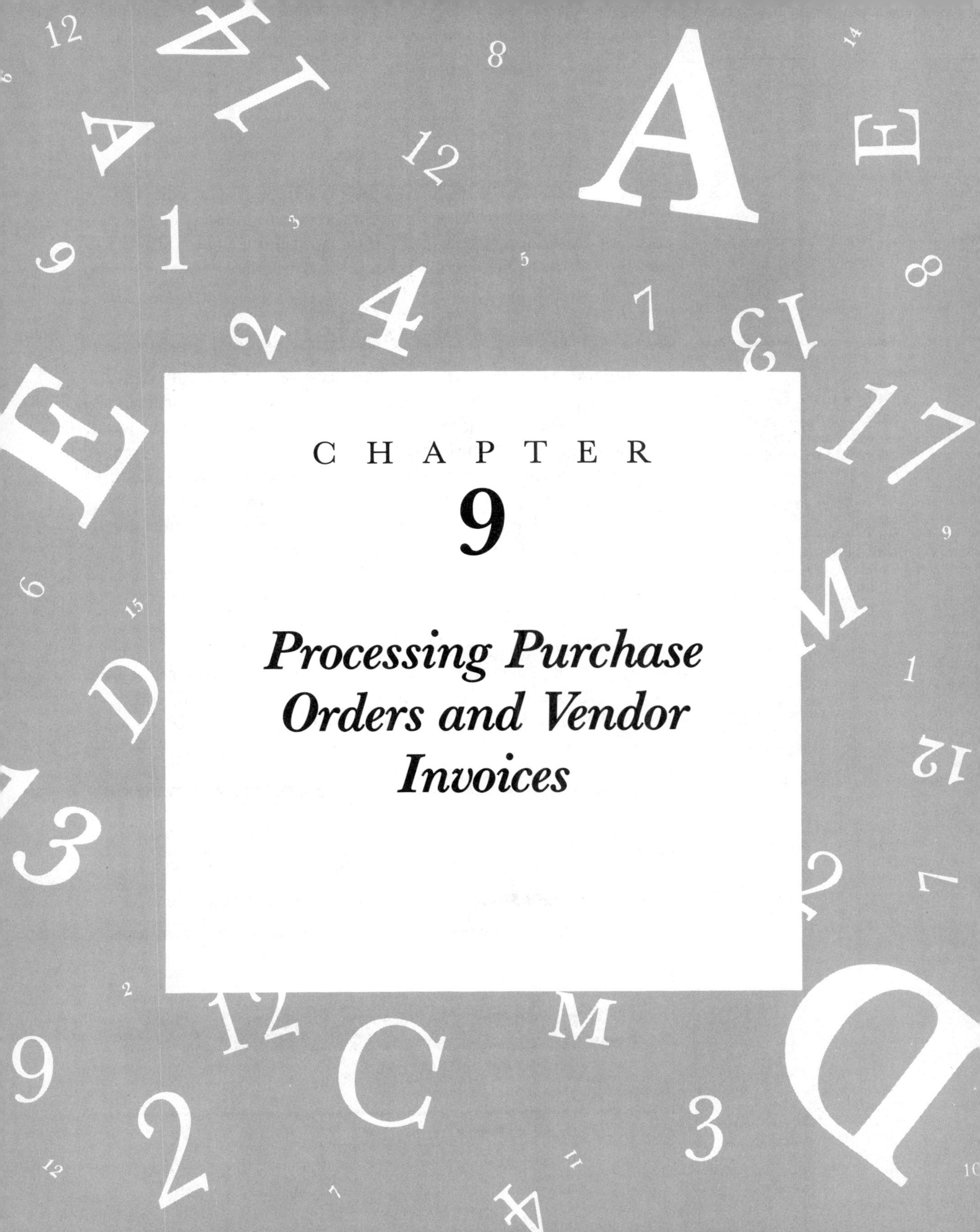

CHAPTER

9

Processing Purchase Orders and Vendor Invoices

PROCESSING PURCHASE ORDERS AND VENDOR invoices involves entering your orders, recording receipt of the merchandise or service, and entering purchase returns. DacEasy creates purchase orders and vendor invoices and updates the vendor and product records.

ENTERING PURCHASE ORDERS

* From the Transactions menu, select Purchasing. From the Entry submenu, select Purchase Orders.

3.1 From the Transaction menu, select Purchasing. From the submenu, select Enter Purchase Orders.

Purchase orders are a means of confirming an order placed with a vendor and controlling what is purchased. A purchase order helps you track when you ordered merchandise, the quantity you ordered, the quoted price, and the delivery method. You can print a purchase order status report, which lists all outstanding purchase orders, to help you follow up on deliveries that are behind schedule.

Keep in mind that entering a purchase order does not affect inventory or accounting; it simply updates the amount of units on order in the product record. Your Accounts Payable and product files are not updated until you enter the merchandise (or service) as received, as discussed later in the chapter.

To enter a purchase order, select the Purchasing option from the Transactions menu, and then choose Purchase Orders from the Entry submenu. You will see the Purchase Orders screen, shown in Figure 9.1. The fields in this screen are described in Table 9.1.

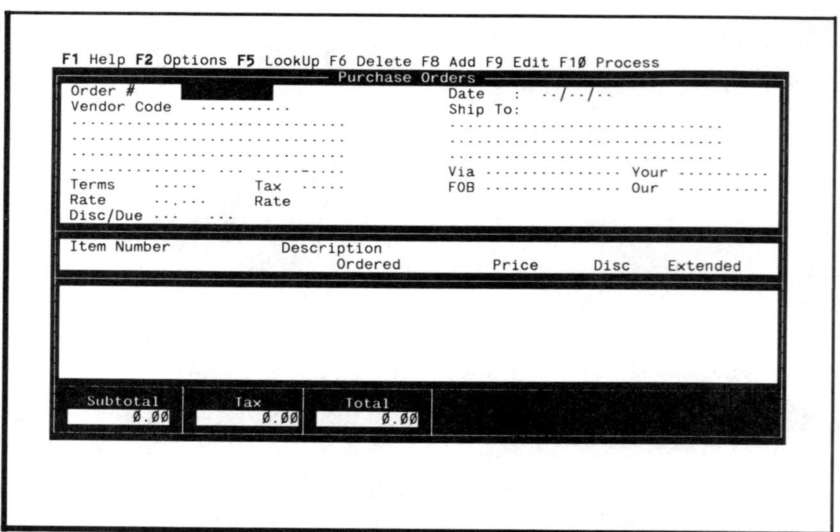

Figure 9.1: Purchase Orders screen

Table 9.1: Fields on the Purchase Orders Screen

Field	Description
Order #	The program assigns a number to the purchase order. To edit an existing purchase order, enter its number here.
Vendor Code	The code of the vendor you are placing an order with. After you enter the code, the program displays the name, contact person, and address from the vendor record. You can enter an override for any item for the current transaction.
Terms	The program supplies the terms code from the vendor record. You can enter an override for this order.
Rate	The program supplies the discount rate indicated by the terms code. This is the percent you can deduct from the total invoice when making an early payment. For example, 2.0 is 2 percent.
Disc Due	The program supplies the days allowed indicated by the terms code. The first figure is the maximum number of days after the invoice date that you can take a discount for early payment. The second figure is the number of days after the invoice date you must pay the invoice in full (or the day of the month the invoice is due, according to the definition of the terms code).
Tax/Rate	The program supplies the tax code from the vendor record and the related sales tax percent from the tax table. You can enter an override for this order.
Ship To	Any notation or instructions to the vendor pertaining to this purchase order. For example, *Deliveries accepted on weekdays only*.
Via	How the purchase is to be shipped, for example, UPS.
Your	The vendor's reference, possibly the initials of the person accepting the order. This appears on the purchase order after the heading Your #.
FOB	The name of the city where your freight charges originate (freight on board).
Our	You own reference, if any. This appears on the purchase order after the heading Our #.
Item Number	The inventory number of the product being ordered. Other entries possible in this field are *C* plus a purchase order code for a nonproduct or service item, *M* plus a message code from your messages table, and *D* plus up to 40 characters of free text.
Description	The program displays the description from the product record or purchase order codes table.
Ordered	The quantity you are ordering using the unit and fraction of purchase measure for that item. For example, one and one-half cases is 1.12, assuming 24 items in a case.
Price	The program supplies the sale price from the product file. You can enter an override for this order.
Disc	The percent by which the vendor has reduced the price normally charged for this item. For example, 15.50 is 15½ percent.

Table 9.1: Fields on the Purchase Orders Screen (continued)

Field	Description
Extended	The program calculates the amount due for this item (ordered × price − the calculated price discount).
Subtotal	The program calculates the subtotal of all items before sales tax.
Tax	The program calculates the sales tax according to the tax code entered above for each item that is defined as taxable.
Total	The program calculates the total amount of the order (subtotal + tax).

Version 3.1: The Terms field does not exist. The discount rate appears in the Disc. % field. Instead of a Ship To field, there is a Remark field for notations.

PURCHASING INVENTORY ITEMS

Before you start ordering products haphazardly, print a product alert report to determine which items are below minimum stocking levels. From the Reports menu, select the Inventory option. From the submenu, select Alert Report.

Products that you purchase and resell are defined in the product file as part of your inventory. Items you buy for use within your company are defined in the purchase order codes table. Purchase orders for fixed assets are described in the next section.

As an example, suppose that you are purchasing items for a pet store. The vendor gives you a volume discount on cat kibble, but you don't want to have so much on hand that it goes stale. You place an order taking advantage of the quantity discount, but include instructions to ship the order in fourths. The vendor charges you a packaging and handling charge for the special delivery method. The completed purchase order is shown in Figure 9.2.

The following procedure is used to enter the sample order:

1. Press ↵ in the Order # field to assign a purchase order number.

3.1 The Date field does not exist.

2. Press ↵ to accept the system date in the Date field or enter an override.
3. For Vendor Code, enter **FOUR**, the identification of the vendor you are ordering the merchandise from. If you enter the code of a vendor who has a message attached to the record, DacEasy displays a window with the message, as well as your credit limit, current balance, and credit available.

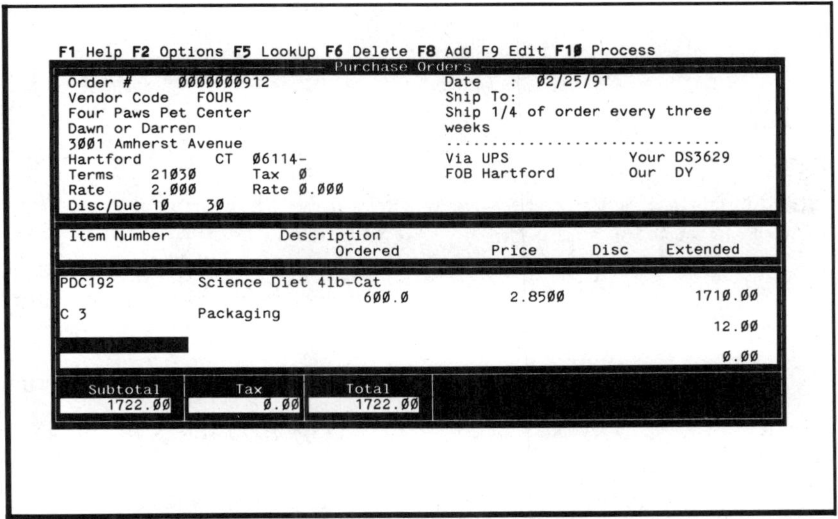

Figure 9.2: A completed purchase order for a resale item

As with customer accounts, seeing the current status of a vendor account is just a side benefit of having the message display. It's a good idea to create a credit-related message for vendors who impose a credit limit to ensure the message and limit display when you enter purchase orders. Be aware that DacEasy does not update the credit limit usage in the vendor record until the merchandise is received and posted to Accounts Payable. Therefore, you could exceed your limit when ordering without being aware of it if several orders are placed before any merchandise is received.

4. The vendor name, Four Paws Pet Center, as well as the contact and address, appear for verification. You can edit the information that will print on this purchase order without affecting the vendor record.

5. Press ↵ four times to accept the default Terms, Rate, and Disc/Due entries that appear from the vendor record. You can override the terms code for this order if the terms differ from those defined for the code in the vendor record.

6. Press ↵ again to accept the Tax field entry. In the Tax and Rate fields, the program inserts the tax code from the vendor

record and rate from the tax table. You can override the tax code, or change the actual sales tax after the program calculates it for this item. Typically, products bought for resale are not taxable when you purchase them.

3.1 You must type the shipping address or notations in the Remark field.

7. In the Ship To field, enter **Ship 1/4 of order every three weeks**. You can use this field for any remarks relating to the order or instructions to the vendor. The text will print on the purchase order. To insert your shipping address, press F5 and select it from the list of alternate addresses you defined for your company.
8. Enter **UPS** in the Via field to indicate the method of shipment.
9. The Your field refers to the vendor's reference on this purchase order. Enter **DS3629**, the initials of the person accepting your phone order followed by the confirmation number.
10. Enter **Hartford** for FOB, the city from which you pay shipping costs.
11. The Our field is used for your own internal reference. Enter **DY**, the initials of the employee who authorized the order.
12. Enter **PDC192** for the Item Number. This is the inventory number of the cat kibble you are ordering. The description appears from the product record.
13. Enter **600** in the Ordered field to indicate the number of bags you are ordering. The units on order field in the product record will be updated.
14. In the Price field, the program displays the price of the last shipment you received of this item (from the last purchase price in the product record). Press ↵ to accept it. You can enter an override that applies to this order only. It will not change the amount in the product record until you actually post the price when the merchandise is received.
15. Press ↵ to move past the Disc field. If the vendor gives you a price break for this item, you would enter the percent of discount allowed. The program calculates the Extended amount (quantity ordered × price – calculated price discount), and then moves to the next Item Number field.

16. For Item Number, type **C**, press the spacebar, and enter **3**, the purchase order code that represents packaging. The description from the purchase order codes table appears. Because the packaging charge fluctuates from order to order, there isn't an amount defined for it in the purchase order codes table. If there was an amount defined in the table, it would also appear.
17. Press ↵ to accept the description and enter **12** for $12 in the Extended field as the packaging charge on this invoice. Because the account numbers are defined in the purchase order codes table, the program knows which general ledger account to debit for this expense when you post.
18. The program calculates and displays the subtotal after each item. Press F10 to process the items.
19. The program calculates the sales tax on the items defined as taxable in the product record according to the sales tax defined for the tax code in the vendor record. Press ↵ to accept the entry in the Tax field. There is no tax on this order.
20. The program calculates the total (subtotal + sales tax). Press F10 to process the purchase order. If you wanted to print the order now, you would press F7 to process and print it.

The entry becomes an open purchase order, which will appear in the purchase order status report (the listing of open purchase orders). You do not post purchase orders because they do not affect your vendor balance or your accounts payable. When the merchandise is received or the service is rendered, you must enter a merchandise-received transaction to record the vendor invoice and clear the purchase order, as explained later in the chapter.

PURCHASING SERVICES AND FIXED ASSETS

Services and assets that you purchase from vendors are defined in the purchase order codes table. (In contrast, the services you sell are defined in the services file.) When you enter a purchase order to buy a service or asset, you must use the code in the purchase order codes table.

In the Item Number field of the Purchase Orders screen, enter C, followed by the code. The procedure is the same as the one used to enter the vendor's packaging charge in the previous example (steps 16 and 17 above). Figure 9.3 shows an example of the entries to purchase services. Figure 9.4 shows an example of a completed purchase order for a fixed asset.

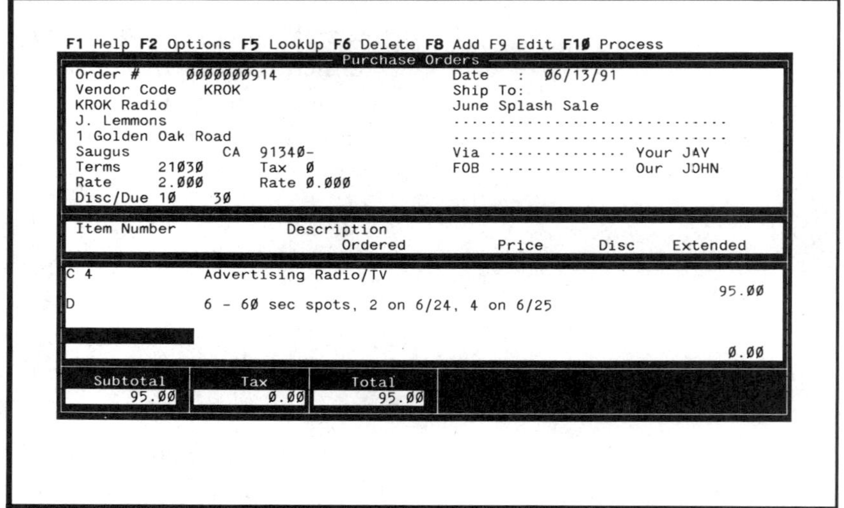

Figure 9.3: Completed purchase order for services

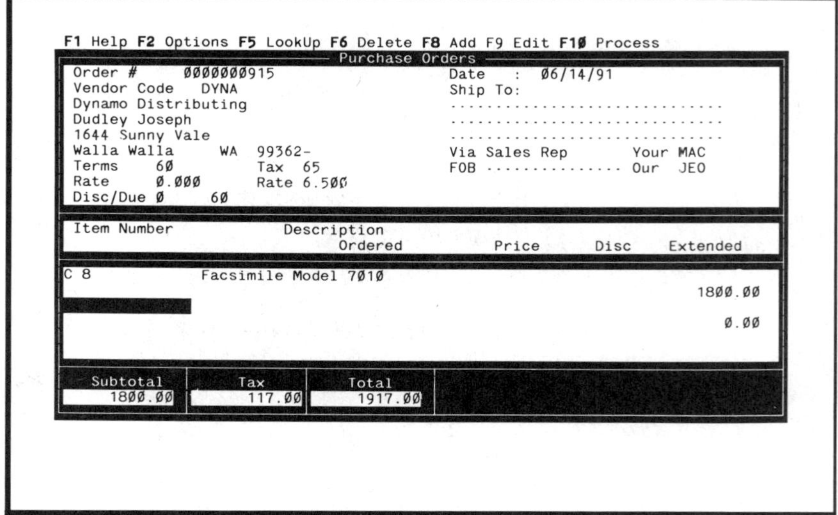

Figure 9.4: Completed purchase order for a fixed asset

It is best to enter each major item (service or fixed asset) that requires a purchase order code on a separate purchase order. This is because you must accept receipt of the entire order. You can't back order purchase order code items. For example, suppose that you are ordering a computer and a printer, both fixed assets, on the same purchase order. The printer comes in and you are invoiced, but the computer won't arrive for another month, so you don't have an invoice for it. Under these circumstances, you are between a rock and a hard place because you must enter receipt of both items or neither.

When you enter the asset as received, you actually incur the liability and increase your fixed-assets account. Don't forget to set up a depreciation schedule for this asset and to enter depreciation into the general ledger regularly.

CORRECTING OR DELETING PURCHASE ORDERS

Before you enter receipt of a product, service, or asset that you ordered, you can edit or delete the purchase order using the procedure described in Chapter 5. After anything has been received on a purchase order, you must make your changes through the Merchandise Received option, as explained later in the chapter.

When you delete a purchase order, the units on order field in the product record is decreased by the quantity on the deleted purchase order. The purchase order number is deleted from the system. It will not appear on reports, but you cannot reuse that number.

ENTERING SERVICES OR MERCHANDISE RECEIVED

* From the Transactions menu, select Purchasing. From the Entry submenu, select Merchandise Received.

When your orders arrive or the service is rendered, you record the transaction as merchandise received. This procedure creates an invoice that will appear on the vendor's record and become part of your accounts payable obligations. It also updates your inventory records and closes out the related purchase order. These last two

3.1 From the Transaction menu, select Purchasing. From the submenu, select Enter Merchandise Received.

operations do not occur when you record invoices for merchandise in the Accounts Payable module, as discussed in the next chapter.

To enter merchandise received or a service rendered, select the Purchasing option from the Transactions menu, and then choose Merchandise Received. You will see the Merchandise Received screen, shown in Figure 9.5. The fields on this screen are described in Table 9.2.

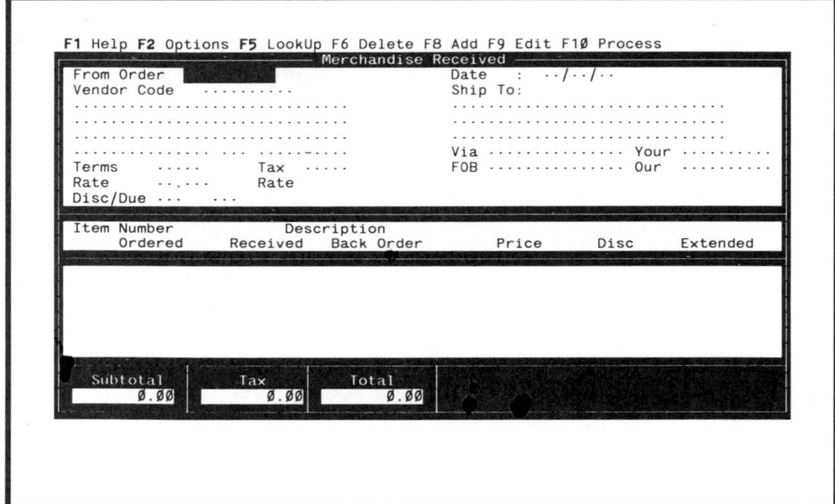

Figure 9.5: Merchandise Received screen

Table 9.2: Fields on the Merchandise Received Screen

Field	Description
From Order #	The purchase order number for the merchandise you received. If no purchase order was issued, press ↵ to assign a new receipt number. Purchase orders and merchandise-received slips use the same numbering series.
Vendor Code	The code of the vendor the order was placed with. The program supplies the vendor name and address from the purchase order or vendor record. You can enter an override for the current transaction.
Terms	The program supplies the terms code from the purchase order or vendor record.
Rate	The percentage you can deduct from the invoice for paying early.

Table 9.2: Fields on the Merchandise Received Screen (continued)

Field	Description
Disc Due/Days	The first figure is the maximum number of days in which you can take an early payment discount. The second figure is the number of days in which the invoice accompanying this merchandise must be paid (or the day of the month on which the invoice is due).
Tax/Rate	The program supplies the tax code from the vendor record and related sales tax percentage from the tax table. This is the percent that will be charged on every item defined as taxable in the product and purchase order code records.
Ship To	Use for comments regarding the order.
Via	The shipping company that delivered the merchandise.
Your	The number of the invoice that accompanies this merchandise.
FOB	The city where the shipping charges originate.
Our	Your reference for the order.
Item Number	The inventory number of the item you received. You can also enter *C* plus a purchase order code, *M* plus a message code, or *D* and free text.
Description	The program supplies the description of the item.
Ordered	The quantity on the original purchase order.
Received	The quantity actually received using the unit and fraction of purchase measure. If you are entering an invoice for an item identified by a purchase order code, this field is unavailable.
Back Order	The program calculates the number of ordered items that were not received (ordered minus received) if this is for merchandise. If it is for an item identified by a purchase order code, this field is unavailable.
Price	The price of the item as billed on the vendor invoice.
Disc	The price discount.
Extended	The program calculates the extended amount (quantity received × price – calculated price discount).
Subtotal	The program calculates the subtotal of the items before taxes.
Tax	The program calculates the sales tax on taxable items according to the tax code entered above. You can enter an override.
Total	The program calculates the amount due on the invoice (subtotal + sales tax).

Version 3.1: The Terms field does not exist. The discount rate appears in the Disc. % field. Instead of a Ship To field, there is a Remark field for notations.

On this screen, you enter the number of the purchase order for the merchandise or service. DacEasy will automatically supply the rest of the information from the purchase order. You can verify the quantity and price on the vendor invoice and override the entries if necessary. You can also add merchandise that was not included on the original purchase order.

Because merchandise received and purchase order numbers are two sides of the same coin, they share the same series of numbers.

If you did not issue a purchase order for the merchandise received or service rendered, you can enter the vendor invoice directly through the Merchandise Received screen. Press ↵ in the From Order field to assign a new receipt number. Then complete the fields on the screen (see Table 9.2 for field descriptions).

RECORDING RECEIPT OF INVENTORY ITEMS

When you enter merchandise received, the stock-on-hand count in the product file is updated immediately. This feature ensures you won't lose sales because your records show you are out of stock while the merchandise sits in your warehouse.

For example, suppose that you issued a purchase order for a gold-mining dredge and three metal detectors. Later, the salesman called to tell you about a promotion on plastic gold pans. You can get a dozen for $1.50 each, which is a 50 percent savings off your regular price of $3.00. You tell him to send the pans with your next shipment, even though they are not on the original purchase order. The merchandise arrived this morning. Figure 9.6 shows the entries to record the receipt of the merchandise.

The following procedure is used to enter the merchandise received in the example. Note that you may have to handle recording receipt of fixed assets and services differently, as explained in the next section.

1. In the From Order field, enter **918**, the purchase order number that was used to order the treasure-hunting supplies. You can press F5 to look up the numbers of outstanding purchase orders. If you don't enter the purchase order number to charge the receipt against, you will end up with an open purchase order that you will have to delete from your files.

The information on the purchase order appears. You can press F10 to move the cursor immediately to the line items, or you can

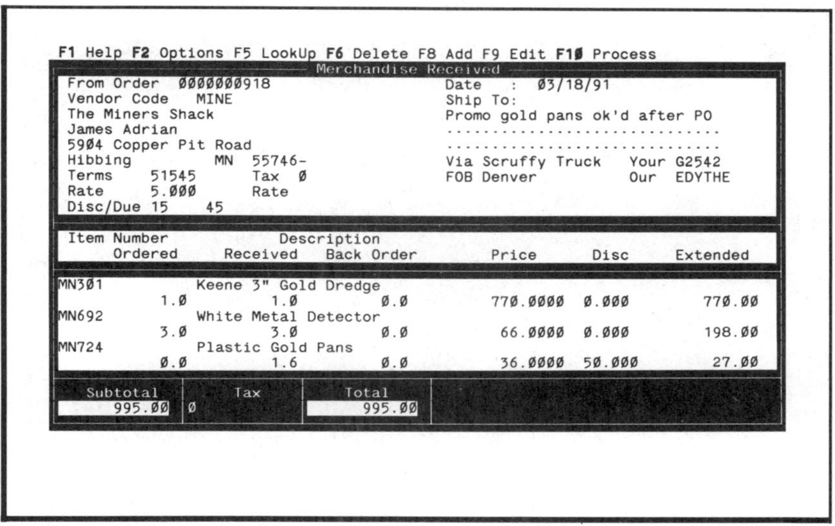

Figure 9.6: Entering merchandise received

press ⟵ to move field by field through the header if you need to make changes. Any overrides you enter here affect this merchandise-received entry and the related purchase order. They are not reflected anywhere else in your records. The name and address in the vendor record are the ones used when you make a payment on this invoice.

2. Press ⟵ to accept the system date as the date of the transaction or enter an override.
3. Press ⟵ to accept the name and address.

The terms shown in the Terms, Rate, and Disc/Due fields are used to calculate the amount of the early payment discount, the date the discount expires, and the date the invoice is due. The tax rate indicates there is no sales tax charged to you for this resale item.

4. Press ⟵ through the Terms and Tax fields.
5. In the Ship To field, enter **Promo gold pans ok'd after PO** to note the added items. If you entered comments on the original purchase order, they would appear in this field. You could override the original text or move the cursor below it and add another remark.

6. Press ↵ to accept the Via entry. You can change the information if the merchandise was delivered by another freight company.
7. Override the information in the field titled Your by entering **G2542**, the number of the invoice for this merchandise.

When you enter a purchase order, you should use the Your field for a confirmation number or the name of the vendor's order clerk; however, when you receive the merchandise, you should change your reference to the vendor's invoice number. If you are purchasing an expensive item on an installment plan, use the number on the contract. The entry here identifies the payable you are incurring with this vendor. It appears as the invoice number in the Accounts Payable aging report and on the Payments screen when you enter payments in Accounts Payable (see Chapter 10). If you leave this field blank, the merchandise-received number will be substituted.

8. Press ↵ to accept the entries in the FOB and Our fields.
9. Enter **1** in the Received field on the line for the gold dredge to record the quantity you received of that item. Next, the program calculates the number of back-ordered items. When you enter receipt of any inventory item, all remaining inventory items are listed as back orders until you enter the quantity received.

Be careful not to override an item number. If you do, the item is deleted entirely from the purchase order, and the units on order in the product record are reversed.

10. Press ↵ in the Price, Disc, and Extended fields to accept the entries.
11. Enter **3** in the Received field for the next item, metal detector, and press ↵ to move through the remaining fields on the line.

Do not enter unordered items as free text lines (text preceded by the code D). These entries will not affect your inventory.

12. In the next Item Number field, you should enter the code for the gold pans. Because this item isn't listed in the product file (you forgot to enter the promotional item when you approved the order), press F8 to add a code for the gold pans.

3.1 Enter the new code in the Item # field. Enter Y when asked if you want to create a new code.

13. Select Products for the new code category. Enter **MN724**, as the new code, enter the product name, complete the other fields, and press F10 to record the new product record.

14. For Received, enter **1.6**, for receipt of one and one-half dozen gold pans.
15. Enter **36** for Price, to represent the price per dozen you are normally charged for these gold pans.
16. The vendor is giving you a special 50 percent discount on the regular price of these promotional items, so enter **50** in the Disc field.
17. Press ⏎ through the Extended field to accept the discounted total the program calculates for this item, and then press F10.

Although you enter the regular price for this item separately from the price discount you receive on a special order, DacEasy records the discounted price as the last purchase price in the product record. If you are valuing your inventory by last purchase price, this entry will distort the true value. Unfortunately, there is no way around this.

The program calculates the subtotal for all the items, and then the sales tax according to the tax code in the vendor record. You can override the sales tax amount. For example, an item might be defined as nontaxable in your product and purchase order code files because you usually buy it for resale. But this time you are going to use it in your own business and, therefore, must pay sales tax. Next the program calculates the Total field.

If you canceled the order for one of the items after you processed the purchase order, you must delete the item from the merchandise-received entry, or it will remain as an unfilled order on your records. Place the cursor on the line for that item and press Shift-F6.

3.1 Press Alt-D to remove a line item.

18. Press F7 to process and print the slip. You can also print all your merchandise-received slips at once later, when the printer has the proper forms in it.

Remember to print copies of your merchandise-received slips, or you will not have a reference to use to locate and review the detail of these transactions on the screen.

As soon as you process the merchandise-received entry, the inventory items received are removed from the units on order field in the product record and added to the units on hand field, and the vendor invoice is available for payment. However, the latest purchase price is not updated until the transaction is posted.

When a purchase order is marked *Backorder* in the purchase order status report, at least some of the items on the original purchase order have been received.

Inventory items placed on back order, like the second item in Figure 9.7, are left in the units on order field in the product record. When the merchandise-received transactions are posted, back-ordered items are left in the open purchase order file, under the original purchase order number. Received items are deleted from the purchase order, and only the outstanding items appear. This is why it is so important to print purchase orders and merchandise-received slips when they are first entered; they provide a complete record of the history of the purchase.

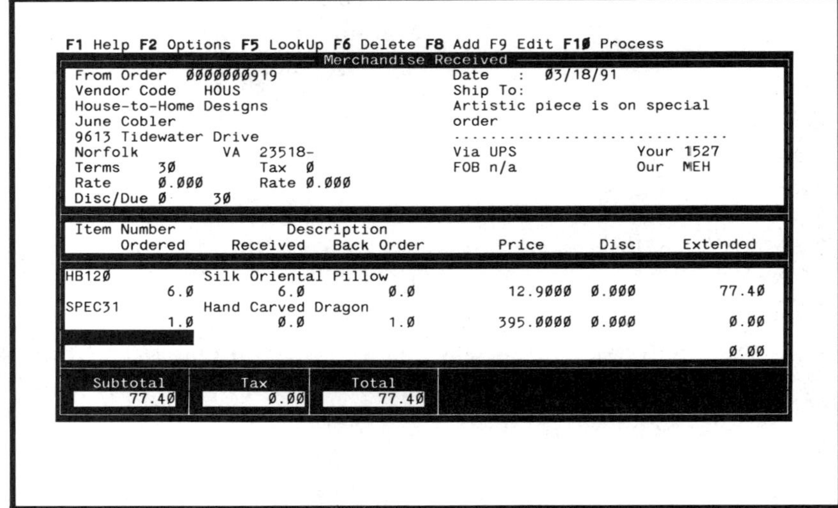

Figure 9.7: Recording partial delivery of merchandise

RECORDING RECEIPT OF SERVICES AND FIXED ASSETS

The main difference in recording receipt of items entered using a purchase order code, usually services or fixed assets, is that the Received and Back Order fields are unavailable. This means that you cannot indicate back orders on these items. You must accept delivery of every purchase order code item on the purchase order—each service or asset—or delete it from the order entirely. If you want to continue to track the deleted item in the open purchase order file, you must reenter it separately under another purchase order number.

In DacEasy, services are ordered by total dollar amount, not by quantity.

For example, you cannot enter a partially received service. Suppose that you order two days' worth of labor from a janitorial service. The workers come one day this week, give you a bill, and plan to return next week to complete the job. You cannot make an entry that will result in a back order to reflect the partial billing. If you changed the amount of the Extended field to reflect the partial billing,

DacEasy would assume that the purchase order is satisfied and remove it from the purchase order file when you processed the receipt. The purchase order would no longer appear in the purchase order status report.

One way to track partially completed services is to manually record them. When a service is not completely finished, reprint the original purchase order, keep it in a file, and handwrite on the order each time a portion of the service is rendered. When the service you ordered is finally complete, enter it through the Merchandise Received option.

Another difference in entering services rendered is that there are no inventory totals for DacEasy to update. Services aren't something you store on a shelf waiting to resell to a customer. However, you may hire subcontractors to provide services to your customers. In these cases, you record the subcontractor's invoice using the Merchandise Received option, and then in the Billing module, prepare an invoice to send to your customer (preferably for more than you had to pay the subcontractor). In the Shipped To field, you might enter the name of the subcontractor who performed the work.

Also, the shipping-related fields titled Via and FOB are not applicable to services. You use a purchase order code, not an inventory item number, to indicate the services for which you are being billed.

As explained earlier, the best way to avoid problems with partial receipt of services or fixed assets is to enter separate purchase orders for each item and its related charges.

CORRECTING OR DELETING MERCHANDISE-RECEIVED ENTRIES

If a merchandise-received entry has been processed but not posted, you can correct or delete it using the procedure described in Chapter 5. If you delete a merchandise-received entry, the units on hand and dollar value in the product record are decreased by the amounts entered as received. The original purchase order itself is also deleted.

If you want to retain the purchase order but cancel the merchandise-received entry (for example, because you entered the receipt on the wrong purchase order), you should reverse the entry instead of deleting it, as explained below.

REVERSING A MERCHANDISE-RECEIVED ENTRY

You can change an unposted merchandise-received slip by recalling the transaction and making entries to reverse all or part of it. For example, suppose that you wanted to test a new product and ordered a musical keyboard for one of your stores. Your downtown store manager thinks it would sell in his location also, so you ordered another one for that store. When one keyboard arrived, the bookkeeper applied it to the wrong purchase order. You want to leave that purchase order in the open file and apply the receipt to the correct purchase order. The reversing entries are shown in Figure 9.8.

```
F1 Help F2 Options F5 LookUp F6 Delete F8 Add F9 Edit F10 Process
                         Merchandise Received
From Order  0000000921                        Date   :  05/17/91
Vendor Code    SOUN                           Ship To:
Sounds of Music                               ..............................
Diane-Susan                                   ..............................
Galaxy Terrace Plaza                          ..............................
Oklahoma City   OK  73159-                    Via ................ Your 236
Terms      15130     Tax  0                   FOB ................ Our  JASON
Rate       1.500     Rate
Disc/Due 10     30

Item Number                  Description
        Ordered      Received    Back Order        Price        Disc        Extended
M74                Casio Keyboard
             1.0         1.0         0.0         525.0000    0.000          525.00
C 1                Freight
                                                                             15.00
M74                Casio Keyboard
             0.0        -1.0         1.0         525.0000    0.000         -525.00
C 1                Freight
                                                                            -15.00

                                                                              0.00
   Subtotal            Tax              Total
       0.00            0.00              0.00
```

Figure 9.8: Reversing an unposted merchandise-return entry

Notice the reversing entries mirror the originals, with three exceptions: the minus sign you enter with the amount received, the minus sign preceding the extended amount the program calculates for the product, and the minus sign you enter for the freight amount. These reversals are reflected in the Total field, which balances to zero.

Reversing a merchandise-received entry cancels the receipt of the merchandise and returns the purchase order to the open file with a back-order status. The dollar and quantity amounts are deducted from the product record and the vendor balance and historical data, with the exception of the number of invoices this year, which remains unchanged.

Familiarize yourself with the differences in deleting a merchandise-received transaction, reversing it, and offsetting it with a purchase-return entry. An understanding of these three options can save you future frustration.

If the merchandise-received entry has been posted, you can neither delete nor reverse it. You must create a purchase-return entry, which offsets the merchandise-received transaction. The difference between reversing a merchandise-received transaction and entering a purchase return is the resulting status of the related purchase order. The amounts in the vendor and product record are still reduced, but the closed purchase order does not return to the open file, nor will it reappear in the purchase order status report when you make a purchase return.

RECORDING RETURNED MERCHANDISE

From the Transactions menu, select Purchasing. From the Entry submenu, select Purchase Returns.

3.1 From the Transaction menu, select Purchasing. From the submenu, select Enter Returns.

When you return merchandise to the vendor, you should enter a purchase-return transaction. This entry automatically creates a debit in the Accounts Payable file to reduce your accounts payable and the vendor balance so you won't pay the vendor by mistake. It also reduces your on-hand inventory amounts.

To enter a purchase return, select the Purchasing option from the Transactions menu, and then select Purchase Returns from the Entry submenu. You will see the Purchase Return screen, shown in Figure 9.9. The fields on this screen are described in Table 9.3.

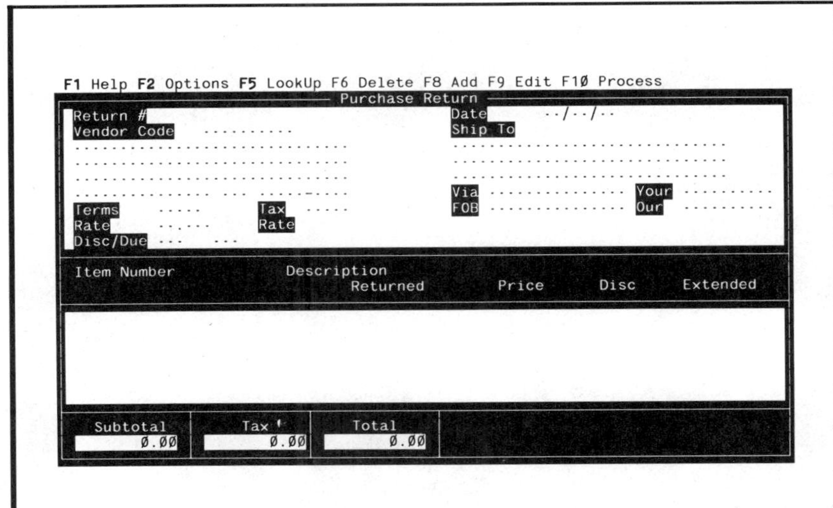

Figure 9.9: Purchase Return screen

Table 9.3: Fields on the Purchase Returns Screen

Field	Description
Return #	The program assigns a number to the return slip.
Date	The program supplies the system date. You can enter an override.
Vendor Code	The code of the vendor you are returning the merchandise to.
Terms	The program supplies the terms code from the vendor record.
Rate	The program supplies the discount percent indicated by the terms code.
Disc/Due	The program supplies the allowable discount and due days indicated by the terms code.
Tax/Rate	The program supplies the tax code from the vendor record and the sales tax rate from the tax table.
Ship To	The address the merchandise is being returned to.
Via	The shipping method.
Your	The invoice number this return relates to.
FOB	The city where shipping charges originate.
Our	Your reference for the return. It could be the number of the purchase order used when you bought this merchandise or the initials of the individual in your company requesting the return.
Item Number	The product number of the merchandise you are returning.
Description	The program supplies the description from the product record.
Returned	The quantity returned using the unit and fraction of purchase measure.
Price	The program supplies the price from the product record. Enter the price from the original merchandise receipt.
Disc	The discount percent on the purchase price given for this item on the original receipt.
Extended	The program calculates the extended amount (shipped × price − calculated price discount).
Subtotal	The program calculates the subtotal of the items before taxes.
Tax	The program calculates the total sales tax on all taxable items from the tax code entered above. You can enter an override.
Total	The program calculates the total (subtotal + sales tax).

Version 3.1: The Terms field does not exist. The discount rate appears in the Disc. % field.

For example, suppose that you ordered shoes, but the vendor sent the wrong style. When you called the vendor's salesman about the mistake, he promised to send the correct style right away. You are shipping the wrong shoes back. The entries for this return are shown in Figure 9.10.

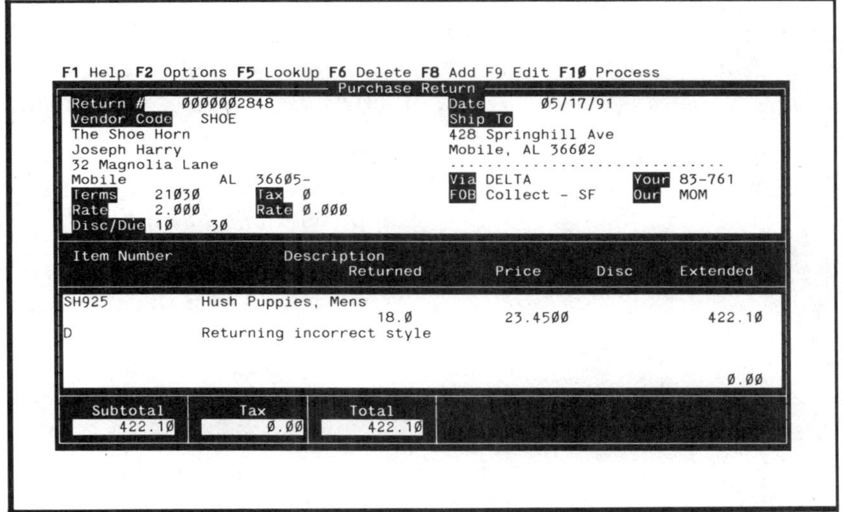

Figure 9.10: Completed purchase return

The following procedure is used to enter the sample return:

1. In the Return # field, press ↵ to assign a number. You do not relate the return to the number of the merchandise-received entry. The transaction is given its own return-slip number. It is, however, applied to the invoice noted on the merchandise-received entry.
2. Press ↵ to accept the system date as the transaction date.
3. Enter **SHOE** for the code of the vendor you are returning the merchandise to. The vendor name, contact, and corporate address appear. If you enter an override, it only affects what is printed on the merchandise-return slip; the vendor record remains unchanged.
4. Press ↵ through the Terms, Rate, and Disc/Due entries, which represent the payment terms. The program defaults to

the terms in the vendor record. However, if the return is applied to a specific invoice, it takes on the terms of the invoice. Otherwise, DacEasy treats all unapplied returns as current.

5. Press ↵ to accept the tax rate code. If the tax on the original purchase differed from the rate in the vendor record, you should enter an override here to match the original invoice.
6. In the Ship To field, enter **428 Springhill Ave, Mobile, AL 36602** for the address of the warehouse the merchandise is being returned to.
7. Enter **DELTA** in the Via field. The merchandise is being shipped back on Delta Freight Lines.
8. Enter **83-761** in the field titled Your. This is the vendor's invoice number for this merchandise.

You do not have to return merchandise against a specific invoice; however, it is a good idea to do so. If the invoice is still in the open-payables file, the invoice amount will be reduced by the amount of the return. If the invoice has been paid, or if you enter the return without applying it to the previous invoice, it will appear in the open-payables file as a separate line item. Whatever you enter here appears on the screen as the invoice number when you enter vendor payments, in the Accounts Payable aging report, and on the statement.

9. In the FOB field, enter **Collect - SF** to indicate the charges are collect from San Francisco because the vendor agreed to pay the return freight charges.
10. In the Our field, enter **MOM**, the initials of the person in your company who obtained the authorization or requested the return.
11. For Item Number, enter **SH925**, the code that identifies this merchandise in your product record. The description and the last purchase price appear.
12. For Returned, enter **18**, the quantity you are returning. The program will not allow you to return more than you have on hand.

13. For Price, press ↵ to accept the last purchase price from the product record. If that is not what you paid for this item, enter the actual price you were charged for the merchandise when it was received.

14. Press ↵ in the Disc field. We did not receive a price discount on this merchandise.

The program calculates the extended amount for the line (quantity returned × price − calculated price discount).

15. Press ↵ to accept the extended amount.

If you are charged a restocking charge, enter the appropriate code from the purchase order codes table and the amount.

16. Enter **D** under Item Number to open a window for free text.

17. Type **Returning incorrect style**, press ↵, and press F10.

The program calculates the sales tax for the items entered if the product file indicates the item is taxable. The tax is calculated using the sales tax percentage for the tax code in the vendor record. You can enter an override if necessary. The program also calculates the total (subtotal + sales tax).

18. Press F7 to record and print the return as soon as you enter it (because you'll probably only have one on any given day). However, you can save it for printing at the end of the session by pressing F10 instead. If you want to print a packing slip to accompany the returned merchandise, see the section about printing merchandise-return slips later in the chapter.

The units on hand, dollar value, and statistical information in the product record are immediately updated when you process the return. The return is applied to the open invoice in the vendor record. However, the statistics in the vendor record are not affected until you post the return. Then the credit available increases, and balances and dollars purchased are decreased.

Whenever you enter a payment to this vendor through the Cash module, an unapplied purchase return will appear as an amount preceded by a minus sign, indicating a decrease of the account balance.

CORRECTING OR DELETING PURCHASE-RETURN ENTRIES

You can correct or delete a purchase-return entry after it has been processed, even if the Purchase journal has been printed, using the procedure outlined in Chapter 5. If you posted the return, you must reverse the transaction, as explained later in the chapter.

3.1 The deleted purchase-return number will not appear on any listings.

Note that during data entry, the purchase-return number is used as soon as you process the transaction. If you delete the transaction, the program removes the transaction and its related number from the file. The return number will be listed in the Purchase journal as DELETED.

PRINTING PURCHASING DOCUMENTS

* From the Transactions menu, select Purchasing. From the submenu, select Print, and then select Purchase Orders, Merchandise Received, or Purchase Returns.

3.1 From the Transaction menu, select Purchasing. From the submenu, select Print Purchase Orders, Print Merchandise Received, or Print Returns.

You can print purchase orders to send to the vendor to confirm your order. The packing slip version of the purchase order, which lists items but no dollar amounts, can be used by your receiving department to verify against the shipment when it arrives.

Your accounting department can use merchandise-received slips to compare with vendor invoices. When you receive an incomplete shipment, you should also keep copies of your merchandise-received slips in a separate back-orders file for follow up. They are the only detailed records you have in print for back-ordered merchandise. The purchase order status report shows only dollar amounts, not items.

You should print two copies of your purchase-return slips. One copy can go to the vendor's business office (as a reminder that you should be issued a credit memo for the returned merchandise), and another copy can be retained by your accounting department to compare with the vendor's credit memo.

A packing slip should accompany returned merchandise to the vendor's warehouse. A copy of the packing slip can also serve as a pick list for your own warehouse to accumulate and package the merchandise for shipment.

To print a purchase order, merchandise-received slip, or purchase-return slip, select the Purchasing option from the Transactions menu, choose Print, and then select Purchase Orders, Merchandise Received, or Purchase Returns. See Chapter 5 for details on printing documents.

PRINTING THE PURCHASING JOURNAL

* From the Journals menu, select Purchasing.

3.1 From the Journals menu, select Purchase Journal.

You should print the Purchase journal, review the entries, and make any corrections before posting the transactions. This report is in two parts: a summary by vendor of all merchandise received or returned and a summary by inventory code of the activity.

To print the journal, select Purchasing from the Journals menu. The journal is ready to print. Select the report disposition and press F10 to start printing or press Esc to cancel the printing.

POSTING PURCHASING TRANSACTIONS

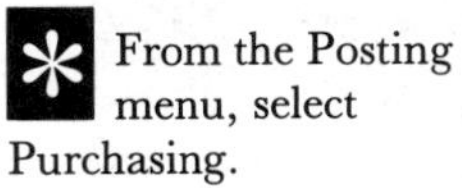

* From the Posting menu, select Purchasing.

3.1 From the Posting menu, select Purchase Orders.

When you post your merchandise-received and purchase-return entries to the Purchase Order module, DacEasy updates the appropriate product and vendor files. The purchase order file is cleared of received merchandise, and the remainder is placed on back order. The entries are also added to the general ledger transaction file in a journal labeled PO to await posting to the general ledger.

You must print all purchase orders, merchandise-received, and purchase-return documents and the Purchase journal before posting the transactions. You should also make a habit of backing up your files before posting.

To post your purchasing transactions, select the Purchasing option from the Posting menu and respond to the prompts. For a description of the procedure for posting, refer to Chapter 5.

REVERSING A POSTED PURCHASE-RETURN SLIP

To delete a posted purchase-return slip, you must prepare a reversing entry. For example, suppose that you received a shipment of china teapots to give away as promotional items. When you discovered a chipped teapot, you entered and posted a purchase-return slip. The display clerk saw the teapot being packaged for return and decided to repair the damaged merchandise and use it in a window display. You want to delete the posted purchase-return slip. The entries for reversing the transaction are shown in Figure 9.11.

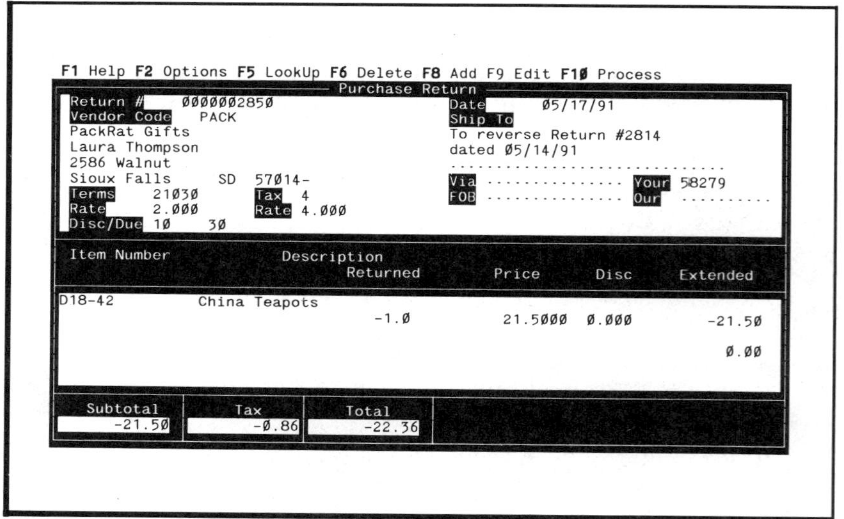

Figure 9.11: Reversing a posted purchase return

The following procedure is used to reverse the sample purchase-return entry:

1. In the Return # field, press ↵ to assign a number to the transaction. The old transaction has been posted and doesn't exist in the open file any longer, so you need to use a new number.
2. Press ↵ to accept the system date in the Date field.

3. Enter **PACK**, the vendor code for the giftwares distributor who sold you the merchandise. The vendor name, contact, and address appear from the vendor record.
4. Press ↵ through the Terms and Tax fields.
5. In the Ship To field, enter **To reverse Return #2814 dated 05/14/91** to describe the reversing entry.
6. In the Your field, enter **58279**, the number of the invoice you applied the original return against. This field must contain the same information as the original purchase return to clear your records accurately. Otherwise, you will have an unapplied item sitting in your open-payables file.
7. Press F10 to move the cursor to the Item Number field and enter **D18-42**. Be sure this is the number of the product on the original return slip.
8. In the Returned field, enter **– 1**, the quantity on the original return slip, but preceded with a minus sign to make it a reversal.
9. Enter **21.50** for the price, exactly as it was on the original return slip. Don't use a minus sign here. The price is not affected by a reversal. The extended amount will reflect the reversal.
10. Press ↵ to move through the Disc field. If you had indicated a price discount on the original return slip, you would enter that exact percentage here.

The program calculates the extended amount (shipped × price – price discount). Here, the amount is preceded by a minus sign to indicate a reversing entry.

11. Press F10 when all items on the original purchase return have been reversed. The program calculates the sales tax on the reversed items and precedes it with a minus sign to indicate a reduction in the amount of tax. You can enter an override if it does not agree with the amount on the original return slip.

12. Press F7 to record and print a copy of the reversing entry and attach it to the original purchase-return slip.

The units on hand, dollar value, and statistical information in the product record and the open-payables file are updated immediately when you record the transaction. The vendor record is updated when you post purchasing transactions.

PRINTING THE PURCHASE ORDER STATUS REPORT

* From the Transactions menu, select Purchasing. From the submenu, select Print, and then select Purchase Order Status.

3.1 From the Journals menu, select P.O. Status Report.

The purchase order status report is not an accounting journal. It simply lists open purchase orders, which are those that include items you have not received. The merchandise-received transaction must be posted before the purchase order's status will be updated on the report.

This listing helps you follow up on orders you have placed with vendors. All unfilled purchase orders are marked with the notation *On Order*. If a partial shipment has been received on a purchase order, the purchase order is marked *Backorder*.

To print the status report, select the Purchasing option from the Transactions menu, select Print, and then choose Purchase Order Status. The report is ready to print. Select Printer as the report disposition, and then press F10 to start printing or press Esc to cancel.

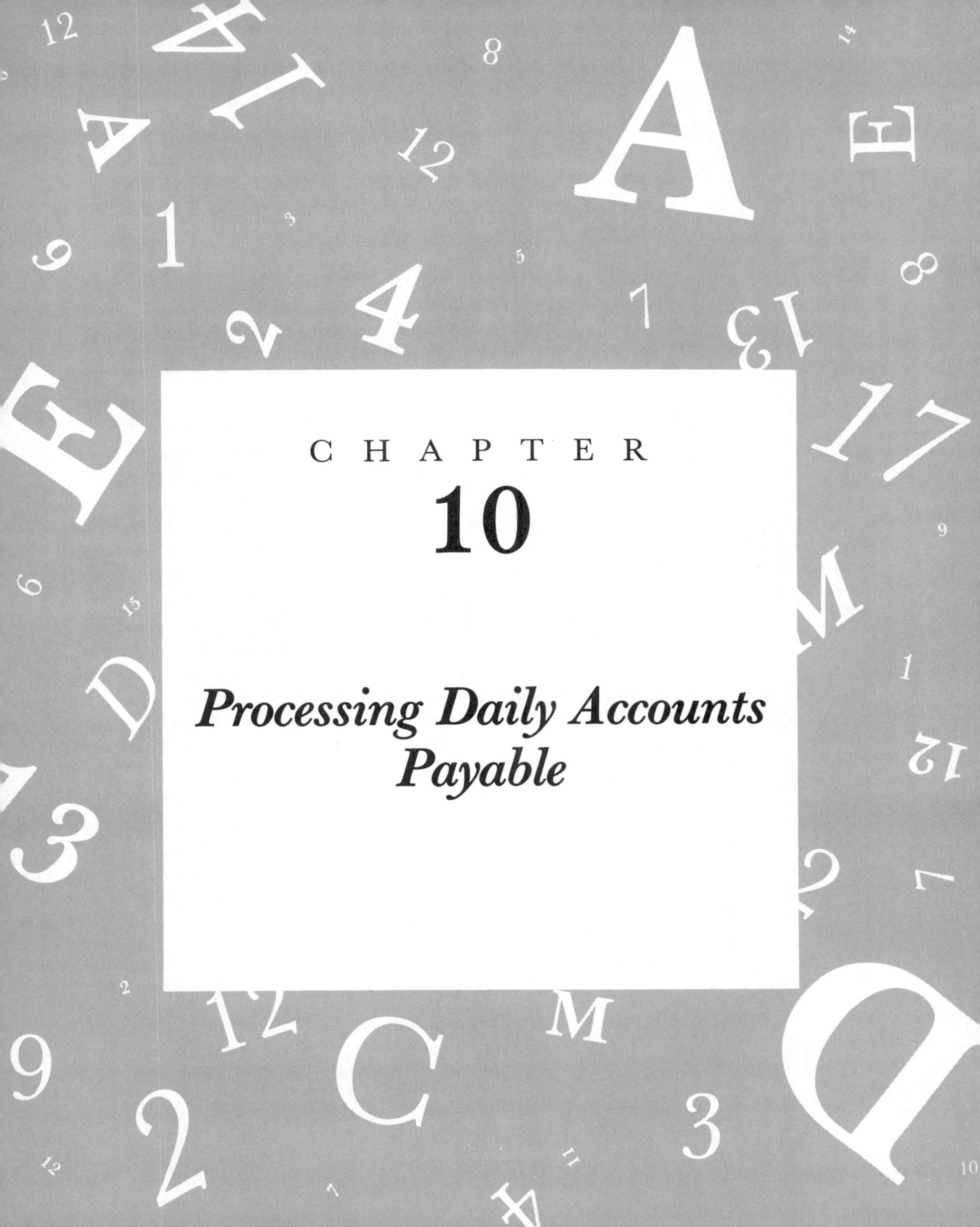

CHAPTER

10

Processing Daily Accounts Payable

3.1 Vendor payments are also processed through the Accounts Payable module. (The Cash module does not exist.)

IN THE ACCOUNTS PAYABLE MODULE, YOU ENTER miscellaneous invoices, debits, and credits. You process payments to vendors through the Cash module.

ENTERING MISCELLANEOUS ACCOUNTS PAYABLE TRANSACTIONS

* From the Transactions menu, select Payables.

3.1 From the Transaction menu, select Accounts Payable. From the submenu, select A/P Transaction Entry.

Miscellaneous Accounts Payable transactions are those that do not involve resale products or purchase order items, such as utility bills, reimbursement of employee expenses, vendor late charges, and miscellaneous credits. These transactions can be entered directly into Accounts Payable.

The Accounts Payable module does not adjust inventory, update your costs, or clear your purchase orders. This is the primary difference between entering vendor invoices here and entering them through the Purchase Order module. You should record any invoices for resale items and products and services ordered on a purchase order by using the Merchandise Received option on the Purchasing Entry submenu, as explained in Chapter 9. This ensures that your inventory and purchase order information is up to date. However, if you do not purchase items for resale (and therefore do not track cost of goods sold) or do not issue purchase orders, you can routinely enter vendor invoices directly into Accounts Payable.

To enter a miscellaneous transaction, select the Payables option from the Transaction menu. You will see the Accounts Payable Transaction Entry screen, shown in Figure 10.1. The fields on this screen are described in Table 10.1.

ENTERING INVOICES DIRECTLY INTO ACCOUNTS PAYABLE

One typical use of the Accounts Payable Transaction Entry screen is to record employee expenses that you must reimburse. For example, suppose that your manager in charge of leasing properties

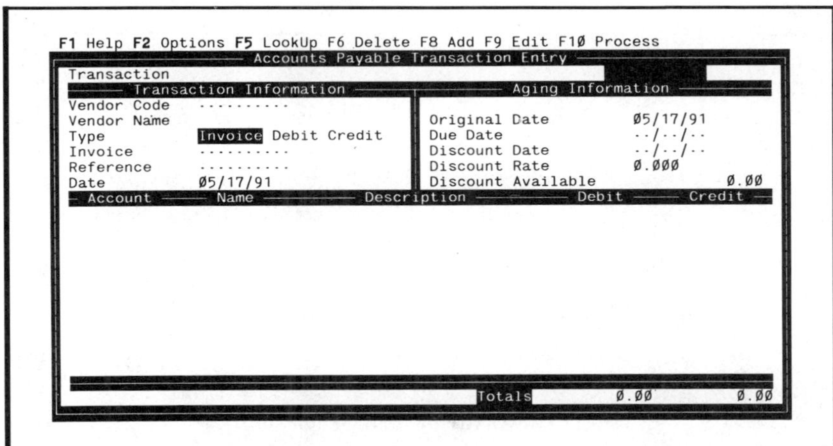

Figure 10.1: Accounts Payable Transaction Entry screen

Table 10.1: Fields on the Accounts Payable Transaction Entry Screen

Field	Description
Transaction	The program assigns a transaction number. To edit an existing transaction, enter its number here.
Vendor Code	The code of the vendor for this transaction.
Vendor Name	The program displays the name from the vendor record.
Type	Select Invoice, Debit, or Credit.
Invoice	The number of the vendor's invoice this entry pertains to. What you enter here appears as the invoice number on the Payments screen, the Accounts Payable aging report, and the payments report.
Reference	The number of a check that prepaid this invoice, if applicable. Otherwise, a notation that further helps identify the transaction. This entry appears under Ref. # on the vendor statement.
Date	The program displays the system date. The transaction date is the date reflected in the Accounts Payable journal. You can enter an override to use the date the transaction took place.
Original Date	The program displays the system date. The actual date on the invoice is used to determine the discount and due dates for the invoice.
Due Date	The program calculates the due date from the terms code in the vendor record. The due date is used to determine if an item is listed as past due on the aging report (except for unapplied debits, which always appear as current). Applied debits and credits take on the terms of the invoice they relate to. You can enter an override for the current transaction.

Table 10.1: Fields on the Accounts Payable Transaction Entry Screen (continued)

Field	Description
Discount Date	The program calculates the discount date from the terms code in the vendor record. You can enter an override for this transaction. Although the program calculates a discount date on all entries, it is only applicable to invoices.
Discount Rate	The program supplies the discount percent indicated by the terms code. You can enter an override.
Discount Available	The program calculates the discount available from the terms code in the vendor record for invoices only.
Account	The program supplies the Accounts Payable account number in your general ledger interface table as the first account number entry.
Name	The program supplies the name for the account number entered.
Description	A description of the transaction. This appears with the transaction in the Accounts Payable journal.
Credit	The amount of the credit for the transaction.
Account	The account number of the offsetting general ledger account for the transaction.
Name	The program supplies the name for the account number entered.
Description	After the first entry, the program displays the same description as that of the previous line. You can enter an override.
Debit	The amount of the debit to be charged to the general ledger account.
Totals	The program calculates the total debits and credits entered. They must be equal in order to save the entry.

Version 3.1: The Type field is called Trans. Code. Enter I for invoice, D for miscellaneous debit, or C for miscellaneous credit. The Discount Rate field does not exist.

periodically visits each site. Figure 10.2 shows the entries to record an expense report for one of the manager's trips. The transaction increases your liability because now you owe the employee for these business expenses.

The following procedure is used to enter the sample invoice:

1. In the Transaction field, press ↵ to assign a number to the transaction.
2. For Vendor Code, enter **BRAN**, the code for the employee, who has been set up as a vendor in our records.

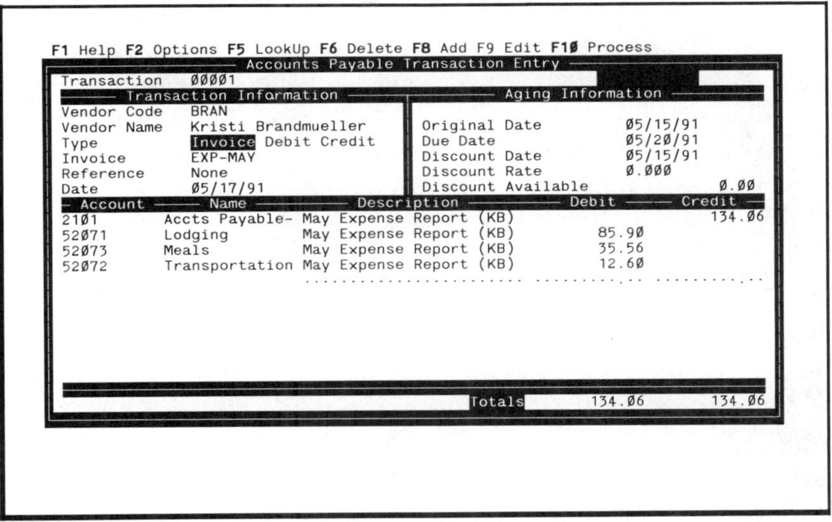

Figure 10.2: Entering a miscellaneous invoice in Accounts Payable

3. Press ↵ to accept the name that appears from the vendor record. You can enter an override for the current invoice.

3.1 Enter I for invoice in the Trans. Code field.

4. For Type, select Invoice.
5. Enter **EXP-MAY** as the Invoice. In this case, it notes the employee's May expense report. If this were from an outside vendor, you would enter the vendor's invoice number.
6. Enter **None** for Reference. If you already paid this invoice, you could enter the check number for reference. You must enter something in this field. If you have no applicable reference, use the word *None* or some other notation to satisfy the requirement.
7. Press ↵ to accept the system date as the data entry date.
8. In the Original Date field enter **051591** as the date on the invoice.

For Account, the program inserts the Accounts Payable number from the general ledger interface table as the first entry. The account name appears.

9. Press ↵ to accept the due date (in our example, employee expenses are reimbursed within five days) and the discount date calculated by the program from the terms in the vendor record. You can override these terms for this invoice. The program supplies the discount rate from the terms in the vendor record.
10. Enter **May Expense Report (KB)** as the description for this transaction (KB are the employee's initials).
11. Enter **134.06** in the Credit column. Because an invoice increases your accounts payable obligations, the first entry is a credit to Accounts Payable.

Remember, you can only make entries to accounts defined as detail accounts in your general ledger. You cannot post to general accounts.

The program calculates the discount available from the terms in the vendor record after you enter the Accounts Payable amount. Next you enter the general ledger accounts for the offsetting entries of this transaction. These entries are typically debits to expense accounts.

12. In the Account field, enter **52071**, the account number for lodging expense. The account name appears from the general ledger account record.
13. The description that appears is the one you entered on the previous line. You can enter an override, but the same description is appropriate in our example. Press ↵ to accept it.
14. Enter **85.90** in the Debit column. Remember, a debit entry increases the balance in an expense account.
15. In the next Account field, enter **52073**, the account number for meals; press ↵ to accept the description; and enter **35.56** in the Debit column.
16. As the final item, enter the account number **52072**, for transportation expenses; press ↵ to accept the description; and enter **12.60** in the Debit column. You could press F7 to automatically enter the balancing amount as the last debit. The program calculates the total debits and credits in the Totals field.
17. Press F10 to record your entries and process the transaction.

If your debits do not equal your credits, you will not be able to process the transaction. DacEasy will display the message

Transaction is out of balance and may not be saved.

Review the amounts you entered against your source document and make the necessary corrections.

When you process the transaction, the invoice becomes an open item on the vendor's account immediately, but the balance in the vendor record is not updated until you post your Accounts Payable transactions.

ENTERING MISCELLANEOUS DEBITS

A credit memo from a vendor is a reduction of the amount you owe. To reduce the accounts payable liability on your books, you enter a debit. Therefore, a credit memo from a vendor becomes a debit entry in Accounts Payable.

A miscellaneous debit in Accounts Payable is a transaction that reduces your liability. It could be a price decrease on a previously posted invoice or any other credit memo from your vendor. If you do receive a price adjustment after the invoice is posted, you cannot update the last purchase price field in the product record.

As an example, suppose that you rented a paging device. The store has been billing you in advance, and your accounting clerk paid the last invoice before you told him you had canceled the rental. Instead of writing you a refund check, the vendor issued a credit memo to be applied against the cellular phone you plan to buy. The completed entry for the miscellaneous debit is shown in Figure 10.3.

The following procedure is used to enter the vendor's credit memo as a miscellaneous debit:

1. Press ↵ in the Transaction field and enter **TELE** as the Vendor Code.
2. Select Debit as the Type.
3. Enter **CM2874** for Invoice, the number from the vendor's credit memo.

3.1 Enter D for miscellaneous debit in the Trans. Code field.

In this example, the credit memo number will appear as an unapplied debit on the vendor's account. However, if the original invoice were still unpaid and in your open-payables file, you would enter the number of the related invoice. Then this entry would appear beneath the transaction it relates to and be deducted from it on the aging

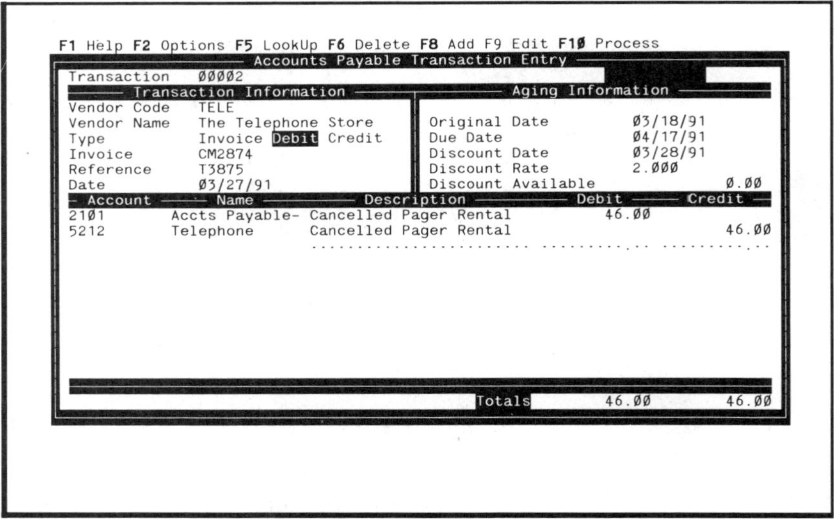

Figure 10.3: Entering a miscellaneous debit in Accounts Payable

report and the vendor statement. What you enter here becomes the identifier for an unapplied open item on the vendor record and will appear when you are selecting items to pay. (Remember, on an open-item vendor account, each debit transaction—invoice or miscellaneous debit—must have a payment or credit applied to it so that the amount due is zero before it can be removed during period-end processing.)

4. For Reference, enter **T3875**, the number of the previously paid invoice that the credit is for.
5. Press ↵ to accept the system date as the date you are entering the transaction.
6. Override the system date by entering **031891** in the Original Date field. This is the date on the memo.
7. Press ↵ in the Due Date, Discount Date, and Discount Rate fields. Although the program calculates the due and discount dates from terms in the vendor record, neither pertain to unapplied debit memos. The discount available is only calculated on invoices.
8. After the program displays the Accounts Payable account number and name, enter **Cancelled Pager Rental**.

9. In the Debit field, enter **46**, for the amount of the credit memo from the vendor.
10. In the Account field, enter **5212**, the general ledger account number for telephone expense. The account name appears.
11. Press ↵ to accept the description from the first entry.
12. In the Credit field, press F7 to automatically enter the same figure that is in the Debit field, and then press ↵ to accept the amount. (If you are reducing the amount of an expense, the entry is a credit to the expense account.)
13. The total debits and credits are calculated by the program. When all the items are entered and your debits and credits match, press F10 to record your entries and process the transaction.

3.1 Use F9 to automatically enter the amount.

3.1 Open items are viewed on the Payments and Adjustments screen.

The debit immediately becomes an open item on the vendor's account, but the balance in the vendor record will not be updated until you post Accounts Payable transactions. If the miscellaneous debit is applied to an open invoice, it automatically decreases the invoice amount displayed on the Accounts Payable open invoices lookup screen (which will be discussed later). You must print the Accounts Payable journal to have a record of the individual transactions that make up the outstanding amount on an invoice. However, an unapplied miscellaneous debit appears as an open item on the payments screen as a separate amount preceded by a minus sign. It can be used against the amount due on any invoice.

Debit amounts, whether applied or unapplied, appear on the Accounts Payable aging report and the payments report preceded by a minus sign to indicate a reduction in the balance.

ENTERING MISCELLANEOUS CREDITS

A debit or charge from a vendor increases what you owe. A credit posted to Accounts Payable increases your liability. Therefore, a debit memo from a vendor becomes a credit entry to your accounts payable.

A miscellaneous credit in Accounts Payable is a transaction that increases your liability. It could be a restocking fee for returned merchandise or any other debit memo from the vendor.

To enter a miscellaneous credit memo, select Credit in the Type field of the Accounts Payable Transaction Entry screen. Figure 10.4 shows an example of the entries for a miscellaneous credit to add late charges to a vendor's account.

3.1 Type C in the Trans. Code field to enter a credit memo.

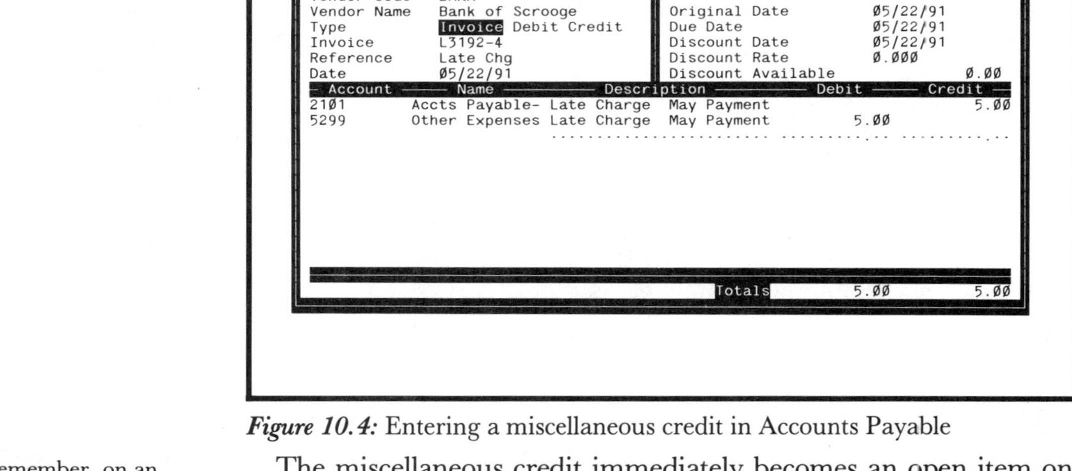
F1 Help F2 Options F5 LookUp F6 Delete F8 Add F9 Edit F10 Process
Accounts Payable Transaction Entry
Transaction 00004
Transaction Information
Aging Information
Vendor Code BANK
Vendor Name Bank of Scrooge
Type Invoice Debit Credit
Invoice L3192-4
Reference Late Chg
Date 05/22/91
Original Date 05/22/91
Due Date 05/22/91
Discount Date 05/22/91
Discount Rate 0.000
Discount Available 0.00

Account	Name	Description	Debit	Credit
2101	Accts Payable- Late Charge	May Payment		5.00
5299	Other Expenses Late Charge	May Payment	5.00	
		Totals	5.00	5.00

Figure 10.4: Entering a miscellaneous credit in Accounts Payable

Remember, on an open-item vendor account, each credit transaction (merchandise return or miscellaneous credit) must be applied to an invoice or debit so that the amount due is zero before it can be removed during period-end processing.

The miscellaneous credit immediately becomes an open item on the vendor's account, but the balance in the vendor record will not be updated until you post your Accounts Payable transactions.

If the miscellaneous credit is not applied to an open invoice (you did not enter the original invoice number in the Invoice field), it will appear on the Accounts Payable open invoices lookup screen as a separate amount due. It must be cleared by applying a payment or debit against it. Miscellaneous credits applied to open invoices immediately increase the amount of the invoice and do not appear as a separate line item. You must print the Accounts Payable journal to have a record of the individual entries that make up the outstanding amount shown for each invoice.

CORRECTING AND DELETING ACCOUNTS PAYABLE TRANSACTION ENTRIES

You can correct or delete a miscellaneous Accounts Payable transaction after it has been processed, even if the Accounts Payable journal has been printed, using the procedure outlined in Chapter 5. However, you must reverse the transaction if it has been posted, as explained later in the chapter.

3.1 The deleted number will not appear on any listings.

Note that when you delete a miscellaneous transaction, the program removes the transaction and transaction number from the file and the amount from the vendor account. The number appears on listings with the notation DELETED.

PRINTING THE PAYMENTS REPORT

* From the Reports menu, select Payables. From the submenu, select Payments.

3.1 From the Reports menu, select Accounts Payable. From the submenu, select Payments Report. Enter 1 to print subtotals by vendor at the Enter Your Selection prompt.

Unfortunately, you cannot restrict the payments report to a vendor range.

The payments report lists all open items: invoices, applied and unapplied memos, and advance payments. The discount and due dates for each item are listed with their respective payment amounts. You can use this listing to plan your payments in a timely manner and take advantage of the discounts offered. Select to print subtotals by due or discount date or by vendor at the subtotals prompt.

To print the payments report, select the Payables option from the Reports menu, and then choose Payments. The first prompt allows you to choose between totaling your outstanding invoices by vendor, by the date they are due, or by their discount date. You can use the date subtotals as a cash-requirements report to determine how much money you need on a given date to pay your bills on time. Grouping the information by vendor will help you select items for payment. On the report, mark the items and amount to pay and the debits or advance payments to use, and then refer to it when you are entering payments.

Next, you can restrict the report to items due in a specific date range. For example, you can exclude items that are not due until next month. In the From field, enter the first due date you want included on the report. Press ↵ if you want to start with the earliest date in the open-payables file. In the To field, enter the last due date you want included on the report, or press ↵ to end with the last date in the file.

MAKING PAYMENTS TO VENDORS

* From the Transactions menu, select Cash. From the Entry submenu, select Payments.

There are two ways to make payments to vendors: by writing a check manually or by printing computer-generated checks. You can also make advance payments and apply them to invoices received later.

To enter a payment, select the Cash option from the Transactions menu, choose Entry, and then choose Payments. You will see the Payments screen, shown in Figure 10.5. The fields on this screen are described in Table 10.2.

3.1 Entering vendor payments through the Accounts Payable module is described in separate subsections.

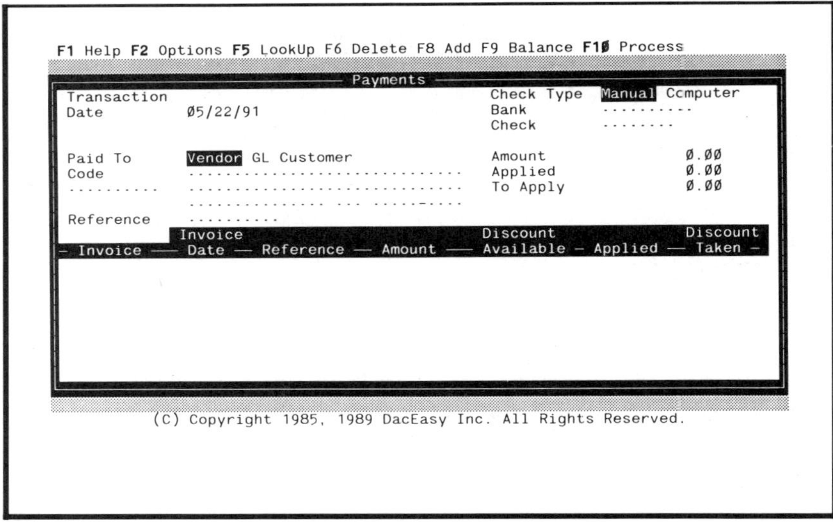

Figure 10.5: Payments screen

Table 10.2: Fields on the Payments Screen

Field	Description
Transaction	Press ↵ to assign a number to this transaction.
Date	The program supplies the system date. You can enter an override.
Check Type	Select Manual if you wrote a manual check and are recording it, select Computer if you want DacEasy to print the check for you.
Bank	The program supplies the general ledger cash account number from the interface table. You can enter an override. This field is not applicable to computer-generated checks.
Check	The number of the manual check written to this vendor. The program assigns a check number to each payment when the checks are printed.
Paid To	Select Customer to write a refund check to a customer or Vendor to make a payment to a vendor. Select General Ledger if the payment is for a miscellaneous expense that does not affect a customer or a vendor record.
Code	If you selected Customer or Vendor, enter the code for that record.
Name	The program displays the name from the vendor or customer record.
Amount	The amount of a manual check. This field is not applicable to computer-generated checks. The program calculates the check amount for computer-generated checks after you enter the amount applied to each invoice.

Table 10.2: Fields on the Payments Screen (continued)

Field	Description
Applied	The program calculates the total of the amounts you apply to the invoices.
To Apply	The program calculates the amount left to apply from a manual check.
Reference	A reference to identify the payment that appears on the check stub.
Invoice	The program displays the identifier for the document that is due. This identifier is from the open-payables file. It could be the invoice number from a merchandise-received or Accounts Payable transaction entry. It could also be the merchandise-received number (if no vendor reference was noted), the number of a purchase-return slip, or the invoice number on an unapplied miscellaneous debit or credit.
Invoice Date	The program displays the date from the invoice.
Reference	The program displays the reference from the original item. You can enter an override.
Amount	The program displays the total outstanding amount of the document.
Discount Available	The program calculates the discount available from the terms on the original document.
Applied	The amount you want to pay on this invoice.
Discount Taken	The amount of discount you want to take on this invoice.

Version 3.1: The screen is called Payments and Adjustments. The Bank field is called Account #, and it is not applicable to computer-generated checks or adjustments. The Paid To field does not exist. An additional field is Transac. Type. Enter P for manual check, K for computer-generated check, or A for adjustment.

ENTERING COMPUTER-GENERATED PAYMENTS

Before you can print computer-generated checks, you must enter the payments through the Payments screen. This is where you select the invoices you want to pay. For example, suppose that you want to pay two invoices, and you need to handle the discount for each invoice differently. One includes shipping insurance, which the vendor does not discount. You must figure a discount only on the merchandise and ignore the discount available calculated by DacEasy. For the other invoice, you can take the full discount calculated by the program. Figure 10.6 shows the entries for paying the invoices.

The following procedure is used to enter the sample transaction:

1. Press ↵ to assign a number in the Transaction field.

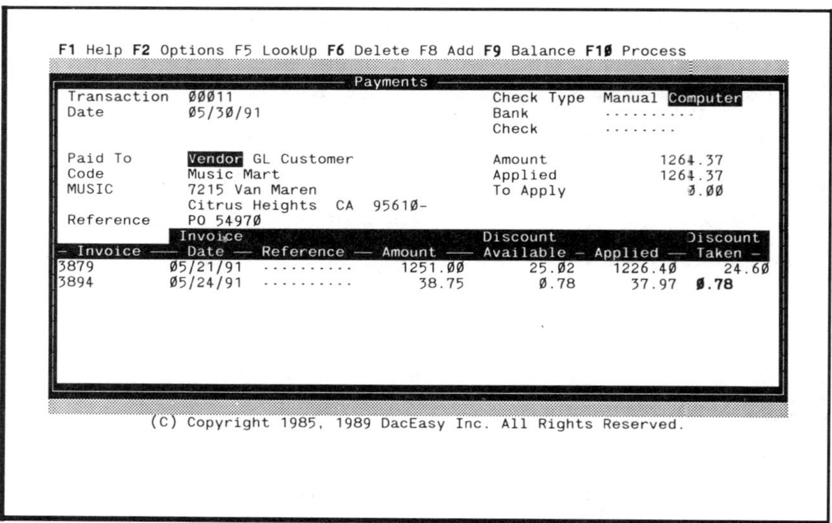

Figure 10.6: Taking a discount when selecting invoices to pay

2. The program displays the system date in the Date field. Press ↵ to move past the date, which is not applicable to computer-generated checks.
3. Select Computer for Check Type.

The Bank and Check fields are not available when you are selecting payments to be made by computer-generated checks. When you print the checks, you select the cash account to use, and the program assigns a check number to each payment.

4. Select Vendor in the Paid To field. You can also enter payments (refunds) to a customer by selecting Customer in the Paid To field, entering the customer code in the Code field, and completing the fields.
5. Enter **MUSIC** as the Code (Music Mart is the company to be paid). The program displays the vendor name and address.
6. Enter **PO 54970** in the Reference field. This reference will appear on the check stub to help identify the payment.

DacEasy calculates the Amounts Applied and To Apply field entries after you enter the amount you want to pay on each invoice. The program displays the outstanding items for this vendor, as shown in Figure 10.7.

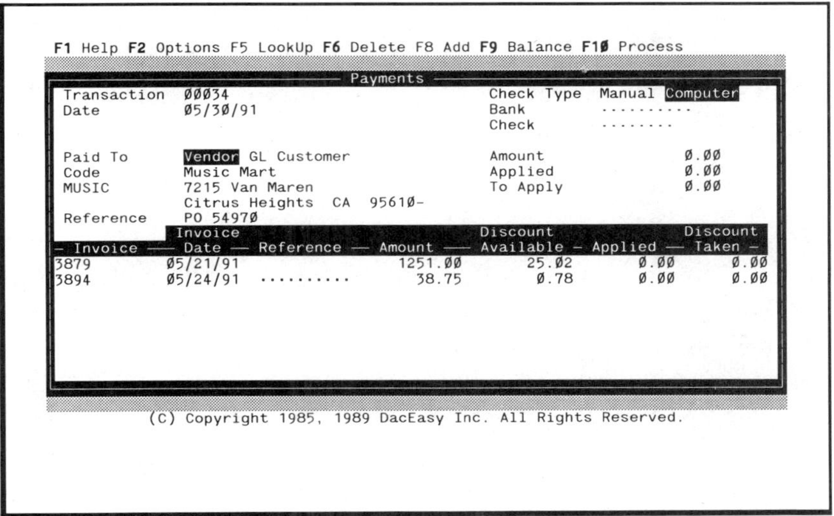

Figure 10.7: Open items on a vendor's account

The program displays the identifier for the document that is due in the Invoice field, the total amount outstanding in the Amount field, and the discount available (according to the terms on the original document) in the Discount Available field.

> The program calculates the early payment discount on the total invoice, including sales tax and auxiliary charges such as freight. Sales tax is rarely discounted. To pay the invoice correctly, you must deduct the nondiscountable amounts, refigure the discount allowed, and determine how much to pay.

7. Press ↵ to move past the blank Reference field next to the invoice date. If a notation were entered with the original invoice, it would appear in this field. You can override it and enter a new notation. This reference will accompany the line item into the Cash journal. Do not confuse the purpose of this Reference field with the one in the header.
8. In the Applied field on the line for invoice 3879, enter **1226.40**, the amount you want to pay on this invoice. When a discount is available, subtract that amount from the invoice total to determine the actual amount to pay on the invoice.
9. For Discount Taken, enter **24.60**, the actual discount available considering the insurance fee. This leaves a discount

available on the invoice. Because you have paid the invoice in full, the invoice and the remaining discount notation will be removed during period-end processing.

10. Again, press ↵ to leave the Reference field blank for invoice 3894.
11. Enter **37.97** in the Applied field.
12. Enter **.78** in the Discount Taken field to take the allowable discount.
13. Press F10 to record and process your entries.

You should continue and enter all the payments you want to make. Repeat the process for each vendor that will be sent a check. Then print the Checks to Print journal, as described later in the chapter.

ENTERING MANUAL PAYMENTS

Manual checks are those produced without the benefit of DacEasy. Any checks that you write elsewhere should be entered through the Payments screen to keep your general ledger cash account and records up to date. Whenever possible, enter the invoice or miscellaneous charge through the Accounts Payable Transaction Entry screen before entering the manual check so you can apply the check against the bill immediately. Otherwise, you will also have to process an adjustment to apply the payment to the bill.

To enter a manual check payment, select Manual in the Check Type field of the Payments screen. You may want to override the system date in the Date field to enter the date the check was written. In the Bank field, the program displays the number of the cash account from your general ledger interface table. If you wrote the check on another checking account, change the default number in the field to the general ledger account number for the appropriate cash account. The program tracks check numbers when generating computer checks and defaults to the next number in the Check field. However, it does not increment the number when you write a manual check. Always verify that the number supplied by the program is the actual check issued for the vendor and override the default if it is incorrect.

As an example, suppose that you received a special order from your vendor. You had a check waiting for the amount of the invoice, but there was also a C.O.D. charge. Figure 10.8 shows the entries to record the manual check to the delivery service.

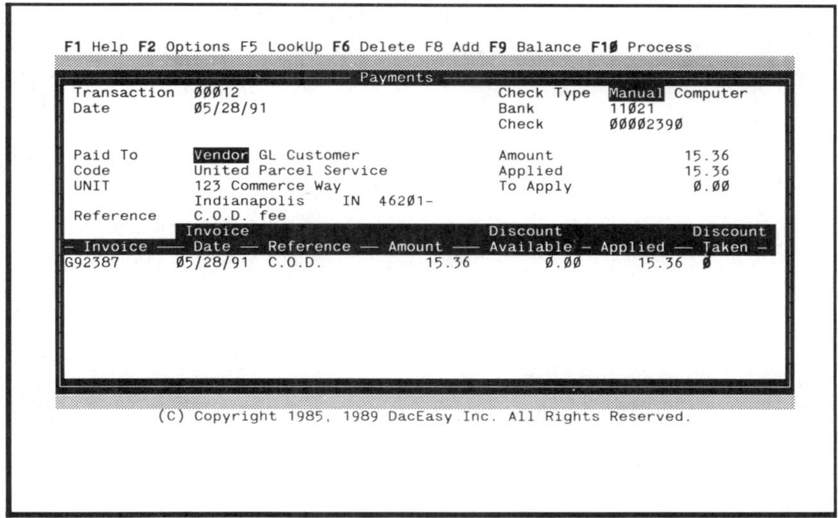

Figure 10.8: Entering manual checks

MAKING PAYMENTS TO VENDORS IN VERSION 3.1

3.1 From the Transaction menu, select Accounts Payable. From the submenu, select A/P Payments.

To enter a vendor payment in version 3.1, select the Accounts Payable option from the Transaction menu, and then choose A/P Payments. You will see the Payments and Adjustments screen. See Table 10.2 for a description of the fields.

To set up the transaction for a computer-generated payment, press ↵ to assign a number in the Transaction # field and enter the vendor code. Enter K for check in the Transac. Type field. The Account #, Date, and Check # fields are not available when you are selecting payments to be made by computer-generated checks. The program calculates the Amount and Applied field entries after you enter the amount you want to pay on each invoice.

In the open-items list, the program displays data for each uncleared item. Enter the amount you want to pay on the invoice in the Amt. Applied field. When a discount is available, subtract that amount from the invoice total to determine the actual amount to pay on the invoice. For Disc. taken, enter the actual discount available on the merchandise. Press F10 to record and process your entries.

To enter a manual check payment, enter P in the Transac. Type field of the Payment and Adjustments screen. If you wrote the check on another checking account, change the default number in the Account # field to the general ledger account number for the appropriate cash account. You may also want to override the system date in the Date field to enter the date the check was written. In the Check # field, enter the number of the check you wrote.

MAKING ADVANCE PAYMENTS TO VENDORS

If a vendor requires an advance payment, you should enter it through the Payments screen. You can enter a payment made by manual check or one to be printed in your next check run. Select the appropriate indicator, Manual or Computer, in the Check Type field and complete the header for the transaction. If no outstanding invoices exist, you will be asked if you want to create an advance. Press ↵ to accept the default, Yes. In the invoice Reference field, press F10 to record an advance.

The amount of a manual check is automatically entered on the vendor's account with the identifier ADVANCE. You can enter a reference to accompany the distribution detail in the journal.

If you entered a manual check, the transaction is complete. If you requested a computer check, it will be included in the Checks to Print journal and printed in your next check run.

As an example, suppose that the transmission failed in your old delivery truck, and you had it towed to your regular repair shop. The manager says you must pay in advance for special-order parts. You give him a down payment for a rebuilt transmission. You will get an invoice including the parts and labor when the repair is complete. Figure 10.9 shows the entries for this advance payment. In the vendor record, the advance is listed as an open item.

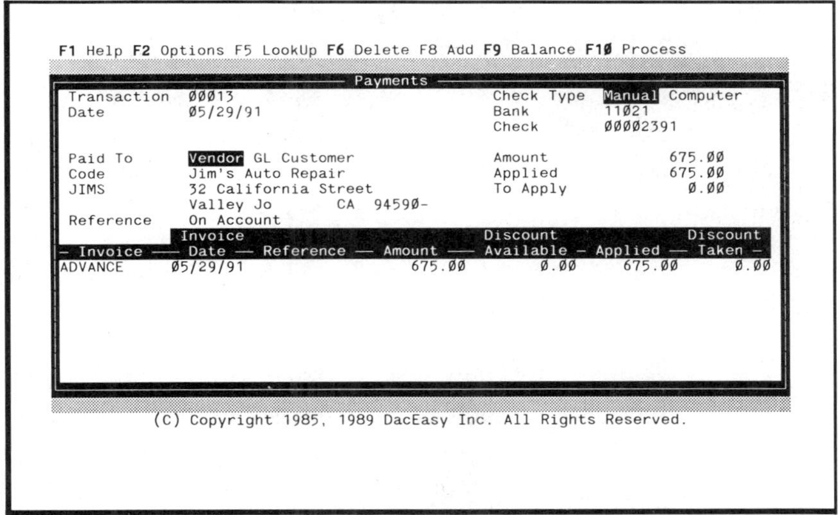

Figure 10.9: Entering an advance payment to a vendor

MAKING ADVANCE PAYMENTS IN VERSION 3.1 In version 3.1, you enter an advance payment to a vendor through the Payments and Adjustments screen. Enter the appropriate code, P for manual payment or K for a computer-generated check to be printed in your next check run, in the Transac. Type field and complete the header for the transaction.

If there are no open invoices on this vendor's account, when you enter the check amount in the Amount field, the program displays the prompt

No Open invoices exist, Do you want to create an advance N

Enter Y. If you have open invoices on this account, the program displays them. To enter an advance when there are open invoices, press F2 in the Amt. Applied field on the first line.

The amount of a manual check is automatically entered on the vendor's account with the identifier ADVANCE. If you are paying by a computer-generated check, you must enter the amount of the advance yourself.

In the vendor record, the advance is listed as an open item. The amount is preceded by a minus sign to indicate a reduction in the vendor balance.

APPLYING ADVANCE PAYMENTS OR UNAPPLIED DEBITS

From the Transactions menu, select Cash. From the Entry submenu, select Vendor Adjustment.

When you receive an invoice that you made an advance payment on, you must apply the advance to it. You accomplish this by entering an adjustment in the Vendor Adjustments screen. The net result of this transaction is zero, and the balance in the cash account is not affected. The advance has already been recorded as a check, which decreased your checking account. The adjustment just moves amounts from one line item to another, without affecting the account balance.

If you do not apply a purchase return or miscellaneous debit to a specific invoice when you enter it, the item will be listed separately on the Accounts Payable open invoices lookup screen. The return or debit is identified by the number of the return slip or the vendor's credit memo number. You can apply these items to any outstanding charges.

You cannot adjust items that have not been posted.

To transfer amounts from one transaction to another, select the Cash option from the Transactions menu, and then select Vendor Adjustment.

Figure 10.10 shows the entries to apply the advance payment for truck repair made in the previous example. The following steps are used to enter the sample adjustment:

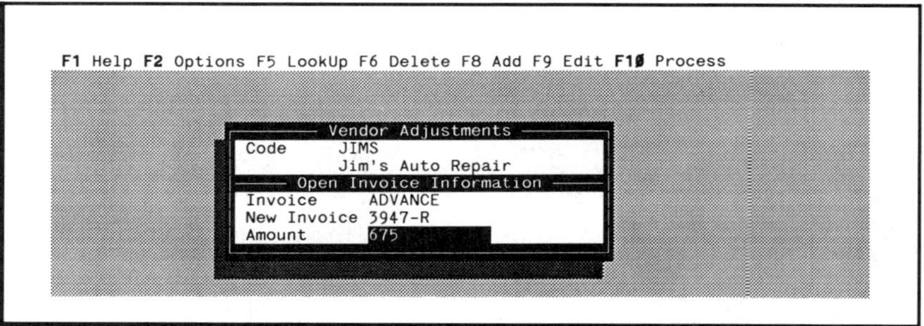

Figure 10.10: Applying an advance payment to an open invoice

1. Enter **JIMS** for the vendor code.
2. In the Invoice field, press F5 to display the open items on the vendor's account. Figure 10.11 shows an advance and an

unpaid invoice listed on the lookup screen. Instead of using the lookup screen, you could enter ADVANCE, the identifier of the advance payment (or the number of the debit memo), you want to apply.

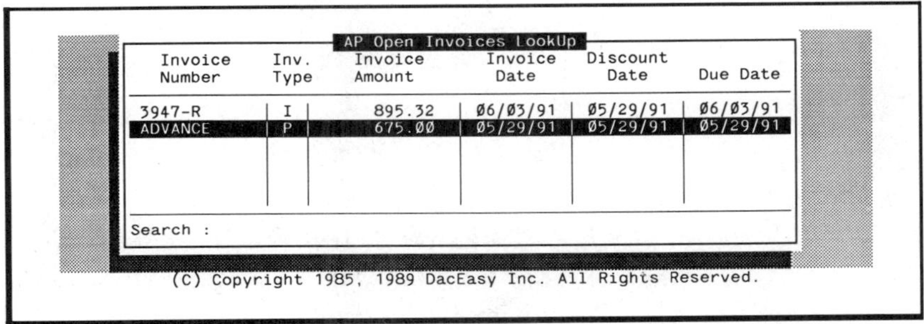

Figure 10.11: An advance payment and an unpaid invoice on a vendor's account

3. Highlight the advance you want to apply to the invoice and press ↵ to select it.
4. In the New Invoice field, enter **3947-R**, the number of the recent invoice to which you want to apply the advance payment. The full amount of the advance appears in the Amount field.
5. Press ↵ to apply the full amount of the advance to the invoice. You can override the default and use less than the full amount of the advance or debit memo.

If the advance or debit memo is greater than one invoice, you can apply it to several invoices. Enter the amount to be applied to this invoice and save the transaction. Then repeat the steps, selecting another invoice as the New Invoice to which a portion of the advance is to be applied.

After you apply the payment, the invoice number will appear twice on the open invoices lookup screen, as shown in Figure 10.12. These two line items, the original invoice identified by the invoice type I and the payment identified by P, offset one another. In the Payments journal, the advance and the invoice it was applied to will appear as offsetting entries.

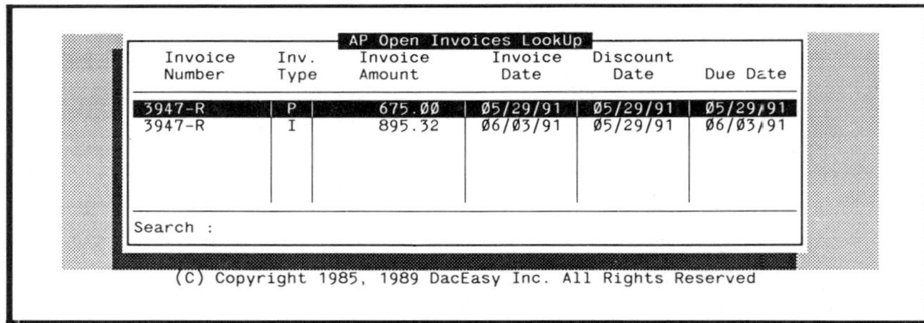

Figure 10.12: Offsetting entry indicates use of advance payment

APPLYING ADVANCE PAYMENTS OR UNAPPLIED DEBITS IN VERSION 3.1 To apply an advance payment to an invoice in version 3.1, enter A in the Transac. Type field on the Payments and Adjustments screen. This indicates the transaction is an adjustment. The Account # and Amount fields are not applicable to an adjustment. The Check # field is not applicable either, but the program requires an entry. You could enter the word *Adjust* to satisfy the requirement. The program calculates the Applied and To Apply fields.

Move the cursor to the line item identified as ADVANCE, and enter the amount of the advance you want to use preceded by a minus sign. You do not have to use the entire amount of an advance payment. However, you cannot process an advance payment transaction until the amount you selected to use has been completely applied.

Next, move the cursor to the Amt. Applied column on the line for the invoice that you want to apply the advance to, and enter the amount you want to apply to that item.

The invoice is reduced, but two entries labeled ADVANCE remain on the account. These two line items, one for a positive amount and one for a negative amount, offset one another. They will be removed during month-end processing.

Unapplied debits are identified by the number of the return slip or the vendor's credit memo number and appear as an amount preceded by a minus sign. When making payments, you can use these unapplied entries against any outstanding charges.

To use unapplied debits, move the cursor to the debit line item and enter the amount you want to use preceded by a minus sign in the

3.1 Don't be misled by an advance remaining in the open-items list after it has been used. If you, in error, reuse the advance, DacEasy will deduct the amount from the invoice you applied it to, but it will also create an offsetting entry labeled ADVANCE. This will remain as an unpaid, open item, ensuring that your balance is correct, even though your individual line items are not.

Amt. Applied field. The Amount field in the header, which indicates the amount of the check that will be written to this vendor, is reduced by the amount of the debit. Any return or vendor credit memo used in making the payment will be listed on the check stub as a separate line item.

VERIFYING CHECKS TO PRINT

* From the Journals menu, select Cash. From the submenu, select Checks to Print.

3.1 From the Transaction menu, select Accounts Payable. From the submenu, select Checks to Print Journal. Enter the transaction numbers of the first and last payments you want to print, including leading zeros, in the Transaction # From and To fields (or press ↵ for the first or last transactions).

Before you print checks, you should review the Checks to Print journal to verify the documents. This listing shows each invoice, the amount to be paid, the discount taken, and any returns or vendor credit memos used in the payment. It also totals the amount of cash you will need to pay those invoices.

To request a listing of checks to print, select the Cash option from the Journals menu, and then choose Checks to Print. Select Printer as the Report Disposition and press F10 to print the journal.

Review the list to make sure each vendor will be paid as you intended and the total is what you expected. You can change the amount to pay on an invoice or remove a payment entirely before actually printing checks. To do so, select Cash from the Transaction menu, and then Payments from the Entry menu. Recall the payment by the transaction number, then use the procedure for correcting and deleting transactions outlined in Chapter 5. Don't forget to print another Checks to Print journal for final review.

PRINTING CHECKS

* From the Transactions menu, select Cash. From the submenu, select Print, and then select Checks.

After you have verified the invoices and amounts selected for payment, you are ready to actually print the checks. DacEasy calculates the amounts and prints the payments for you.

To print checks, select the Cash option from the Transactions menu, choose Print, and then choose Checks. You will see the Checks Printing screen, shown in Figure 10.13.

3.1 From the Transaction menu, select Accounts Payable. From the submenu, select Print Checks.

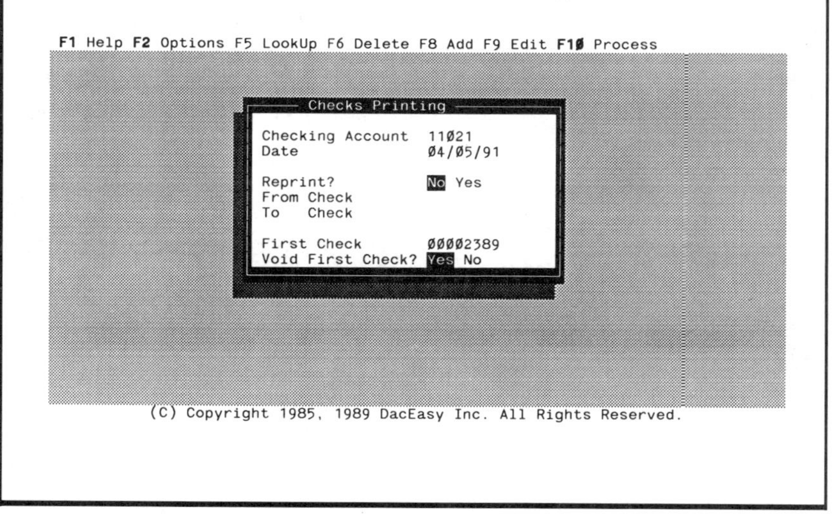

Figure 10.13: Defining checks to print

In the Checking Account field, the program inserts the cash account defined in the general ledger interface table. If you are writing these checks out of another account, enter the number of the general ledger cash account for that checking account. The program displays the system date in the Date field. You can enter an override. The date here will print on your checks. It also is the transaction date that will be recorded in your Accounts Payable Payments journal.

Select No for the Reprint field. For First Check, enter the number of the first check you have in the printer.

3.1 The Void First Check option does not exist. Although the program prompt indicates that you can press F6 to skip the alignment test, it still automatically voids the first check number and prints *VOID* on the first check.

In the Void First Check field, if you respond Yes, the program will use the first check to verify the alignment of the forms in your printer. The program prints a line across the perforation of the top of the check, prints *VOID* on the body of the check, and voids the first check number. Select No if you do not need an alignment test. Press F10 and select Printer as the Report Disposition. If you have defined more than one printer, select the one that is loaded with the checks and press F10 again to begin printing.

DacEasy will print the name and address in the vendor record on each check. Any override you entered on the Purchase Order or Merchandise Received screen is not applicable to check generation.

3.1 If you want the check payable to someone else, you must write a manual check using the correct name, and then apply it against the vendor's account.

If you want the check payable to someone else, you must enter an alternative address in the vendor record and make it the default. If the vendor's company name or address has changed, you should update the vendor record before processing payment (refer to Chapter 4 for the procedure).

REPRINTING CHECKS

If your first printing is incorrect because your printer mangled the checks or you ran them on plain paper by accident, you can print them a second time. The program will void the record of the original checks and print new ones starting with the number you indicate. You must physically nullify the original checks.

To reprint checks, return to the Checks Printing screen. Select Yes in the Reprint field. Enter the number of the first and last check you want to reprint in the From Check and To Check fields. The program will void the checks in the range you enter and print new ones with new numbers.

For First Check, enter the number of the first check in the series you have placed in the printer for the second printing. Indicate whether or not to void the first check for the alignment test, press F10, select Printer as the Report Disposition, and press F10 to reprint the checks.

VOIDING A PRINTED CHECK

Before you post Cash transactions, you can void a printed check. After posting, you must make an adjustment, as explained later in the chapter.

To void a check, you simply delete the original payment selection. On the Payments screen, press F5 in the Transaction field and select the transaction number of the original selection (you also can find the transaction number in the Checks to Print and Cash journals).

After the computer-generated checks are printed, the number of the check printed for this vendor appears in the Check field on the Payments screen. Verify that it is the check you want to void. If it is, press ↵ through all the fields in the header until the cursor rests in the Invoice field. Press F6 to delete the entire transaction, and then press ⟵ to accept the default Yes to void the check (or select No to cancel the deletion). Remember to physically void the printed check as well.

The transaction and check are removed from the Cash transaction file. The check is listed as VOID on the lookup screen and in the check register.

PRINTING A CHECK REGISTER

* From the Transactions menu, select Cash. From the submenu, select Print, and then select Register.

3.1 A check register does not exist. The Accounts Payable Payments journal provides a record of checks that were written.

The check register lists both check and deposit information including the check number, customer or vendor code, transaction number and reference, check date and amount, deposit number, deposit date, and amount. The notation BI in the deposit number column identifies customer payments recorded in the Billing module. The transaction status field marks checks and deposits as O for outstanding or C for cleared. Manual check transactions and computer printed checks do not appear on the check register until you post Cash.

To print a check register, select Cash from the Transactions menu, select Print, and then choose Register. At the prompt to enter bank account to print, enter the general ledger account number for the bank account you want to list. Press F10, and then select the report disposition.

PRINTING ACCOUNTS PAYABLE JOURNALS

* From the Journals menu, select Payables. From the Journals menu, select Cash, and then select Cash Journal or Disbursements Report.

The invoices and miscellaneous transactions you enter directly into Accounts Payable are contained in the Accounts Payable journal. Computer-generated payment selections are listed in the Checks to Print journal until you actually run the checks, as explained earlier. The checks you write to your creditors are contained in the Cash journal and are also listed in the cash disbursements report.

You can print these journals, review the entries, and make any corrections before posting the transactions to Accounts Payable or Cash. To print the Accounts Payable journal, select the Payables

3.1 From the Journals menu, select A/P Transactions or A/P Payments. The cash disbursements report does not exist.

option from the Journals menu. To print the Cash journal and cash disbursements report, select Cash from the Journals menu, and then select Cash Journal or Disbursements Report from the submenu. Next, respond to the prompts, as described in the section about printing journals in Chapter 5.

POSTING TRANSACTIONS AND PAYMENTS

* From the Posting menu, select Payables or Cash.

3.1 From the Posting menu, select Accounts Payable.

3.1 Accounts Payable transactions and payments are both handled through the Accounts Payable option. When DacEasy completes the posting process, it prints a listing titled *Posted to G/L*, which shows the total debits and credits posted. However, the heading is misleading. The transactions were posted to Accounts Payable, not to the general ledger. You must still post to the general ledger, as discussed in Chapter 13.

Before you post your transactions and payments, remember to print the Accounts Payable and Cash journals so that you have a record of each individual entry. The detail is removed after you post. If you selected invoices for payment, you must print the checks for the payments you entered before posting.

When you post to Accounts Payable and to Cash, the entries in the Accounts Payable and Cash journals are posted to the appropriate vendor files and placed in the AP or CH journal respectively, to await posting to the general ledger.

To post your Accounts Payable transactions, select the Payables option from the Posting menu and respond to the prompts. To post Cash transactions, select Cash from the Posting menu and respond to the prompts. The total debits and credits posted are displayed on the screen when the posting process is finished. Chapter 5 describes posting in more detail.

REVERSING A POSTED TRANSACTION

To reverse a posted invoice that was entered through the Accounts Payable Transaction Entry screen, enter a miscellaneous debit to offset the entries on the original document. Be sure to enter the original invoice number in the Invoice field. Figure 10.14 shows an example of entries to reverse an invoice posted to the wrong vendor.

The transaction description will appear in the Accounts Payable journal as an explanation of the entry. Of course, you must also reenter the invoice using the correct vendor code.

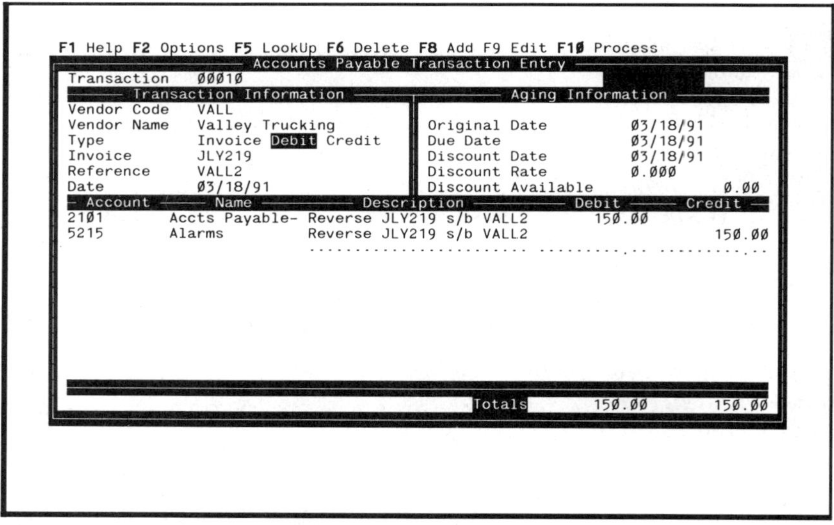

Figure 10.14: Reversing a posted invoice entered in Accounts Payable

If you want to reverse a posted miscellaneous debit, simply enter a miscellaneous credit through the Accounts Payables Transaction Entry screen to offset the entries on the original document. In the Invoice field, type the exact identifier of the item you are reversing, or the reversal will not be properly applied.

REVERSING A POSTED CHECK

3.1 Checks are finalized when you post to Accounts Payable.

When you post to Cash, the checks you printed are finalized. If you want to void a posted check, you must make a reversing entry through the Accounts Payable Transaction Entry screen. What you actually do is return the amount of the paid invoice to the open-payables file and make adjusting entries to your general ledger cash account and purchases and discounts.

Figure 10.15 shows an example of the entries to reverse a posted check. The following procedure is used for this reversal:

1. Press ↵ in the Transaction field to assign a number to this transaction.
2. In the Vendor Code field, enter **MINE**, the code for the vendor the check was written to. The vendor name appears for verification.

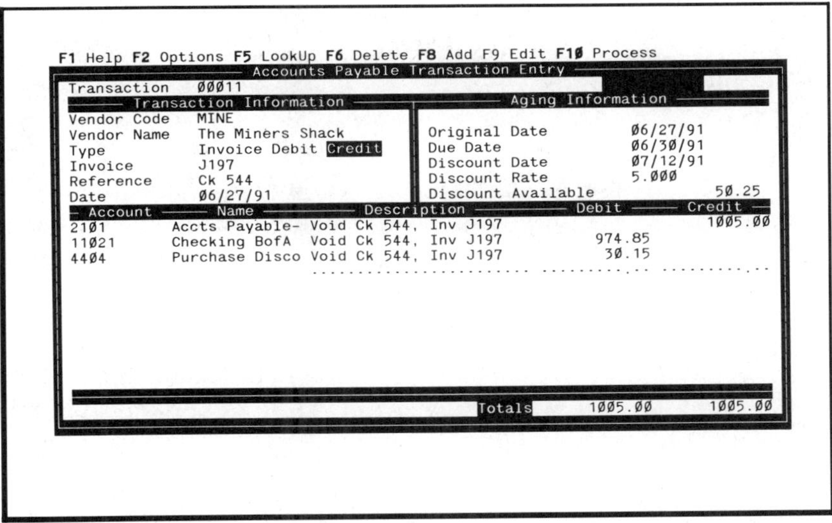

Figure 10.15: Reversing a posted check in Accounts Payable

3.1 For Trans. Code, enter C for credit.

3. Select Credit for Type. You are increasing your liability by removing the payment from the vendor's account; therefore, you want to enter a credit.
4. In the Invoice field, enter **J197**. The check pertained to one invoice, so you can enter that number here. If the check covered several invoices, the entry would not be so straightforward. What you enter here will show as the identification of the unpaid line item on the vendor's account after the reversal. You could enter *CKREV* to indicate that the entry covers a check reversal affecting several invoices. If you want to be exact, you can enter a separate credit for each invoice.
5. For Reference, enter **Ck 544**, the number of the check you are voiding.
6. Press ↵ to accept the system date as the transaction date and original date. Enter an override for the original date if you voided the check on another date.

3.1 The discount available that showed on the vendor's account when you selected the invoice for payment will no longer appear after a check has been written and reversed.

The Due Date, Discount Date, Discount Rate, and Discount Available entries are calculated from the terms in the vendor record and the reversal transaction date. You can override the due date and enter the date applicable to the invoices paid by this check. The discount date and discount available are not applicable to miscellaneous credits.

7. For Due Date, enter **063091**, the due date on the original invoice. Again, if more than one invoice is involved but you are making one all-encompassing adjusting entry, deciding on a date isn't easy. You may want to use the earliest due date on the various invoices being returned to the open-payables file.
8. The program defaults the first entry to 2101 in the Account field. The account name appears.
9. For Description, enter **Void Ck 544, Inv J197** to describe the reason for the transaction.
10. Enter **1005.00** in the Credit field.
11. Enter **11021** in the next Account field. This is the general ledger account number for the cash account you wrote this check against.
12. Accept the description from the previous line by pressing ↵. In the Debit field, enter **974.85**, the amount of the check. You are increasing the balance in your cash account by voiding a check, so you debit your cash account.
13. In the Account field, enter **4404**, the number of the account used to track discounts taken when paying vendors, and then press ↵ to accept the description. Because a discount was taken when the check was written, you must also make an adjustment to your purchase discounts account.
14. Enter **30.15** in the Debit field to reduce the income account, and then press F10 to record the adjustment. The check will be listed as VOID on your listings.

3.1 The reversed check will not appear on any of your listings as being voided. You should mark the check as void and keep it on file.

The original invoice related to a reversed check remains in the open-invoice file as a cleared invoice until period-end processing. Don't confuse it with the reversing entry that is identified by the same invoice number.

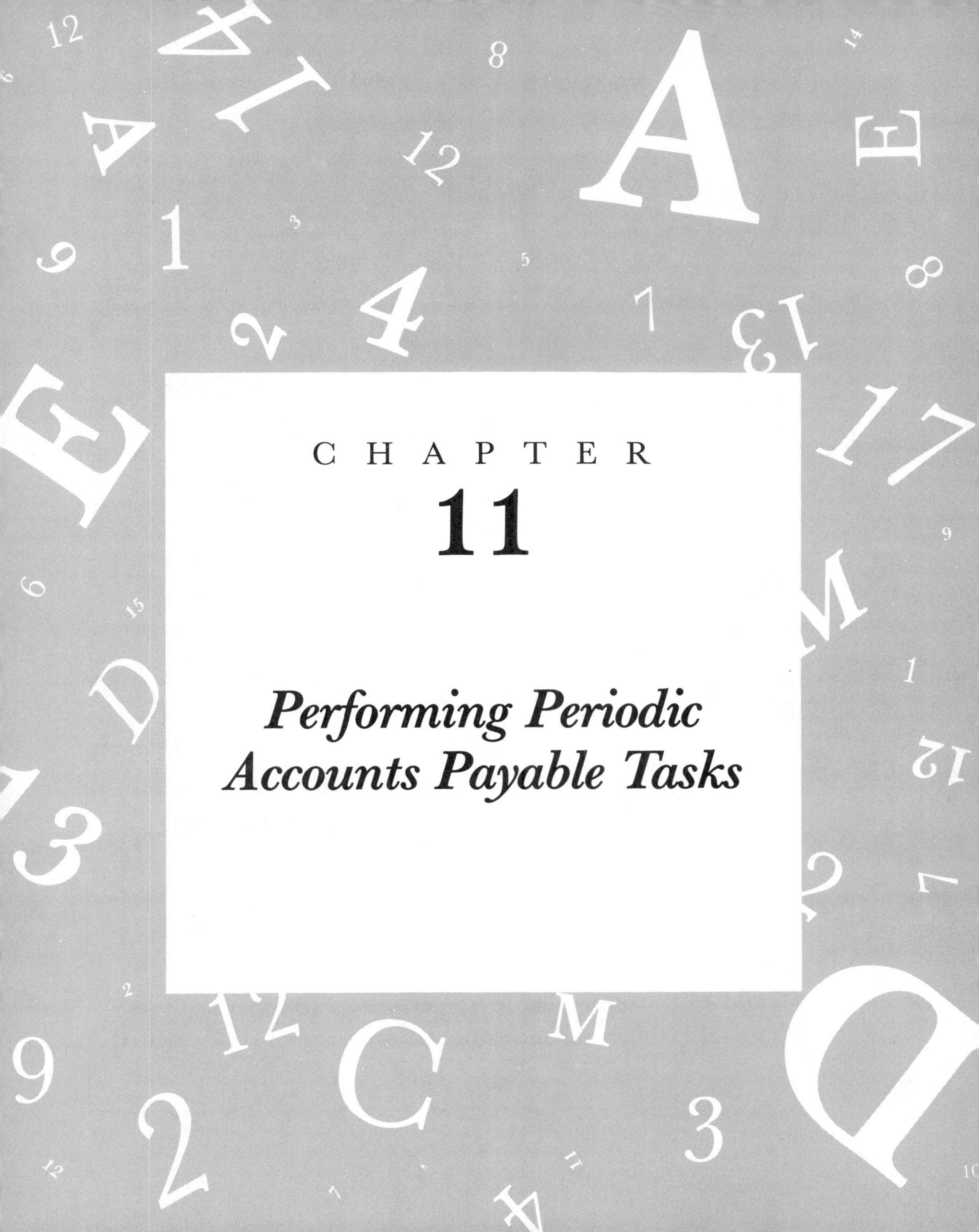

CHAPTER

11

Performing Periodic Accounts Payable Tasks

PERIODIC ACCOUNTS PAYABLE FUNCTIONS INCLUDE monthly routines, such as printing vendor statements and closing periods; tasks that you will perform as necessary, such as reconciling your bank account; printing aging reports, vendor labels, and statistical reports; and yearly printing of 1099 forms. This chapter describes how to perform these functions. The Accounts Payable forecasting and year-end functions are covered in Chapter 14.

RECONCILING A BANK STATEMENT

* From the Transactions menu, select Cash. From the submenu, select Reconciliation.

3.1 The Reconciliation option does not exist. Refer to the next section.

The Reconcile field in the general ledger cash account must contain Yes in order to use the Reconciliation function for the related bank account.

Before attempting to reconcile a bank statement to your DacEasy records, you should print a check register, as described in Chapter 10. Then select Cash from the Transactions menu and Reconciliation from the submenu. In the Bank field, enter the general ledger account number of the cash account related to the bank account you are reconciling. The program displays the account description. In the Balance field, enter the ending balance shown on the bank statement. The outstanding checks and deposits will appear, as shown in Figure 11.1.

Transactions entered through the Receipts or Payments option on the Cash submenu appear on the Reconciliation screen. Transactions affecting cash that were entered through the General Ledger option on the Transactions menu will not appear.

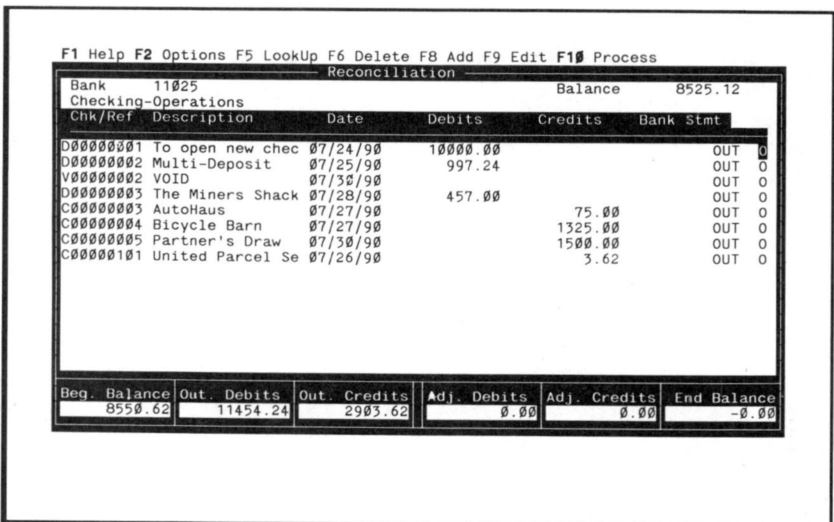

Figure 11.1: Outstanding checks and deposits listed on Reconciliation screen

In the example, the three entries beginning with D are deposits, numbered as they were on the Receipts screen. These deposits illustrate the three types of cash receipts: those paid from the general ledger, from a customer, and from a vendor. The first deposit is the owner's investment of cash to open the checking account. The second deposit, described as Multi-Deposit, is made up of several checks from various customers. The third deposit is one check from a vendor to refund money for damaged merchandise.

All checks, except voided ones, are preceded by C. Checks 3, 4, and 5 were computer-generated. Check 2 was voided in the alignment test and is identified by a V preceding it. Check 101 is from another series of checks set aside specifically for manual checks on the same account.

Record each item on your bank statement as cleared in DacEasy by placing the cursor on the line for that item and pressing F3 to change the status from outstanding (O) to cleared (C), as shown in Figure 11.2. You must also "clear" any voided checks to remove them from the file.

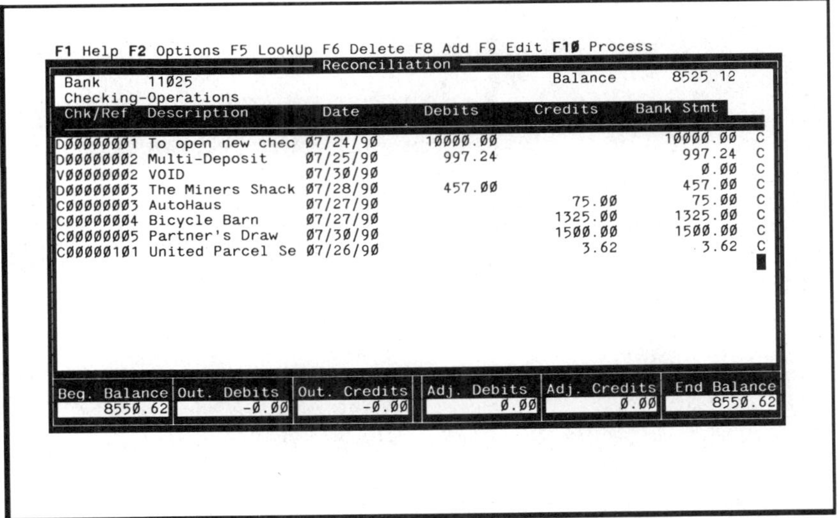

Figure 11.2: Cleared checks and deposits

If a check or deposit amount is wrong in your records, or if there are items on the bank statement that you have not yet recorded in DacEasy, you can make an adjustment. Figure 11.3 shows an adjustment to record bank charges for personalized checks.

The system date in effect when you selected the Reconciliation option will be the date used to post any adjustments you make during reconciliation.

Press F7 to display the adjustment window. Enter a description and the date of the entry. Enter the amount in the Debit or Credit field, depending on the affect it should have on your cash account. In the example, we are reducing the cash account by the amount the bank took out, so we credit the cash account. In the Account field, enter the number of the other general ledger account affected by the transaction, in this case 5303, Bank Charges, an expense account. This account will be debited because you have credited the cash account. It would be credited if the entry were a debit to cash. Press F10 to record the adjustment.

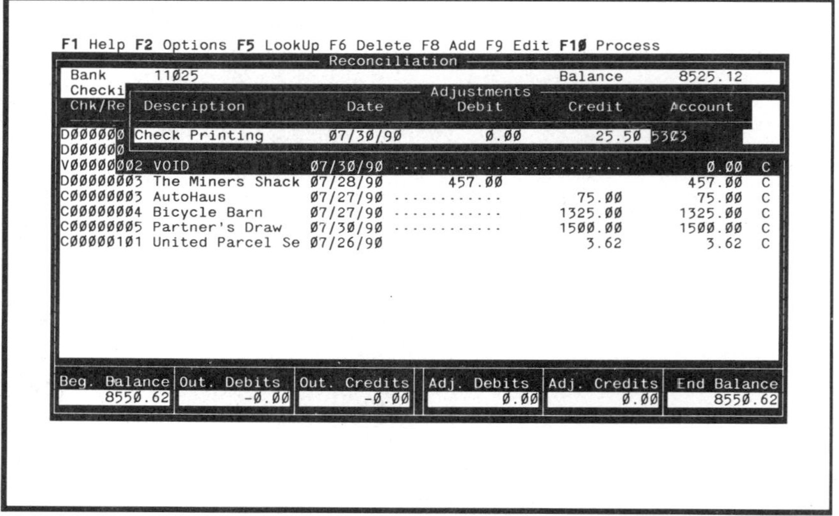

Figure 11.3: Adjusting the cash account during reconciliation

When the balance you entered from the bank statement and the figure calculated by the program in the End Balance field agree, press F10 to record the reconciliation. Any adjustments are automatically posted to the general ledger cash account and the offsetting accounts you selected. When prompted

Do you wish to purge the Check Register File? Yes No

press ↵ to accept the default No or select Yes to remove all the cleared items from the file. When you purge the check register file, cleared items no longer appear on the printout.

RECONCILING A BANK STATEMENT WITH VERSION 3.1

There is no easy way to reconcile deposits made or checks written to your bank statement with version 3.1. You must use a combination of the Accounts Payable Payments journal, the Accounts Receivable Cash Receipts journal, the Sales journal, and the general ledger activity report to piece together how much money came into and went out of each checking account.

The Accounts Payable Payments journal is the only record you have of written and voided checks, and this information is intermixed with adjustments and detail for each cash account.

In the Accounts Receivable Cash Receipts journal, each payment amount is divided between the invoices it paid. A $50 payment would appear as two entries, one for $10 paid against an invoice and another for a $40 advance, rather than the actual $50 check from the customer. If you post your receipts to more than one cash account, the transactions for each account are intermixed. The Check Amount column total reflects all payments received, regardless of depository.

Payments you entered with invoices in Billing appear in the Sales journal and are posted to the cash account set up in your general ledger interface table. You might need to transfer money from the primary cash account to other cash accounts. You would do so with a general ledger entry, along with bank charges and other cash adjustments.

The general ledger account activity detail report can be printed for each cash account separately, but voided checks are not listed. Also, payments are not listed as they were received from the customer, but as they were applied, the same as in the Accounts Receivable Cash Receipts journal. This makes it impossible to track where an error or omission occurred in your deposits.

PRINTING VENDOR STATEMENTS

* From the Reports menu, select Payables. From the submenu, select Statements.

Vendor statements are most useful for auditing purposes. They provide detail on a given vendor in one concise report. You can print statements to have a permanent record of all activity on each vendor. This

3.1 From the Reports menu, select Accounts Payable. From the submenu select Statements.

record is especially important for balance-forward vendor accounts because all their detail is removed during period-end processing.

On the statement, an invoice is described as a purchase and listed as a debit amount. A miscellaneous debit entry is described as a debit; however, the amount is listed in the column for credits. A miscellaneous credit is described as a credit, but listed in the debit column. At first glance, this can be confusing. Keep in mind that the description matches how you entered the transaction; the placement of the amount on the statement reflects how the vendor views the transaction.

To print a vendor statement, select the Payables option from the Reports menu, and then choose Statements. The procedure for printing vendor statements is the same as the one for printing customer statements (described in Chapter 8).

Because vendor statements are an internal document, you probably won't want to go to the expense of having special forms printed. Prior to printing statements, you can change the default form type (as described in Chapter 5) so you can print them on plain paper. Reset the form type when you are finished. To have a complete record of vendor activity, you should include vendors without any amount due on their accounts. Charges and payments could have been posted to the account this period, even if the balance is now zero.

PRINTING ACCOUNTS PAYABLE YEAR-TO-DATE STATISTICS

* From the Periodic menu, select Payables. From the submenu, select Print Statistical YTD.

3.1 From the Periodic menu, select Accounts Payable. From the submenu, select Forecasting. From the next submenu, select Print Statistical YTD.

The Accounts Payable statistical year-to-date report compares your actual activity for the current year with the forecast for number of invoices and dollars purchased from each vendor. The statistics are based on the three-year history retained by DacEasy and reflect the same information that you see at the bottom of the screen in the vendor record.

If the report shows that you are spending more than expected, you can research your records to discover the reason. Perhaps the vendor is charging you more, in which case you could look for alternative suppliers who offer better prices. Or maybe you are buying more, and you could use the figures to negotiate a lower price with your current vendor because of the increased volume of business.

To track your purchasing activity closely, you should print the statistical report at the end of each period. To print the report, select the Payables option from the Periodic menu, and then choose Print Statistical YTD. In the Sort field, select to sort by code, type, or territory. In the From and To fields, enter the first and last records you want to include in the report (or press ↵ to print from the first record and to the last record). Press F10 and select Printer as the Report Disposition.

PERIOD-END PROCESSING

* From the Periodic menu, select Payables. From the submenu, select Period End.

3.1 From the Periodic menu, select Accounts Payable. From the submenu, select End Month.

You must close each period in Accounts Payable, just as you do in Accounts Receivable. When you close the period, all transactions with a zero amount remaining will be removed from your open-item vendor accounts, leaving only the items that have a balance due. Figure 11.4 shows an example of an Accounts Payable open invoices lookup screen listing three invoices. Two of these invoices have no balance due; the invoice number is listed twice, once with the notation I for the original invoice and once with P for the payment applied to it. Both the invoice and the offsetting payment will be removed when the period-end routine is performed.

For balance-forward vendor accounts, the program calculates the balance remaining at the end of the period, and then removes the supporting detail for every invoice and payment, leaving only a balance-forward amount. That is why you should print vendor statements to preserve the detail on paper before running this routine.

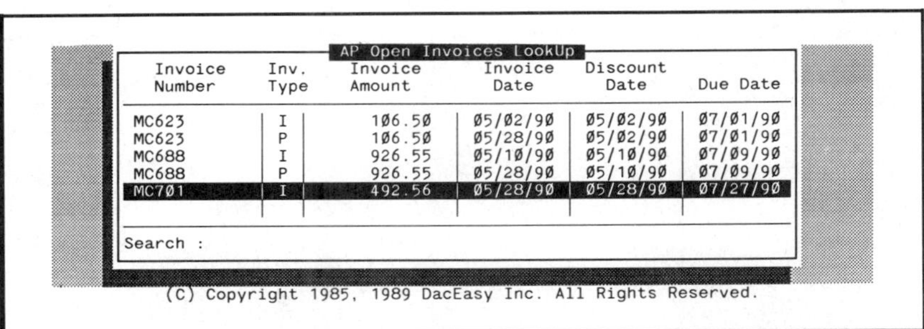

AP Open Invoices LookUp

Invoice Number	Inv. Type	Invoice Amount	Invoice Date	Discount Date	Due Date
MC623	I	106.50	05/02/90	05/02/90	07/01/90
MC623	P	106.50	05/28/90	05/02/90	07/01/90
MC688	I	926.55	05/10/90	05/10/90	07/09/90
MC688	P	926.55	05/28/90	05/10/90	07/09/90
MC701	I	492.56	05/28/90	05/28/90	07/27/90

Search :

(C) Copyright 1985, 1989 DacEasy Inc. All Rights Reserved.

Figure 11.4: Open items listed before period-end

Print the Accounts Payable aging report *after* you have closed the period, so that redundant detail, such as both the charge and the payment for a closed invoice, will have been removed from the file.

Before you close the period, print the Accounts Payable journal and the Payments journal and post all your Accounts Payable activity for the period. Print the Accounts Payable statistical year-to-date report and the vendor statements to keep a printed historic record of the activity for the period. Also, remember to back up your files first, as described in Chapter 3.

To close the period, select the Payables option from the Periodic menu, and then choose Period End. Respond to the prompts as described in Chapter 5.

PRINTING THE ACCOUNTS PAYABLE AGING REPORT

* From the Reports menu, select Payables. From the submenu, select Aging.

3.1 From the Reports menu, select Accounts Payable. From the submenu, select Aging.

The Accounts Payable aging report separates your vendor balances into the time periods you designate. You can use it to determine which accounts are coming due and prepare to make payments. The aging periods can be manipulated so that the listing becomes a cash-requirements report. For example, if you enter periods that are only one week long, you can predict how much money you will need for bills due this week, next week, and the week following.

You can also use the Accounts Payable aging report in conjunction with the Accounts Receivable aging report as a cash-flow analysis tool. You'll want to have the same aging periods in both reports to facilitate the comparison. Together, the reports show you when you can expect money to come in and when money is due to go out.

Before printing the aging report, close the period to remove transactions with no balance from the files. To print the report, select the Payables option from the Reports menu, and then choose Aging. The procedure for printing an Accounts Payable aging report is the same as the one for printing an Accounts Receivable aging report (described in Chapter 8).

On this report, advance payments and unapplied miscellaneous debits always appear as current, regardless of their date. Miscellaneous debit amounts are listed with a minus sign following them. Unapplied miscellaneous credits are aged by the due date entered when they were created, although that date doesn't appear on the report. Unposted items appear with an asterisk (*).

PRINTING A VENDOR DIRECTORY

* From the Reports menu, select Payables. From the submenu, select Directory.

3.1 From the Reports menu, select Accounts Payable. From the submenu, select Directory.

The vendor directory is a listing of your vendors, including terms, credit limit, balance, vendor type (such as 1099), contact, address, and telephone number. Your purchasing department can use it to determine which vendors give you the best terms.

To print the vendor directory, select the Payables option from the Reports menu, and then choose Directory. Enter the sorting and ranking criteria, press F10, and choose Printer as the Report Disposition. Refer to Chapter 5 for a description of the sorting and ranking options.

PRINTING VENDOR LABELS

* From the Reports menu, select Payables. From the submenu, select Labels.

3.1 From the Reports menu, select Accounts Payable. From the submenu, select Labels.

DacEasy will print vendor labels, which you can use for mailings (notifications of your new shipping address, for example) and for reference in the warehouse (put them on index cards). Each label includes the vendor code, vendor name, contact, address, city, state, zip code, and telephone number. As with customer labels, you can choose not to include the code and the telephone number. The information fits on a 1-inch (or larger) label.

To print labels, select the Payables option from the Reports menu, and then choose Labels. Next specify the sorting and ranking criteria. If you are printing labels for a bulk mailing, sort by zip code. If they are for reference, sort them alphabetically. Then respond to prompts regarding label size and what to include (refer to the section about printing customer labels in Chapter 8 for a description of the prompts). Load the labels, press F10, and select Printer as the Report Disposition.

PRINTING 1099 FORMS

* From the Reports menu, select Payables. From the submenu, select 1099's.

The Internal Revenue Service (IRS) requires you to submit a 1099 form for every vendor you pay more than a given amount during the year. Recently, the amount has been $600, but it is subject to change. Check your IRS regulations.

3.1 From the Reports menu, select Accounts Payable. From the submenu, select Print 1099's. You must enter your IRS-assigned employer number.

To print 1099 forms, select the Payables option from the Reports menu, and then choose 1099's. The program supplies the IRS-assigned employer number in the Employer ID field and inserts 600.00 as the Minimum Payment Amount. You can enter an override for the minimum payment amount to report. Proceed by pressing F10 and selecting Printer as the Report Disposition.

Finally, place the forms in the printer and print the alignment test, or press F7 to skip alignment. You must use preprinted forms when printing the 1099 information. The alignment test prints across the perforation on the 1099 forms.

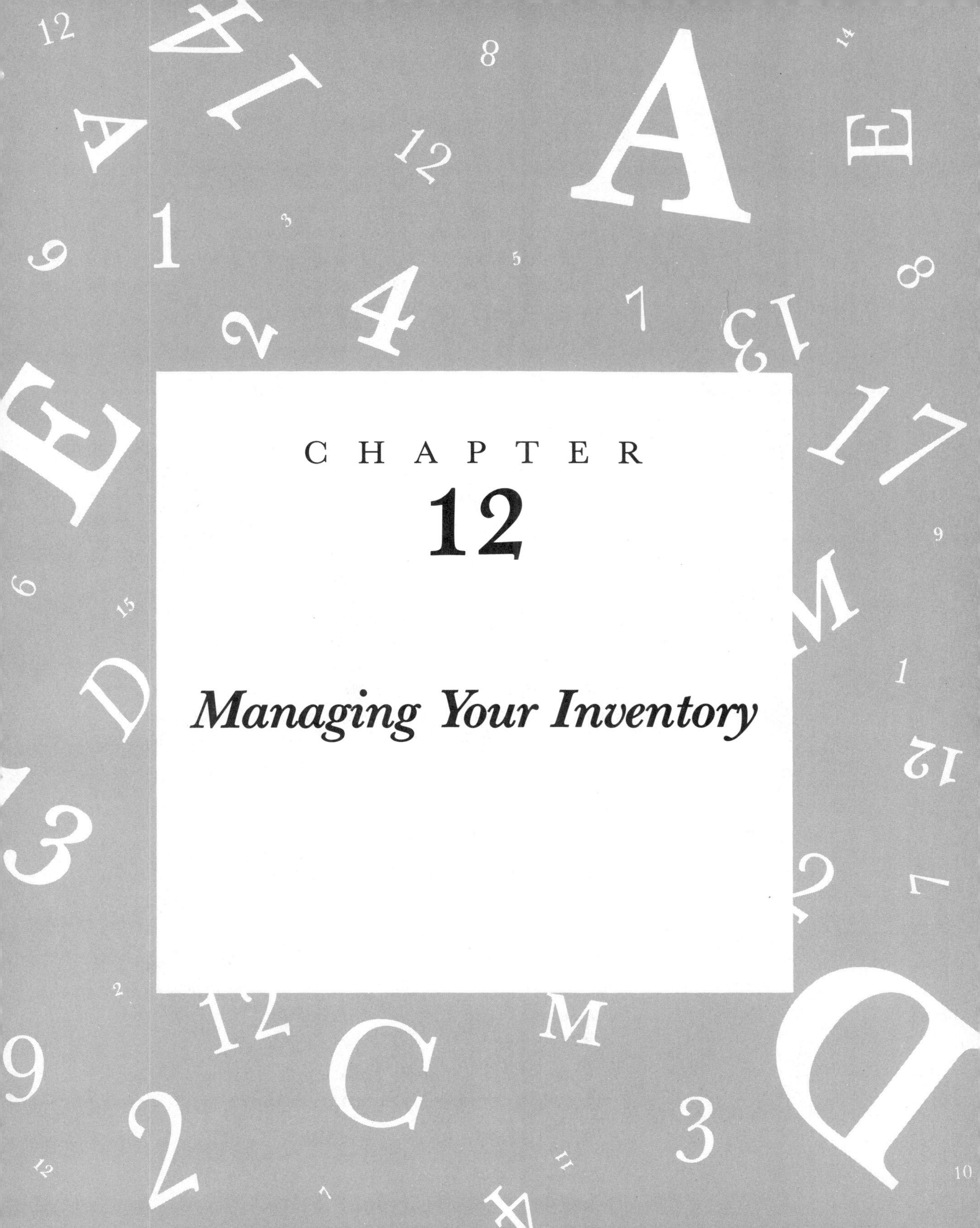

CHAPTER

12

Managing Your Inventory

MANAGING YOUR INVENTORY INVOLVES ENTERING assembled products, reconciling your inventory records with your actual merchandise in stock, reviewing product and services reports, changing product prices, and printing statistical reports. This chapter describes how to accomplish these tasks. Forecasting and year-end functions for inventory are discussed in Chapter 14.

MANAGING PRODUCT ASSEMBLY

3.1 Product assembly is not available.

As discussed in Chapter 4, if you plan to sell an assembled product, you must define the finished goods and its components. After these products have been defined, you must enter an assembly transaction, print the Assembly journal, and post the transactions.

ENTERING ASSEMBLY TRANSACTIONS

* From the Transactions menu, select Assembly.

You must post all merchandise received and customer invoices before you can assemble products. When you are ready to assemble a product, select the Assembly option from the Transactions menu.

As an example, we'll assemble the gold-mining souvenirs we defined in Chapter 4. The completed transaction is shown in Figure 12.1. The following steps are used to enter the sample assembly transaction:

1. Press ↵ to assign a transaction number.
2. Enter **Mar Stock** in the Reference field to indicate that this transaction is to assemble stock you need for March sales.
3. Press ↵ to accept the system date as the date of the transaction. You can also press F4 to change the date.
4. In the Product Information section of the screen, select Assemble as the Action. If you wanted to disassemble an assembled product, you would select Disassemble as the Action.
5. Enter **S395**, the code for the assembled souvenir, in the Product Code field. The description in the product record appears.

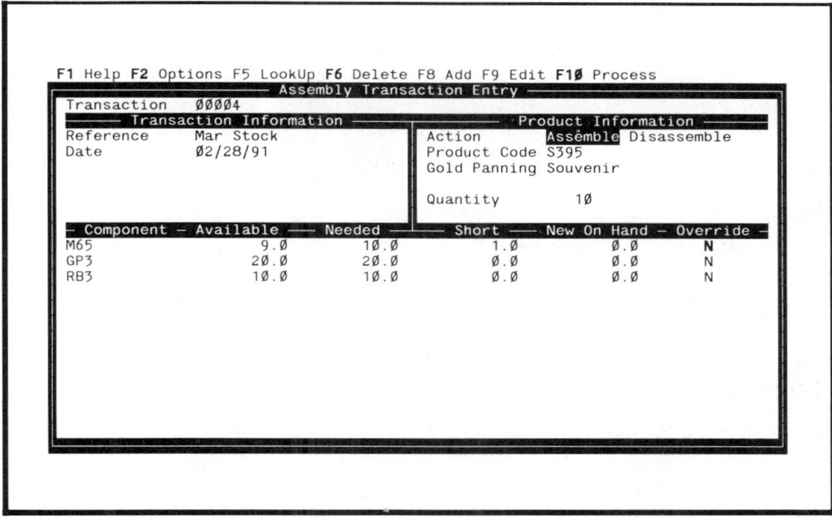

Figure 12.1: Entering an assembly transaction

6. Enter **10** in the Quantity field as the number of units you want to assemble.

The program displays all the components that make up the finished goods and their status, based on your current inventory. If you do not have enough of any component, as in our example, you can override the requirement by entering a Y in the Override field and assemble the product using what you do have in stock. However, there are two reasons to avoid using the Override option:

- You must physically assemble the finished goods from the exact number of components shown in the assembly transaction or your book inventory will not agree with your actual inventory.
- If you later disassemble the goods, your files will indicate that *all* components typically included in the finished goods (according to the definition in the product record) are returned to stock, even if you were short one or more of them during the assembly process. Again, the result is an incorrect book inventory.

Instead of overriding the missing components, it is recommended that you decrease the number of finished goods you are requesting. You must first delete the current transaction (press F6) and then repeat the process. When you get to the Quantity field, enter the number that can be assembled from the components you have available.

7. When you have enough components for the requested number of finished goods, press F10 to process the transaction.

DacEasy marks the components used in the assembly as committed and places the transaction in the assembly transaction file. You can enter several transactions before posting. However, you must post the transactions before the on-hand fields of the inventory files are updated.

PRINTING AND EDITING ASSEMBLY TRANSACTIONS

From the Journals menu, select Assembly.

A product assembly transaction must be posted before your product file reflects the creation of finished goods. As with every transaction in DacEasy, you must print the journal before posting. To print the journal, select Assembly from the Journals menu. Press ↵ in the From and To fields to select all transactions for posting. Press F10 and select Printer as the Report Disposition.

Review the listing before posting. If you discover errors, you can edit the transaction. Select Assembly from the Transactions menu and enter the number of the assembly transaction that contains errors, make corrections, and press F10 to save your entry.

POSTING ASSEMBLY TRANSACTIONS

From the Posting menu, select Assembly.

You cannot post an assembly transaction if any component was short and you did not override it.

When you are satisfied that all the assembly transactions are correct, you can post them. Select Assembly from the Posting menu, then enter the date on which you want the transactions posted and a reference.

When posting is complete, the committed units in the component file are released, and the on-hand units are reduced. The number of assembled products are added to the on-hand units in the finished goods record. The last purchase price field is updated. The program calculates the amount by adding the cost of all the components together and dividing by the number of finished goods assembled.

MAKING ASSEMBLY ADJUSTMENTS

* From the Periodic menu, select Inventory. From the submenu, select Assembly Adjustment.

After you have defined products that require assembly in your product file, you can alter the definition of several products at once by adding, replacing, or deleting a component. To make such changes, select the Inventory option from the Periodic menu, and then choose Assembly Adjustment.

As an example, suppose that you have several camera packages that include a particular brand of camera, a wide-angle lens for that camera, and a camera bag. For a brief period of time, as a promotion, you are including five rolls of film with every camera sale. You would include the film by completing the fields on the Assembly Adjustment screen, as shown in Figure 12.2. The following steps are used to enter the sample adjustment:

1. In the Component field, enter **ASA400**, the code for the film you want to include in the finished goods. If you were replacing one component with another, you would enter the code for the old component in the Component field.

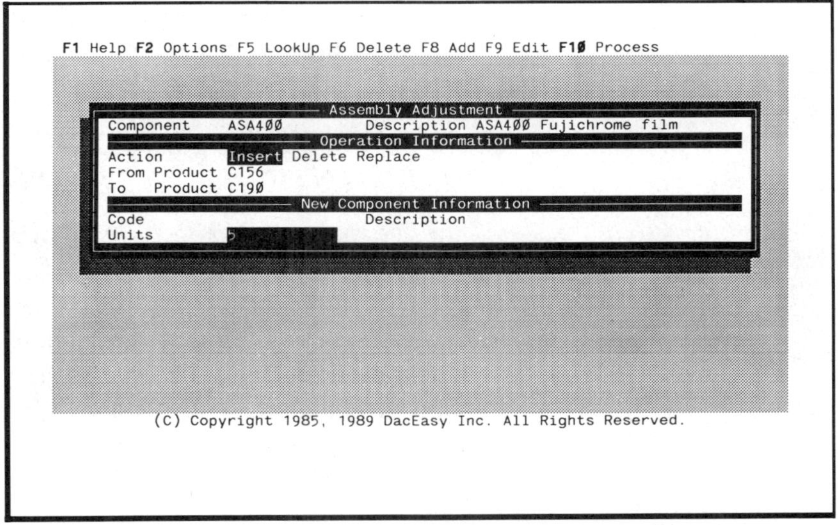

Figure 12.2: Adjusting the components in the finished goods definition

2. Verify that you have entered the correct code by reviewing the description supplied from the product record.
3. Select Insert as the Action. The other options, Delete and Replace, allow you to delete one component from one or several products or replace one component with another.
4. Enter **C156**, the code of the first finished product to which you want to add film, in the From Product field.
5. Enter **C190**, the code of the last finished product to which you want to add film, in the To Product field.

To group products for actions, you must have coded your finished goods in a manner that allows you to indicate a range (refer to the section about coding and sorting considerations in Chapter 1). All products within the range you enter will be affected, whether or not they are related.

The Code field in the New Component Information section of the screen is for the code of a product that is to replace an existing component. Leave it blank if you are inserting or deleting a component.

6. Enter **5** in the Units field to indicate that you want to add five rolls of film to the camera packages. Use the selling fraction in this field.
7. Press F10 to process that adjustment.

You can print an assembly report, as described in the next section, to verify the transaction. Any product assembly transaction you generate after you process the adjustment will include the film. When the promotion is over, you can use the Assembly Adjustment option on the Periodic menu to delete the film from the camera packages.

PRINTING THE ASSEMBLY AND COMPONENT ANALYSIS REPORTS

From the Reports menu, select Inventory. From the submenu, select Assembly.

The assembly and component analysis reports complement each other. They both list the finished goods and their components. The assembly report is sorted by finished goods, and the component analysis report is sorted by component. These reports help you keep track of which inventory items are sold separately as well as included in a finished product, which are included in a finished product but not sold separately, and which products are made of components that need to be assembled periodically.

To print either report, select Inventory from the Reports menu, and then choose Assembly. Both reports are listed on the submenu. You can restrict either report by entering a range to print.

KEEPING TRACK OF YOUR PHYSICAL INVENTORY

Your inventory is originally established when you create a record for each product and enter the on-hand units, as described in Chapter 4. Thereafter, activity posted for merchandise received and customer sales updates your on-hand data. This running total of items in inventory is called the *perpetual*, or *book*, *inventory*. It may or may not agree with what is actually in your warehouse and store.

The quantity of stock you keep on hand and the rate at which it turns over determine how often you reorder merchandise. A regularly scheduled reorder day will ensure that you don't unexpectedly run out of an item. Keeping close tabs on your stock eliminates managing customer back orders or worse, losing a sale because you didn't have the merchandise.

Because your inventory is an asset, keeping track of it is an important function. DacEasy adds and subtracts items from the perpetual inventory as you buy and sell each item. However, discrepancies occur between what you really have and what your records say you have. The difference is caused by breakage, spoilage, and, unfortunately, theft. You should take regular physical counts of each item and change the totals in your records. This ensures that the worth of your business assets is accurately stated on your financial reports.

Count each inventory item and compare the results to the inventory amounts in your records at least once a year. A more frequent count, even monthly, will protect you from undetected losses and help you take steps to rectify unsatisfactory inventory handling before it becomes a major problem.

There are several steps involved in taking the inventory, recording it, and adjusting your records, as explained in the following sections.

PRINTING INVENTORY COUNT SHEETS

From the Reports menu, select Inventory. From the submenu, select Count Sheets.

3.1 From the Reports menu, select Inventory. From the submenu, select Print Count Sheets.

Taking a physical inventory is easier when you have a list of all your inventory items, or count sheets, for reference. DacEasy provides count sheets that list the product code, description, location, department, and the vendor, with room to write the results of your physical inventory count. Each inventory item is listed with space for units, selling fractions, and remarks. Figure 12.3 shows an example of a printed count sheet.

```
Date : 06/25/91                         The Emporium                              Page 1
Time : 8:49 AM                         321 Main Street
                                       P. O. Box 4512
                                   Yourtown, Anystate 95842

Sorted by: Bin                          Count Sheets               Ranked by: Inventory Number


Inventory Nbr. Description                   Unit     Fraction Dept.  Bin      Vendor     Units      Fractions Remarks
-------------- ----------------------------- -------- -------- ----- -------- ---------- ---------- ---------- ------------------
D18-42         China Teapots                 Each     1        02    D8       PACK       ________.__________ __________________
D23-10         Rockwell-Cobbler              Each     1        02    D8       PACK       ________.__________ __________________
Subtotal  D8 : 2

P261287        Clawtuff Cat Condo            Each     1        02    P3       FOUR       ________.__________ __________________
Subtotal  P3 : 1

P11001         Petromalt 50g - Cats          Box      4        02    P5       FOUR       ________.__________ __________________
PDC192         Science Diet 4lb-Cat          Bag      1        02    P5       FOUR       ________.__________ __________________
Subtotal  P5 : 2

MN301          Keene 3" Gold Dredge          Each     1        01    R        MINE       ________.__________ __________________
MN692          White Metal Detector          Each     1        01    R        MINE       ________.__________ __________________
MN700          Plastic Gold Pans             Dozen    12       01    R        MINE       ________.__________ __________________
Subtotal  R : 3

Total Products :  8
```

Figure 12.3: Count sheet for a physical inventory

To print the list, select the Inventory option from the Reports menu, and then choose Count Sheets. Choose the sorting and ranking criteria using the procedure outlined in Chapter 5. By selecting the appropriate criteria, you can print count sheets for a department, location, or vendor, as well as for your entire inventory. You might want to sort by item location (bin) to make counting easier, as shown in Figure 12.4.

ENTERING PHYSICAL INVENTORY

* From the Transactions menu, select Physical Inventory.

As you receive completed inventory count sheets, you should enter the information into DacEasy. The previous count will be incremented by the current count when you enter the amounts from additional sheets. If a listed product is not in stock, still record the item

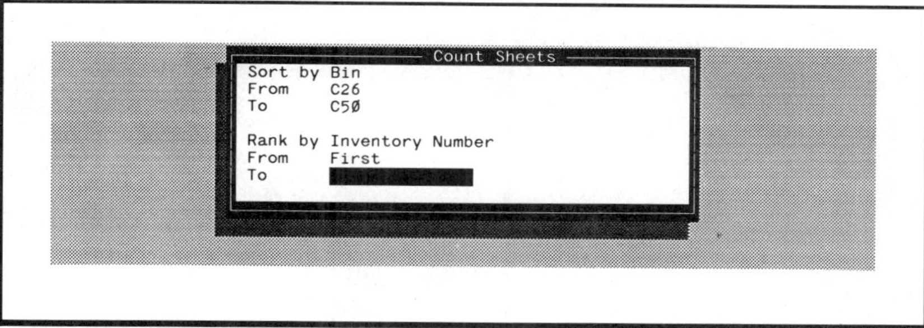

Figure 12.4: Sorting count sheets by location

3.1 From the Transaction menu, select Inventory. From the submenu, select Enter Physical Inventory.

3.1 To completely delete the count for any item, enter the product number and press F6. All accumulations for the item will be deleted. Press Esc to record the entries.

number and enter zero for the amount on hand. Your inventory records may show that there are units on hand, and this discrepancy will be adjusted along with any others when you post your physical inventory.

To record physical inventory amounts, select the Physical Inventory option from the Transactions menu. You will see the Physical Inventory screen.

Enter the product number of the counted item in the Code field, and the product description will appear in the Description field. The program displays the accumulated count from previous entries in the Previous Count field. Enter the amount of items counted in the Counted field using selling fractions. You can enter an amount preceded by a minus sign to reverse an earlier entry. In the Total field, the program displays the new total of items. When you have recorded the information on the count sheet, press F10 to record the entries.

Figure 12.5 shows an example of a Physical Inventory screen. Let's review some of the entries in the figure. On the sixth line, the data-entry person corrected an error on the line above for baseball shirts, size small, by reentering the amount preceded by a minus sign to reverse it. On the next line, she entered the correct amount. A zero amount has been entered on the eighth line for baseball shirts, size extra large. They were listed on the count sheet, but there is no stock on hand. The inventory records might not agree with this total, so it must be recorded. Finally, the last line records a second entry for Reebok aerobic shoes, the same product as listed on the first line. The clerk found more later in the wrong location.

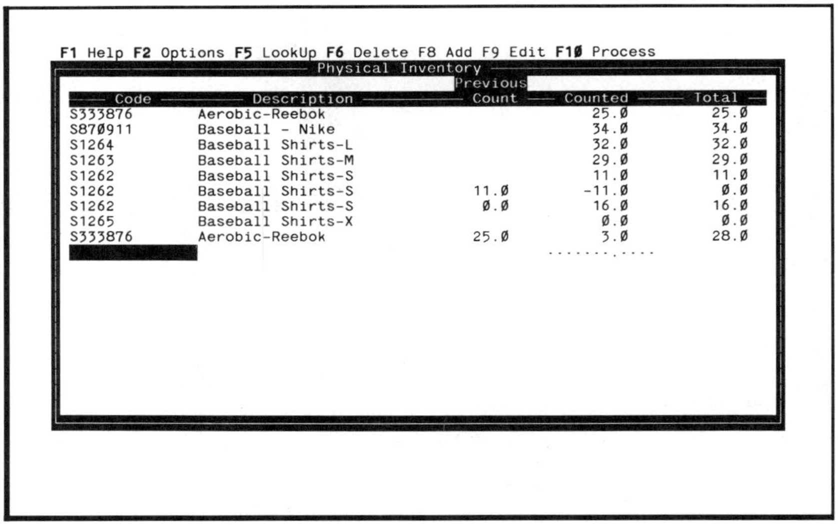

```
F1 Help F2 Options F5 LookUp F6 Delete F8 Add F9 Edit F10 Process
                         Physical Inventory
                                               Previous
   Code              Description                 Count      Counted      Total
S333876       Aerobic-Reebok                                   25.0        25.0
S870911       Baseball - Nike                                  34.0        34.0
S1264         Baseball Shirts-L                                32.0        32.0
S1263         Baseball Shirts-M                                29.0        29.0
S1262         Baseball Shirts-S                                11.0        11.0
S1262         Baseball Shirts-S                   11.0        -11.0         0.0
S1262         Baseball Shirts-S                    0.0         16.0        16.0
S1265         Baseball Shirts-X                                 0.0         0.0
S333876       Aerobic-Reebok                      25.0          3.0        28.0
```

Figure 12.5: Entering the physical inventory count

PRINTING THE INVENTORY JOURNAL

* From the Journals menu, select Physical Inventory.

After you enter the physical inventory count, you should review the Inventory journal to be sure the final count is right. The report lists the physical count, perpetual inventory, and difference in units and fractions between the two.

3.1 A similar inventory comparison report is available. From the Reports menu, select Inventory. From the submenu, select Physical Perpetual Compare. After you enter the sorting criteria, the report will print.

To print the journal, select the Physical Inventory option from the Journals menu. Review any differences to be certain the physical count is accurate. The book inventory will be adjusted to match the physical count when you post inventory adjustments. Make any corrections as explained in the preceding section and reprint the journal.

POSTING ADJUSTMENTS TO INVENTORY

* From the Posting menu, select Physical Inventory.

The purpose of taking a physical inventory and comparing it to your perpetual inventory is to correct discrepancies. After you check the physical count, you should post the results. DacEasy will adjust the inventory file in your system to match the count you took of the stock on hand.

Before you begin posting, make certain that every inventory item has been entered through the Physical Inventory option on the Transactions menu, even if none of the product is in stock. Print the Inventory journal. Be sure that the physical count is correct; your records will be changed to match it. Of course, back up your files.

To post your inventory adjustments, select the Physical Inventory option from the Posting menu and respond to the prompts. Chapter 5 describes the posting procedure in more detail.

The units-on-hand information and dollar value of the inventory are updated in each product record, and the transactions are placed in the IN journal to await posting to the general ledger.

POSTING INVENTORY ADJUSTMENTS TO THE GENERAL LEDGER

* From the Posting menu, select General Ledger.

3.1 When prompted, choose to print the IN journal.

When you post your inventory adjustments to the general ledger, they are posted to the appropriate cost of goods account for each product and to the inventory account defined in the general ledger interface table.

Before posting these adjustments to the general ledger, you should print the general ledger listing to keep a printed detail of the transactions created by the inventory adjustment. Select General Ledger from the Journals menu. Then choose Listing as the Journal Type and IN as the Journal Code.

To post to the general ledger, select the General Ledger option from the Posting menu and respond to the prompts. All transactions in the general ledger transaction file, including the inventory adjustments, will be posted.

REVIEWING PRODUCT REPORTS

From the Reports menu, select Inventory. From the submenu, select Alert Report, Product Listing, Price List, or Activity Report.

DacEasy produces several helpful product listings. You can refer to them when ordering merchandise, determining inventory value, and adjusting product prices.

PRINTING THE PRODUCT ALERT REPORT

3.1 From the Reports menu, select Inventory. From the submenu, select Product Alert Report, Product Listing, Product Price List, or Product Activity Report.

The product alert report lists inventory items that have met or fallen below the minimum stocking level you entered in the product record. It includes the number of items on order, optimum reorder amount you established, available units, minimum quantity, number of units under minimum, price, and extended purchase amount for the recommended reorder quantity.

You can use this report as a guide when ordering merchandise to determine the amount to order, the vendor to order from, what your last purchase price was, and your cost if you order the recommended quantity. This information should prevent you from overstocking or understocking items.

3.1 As soon as you enter the sequencing criteria, DacEasy will print the product reports.

To print the report, select the Inventory option from the Reports menu, and then choose Alert Report. Enter the sorting and ranking criteria, as described in Chapter 5. Press F10 and select the report disposition.

PRINTING A LISTING OF YOUR PRODUCTS

The product listing includes information from each product record. It lists the sales price, minimum and reorder quantities, last sale and purchase dates, last purchase price, standard cost, and average cost for each item.

Management can use the detail listing to analyze the total inventory value in the general ledger. The purchasing department can refer to it to review the product lines you carry.

To print the report, select the Inventory option from the Reports menu, and then choose Product Listing. Select the sorting and ranking criteria, press F10, and select the report disposition.

PRINTING A PRICE LIST

The price list summarizes pricing information for each inventory item. It lists the department, if the product is taxable, the sales price, and the unit cost. You can encrypt the unit costs to ensure confidential pricing. This report is useful as a catalog, a price list, and a guideline for increasing or decreasing prices.

To print the price list, select the Inventory option from the Reports menu, and then choose Price List. After you select the sorting and ranking criteria, you can make an entry in the Cost Code field. This entry specifies the encrypting method to be used when printing the cost for each product. If you leave the Cost Code field blank, no cost will be printed. To print the actual cost, enter 1234567890.

If you want to print costs in code, enter the code as the Cost Code. Whatever characters you enter represent 1 through 0, reading left to right. You could use letters or symbols for numbers, or even numbers to represent other numbers. For example, you might use the row of letters below the top row of numbers on the keyboard to represent those numbers, as shown in Figure 12.6. In the example, Q=1, W=2, and so on to P=0. Using this coding method, a cost of $249.50 would print as WRO.TP.

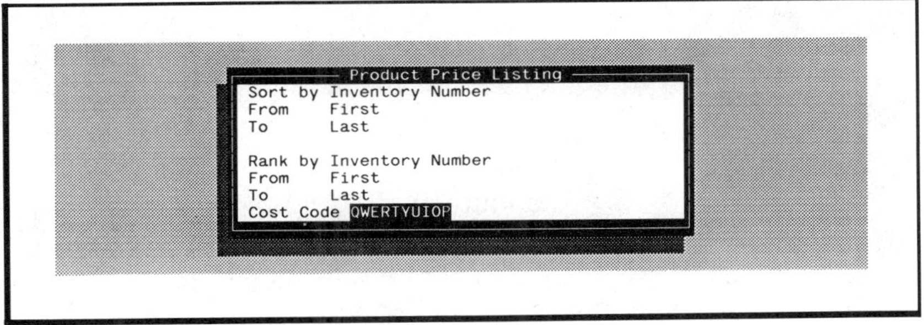

Figure 12.6: Entering a cost code for a price list

PRINTING A PRODUCT ACTIVITY REPORT

3.1 The turn rate and gross return on investment are included in the activity report.

The activity report is a status report on your inventory. It is the only report that lists units currently on hand for every product. It also includes unit price and cost, year-to-date purchases, sales, and costs.

This report helps you to determine how an item is doing. You can adjust your prices wisely after you see how each product sells. To move a slow item, you might need to lower the price. If an item is popular, a small price increase might bring in more profit per sale without lowering the number of sales.

To print the activity report, select the Inventory option from the Reports menu, and then choose Activity Report. Enter the sequencing criteria, press F10, and choose the report disposition.

ASSIGNING NEW PRICES TO INVENTORY ITEMS

* From the Periodic menu, select Inventory. From the submenu, select Price Assignment.

3.1 From the Transaction menu, select Inventory. From the submenu, select Price Assignment.

You must change prices for services in each individual record. They cannot be changed by using the Price Assignment option.

3.1 You can both sort and rank your selections.

3.1 Press the spacebar to change the method.

Products you purchase for resale must be priced to cover not only your purchase price, but your overhead as well, and still leave a profit for you. You will need to adjust prices when your business costs change. Use the product price list and activity report to help you determine whether or not to change your sales prices.

DacEasy provides a very flexible method of changing the price on each product. You can quickly increase or decrease the price of every product individually within the category you select.

Profits are best controlled by pricing items individually, although DacEasy does allow you to change prices identically for a range of items. DacEasy uses the last cost as the base for calculating the new sales price. You can increase or decrease the price by a flat dollar amount or mark it up or down by a percentage.

To change prices, select the Inventory option from the Periodic menu, and then choose Price Assignment. Enter the sorting criteria in the Sort by field and the codes for the first and last products to be priced in the From and To fields. Select the ranking criteria from the choices listed and enter the range in the From and To fields. DacEasy will display the product number, description, price, and last cost for each item in the criteria range.

The % or $ field indicates the method you want to use in the price change, percent or dollar. Press F9 to change the method from % to $, and then enter the amount to use in the price change. For example, a $12 dollar increase is entered 12.000; a 40 percent markup is entered 40.000.

The program calculates the new price based on your most recent cost. To review the mathematical equation DacEasy uses to calculate the new price, press F1 to display help when the cursor is in the Amount field under the heading % or $. You can override the new

3.1 Press Alt-P to print your calculations and press Esc to exit and save your changes.

price to round it to a logical amount. For example, you might change the calculated price of 8.947 to 8.99.

When you have completed the changes, you can print a report listing your calculations by pressing F7. Press F10 to exit and save your changes. Don't forget to print a new price list and distribute it to customers and staff.

Figure 12.7 shows an example of assigning new prices to some bicycle models. A percentage was used to increase the price for the men's bicycle (a popular seller) and to decrease the price on one women's bicycle (a slow mover) for a special sale. No change was entered for another women's bicycle that was part of the selection range. The price of the child's bicycle was increased by an arbitrary dollar amount.

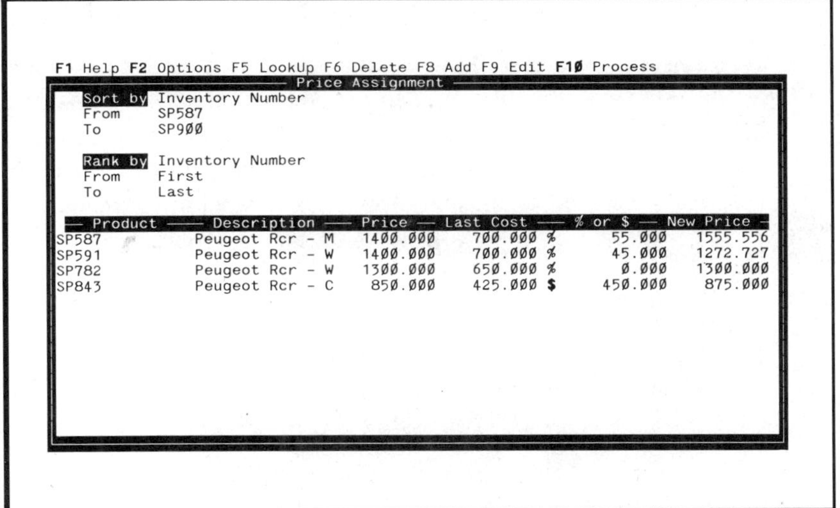

Figure 12.7: Entering price changes based on last cost

PRINTING A LISTING OF YOUR SERVICES

* From the Reports menu, select Inventory. From the submenu, select Service Listing.

The service listing includes your services, sales price, and, optionally, number of units sold and sales dollars. You can use this report as a price list or to evaluate how each service is selling.

3.1 From the Reports menu, select Inventory. From the submenu, select Service Report.

To print the list, select the Inventory option from the Reports menu, and then choose Service Listing. Select the sorting and ranking criteria, as described in Chapter 5. You might want to rank all your services by last sales date to determine if any service is no longer being used by your customers. You can then attempt to promote that service or decide to eliminate it from your offerings.

At the prompt asking if you want to include sales information, press ↵ to accept the default Yes if you want to print the number of units and dollars sold for each item. Otherwise, select No. If you want to use the report as a price list, you probably do not want to include the sales information.

PRINTING INVENTORY OR SERVICE YEAR-TO-DATE STATISTICS

* From the Periodic menu, select Inventory. From the submenu, select Print Statistical YTD.

3.1 From the Periodic menu, select Inventory. From the submenu, select Forecasting, then select Print Statistical YTD. You select whether or not to include costs and profits in the report.

The statistical year-to-date reports list all the data in the historical file for each product or service. By printing inventory and service statistical reports each month, you can trace sales cycles. If you determine high and low sales months for each product and service, you can plan appropriate stocking levels and staff requirements.

To print a statistical report, select the Inventory option from the Periodic menu, then choose Print Statistical YTD. In the Type field, select to print the inventory or service statistics. Select to sort by Code, Department, Vendor, or Bin, and then enter the first and last records in the From and To fields. The historical costs and profits will be included on the report.

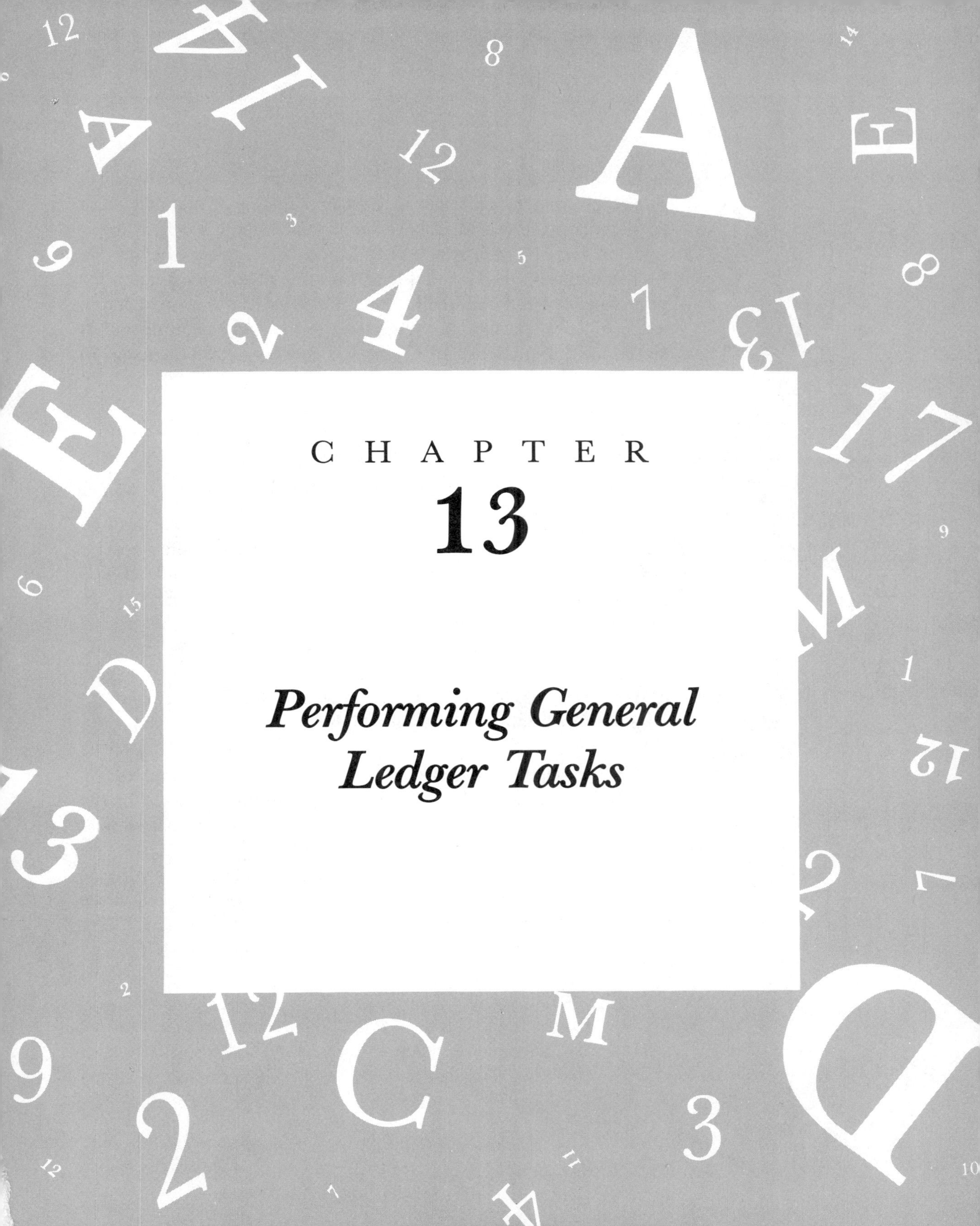

CHAPTER

13

Performing General Ledger Tasks

THE FEW TRANSACTIONS THAT ARE ENTERED directly in the general ledger are usually adjustments that take place at the end of the period. All the activity from the other modules is summarized into journals, which should be posted to the general ledger regularly. The general ledger also holds the information for your financial statements. This chapter discusses various general ledger entries, posting to the general ledger, and printing financial reports. Forecasting and year-end processing are discussed in Chapter 14.

RECORDING MISCELLANEOUS GENERAL LEDGER TRANSACTIONS

* From the Transactions menu, select General Ledger.

3.1 From the Transaction menu, select General Ledger.

Most of your business activity is recorded in your books through one of the subsidiary modules: Purchase Order, Accounts Payable, Billing, Accounts Receivable, Cash, Inventory, and Payroll. Miscellaneous transactions you enter directly into the general ledger are those that are unrelated to sales or purchases. These entries do not affect a specific vendor, customer, or inventory item. For example, you may enter capital investments or withdrawals by the principals, depreciation, return of a utility deposit, and interest on bank accounts. You can also enter payroll information if you do not use DacEasy Payroll.

When you enter a miscellaneous transaction in the general ledger, you must determine if a debit or credit should be posted to the account. Remember, when you have completed the transaction, it must balance; the debits must equal the credits.

To enter a miscellaneous general ledger transaction, select the General Ledger option from the Transactions menu. You will see the General Ledger Transaction Entry screen, shown in Figure 13.1.

ENTERING EARNED INTEREST

A typical use of the General Ledger Transaction Entry screen is to record auxiliary income, such as interest earned on your savings

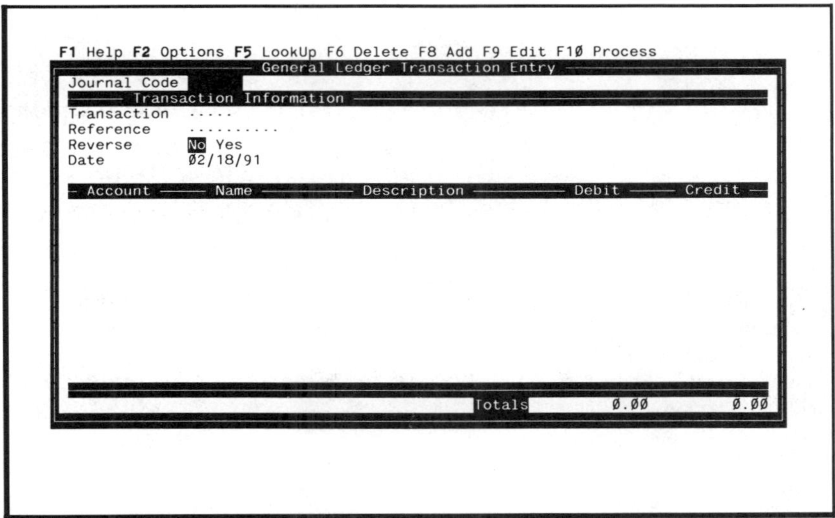

Figure 13.1: General Ledger Transaction Entry screen

account. You must record the income and increase your cash account by the amount added to your savings account.

Figure 13.2 shows an example of the entries for interest that is automatically added to your account each quarter.

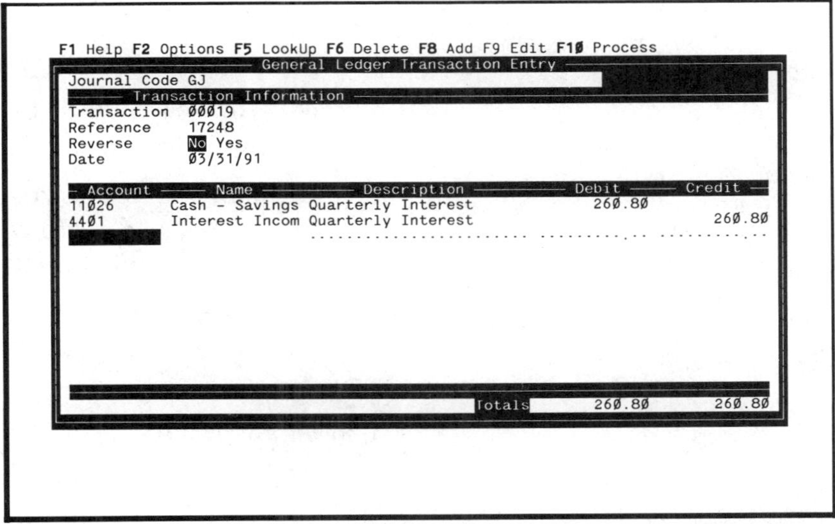

Figure 13.2: Entering miscellaneous income in the general ledger

The following procedure is used to enter the sample transaction:

1. For Journal Code, enter **GJ**, which stands for General journal. You can create as many journal types as you need to categorize your direct entries. However, the journal codes SU, PO, AP, BI, AR, IN, CH, and PY are reserved for transfers from the subsidiary modules; you cannot enter transactions directly from the general ledger into these journals.

> 3.1 Enter a transaction number in the Transaction field. The Reference and Reverse fields do not exist.

2. Press ↵ in the Transaction field to assign a number to the transaction.
3. In the Reference field, enter **17248**, the number of your savings account.
4. Press ↵ to accept No in the Reverse field. We will discuss reversals later.
5. Override the system date in the Date field by entering **033191**, the date the addition was made. Although it is now April 2 in the example, the books have not yet been closed for March, so the activity can be posted as of the day it took place.

> Remember, you can only make entries to accounts designated as detail accounts in your chart of accounts. Also, you cannot enter a transaction directly into the accounts in the general ledger interface table for Accounts Receivable, Accounts Payable, and Inventory.

6. In the Account field, enter **11026**, the general ledger account number for Cash–Savings, and the program displays the account name.
7. Enter **Quarterly Interest** in the Description field.
8. Enter **260.80** in the Debit field to record the amount the bank deposited to your account.
9. Enter the number of the offsetting income account, **4401**, in the Account field, and the program inserts the account's name and the description from the first line.

> 3.1 Use F9 to duplicate amounts.

10. Press ↵ to accept the description, and then press F7 in the Credit field to automatically enter the same amount as the debit entry.
11. When all entries are complete and the debits equal the credits, press F10 to record the transaction.

> 3.1 Use F2 to create a balancing entry.

If you enter numerous items only to find your entries don't balance (debits do not equal credits), DacEasy will not let you process the transaction, but you don't have to lose everything you entered. Just press F3 to enter the unbalanced amount in the Difference account. In this way, you can save your work, and then return to it after you research the error. Be aware, this is just a short-term solution. You must correctly apply the amount held in limbo before you can post to the general ledger.

ENTERING CAPITAL INVESTMENTS AND WITHDRAWALS

If the cash account affected by an investment, withdrawal, or other general ledger transaction is a checking account you are reconciling to a bank statement, use the Receipts or Payments option on the Transactions, Cash submenu instead of the General Ledger option on the Transactions menu and select GL in the Paid From and Pay To fields.

When you invest in your business or withdraw cash from it, you can enter the transaction directly into the general ledger through the General Ledger Transaction Entry screen. For example, suppose that you and another photographer are going into business together, each contributing something to the new company. You invested cash in the business. Your partner provided some darkroom equipment, which has a value of $3,500, and added cash to his investment so it would equal your contribution. The entries to record these capital investments are shown in Figure 13.3.

In a single proprietorship or a partnership, each principal has a drawing account to record how much he or she takes out of the business. As profits are distributed to the principals, their capital

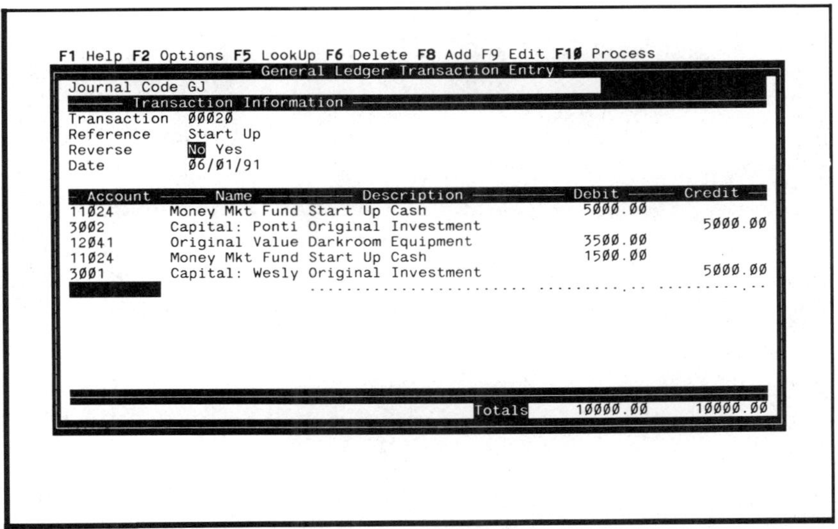

Figure 13.3: Recording capital investments

accounts increase. Most business owners take an amount of cash out of the business on a monthly basis. This transaction is recorded in a drawing account, which acts as a contra account (an offset) to the principal's capital account. An example of the entries for a capital withdrawal is shown in Figure 13.4.

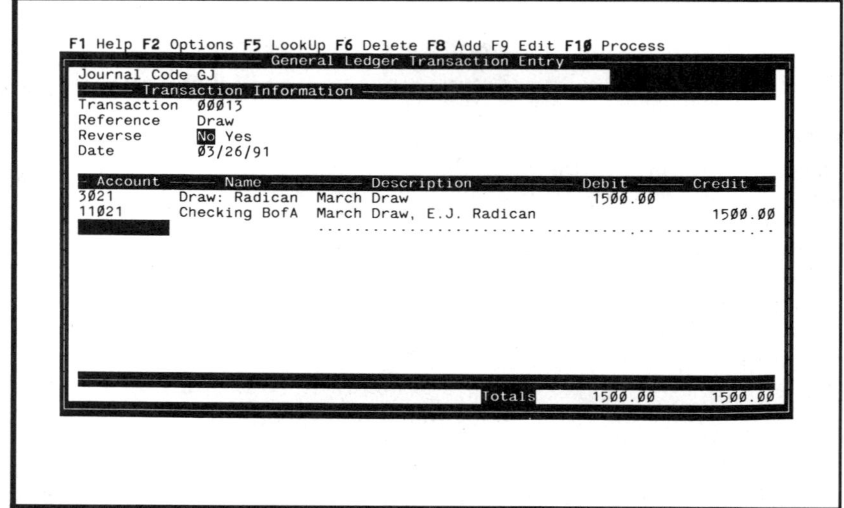

Figure 13.4: Recording capital withdrawals

RECORDING MISCELLANEOUS RECEIPTS IN THE GENERAL LEDGER

* From the Transactions menu, select Cash. From the Entry submenu, select Receipts.

3.1 Enter Miscellaneous receipts through the General Ledger Transaction Entry Option.

If you receive money from a source other that a customer or a vendor, such as a check for money that was held in escrow for property taxes, you record it in the general ledger.

To record miscellaneous receipts, select Cash from the Transactions menu, and then choose Receipts from the Entry submenu. Complete the heading as explained in Chapter 7, but select GL in the Paid From field. You can enter a name to identify the payment in the space next to the Code prompt. After you enter the amount of the cash, the General Ledger Receipts window appears, as shown in Figure 13.5.

The cash account entered in the Bank field of the heading will be debited. Enter the number of the general ledger account to credit in

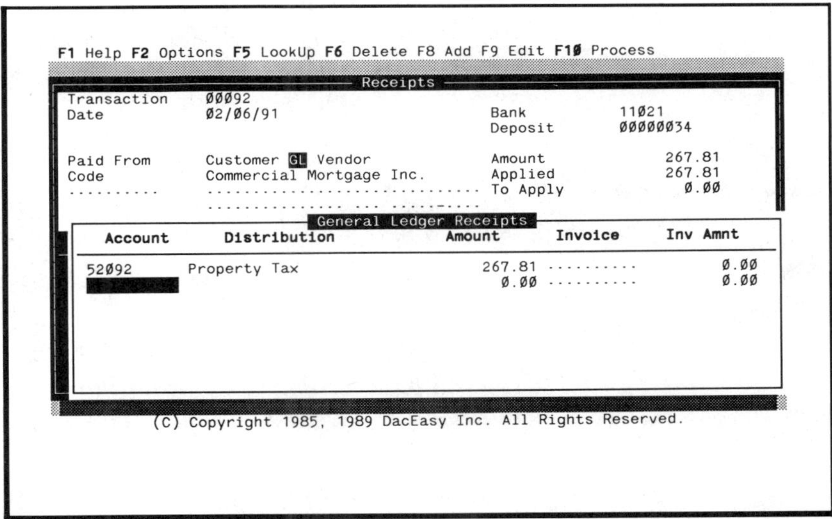

Figure 13.5: Entering miscellaneous receipts in the general ledger

the Account field, and then enter the portion of the receipt to be applied to the account in the Amount field. Enter the original invoice number and its amount in the Invoice and Inv Amnt fields.

CORRECTING OR DELETING GENERAL LEDGER TRANSACTION ENTRIES

You can correct or delete an entire transaction originating in the general ledger after it has been processed, and even if the General Ledger journal has printed, but you must reverse the transaction if it has been posted. You cannot recall and delete a transaction that originated in a subsidiary journal. You must return to the module and make a reversing entry.

To correct an unposted general ledger transaction, recall it by entering the journal code and transaction number in the General Ledger Transaction Entry screen, and make the changes. With the cursor in the Account field, press Shift-F6 to delete a line or F6 to delete the entire transaction. The transaction will appear on listings as DELETED.

3.1 Press Alt-D to delete a line. There is no record of a deleted transaction. You can use the journal transaction number again.

If you used the Difference account to force a general ledger transaction to balance, DacEasy won't let you post until you correct it.

When you are adjusting a transaction that contained an entry to the Difference account, delete the line containing the entry to the Difference account after you have made all your corrections.

PRINTING GENERAL LEDGER JOURNALS

* From the Journals menu, select General Ledger.

3.1 From the Journals menu, select G/L Journal.

3.1 There is only one report, the General Ledger journal. It is similar to the 4.1 general ledger listing, except it is cleared of transactions during month-end processing.

When posting to the subsidiary modules is completed, DacEasy creates summary journals and sends them to the general ledger. The journals from the subsidiary modules are BI from Billing, AR from Accounts Receivable, PO from Purchase Order, AP from Accounts Payable, IN from Inventory, CH from Cash, PY from Payroll (if you use DacEasy Payroll), and when you converted your old system to DacEasy, SU from setup. You enter miscellaneous transactions in the general ledger through other journals, which you designate. These are all contained in the General Ledger journal.

The General Ledger journal and listing show transactions by date. The general ledger listing prints alphabetically by journal code.

In the General Ledger journal, only unposted transactions are included. To print the journal, select General Ledger from the Journals menu. On the GL Journal screen, select Journal as the Journal Type. In the Date field, enter a date within the period you want to review.

The general ledger listing includes posted and unposted transactions. The report can be quite long because the listing includes all the activity from your entire accounting system. You can restrict it by journal and by date.

To print the general ledger listing, select General Ledger from the Journals menu and choose Listing as the Journal Type. Enter the number you want the page numbering to begin with in the Beginning Page field. You may want to keep your journal printouts in a file with consecutive page numbers by the month or year.

In the Beginning Journal Code and Ending Journal Code fields, enter the codes of the first and last journals you want to print, or press ↵ to start with the first or print through the last journal.

In the Beginning Date and Ending Date fields, enter the first and last transaction date to include in the journal. Press ↵ to start with the earliest transaction in the current year in the selected journals or print from the first of the year through the end of the file. Figure 13.6 shows an example of a completed GL Journal screen for printing a listing of transactions in the Petty Cash journal.

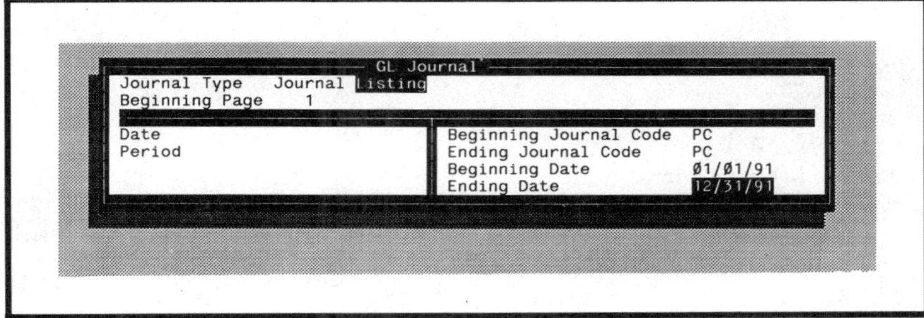

Figure 13.6: Printing a Petty Cash journal

Because the report could be lengthy, you might want to select Screen as the Report Disposition to display the information rather than printing it on paper.

REVIEWING JOURNALS ON THE SCREEN IN VERSION 3.1

3.1 From the Transaction menu, select General Ledger.

In version 3.1, you can display a journal's contents on the screen to see all the transactions for the current month in the general ledger.

To review summarized transactions in a subsidiary journal, select the General Ledger option from the Transaction menu. Enter the journal code and the transaction number assigned to the journal by the program. The transaction number for a subsidiary journal is the month and day it was created in the general ledger. For example, 0823 would be the transaction number for the journal containing transactions posted in a subsidiary module on August 23. This is also how the journal is identified in the General Ledger journal.

In the display, an asterisk next to an account number means that the transaction is posted. You must refer to the paper copy of the journal you printed prior to posting the transactions in the module to review detailed transactions that comprise the summary in a subsidiary journal.

You cannot edit or delete any information displayed from the subsidiary journals or posted miscellaneous general ledger transactions.

PRINTING THE GENERAL LEDGER ACTIVITY REPORT

* From the Reports menu, select General Ledger. From the submenu, select Activity Report.

3.1 From the Journals menu, select G/L Activity.

3.1 Month-end processing removes all the detail for that period from the general ledger activity report.

The general ledger account activity detail report is a listing of every general ledger transaction, grouped by account within the date range you specify. The listing also indicates whether or not the transaction has been posted to the general ledger.

You should review the report after the period's activity has been finalized, but before you close the period. If necessary, make corrections to the general ledger so the summary information in your financial statements is correct.

To print the general ledger activity report, select General Ledger from the Reports menu, and then choose Activity Report from the submenu. In the Print Accounts From and To fields, enter the numbers of the beginning and ending records to include on the report, or press ↵ to start with the first and end with the last. In the Print Dates From and To fields, enter the beginning and ending dates to include on the report (or press ↵).

For Initial Page, press ↵ to begin the page numbering with 1. If you want to start with another number, perhaps to keep the pages running consecutively from report to report throughout an entire month, enter the number for the first page of this report.

At the prompt asking if you want to print by page, select Yes if you want each account listed on a separate page. Select No if you want a running report, with page breaks only at the end of each sheet of paper. In the final field, Ranking, press ↵ to accept the default, Date, which sequences the report by date. Select Journal if you want to print the report by journal code and transaction number.

To print all the activity for the current period, accept the defaults to include the first through last records and enter the first and last dates of the period, as shown in Figure 13.7. Only accounts with activity will appear on the report. If you print more than one period, only transactions that you elected not to delete during period-end processing will appear. Because all activity is posted to detail accounts, no general accounts appear on this report.

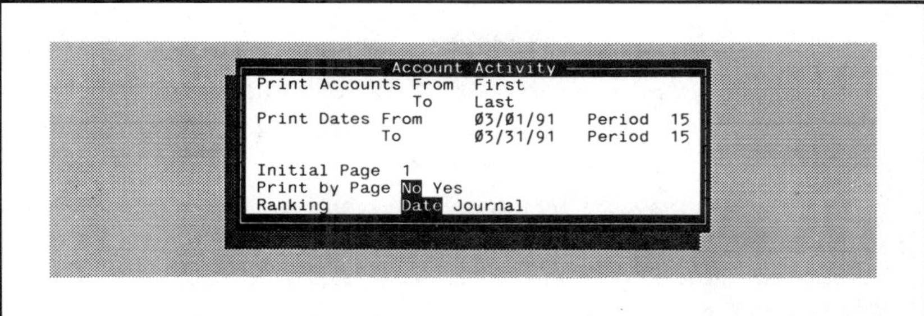

Figure 13.7: Printing a complete general ledger activity report for one month

POSTING TO THE GENERAL LEDGER

* From the Posting menu, select General Ledger.

When you post to the general ledger, all the transactions held in the general ledger transaction file are posted. These transactions include not only those originating in the general ledger itself, but also the transactions posted first to the subsidiary modules and summarized in the journals labeled SU, BI, AR, PO, AP, IN, CH, and PY (if you are using DacEasy Payroll). These transactions do not affect the general ledger accounts until you post to the general ledger. A good practice would be to post each module, print the resulting journals created for the general ledger, and post to the general ledger on a daily basis.

Remember, before posting to the general ledger, you must clear any transactions awaiting assignment in the Difference account. If the balance in the Difference account is not zero, DacEasy will print a list of the journals that are incomplete and cancel the posting process.

3.1 You enter the number of the month (1-12) to be posted. When the posting process is complete, DacEasy prints the total debits and credits posted to the general ledger.

To post to the general ledger, select the General Ledger option from the Posting menu. The procedure for posting to the general ledger is the same as the one for the subsidiary modules, except for the Date to Post prompt. Press ↵ to accept the default of the current period, or enter a date within the period you want to post. You can post to any period you haven't closed.

The posting date you used when posting transactions to the subsidiary modules determines if the transactions will be posted to the general ledger, depending on the period you select to post. The dates of miscellaneous general ledger entries determine whether they will be included.

The general ledger account balance that appears on your financial statements only includes transactions that have been posted to the general ledger. In contrast, the general ledger listing and activity report include all summarized transactions posted to the subsidiary modules and miscellaneous transactions in the general ledger, whether or not they are posted to the general ledger.

When the posting process is complete, DacEasy displays the total debits and credits posted to the general ledger. If you are uncertain of the posting status of any transaction, print a general ledger activity report, which indicates if a transaction has been posted to the general ledger.

REVERSING A POSTED TRANSACTION

After you post a transaction you entered directly into the general ledger, you must make reversing entries through the General Ledger Transaction Entry screen to correct it. Before you make these entries, review the original transaction to be sure you are creating the correct reversal. Until you close a period, you can review posted general ledger transactions on the screen. After the period is closed, posted transactions are removed from the general ledger transaction file. You will have to refer to the paper copy of the General Ledger journal you printed prior to closing the period.

As an example of reversing a posted transaction, suppose that your office staff worked through lunch to finish the period and run financial statements for a presentation. You gave the delivery boy $30 from petty cash to buy sandwiches and a presentation folder. He gave your cashier the change, but not the receipts. Hurrying to close the books, the staff posted the cash shortage rather than research it. Later, the delivery boy turned in the receipts. You need to reverse the posted cash shortage transaction. The original transaction and the correcting entries are shown in Figure 13.8.

The following procedure is used to reverse the sample transaction:

1. Enter **PC**, the code for Petty Cash journal, where the original transaction was posted.
2. Press ↵ in the Transaction field and enter **Register 4** in the Reference field.
3. Press ↵ to move through the Reverse and Date fields and enter **5401**, the general ledger number for the Cash Short account, in the Account field.
4. For Description, enter **6/30 shortage reconciled**.

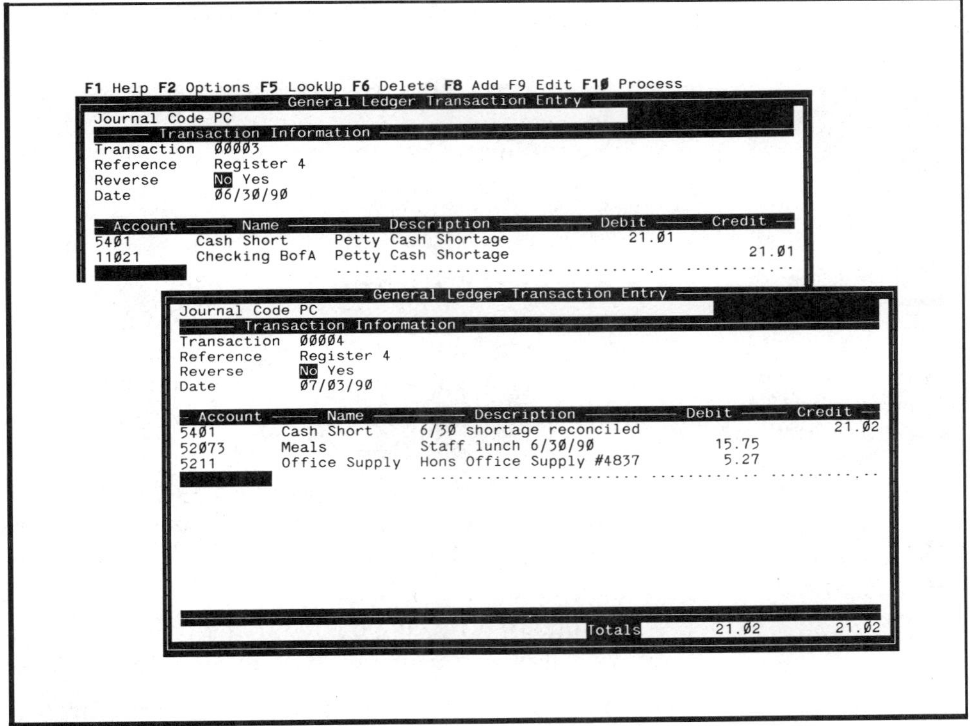

Figure 13.8: Reversing a posted general ledger transaction

5. In the Credit field, enter **21.02** to reverse the original entry, which recorded an expense due to lost cash.
6. In the Account field, enter **52073**, the account number for Meals.
7. In the Description field, press the Ctrl and Backspace keys simultaneously to clear the field, then enter **Staff lunch 6/30/90**.
8. In the Debit field, enter **15.75**, the cost of the lunches.
9. In the Account field, enter **5211**, the account number for Office Supplies.
10. For Description, enter **Hons Office Supply #4837** to identify the invoice from the stationery store.

11. In the Debit field, enter **5.27** to record the expense for the presentation folder.
12. Press F10 to record the transaction.

Notice that although several line items make up the correcting transaction, the total debits and credits match the original entry.

PRINTING A TRIAL BALANCE

* From the Reports menu, select General Ledger. From the submenu, select Trial Balance.

3.1 From the Financials menu, select Trial Balance.

You can print a trial balance at any time to review the current balance, but it is typically printed at the end of the period to determine what adjustments should be made to the general ledger. You cannot print a trial balance for a closed period. The report lists the beginning balance, total of transactions posted this period, and resulting ending balance. Only transactions that have been posted to the general ledger are included; those that are in journals waiting to be posted do not affect the ending balance.

If you are reviewing the trial balance before closing a period, you should also print vendor and customer directories. These list the balance in each record, so you can compare the totals in your Accounts Payable and Accounts Receivable files with the balance in the related general ledger accounts. You should locate and correct any differences while the transactions are still current.

To print a trial balance, select General Ledger from the Reports menu, and then choose Trial Balance from the submenu. Indicate which account levels and accounts you want to include. Chapter 5 describes the procedure for printing financial statements in more detail.

USING RECURRING GENERAL LEDGER TRANSACTIONS

3.0 Recurring transactions do not exist.

Recurring transactions are those that repeat entries to the same accounts for the same amounts at different times in your accounting cycle. In DacEasy, they can be flat amounts or a constant percentage based on the same account each time. Prepaid expenses, accrued revenue, and depreciation (if you use the straight-line method) entries are typical examples of recurring transactions.

After you define the recurring transaction, you can generate it at any time.

CREATING RECURRING TRANSACTIONS

* From the Transactions menu, select Recurring. From the Entry submenu, select General Ledger.

To define a recurring transaction, select Recurring from the Transactions menu, and then choose General Ledger. As an example, suppose that you paid a year's rent in advance. This is a prepaid expense that can be treated as a recurring transaction. You credit your cash account for the payment and debit prepaid expense, another asset account. As each month goes by, you incur the same rent expense and record it by entering a debit to the rent expense account and a credit to the prepaid expense account, reducing the amount of the deposit. Figure 13.9 illustrates an example of the entries. The following steps are used to create the sample recurring transaction:

1. Enter **EOM** as the Group. The group identifies one or more recurring transaction definitions that will be generated together. A single transaction can have a unique group identifier, or several transactions can share the same one.

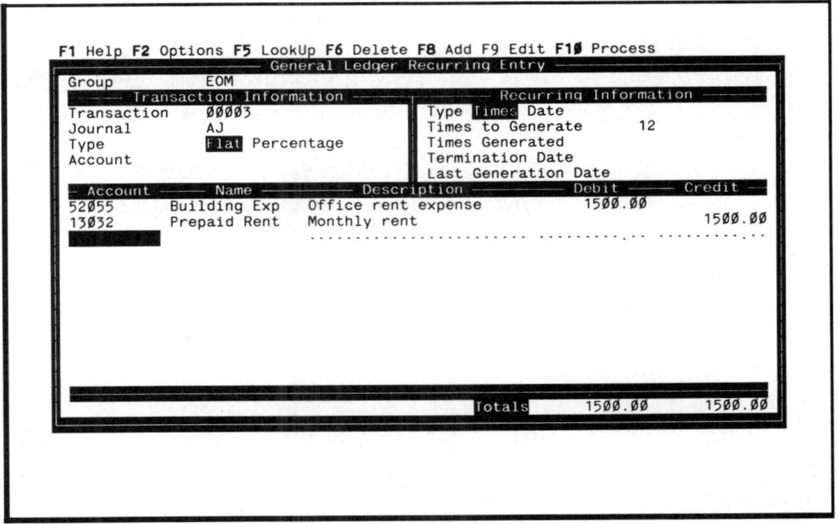

Figure 13.9: Creating a recurring transaction based on a flat amount

2. Enter **3** as the number of the recurring transaction. You can use this number to edit the transaction after it is generated.
3. In the Journal field, enter **AJ** to indicate this particular transaction should go into the Adjustment journal.
4. Select Flat as the Type. You will enter a flat amount in the body of the transaction. You can also use a percentage, as described in the next section. The cursor moves to the Recurring Information section of the screen (the Account field is only used when the transaction is based on a percentage of the amount in a specified account).
5. Select Times as the Type. This means the transaction can only be generated a given number of times. When you select Date, the transaction can be generated any number of times, but only until a given date.
6. In the Times to Generate field, enter **12**. The rent was paid in advance for 1 year, and we want to record the expense on a monthly basis. The cursor moves to the account information section (The Termination Date field applies to date-restricted transactions).

The entries for the Times Generated and Last Generation Date fields are supplied by the program as transactions are processed.

7. In the Account field, enter **52055**. The account name is supplied from the chart of accounts.
8. Enter **Office rent expense** as the Description.
9. Enter **1500** in the Debit field to record the monthly expense.
10. In the Account field on the second line, enter **13032**, the asset account that tracks prepaid expenses.
11. For Description, enter **Monthly rent**.
12. In the Credit field, press F7 to enter the same amount as is in the Debit field.
13. Press F10 to save the definition of the recurring transaction.

You can return to the General Ledger Recurring Entry screen at any time and change the definition or remove it from the recurring transaction file.

USING A PERCENTAGE An example of a recurring transaction that uses the percentage method is shown in Figure 13.10. In the example, the company contributes an amount equal to 3½ percent of the hourly union employees' gross wages to their retirement fund. The transaction differs from the one based on a flat amount in the following ways:

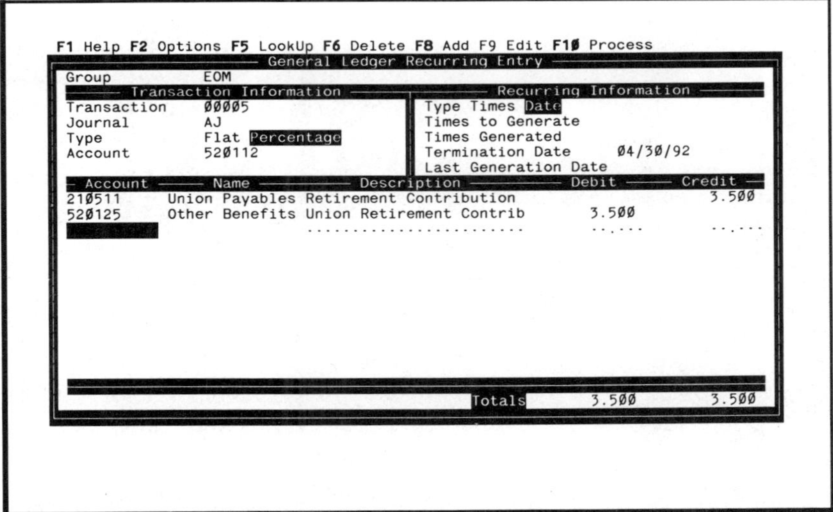

Figure 13.10: Creating a recurring transaction based on a percentage of a specified account

- The transaction type is Percentage.
- A general ledger account, 520112-Hourly Wages, is noted as the account to base the calculations upon.
- The recurring type is Date.
- The Termination Date field indicates the last day on which this transaction can be generated (the final day of the union contract).

- The amounts in the body of the transaction represent percentages, not flat dollar amounts (3.500 represents 3½ percent). The total of the current activity in the Hourly Wages account will be multiplied by 3½ percent, and the result will be the amount that is credited to 210511-Union Payables and debited to 520125-Other Benefits Expense.

The account on which the calculation is based (Hourly Wages in the example) is not affected by the transaction. Different percentages can be applied to various accounts, as long as the total debit percent and the total credit percent are equal.

GENERATING AND EDITING RECURRING TRANSACTIONS

> * From the Transactions menu, select Recurring. From the submenu, select Generate, and then select General Ledger.

After defining a recurring transaction, you can generate it at any time (within the confines of the recurring type you established). It becomes an entry in the general ledger transaction file.

To generate a recurring transaction, select Recurring from the Transactions menu, then Generate, then General Ledger. In the Generate Date field, enter the date you want on the transaction. In the From Group field, enter the first group for which you want to generate transactions. In the To Group field, enter the identification of the last group to be included. Press F10 to generate the transactions.

The resulting transactions can be displayed and edited. Select General Ledger from the Transactions menu and enter the Group and Transaction numbers defined in the recurring transaction record.

You must print the General Ledger journal, then post the general ledger before the generated transactions appear in your account activity.

MAKING PERIOD-END ADJUSTMENTS

> * From the Transactions menu, select General Ledger.

At the end of each period before closing your books, you should create adjusting entries. An adjusting entry is a transaction to record changes in your financial status that are not routine. For example, an adjusting entry to record depreciation denotes the wear and tear on certain fixed assets and reduces their book value.

You should discuss accruals with your accountant. They affect the way your business activity is reported and taxed.

Adjusting entries often involve accruals. An accrual is an amount that accumulates over time, such as the liability for wages owed to your employees for the current, incomplete pay period. Other accruals pertain to expenses and assets. Some of these adjustments record the use of monies paid in advance and revenue earned but not yet received. Many repetitive adjusting entries can be treated as recurring transactions, as discussed in the previous sections.

You make period-end adjustments through the General Ledger Transaction Entry screen. Select the General Ledger option from the Transactions menu and credit and debit the appropriate accounts, as explained in the following sections.

ENTERING DEPRECIATION

When you purchase an asset, you record it in a fixed-asset account. Assets such as equipment deteriorate with use and must be replaced eventually. This deterioration is recorded as an expense called depreciation.

Consult your accountant regarding various depreciation methods and regulations.

Rather than reducing the original value of the asset, the depreciation is captured in a contra account called accumulated depreciation. When you print your balance sheet, the accumulated depreciation is subtracted from the original value to give a book value. Depreciation should be posted regularly. Figure 13.11 shows an example of the entries to record a $150 depreciation for office equipment.

ENTERING PREPAID EXPENSES AND ACCRUED REVENUE

Prepaid expenses, such as those discussed in the section about recurring general ledger transactions, are usually recorded as adjustments at the end of an accounting period. If the amounts do not remain constant, you must enter each transaction individually. The body of the transaction would be similar to the example shown in Figure 13.9.

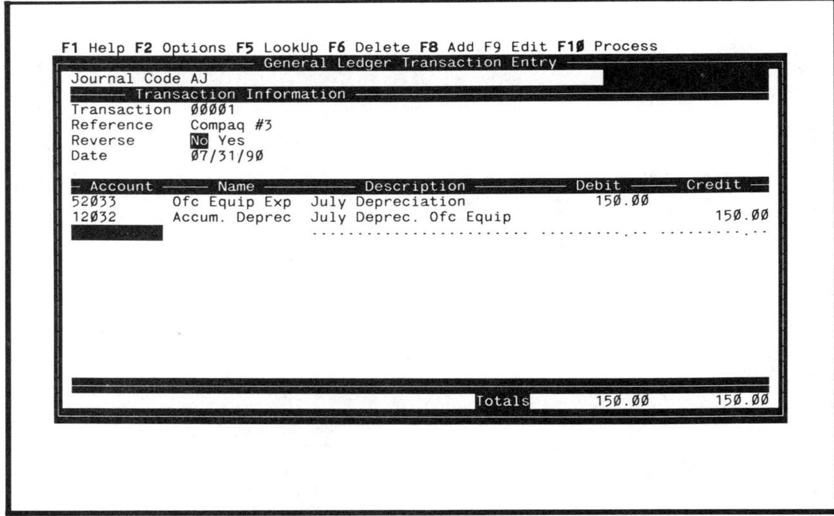

Figure 13.11: Entering depreciation

Another adjustment involves accrued revenue, which is money you have earned but not yet received. Accrued revenue could be interest on an investment that accumulates over time but is not received until the investment matures, or the value of work you perform under a long-term contract that you do not receive payment for until the job is complete.

The entries to record accrued revenue are similar to those for selling merchandise on credit. Accrued revenue is tracked as a receivable until you actually have the money in hand. You debit accrued interest receivable, the asset account, and credit the income account, interest revenue. When you actually receive the money, you credit the accrued interest receivable account, leaving a zero balance, and debit the cash account to record the money you received.

ENTERING ACCRUED SALARY EXPENSE

At the end of a period, wages your employees have earned but not been paid should be entered as a liability to reflect your true financial situation. You also want to include the wages as an expense when calculating your profit and loss for the period. To accomplish this, you debit the payroll expense account and credit accrued salaries, a liability account. Figure 13.12 shows an example of the entries.

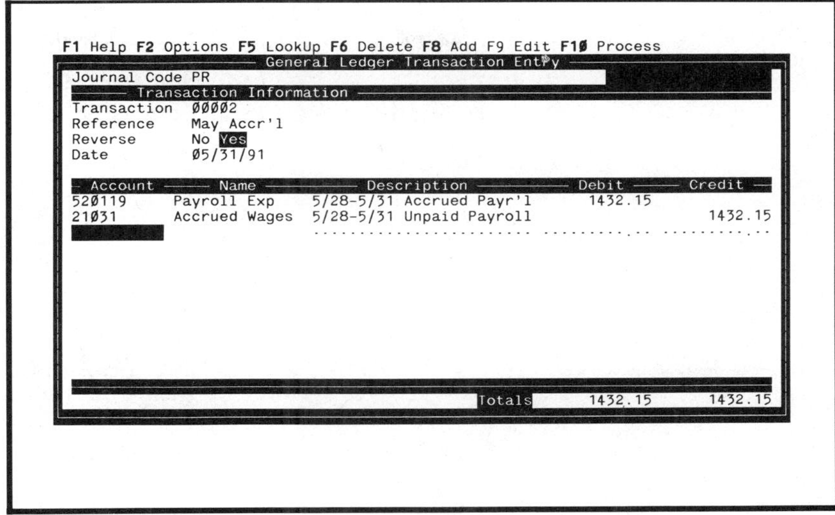

Figure 13.12: Entering accrued payroll expense

3.1 At the beginning of the next month, you must make an entry to reverse the accrual.

When you enter the salary accrual, select Yes in the Reverse field. When the transaction is posted, a new transaction is created, dated the first of the following period, that reverses the entries of the original. The reversing transaction is placed in the general ledger transaction file to await posting. This reversal prevents you from duplicating amounts as you post the specific expenses and liabilities incurred when the payroll checks are written.

PRINTING YOUR CHART OF ACCOUNTS, BALANCE SHEET, AND INCOME STATEMENT

* From the Reports menu, select General Ledger. From the submenu, select Chart of Accounts, Balance Sheet, or Income Statement.

3.1 From the Financials menu, select Chart of Accounts, or Balance Sheet/Income Statement.

To print your chart of accounts, select General Ledger from the Reports menu, and then choose Chart of Accounts from the submenu. Print a trial balance (select Trial Balance from the submenu) to check the account entries for accuracy. You can restrict either report to a range of accounts.

The balance sheet is a listing of your assets, liabilities, and equity. The income statement is a listing of revenue and expense accounts, with the calculated difference stated as a profit or a loss.

To print the balance sheet or income statement, select General Ledger from the Reports menu, then select the report you want from the submenu. Enter the period for which you want a report, indicate the lowest level in your general ledger structure you want to print (generally, a balance sheet is printed in summary form, level 1), and choose whether or not to include general and inactive accounts. Refer to Chapter 5 for a description of the procedure for printing financial statements.

PRINTING FINANCIAL RATIOS

DacEasy provides the following financial reports in addition to the standard balance sheet and income statement:

* From the Reports menu, select Report Generator.

If you did not use the sample chart of accounts supplied with DacEasy, you cannot print the reports provided in the report generator. You can create your own financial reports using the procedure described in Chapter 15.

- Summary balance sheet
- Summary income statement
- Acid test
- Liquidity and current liquidity
- Leverage
- Turnover
- Cash flow
- Sales analysis #1
- Sales analysis #2
- Profitability

The balance sheet and income statement accessed through the report generator are in summary format.

Both the acid test and the liquidity report include an arithmetic and a geometrical ratio. The acid test compares current assets to current liabilities; that is, assets that can be converted to cash during normal business operations over a year are compared with short-term debts that are due within one year. Current assets are divided by current liabilities to determine your ability to pay operating debts as they become due with operating income.

Liquidity is your ability to turn assets into cash to enable you to pay off debts. Liquid assets are those that can be readily converted to cash, such as marketable securities and accounts receivable. Inventory and real estate—assets you normally cannot quickly convert to cash—are not included in liquidity calculations.

The leverage, turnover, and profitability reports show ratios. Leverage is the amount of debt in comparison to the equity in your company. The four types of turnover DacEasy calculates are for inventory, accounts receivable, fixed assets, and total assets. Turnover indicates the rate at which inventory is sold and restocked, how quickly you collect accounts receivable, and the number of times an asset is replaced. Profitability shows earnings as a percent of sales, as a percent of assets, or as a percent of equity before profit. These figures are shown in a mathematical ratio.

The cash flow report lists operating income for year to date and last year to date. The sales analysis #1 report is a list of invoices and amounts by customer. Sales analysis #2 lists sales by item number.

To print one of these financial reports, follow these steps:

1. Select the Report Generator option from the Reports menu.
2. In the Name field, press F5 to look up the predefined reports.
3. Highlight the one you want to print and press ↵.
4. Press ↵ to move through the fields in the layout area.
5. When the cursor is in a column selection field, press F7 to print, then select the report disposition.

PRINTING FINANCIAL REPORTS IN VERSION 3.1

Version 3.1 contains a changes in financial condition report and a general ledger statistical report, which are not available in version 4.1, plus two financial statements, which are identified on the Print Financial Statements screen as BAL and INC.

The changes in financial condition report indicates sources and application of funds. For example, money is derived from sales and expended for inventory. To print the report, select the Changes in Fin. Conditions option from the Financials menu.

The general ledger statistical report prints the 3-year historical information for every account in your chart of accounts and compares your actual activity for the current year with your recorded forecast. Check the resulting variance to gauge if you are under or over your projections.

To print the general ledger statistical report, select the General Ledger option from the Periodic menu, choose Forecasting, and then choose Print Statistical YTD. Enter the first and last account numbers you want to include, and DacEasy will print the report. Unfortunately, inactive accounts are not excluded from the statistical report, so the report may be very long, depending on the size of your chart of accounts.

3.1 If you are not using the DacEasy sample chart of accounts, you must create reports to suit your own account structure. Refer to Appendix D for details.

The BAL report is a comparative balance sheet showing each asset, liability, and equity account as a percent of total assets. The INC report is a comparative income statement showing each revenue and expense account and profit or loss, with its respective percent of the whole. These reports compare year to date to last year and year to date to budget, and calculate each account's percent of the whole.

To print one of these reports, follow these steps:

1. From the Financials menu, select Financial Statements Generator. From the submenu, select Print Financial Report.
2. Place the cursor on the identification code of the custom report you want to print.
3. Press F2 to select the report for printing. An asterisk appears next to reports you have selected to print. (To cancel the request to print the highlighted report, press F3.)
4. Press F10 after marking the reports to print.
5. Select the report format by pressing the spacebar to choose between the three types of data you can print: YTD (year to date) Only; YTD/Last Year, which compares last year to this year; or YTD/Budget, which compares your current budget to this year. Your budget is the amount you entered in the Forecast field of the statistical information portion of each general ledger account record.

6. In response to the prompt asking if you want to include account numbers, press ↵ if you want account numbers to print on the report; otherwise, enter N to print only account descriptions.

All the selected reports will be printed, one after the other.

PERIOD-END PROCESSING

* From the Periodic menu, select General Ledger. From the submenu, select Period End.

3.1 From the Periodic menu, select General Ledger. From the submenu, select End Month.

3.1 The transactions for the period are arbitrarily removed from the file during period-end processing. The amount for this period balance will be added to the previous balance in each general ledger account record.

You must close each period in the general ledger to update and clear your files. If you have any unposted transactions, they must be posted before DacEasy allows you to end the period.

After all the transactions have been posted, print a copy of the entire general ledger listing and activity report. Review the entries before closing the period and make any last minute corrections. Print a copy of the final activity report to store with the period's backup disk. Be sure you have printed all the monthly reports: the trial balance, balance sheet, income statement, and any custom reports. As always, back up your files.

To close the period in the general ledger, select the General Ledger option from the Periodic menu, and then choose Period End. Follow the procedure for closing the period outlined in Chapter 5.

If you selected to remove transactions, items posted to the general ledger that were dated on or prior to the closing date will be removed from the general ledger transaction file and will no longer appear on reports.

CONSOLIDATING MULTIPLE COMPANIES

3.1 The consolidation feature does not exist.

You can consolidate the account balances of two or more companies into a third. For example, you might have several divisions of one corporation. Each division has its own set of books, but you add the data together at the end of each quarter to produce quarterly corporate reports.

Refer to the section about setting up a consolidated chart of accounts in Chapter 4.

Here are some points to remember when you are consolidating account balances:

- Only detail accounts can be used in a consolidation.
- The number you entered in the Consolidation field in the account record of the originating company must correspond to an account in the consolidated chart of accounts.
- The total debits and credits you consolidate must balance. Assets minus liabilities must equal equity plus revenue minus expenses.

MANAGING THE CONSOLIDATION FILE

When you generate a consolidation transaction, the program creates an ASCII file, which you will import into your consolidated chart of accounts.

You only have to make the subdirectory once. Thereafter, it is available to store consolidation files from any company.

Before you attempt to process a consolidation transaction for the first time, you should create a subdirectory where the ASCII files of the consolidation transactions can be stored until you import them into your corporate files. To do so, exit DacEasy. At the C:\DEA4 prompt, enter **md cnsldt** to make a subdirectory named CNSLDT, an abbreviation for consolidate. (You can use any subdirectory name, except *CON*, which is reserved for use by the computer system.)

When you import the data from the ASCII file into your consolidated chart of accounts, the data is copied, not transferred. This means the transaction will remain in the ASCII file, which will increase in size each time you generate a consolidation transaction. You should clear the ASCII file periodically, depending on how much space you have on your disk.

To clear the file you created as a holding area for the consolidation transactions, exit DacEasy and follow these steps:

*Use the erase *.* command with extreme caution!* It will delete everything in the directory where you enter the command.

1. At the C:\DEA4 prompt, enter **cd\dea4\cnsldt** to change to the subdirectory where the consolidated transactions reside.
2. Enter **dir/p** and review the names of the files in the subdirectory to be certain you are in the correct subdirectory.
3. Enter **erase *.*** to erase all the files in the subdirectory.

GENERATING CONSOLIDATIONS

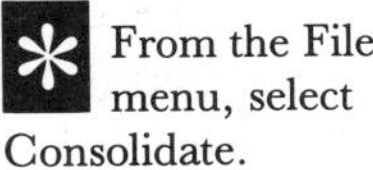
From the File menu, select Consolidate.

To generate a consolidation transaction, select the Consolidate option from the File menu and complete the fields on the File Consolidation screen. Figure 13.13 shows an example of a completed screen. The following steps are used for the sample entry:

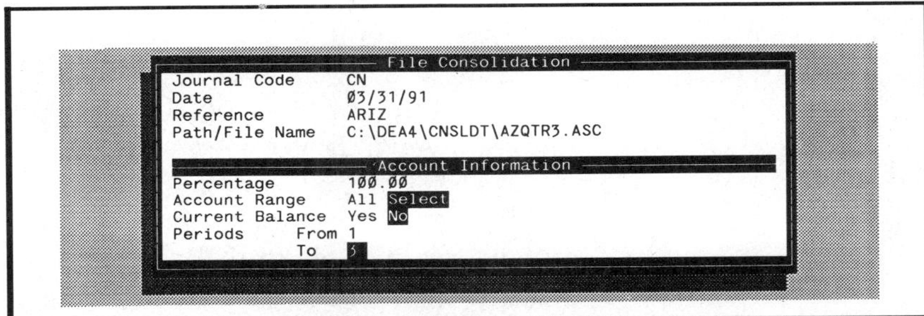

Figure 13.13: Generating a consolidation transaction

1. In the Journal Code field, enter **CN**, a user-defined code indicating this is a consolidation journal for the third quarter of your fiscal year.
2. Press ↵ in the Date Field to accept the system date.
3. Enter **ARIZ** in the Reference field to indicate this transaction originated from data in your Arizona warehouse books.
4. In the Path/File Name field, enter **c:\dea4\cnsldt\azqtr3.asc** to indicate where the consolidated file should be stored—on drive C in the directory DEA4, in the subdirectory CNSLDT for consolidations, in the file AZQTR3 for third-quarter data on the Arizona warehouse, with the extension .ASC to indicate it is in ASCII format.
5. Press ↵ through the Percentage field to accept the default of 100 percent. If you only wanted a percentage of the account balances included in the consolidation, you would enter that percent.
6. Highlight Select in the Account Range field to include only the accounts that have a consolidation account noted in their record. If you wanted to export the balances to a program other than DacEasy, you could select All to include every account in your chart of accounts.

7. Select No at the prompt Current Balance. We do not want the current period only. We want the activity for the entire quarter, which includes three months. If you wanted to use only the current period, you would select Yes.
8. In the Periods From field, enter **1**, the first period in the quarter.
9. In the Periods To field, enter **3**, the last period in the quarter.
10. Press F10 to generate the transaction and place it in the file you indicated in step 3.

You must generate a consolidation transaction for each company you want included in the consolidated account balances. To do so, select Open from the File menu, highlight the name of the next company to process, and press ↵. When the Main menu displays again, you will be in the data files for the next company. Repeat steps 1 through 9 above. Each transaction must have a different name in the cnsldt subdirectory. In the example above, the Colorado warehouse data file could be named COQTR3.ASC.

You can print a listing of the contents of the ASCII file to verify that you have captured all the accounts that you want to import into the corporate books. To do so, first exit DacEasy. Be sure the printer is connected to the computer, loaded with paper, and turned on. At the C:\DEA4 prompt, enter **print c:\dea4\cnsldt\azqtr3.asc**. At the Name of list device [PRN] prompt, press ↵. This prints a list containing the account number, account name, and account balance for the periods requested, with a D to denote a debit amount or a C for a credit.

The ASCII files that are created must be imported into the accounts established for the consolidation, as described in the next section.

IMPORTING CONSOLIDATED TRANSACTIONS

After you have generated all the consolidated transactions, you must import them into the chart of accounts you have established for the corporate consolidation. To import data from your DacEasy files into the DacEasy consolidated chart of accounts, follow the steps below:

1. Select Open from the File menu.
2. Select the files for the corporation where you want to consolidate data.
3. When the Main menu reappears, select the Import option from the File menu.
4. In the Path/File Name field, enter the name of the file in which you stored the consolidation transaction. This must be the same as the destination path you entered when generating the consolidation transaction.
5. Press F10 to import the data.
6. Repeat steps 1 through 5 for each consolidation transaction in the ASCII file.

The transactions will be placed in the general ledger transaction file of the corporation. You must print the General Ledger journal and post the transactions, just as you would any other general ledger transaction.

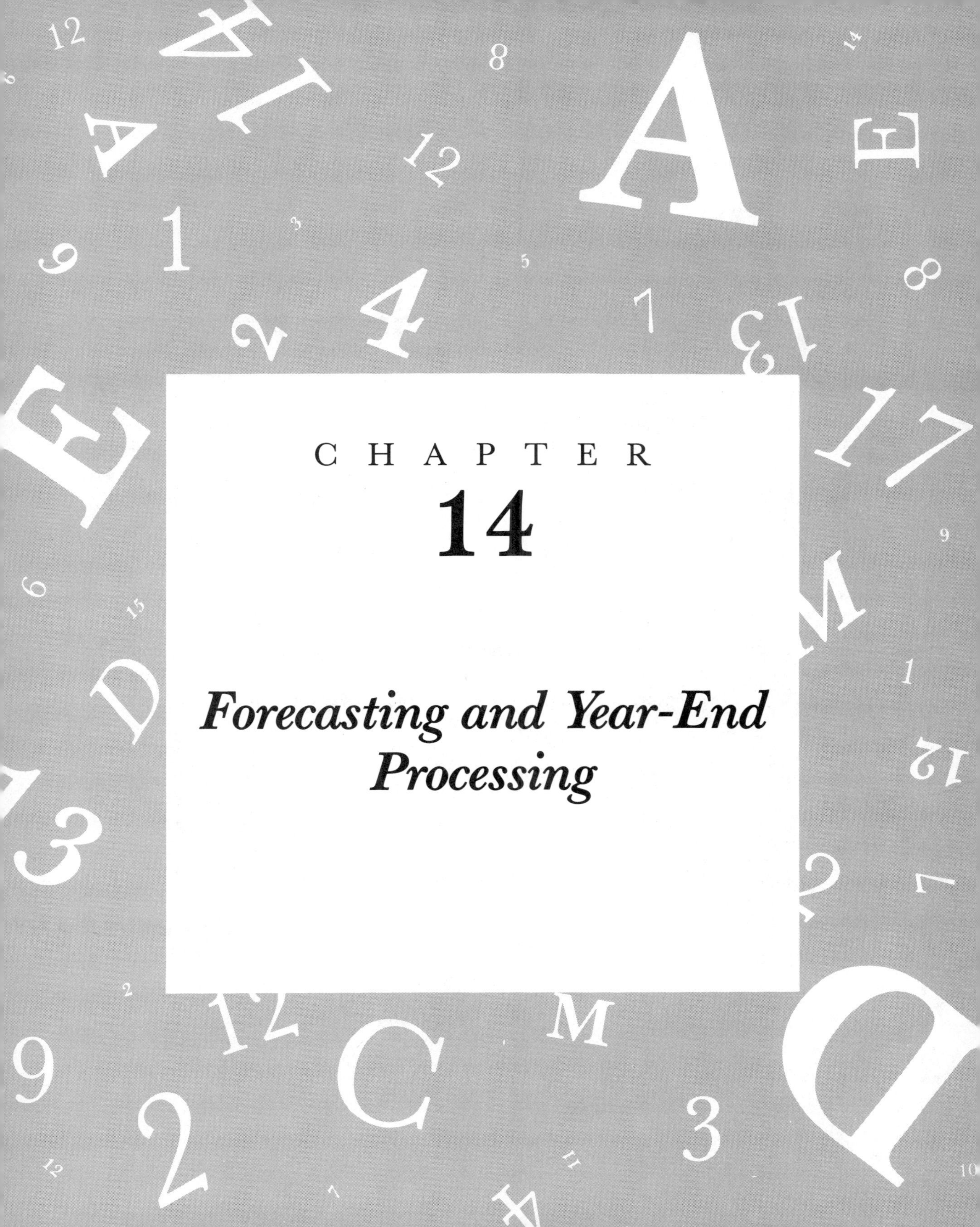

CHAPTER 14

Forecasting and Year-End Processing

YOUR ANNUAL BOOKKEEPING TASKS SHOULD include forecasting, closing the year, and opening a new year. This chapter explains these processes.

FORECASTING

When you process a forecast, DacEasy uses historical data from your records to project activity and dollar amounts for the next year. You can make forecasts for accounts receivable, accounts payable, inventory, and services on an account-by-account basis.

DacEasy will not limit or warn you in relation to the forecast. If the projected amounts represent your budget, you must print the statistical report to see how you're doing in comparison with your forecast.

You can use this forecast as a budget in your subsidiary modules. It shows the variance from your projection for any account. Be aware that the forecast is for an entire year, however, not a period-by-period breakdown.

PREPARING A FORECAST

* From the Periodic menu, select Receivables, Payables, or Inventory. From the submenu, select Forecast Calculation.

3.1 From the Periodic menu, select General Ledger, Accounts Receivable, Accounts Payable, or Inventory. From the submenu, select Forecasting. From the next submenu, select Automatic Calculations.

Before you begin the forecasting process, remember to print the year-to-date statistical report for each module. Keep these copies as final records of the year's activity. Print a second copy to use as a worksheet so you can base the forecasting method on actual experience from this year.

To have DacEasy calculate a forecast, select the option for the module (Receivables, Payables, or Inventory) from the Periodic menu, then choose Forecast Calculation. Select one of the four ways to calculate your projections:

- The Previous Year option simply uses this year's results as a forecast for next year.
- The Previous Year Pct option adds or subtracts a user-specified percentage of this year's activity to this year's results to determine the forecast for next year.
- The Previous Year Trend option requires two years of history on file. The program determines the difference between this year and last year. Then it adds or subtracts that amount from this year as a forecast for next year.

- The Trend Line Analysis option requires all three years of history on file. The program uses a straight-line method with all three years to forecast next year.

You don't have to be a financial wizard to perform the calculations; the program handles the mathematics automatically.

If you chose the Previous Year Pct option, type the percentage you want to add to or subtract from the previous year in the Percent field. Precede a decrease by a minus sign.

Select the sorting criteria in the Sort By field. In the From and To fields, enter the numbers of the first and last records you want included in the forecast. You can press ↵ to default to the first and last records that qualify in the sorting category you selected. You can process a forecast for a limited range of records or for the entire file, and you can use different forecasting methods for various records. Press F10 to calculate the forecast.

After you have completed a forecast, print a forecast report, as described below, and review the results. You can also see the results of the calculations on the screen by accessing the customer, vendor, or product record. After the record appears on screen, press Shift-F3 to see its statistical information. You can process as many forecasts (or what-if analyses) as you want using different figures or different methods. The latest forecast overwrites the results of the previous one.

PRINTING THE FORECAST

*From the Periodic menu, select Receivables, Payables, or Inventory. From the submenu, select Print Forecast.

3.1 From the Periodic menu, select the module. From the submenu, select Forecasting, then Print Forecast. You select whether or not to include cost and profit in the report.

After processing a forecast, you can review it by printing the results. You can use the forecasting methods as a type of what-if analysis. Compare the results of each calculation with those obtained using any of the other three methods, and decide which figures you want to live with for the next year. Print a forecast report after processing the method you finally choose to be certain the forecast is what you intended.

To print the forecast, select the option for the module from the Periodic menu, then choose Print Forecast. Select the sorting criteria in the Sort By field and the numbers of the first and last records you want included in the forecast in the From and To fields (or press ↵). Press F10 and select Printer as the Report Disposition.

YEAR-END PROCESSING

Year-end processing wraps up the activity for either the fiscal or calendar year, whichever you use in your business. Basically, closing the year clears all the statistical information from the current year, calculates profit and loss for the year, and updates your equity account with the result. It is an essential part of the bookkeeping cycle.

Because of the finality of this process, before ending the year, be certain all transactions for the year have been entered and that all the activity balances. You should make final adjusting entries, such as those affecting your inventory and cash and accrual accounts.

Also be sure you have printed the 1099 forms in the Accounts Payable module. Print vendor and customer directories and reconcile the totals in your payables and receivables files with their respective accounts in the general ledger.

The year-end process is separate from the period-end process, and each has a different effect on your records.

Before you end the year, you must close the last period in your year. Calculate the next year's forecast after closing the last period to ensure up-to-date statistics. You must process the forecast prior to closing the year because DacEasy needs data from the current year for its calculations; this data is moved backward into the Last Year field when the year is closed. Be sure to calculate and print the final forecast for each module.

You should also print final copies of all your financial statements—standard and custom—before you end the year. These include the regular and comparative balance sheet and income statement, the financial ratio reports, and any other reports you designed. Year-end reports might be the most important documents you produce in your business; investors, your board of directors, the bank, and the Internal Revenue Service will want to examine them.

Lastly, be certain you have created backup copies of your files and stored them in a safe place. Review the checklist in Table 14.1 before proceeding with year-end processing.

ENDING THE YEAR

From the Periodic menu, select General Ledger, Receivables, Payables, or Inventory. From the submenu, select Year End.

The Year End option has the same effect in each of the three subsidiary modules (Accounts Receivable, Accounts Payable, and Inventory). The program updates the historical data in every record by moving each years' accumulated data backward one year,

Table 14.1: Year-End Checklist

1. Balance the Accounts Receivable file to the accounts receivable account.
2. Balance the Accounts Payable file to the accounts payable account.
3. Count your physical inventory and adjust the perpetual inventory.
4. Balance and replenish the petty-cash fund.
5. Reconcile your bank statement with your cash account.
6. Perform period-end processing for the last period in the year.
7. Print 1099 forms in the Accounts Payable module.
8. Print all your financial statements.
9. Calculate next year's forecast for all modules.
10. Back up your files.

deleting the third year, and leaving the current year fields at zero to begin the next year's activity.

3.1 From the Periodic menu, select General Ledger, Accounts Receivable, Accounts Payable, or Inventory. From the submenu, select End Year.

Note that DacEasy does not give you an error message if you attempt to close a year more than once in the subsidiary modules. It will process a second year closing and, again, move the data in the statistical portion of each record back one year.

3.1 The statistical information in the general ledger is updated in the same manner as the data in the subsidiary modules.

In the general ledger, the program determines the profit or loss, which is the net difference between the revenue and expense accounts, and posts it to the account you designate. In doing so, the offsetting entries bring the balances in your revenue and expense accounts to zero. Typically, the account where the profit or loss is posted is in the equity section of your chart of accounts. In the sample chart of accounts, account 33, Current Earnings, is available for this purpose.

3.1 The Current Date is the date the entries will be effective in your general ledger. If this field does not contain the last day of your fiscal year, exit to the menu and change the date before ending the year. Press ↵ at the prompt to start the closing process.

To close a year, select the option for the module from the Periodic menu, and then choose Year End. Press ↵ to start the year-end process or select Exit to cancel it. If you are closing the year in the general ledger, you will see the prompt

Clear to Account

Enter the number of the account where you want the profit or loss for the year posted and press F10 to begin the process.

OPENING A NEW YEAR

* From the Edit menu, select Defaults. From the submenu, select Open Next Year.

3.1 There is no formal process for opening a new year. Simply date your transactions with next year's date.

You must open the new year before you can enter any transactions. If you have not finalized the prior year, you can still open the next year and begin working in it. DacEasy will keep your records separate and allow you to close last year as soon as you enter and post all your adjusting transactions.

To open a new year, select Defaults from the Edit menu and then choose Open Next Year from the submenu. At the prompt

```
Open Next Year Accounting  Yes No
```

press ↵ to select Yes and F10 to open the year. The periods in the new year will be opened. However, you cannot view them in the periods table until the prior year is closed.

At the start of a new year, you must transfer the earnings from last year into the appropriate equity accounts. The immediate beginning of the new year is also the best time to remove inactive accounts from your records. The following sections describe these procedures.

TRANSFERRING EARNINGS

* From the Transactions menu, select General Ledger.

When you start a year, you need to transfer the amount in the current earnings account that resulted from last year's activity into other equity accounts. This is accomplished through the General Ledger Transaction Entry screen (select the General Ledger option from the Transactions menu).

Before assigning the earnings in a sole proprietorship or a partnership, you should transfer the balance from the drawing account into the capital account. Throughout the year, the drawing account acts as a contra account, which offsets the amount in the capital account to arrive at net equity. Closing this account and transferring the balance into the capital account actually reduces the balance in the capital account. By starting the new year with a zero balance in the drawing account, you can quickly check how much each partner has received during the year. Good management practices dictate that no one withdraws more than the expected profit he will be assigned at year-end. Figure 14.1 shows an example of the entries to close a drawing account.

In a partnership, you should transfer the amount posted to current earnings to the partners according to their percentage of ownership. Figure 14.2 illustrates an example of the entries to transfer earnings to partners.

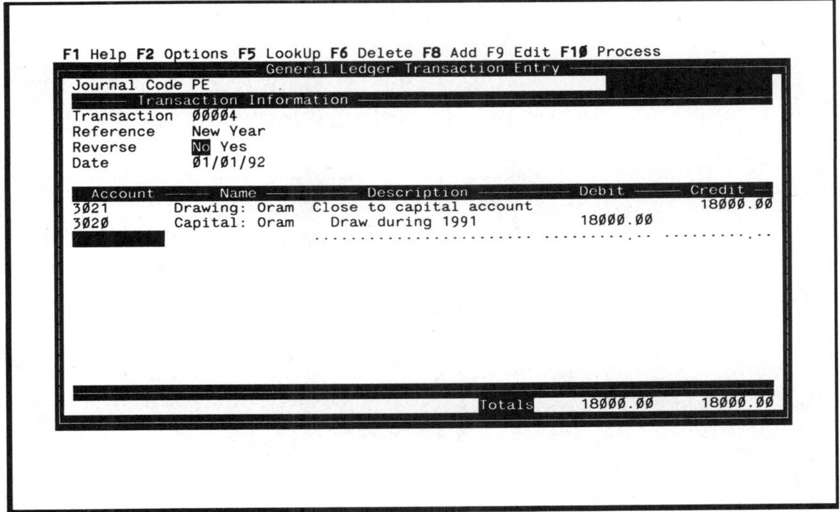

Figure 14.1: Closing a drawing account

```
F1 Help F2 Options F5 LookUp F6 Delete F8 Add F9 Edit F10 Process
                 General Ledger Transaction Entry
Journal Code PE
         Transaction Information
Transaction   00005
Reference     New Year
Reverse       No Yes
Date          01/01/92

Account       Name           Description             Debit       Credit
33            Current Earnin Close to capital accts  84523.00
3020          Capital: Oram    Profit share 1991                 50713.80
3030          Capital: Davis   Profit share 1991                 33809.20

                                              Totals 84523.00    84523.00
```

Figure 14.2: Transferring earnings in a partnership

If your business is incorporated, you would transfer the profit or loss posted to current earnings to various other equity accounts. Optionally, you could designate the only retained earnings account you have as the clearing account for year-end. From there, you might distribute a percentage to your stockholders in the form of dividends. An example of these transactions is shown in Figure 14.3. The current earnings account is debited the exact amount of this year's profit to close that account. Retained earnings, also an equity account, is credited with the profit.

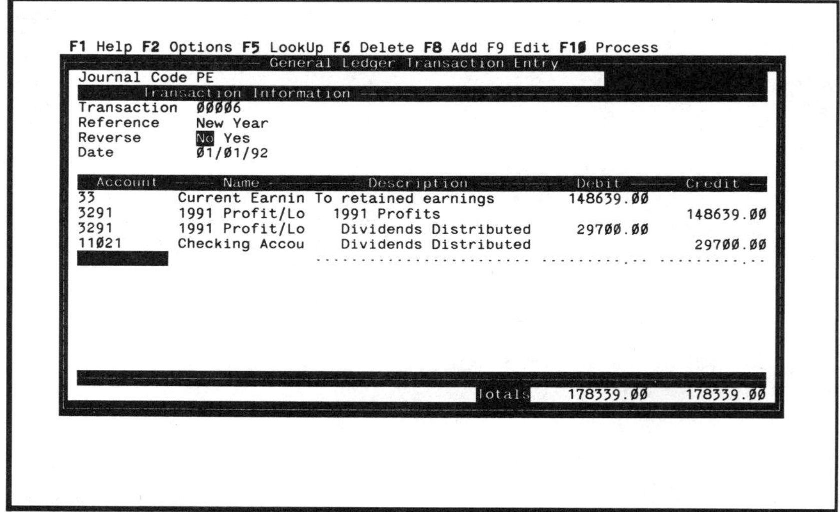

Figure 14.3: Transferring earnings in a corporation

In this example, the company keeps a separate earnings account for each year. On summary reports, the earnings from every year are accumulated into the total retained earnings account. Additionally, a portion of this year's profit has been paid to the stockholders. The retained earnings account is reduced by a debit, and the account that tracks the balance for the bank that paid the dividends is credited.

Notice that in the examples, the transactions for transferring earnings are entered in a journal labeled PE (period end). This keeps them separate from daily transactions and easy to identify.

DELETING INACTIVE RECORDS

Throughout the year, you do not delete inactive records because you want to maintain a statistical picture of the entire year. However, at year's end, you should remove the data from your computer disk.

You can use printed reports and screen displays to decide which records to delete. To create a list of vendors to be purged from your files and then delete them, take the following steps:

3.1 Follow the procedures described in earlier chapters to print the vendor directory, display each record to be purged, and delete it.

1. From the Reports menu, select Payables, and then choose Directory.
2. Select to sort by code.
3. Press ↵ in the From and To fields to sort from the first to the last record.
4. Select to rank by last purchase date.
5. In the From field, press ↵ to rank from the first date.
6. In the To field, enter the last purchase date you want shown on the purge list. For example, you would use 6/30/90 if you wanted a list of all vendors you had not used since June of last year. You must decide how long a record can remain inactive until you purge it at year-end.
7. Press F10 and select Printer as the Report Disposition.
8. Review the list for vendors with a zero balance. You cannot delete records that still have a balance.
9. Place a checkmark beside the names of vendors you want to delete.
10. From the Edit menu, select Vendors.
11. Enter the vendor code. The vendor record displays for verification. Review the record one last time to be certain you want to delete it.
12. Press F6, and in response to the prompt

    ```
    Are you sure you want to delete this Vendor  Yes No
    ```

    press ↵ to accept the default Yes.

To locate and delete inactive customer records, print a customer directory ranked by the last sale date. The service listing can also be restricted to last sale date to locate service records you no longer use.

To locate and delete inactive product records, print a product activity report ranked by last purchase date and look for products with no units on hand. Decide if you are seasonally out of stock or if you no longer carry the product and should remove the record from your files. You might want to print a second report ranked by last sale date to see if you have stock on hand for products that aren't selling, and then take steps to clear your inventory.

When you have transferred your earnings to the appropriate accounts and have purged your files, you are ready to begin processing daily work in your new year.

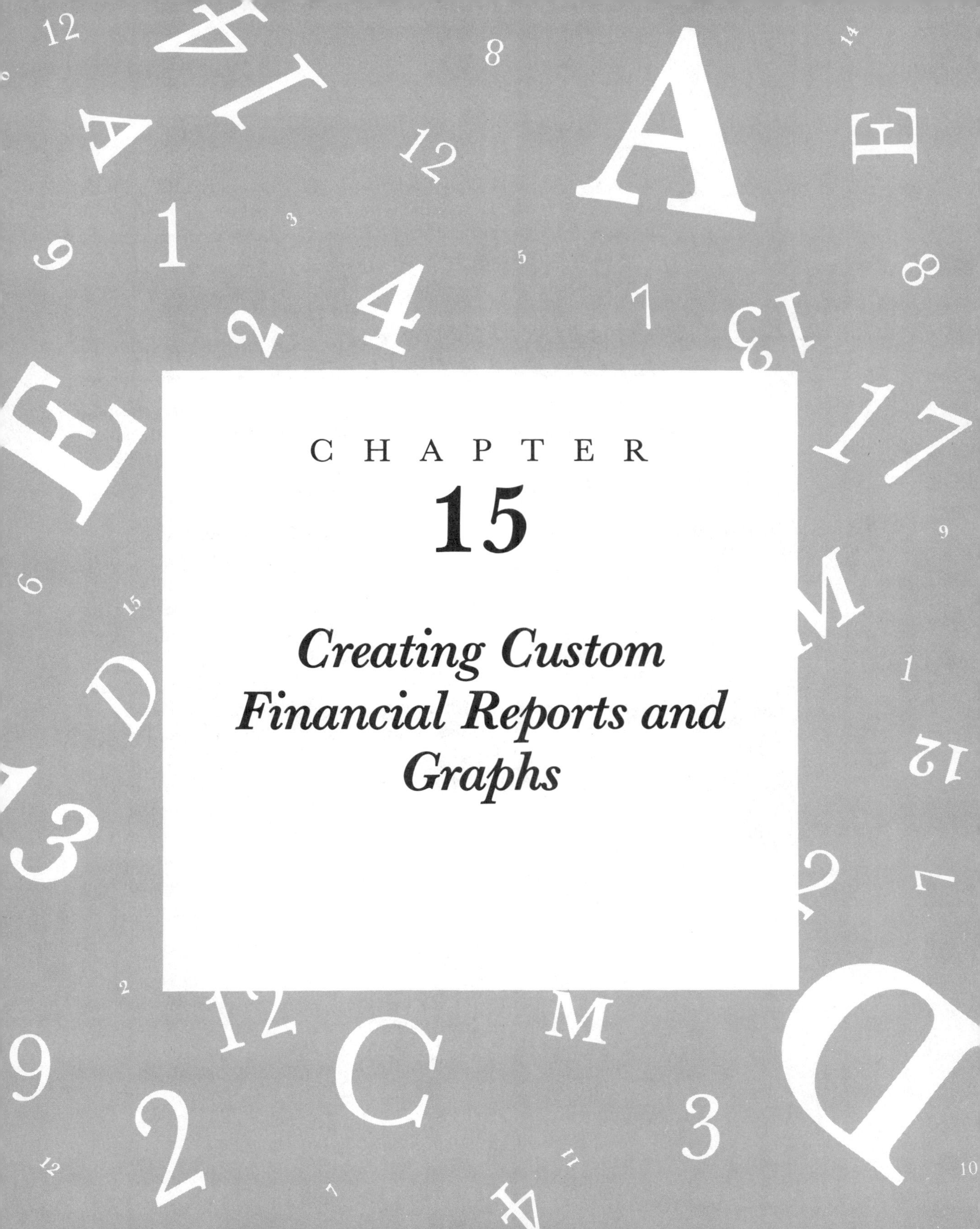

CHAPTER 15

Creating Custom Financial Reports and Graphs

THIS CHAPTER EXPLAINS HOW TO CREATE YOUR own reports to supplement the nine financial reports provided in the DacEasy report generator. It also describes how to create graphs using DacEasy's Graphic option.

CREATING FINANCIAL REPORTS AND LISTINGS

3.1 Adding financial reports is discussed in Appendix D.

You can add, edit, and print financial reports based on the balances in your general ledger and listings based on data in other files.

ADDING A FINANCIAL REPORT

* From the Reports menu, select Report Generator.

For your financial reports, DacEasy can use information from any field in the general ledger file, including period activity, year-to-date balance, last year's balance, and budget.

In addition to account balances, you can use variables that are the result of a calculation. You can enter a formula in a column, however, every amount line in that column will be shown as a percentage of the variable you choose. For example, you could list assets in one column and calculate each asset as a percent of total assets. In a second column, you could list liabilities and calculate each liability as a percent of total liabilities.

Creating a financial report is not a difficult task, but dealing with contra accounts can be tricky. Contra accounts are those that are related to, and deducted from, another account. For example, Accumulated Depreciation is a contra account that reduces its associated account, Fixed Assets. You must remember that all accounts are of a specific type in DacEasy, and each type has a normal balance:

- Debit for asset accounts
- Credit for liability accounts
- Credit for equity accounts
- Credit for revenue accounts
- Debit for expense accounts

If you are dealing with a contra account, the balance is preceded by a minus sign to indicate that it is abnormal (the opposite of what that account type should be), regardless if it is normally a debit or credit balance. Unfortunately, these amounts will also appear on the report preceded by a minus sign, whether or not you are subtracting them in the report. Also, if you want to accumulate the balance of a contra account in a column in your report, you must enter the opposite parameter of what you intend to do; to add the contra account amount, place a minus sign in the Formula field, and to subtract the amount, put a plus sign in this field.

To add a financial report, select the Report Generator option from the Reports menu. You will see the Report Generation screen, shown in Figure 15.1.

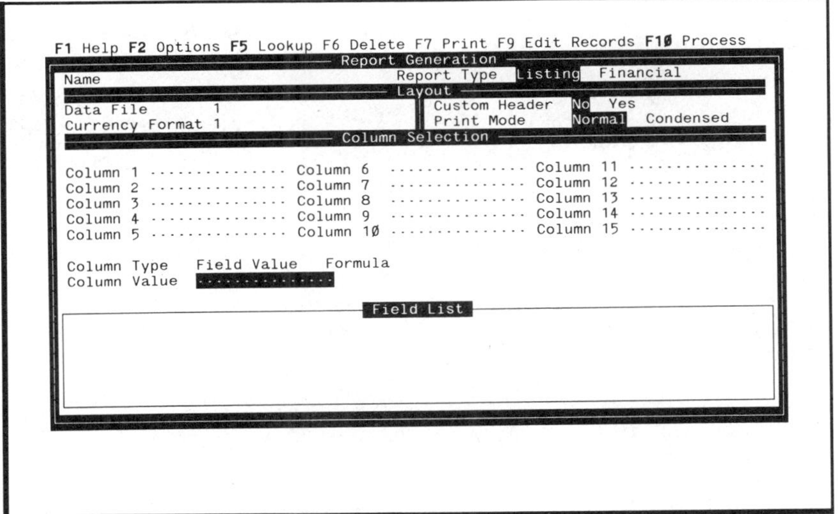

Figure 15.1: Report Generation screen

The format for a simple sales analysis report, which uses accounts from the sample chart of accounts, is shown in Figure 15.2. The report shows sales activity, cost of sales, and the ratio of purchases to sales. Its design illustrates many of the entries you can use to create reports. Figure 15.3 shows a printed report in this format.

The following steps outline the procedure used to create the sample report, and also describe the fields on the Report Generator screen and windows.

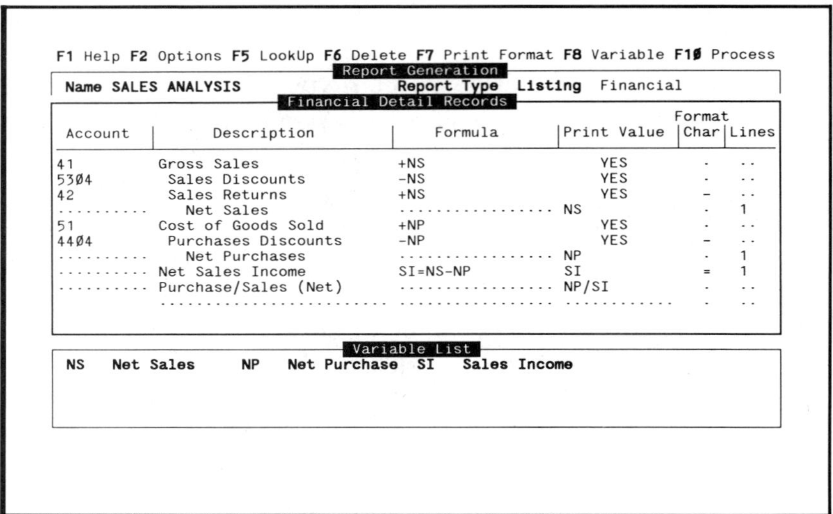

Figure 15.2: Sample design for a financial report

Date : 12/31/90
Time : 09:34 AM

The Emporium
321 Main Street
P. O. Box 4512
Yourtown, Anystate 95842

Page no. 1

SALES ANALYSIS

Account #	Name	December
41	Gross Sales	8,403
5304	Sales Discounts	136
42	Sales Returns	-662

	Net Sales	7,605
51	Cost of Goods Sold	3,800
4404	Purchase Discounts	79

	Net Purchases	3,721
	Net Sales Income	3,884
		==========
	Purchases/Sales (Net)	1

Figure 15.3: Report created from sample format

1. In the Name field, enter **SALES ANALYSIS** for the report name.
2. As the Report Type, select Financial. The Data File field will default to 1, for account balances, the only file used in financial reporting. Other files are available when you create a listing, as discussed later in this chapter.

3. Select 2 as the Currency Format. The amounts will be rounded to the nearest dollar, eliminating cents from the report. Other selections are 1 for dollars and cents, 3 to round to hundreds, and 4 to round to thousands.
4. Select Yes in the Custom Header field. The Edit Custom Header window appears. If you select No for Custom Header, the company name and address (from the company definition) will still be printed at the top, but there will not be a title. Skip to step 8 if you do not want a custom heading.
5. Press ↵ to accept the Yes in the Print Date and Time and Print Page Numbers fields. The date and time the report was requested, as well as page numbers, will print at the top of each page of the report.
6. Title Lines 1 through 4 of the header layout default to your company name and address. These lines will print on your report. You can delete or override them for this report. Press ↵ to accept each of these lines.
7. On Title Line 5, enter **SALES ANALYSIS** as the title, which will print two lines beneath the company information. Figure 15.4 shows the completed window. The window closes, and the cursor moves to Print Mode.
8. Select Normal for Print Mode. If your report has more than 80 characters across, select Condensed instead. Each column of information requires the maximum number of characters possible in the fields you select. You must refer to field definitions prior to creating the report to determine how wide the report will be. The maximum width is 132 characters using condensed (16.7 characters per inch) print mode.
9. Press ↵ to leave Column 1 blank. We only have three columns on our report, and starting in column 2 will result in a more horizontally centered format.
10. In Column 2, press F5 to move the cursor to the Field Selection window.
11. The cursor highlights the first field, Account #. Press ↵ to place the account number in the second column of your report.

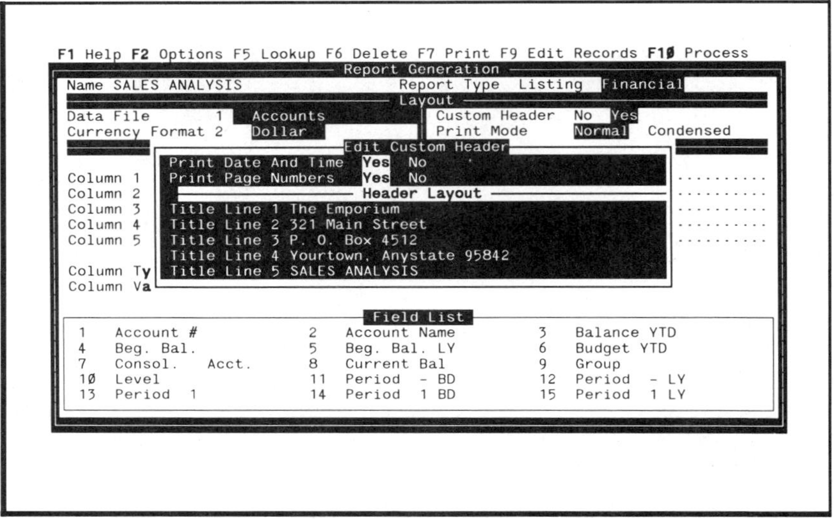

Figure 15.4: Creating a custom report header

You must use F5 and select the field you want from the database and place it in your report. Simply typing the name of the field in the column will not incorporate data from the file into your report.

12. In Column 3, press F5, highlight Account Name in the Field Selection window, and press ↵ to place the field in your report. The text in the Column field will appear as the heading of that column on your report. You can override the field name with a more appropriate (or shorter if the column width dictates) descriptor.
13. Press ↵ in Column 4 to leave a blank column between the description and the balance.
14. In Column 5, press F5, press PgDn to scroll through the fields, highlight Period 12, and press ↵.
15. Move the cursor back to Column 5 and type **December** over the field description. Notice in Figure 15.5 that the Column Value field shows the original field name.
16. Press F9 to display the Financial Detail Records screen, and then press F8 to define the variables you will use in the report.

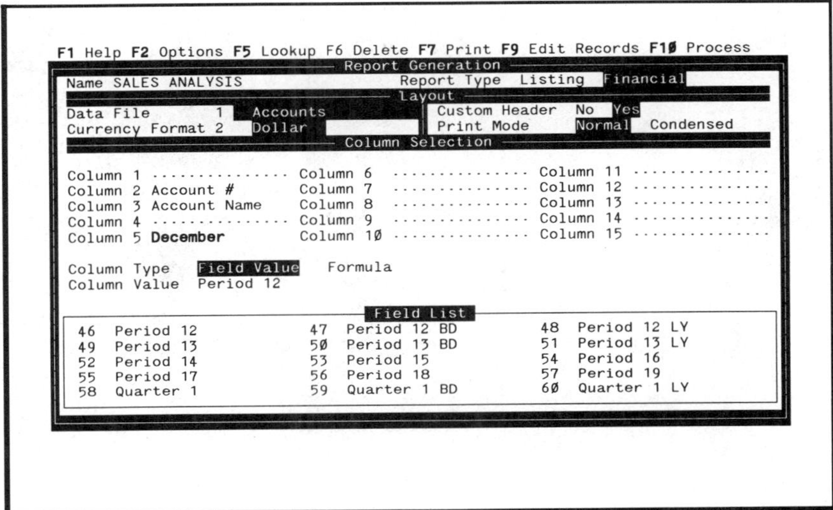

Figure 15.5: Column definitions

17. In the Variable Entry field, enter **NS** as the Name and **Net Sales** as the Description of the first variable. Press F10 to record the definition.
18. Enter **NP** as the Name of the second definition and **Net Purchase** as the Description. Figure 15.6 shows the screen at this point. Press F10 to record the definition.
19. Enter **SI**, **Sales Income** as the final variable, press F10 to record it, and press Esc to return to the Financial Detail Editing screen.
20. Enter **41** in the Account field. This is the number of the general ledger account for total sales. The name from the account record appears under Description. Each account you want included in the report must be added on a separate line.
21. Override the name from the account record by typing **Gross Sales** in the Description field. This changes the title on the report, but not in the account record.
22. In the Formula field, enter **+NS**, which indicates that the amount on this line is to be added to the variable Net Sales.

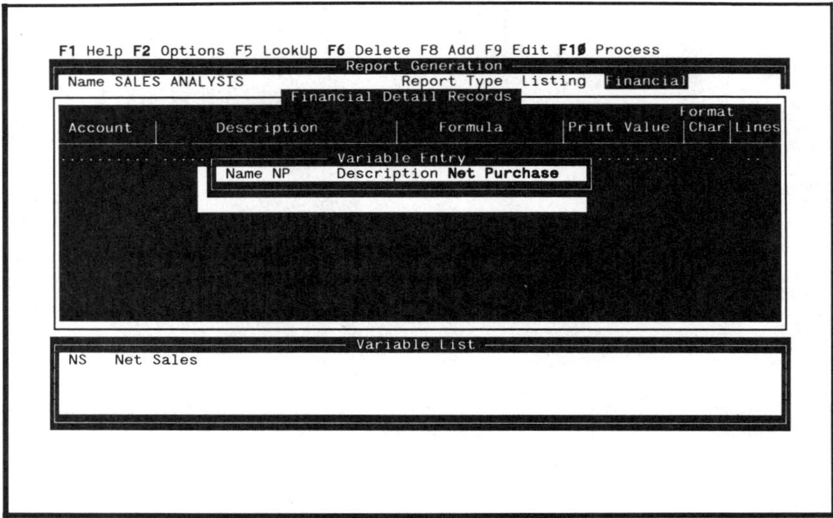

Figure 15.6: Defining variables to be used in a report

In this field, you can use + (plus) to add the amount to the variable), – (minus) to subtract the amount, or = (equal sign) to define another variable.

23. Press ↵ to accept the default Yes in the Print Value field, indicating this line is to print on the report. If you were using this line as part of an accumulation and did not want it to appear on the report, you would select No. An example of using a line for an accumulation is included later in this section.

24. Press ↵ in the Format Char field. You can enter a C in the Format Char field to center a description on the report, a - (hyphen) to print a single line under the amount fields on the report, or an = (equal sign) to print a double line.

25. Press ↵ in the Lines field. You can enter PG to start a new page after the current line, or a number to indicate how many blank lines to insert after the current line when printing the report. The maximum number of lines you can skip is 60.

When this book went to print, the Insert key, for inserting text in a field rather than overtyping, did not work.

26. Enter **5304** in the Account field. The account description, Sales Discounts, appears. Press the spacebar once and retype the account name in the new position. This indents the account name on the printed report.
27. Press ↵ to move to the Formula field and enter **-NS**, which indicates this amount is to be subtracted from Net Sales.
28. Press ↵ three times to accept the defaults in the Print Value, Format Char, and Lines fields.
29. On the next line, enter **42** in the Account field. Press the spacebar once and retype the description, Sales Returns.
30. Press ↵ to move to the Formula field and enter **+NS** to indicate this amount is to be included in the total for Net Sales.

In our report, Sales Returns is a contra account to Sales. It should be used to reduce the amount in the Sales account to present a more accurate picture of sales income. Both accounts are designated as revenue accounts. The Sales Returns account carries a minus sign, however, indicating it has an abnormal (debit) balance for a revenue account.

In order to subtract the Sales Returns amount from the Net Sales amount, we must make the entry for the Sales Returns amount a plus, just the opposite of what we want to do. The other account balance we are adding to the Net Sales amount, Sales Discounts, has a normal balance (debit) for its designation as an expense account. Therefore, we used the normal entry, a plus sign, to add it to the variable.

31. On the same line, move the cursor to the Format Char field and enter a hyphen (-). This will cause a single underline to print in each amount column after the sales return figures. Press ↵ to accept the default Lines field.
32. On the next line, press ↵ past the Account field. This line will contain a variable, not an account balance. Press the spacebar three times in the Description field, and enter **Net Sales** as the description for this entry. Skip the Formula field.
33. In the Print Value field enter **NS**, the identification of the variable that will be calculated from the balances in the Gross

Sales, Sales Discounts, and Sales Returns accounts (lines with NS in the Formula field). Press ↵ through the Format Char field.

34. Enter **1** in the Lines field to skip one line before printing the next line.

35. On the next line, enter **51** in the Account field. Press ↵ to leave the description, Costs of Goods Sold, and enter **+NP** in the Formula field to indicate this amount is to be added to Net Purchases. Press ↵ to move through the other fields on the line.

36. Enter **4404** in the Account field. This is the Purchase Discounts account. For this illustration, we are assuming that discounts for inventory item purchases only, not all purchase discounts, are tracked in this account. Press the spacebar once to indent and retype the description.

37. In the Formula field, enter **-NP** to subtract the amount on this line from Net Purchases. Press ↵ through the Print Value field. In the Format Char field, enter a - to print a single underline in the amount columns under the purchase discount figure. Press ↵ through the Lines field.

38. Press ↵ twice to move to the Description field on the next line. Press the spacebar three times, and enter **Net Purchases**. Press ↵ through the Formula field. For Print Value, enter **NP**, the identification of the variable that will be calculated from the balances in the Cost of Goods Sold and Purchase Discount accounts. Press ↵ through the Format Char field. Enter 1 in the Lines field to skip one line before printing the next line.

39. On the next line, press ↵ and enter **Net Sales Income** in the Description field. In the Formula field, enter **SI = NS-NP** to create the variable Net Sales Income and define it as Net Sales less Net Purchases. In the Print Value field, enter **SI** to print the value of Net Sales Income. In the Format Char field, enter = to print a double underline under the net sales figures. Enter **1** in the Lines field to skip one line before printing the next line.

40. On the last line, press ↵ and enter **Purchase/Sales (Net)** in the Description field to describe the ratio to be calculated and printed on this line. Press ↵ through the Formula field. In the Print Value field, enter **NP/SI**. Thus, Net Purchases will be divided by Sales Income to show the ratio of purchases to sales.

41. Press F10 to save the detail definition, and then press F10 to save the entire report definition.

Another useful function is the ability to do mathematics. Symbols allow you to add (+), subtract (–), multiply (*), divide (/), or do percentages (%). You can enclose operations in parentheses, when necessary. To begin a formula, press F8 in the Column field. The cursor moves to the Column Value field. Press F5 to move to the field list. Select the necessary fields, and enter the appropriate symbols. In the example shown in Figure 15.7, we have subtracted (–) the year-to-date budget (F6) from the year-to-date account balance (F3) to determine the budget variance.

Figure 15.8 shows another example of a report definition. This is a portion of an expense report format, and it illustrates how to center

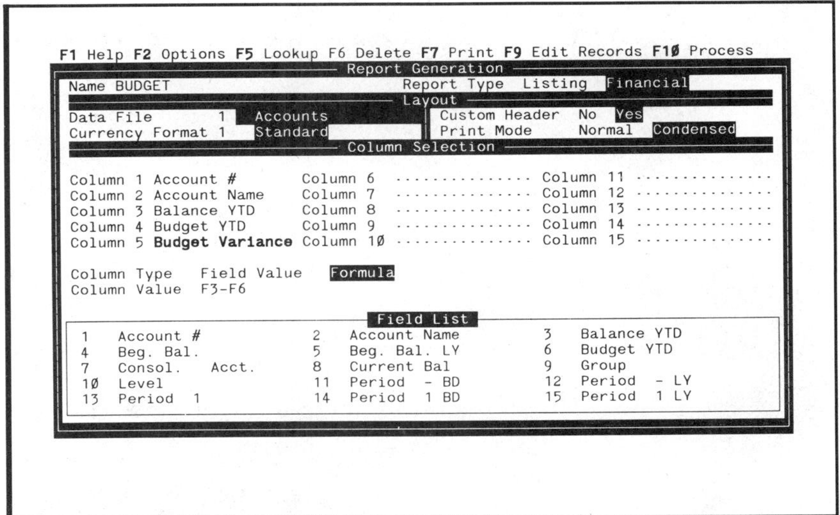

Figure 15.7: Using the formula option

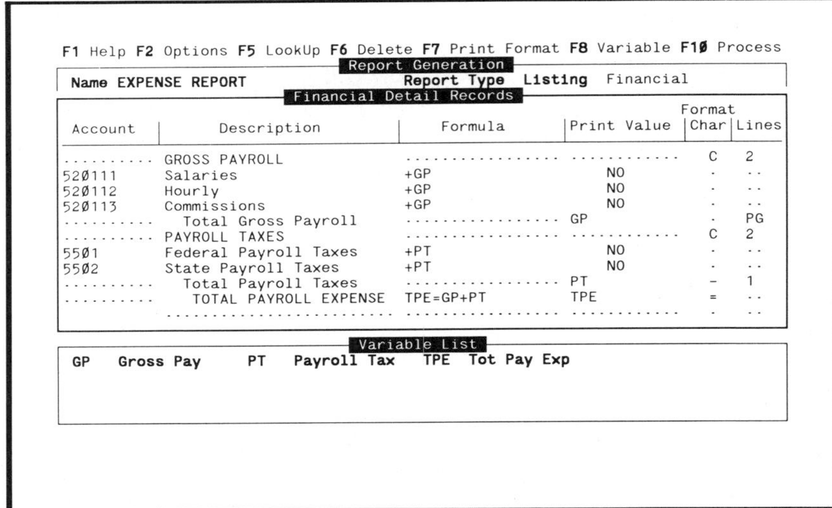

Figure 15.8: Accumulating balances in a financial report

a line description, accumulate balances without printing them individually, print a total of those balances as a variable, and start the next portion of the report on a new page.

Other function keys you can use when creating a report are F3 to insert a blank line above the cursor between existing detail lines, Shift-F8 to place the next account from the chart of accounts on the next line in the financial detail, F9 to toggle between Yes and No in the Print Value field, and Shift-F6 to delete a line in the financial detail.

ADDING A LISTING

Data from files other than general ledger account balances can be printed in a listing. Follow the steps outlined for adding a financial report, with the following three exceptions:

- For Report Type, select Listing.
- Enter a data file number in the Data File field. Figure 15.9 shows the available selections.
- To restrict the information to certain records in the data file, or to sort and rank the data, press F9. The Record Selection

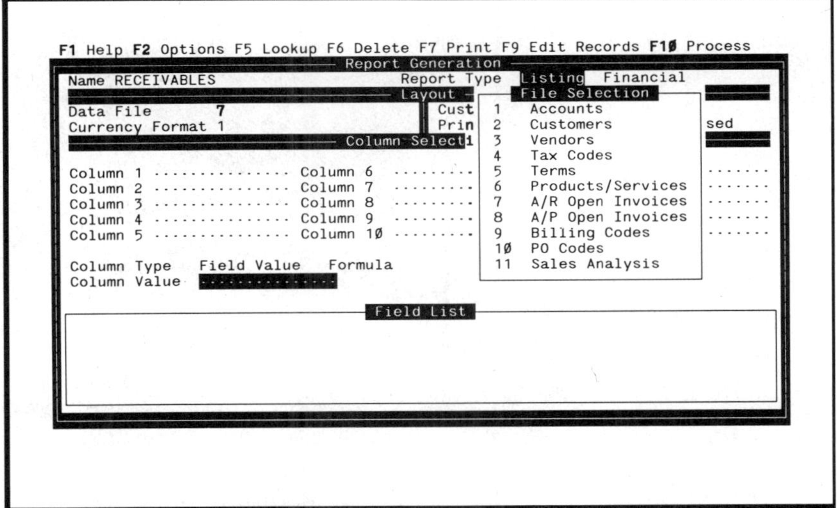

Figure 15.9: Selecting a data file for a listing

window appears. If you want to restrict the report, choose Conditional in the Records To Include field and complete the Field Selection portion of the window. Press F5 to select the field name, and then enter the From and To range for the field. To sort and rank the data, complete the Record Display portion of the window.

Figure 15.10 shows an example of criteria that will print each open invoice from the accounts receivable file for the customers in the range noted if the invoice is due in June and the amount is over $500 (assuming $99,999 is greater than any invoice you may write).

In the Logical Operation fields of the Field Selection portion of the window, you can select And or Or. When you use And as the operator, each criterion must be met. When you use Or as the operator, if any of the criteria is met, the record will be included. If we used the Or operator in our example, invoices would be printed if they were due in June or if they were over $500. Thus, an invoice for $25 that was due in June would be included in the listing.

Because of the Subtotal By and Rank By criteria in the example, the qualifying invoices for each customer will be listed together, sorted by invoice amount, with a subtotal for each customer and a grand total at the end.

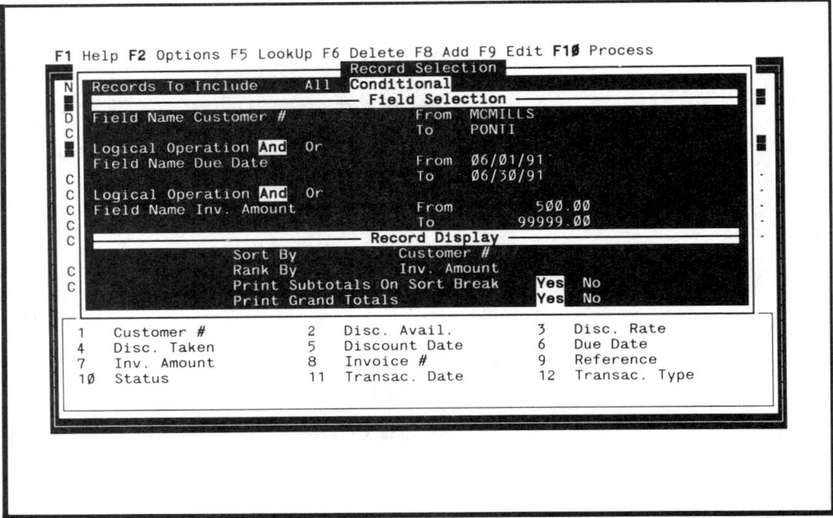

Figure 15.10: Entering criteria for a listing

PRINTING REPORTS AND LISTINGS

To print a report or listing, select Report Generator from the Reports menu. Enter the report name, press F7, and select the report disposition. Chapter 13 describes the steps for printing financial reports in more detail.

EDITING AND DELETING REPORTS AND LISTINGS

You can edit the financial reports and listings you created or the ones supplied by DacEasy. Follow the instructions below to first make a copy of the original report format, and then edit the copy:

1. On the Report Generation screen, enter the name of the report you want to copy.
2. Press Shift-F3 to copy the report.
3. Enter a name for the new report. DacEasy copies the original report and places it in the report list with the new name.

4. Press Esc to exit the original report, and then press ↵ to reselect Report Generator.
5. In the Name field, press F5 and select the new report from the lookup window.
6. Move the cursor to the line you want to edit, make your changes (as listed below), and press F10.

You can use the following techniques to edit a report:

- If you want to change the column heading, type over the existing description.
- If you want to use another field in a column, place the cursor beside the column number, press F5, and select the new field; it will replace the former one.
- To edit a formula, place the cursor beside the column number, press F8, and change the formula.
- If you want to edit the financial detail, press F9. To use another account, type its account number over the existing one. Press ↵, and the new account description will appear.
- To change any of the finanical detail parameters, move the cursor to the column and enter the parameter you want to use.
- To delete the line entirely, press Shift-F6. Use this command with caution as calculations on other lines might depend on the deleted line.
- To insert a new line between existing ones, place the cursor on the line below where you want to insert the new line and press F3. Then enter the data for the new line.
- To delete a variable, press F8, enter the name of the variable, and press F6.

When you are finished editing the report, print it to verify the results. If necessary, make corrections and reprint the report for verification. When you are satisfied with the new report format, you can delete the original report if you won't be using it.

Use caution when deleting because you cannot retrieve a deleted report. Creating reports takes time, but deleting them takes only two keystrokes.

To delete a financial report (one supplied by DacEasy or one you created), enter the name of the report on the Report Generator screen. Press F6 to delete it, and select Yes when prompted to verify your intention to delete the report.

CREATING GRAPHS FROM DACEASY DATA

From the Reports menu, select Graphics.

3.1 You must use Graph+Mate to create graphs.

The Graphics function was incomplete when this book went to print; therefore, the upgraded product may differ somewhat from the examples here. At publication time, only general ledger account balances could be graphed.

You can create graphs in several styles, including pie and bar charts, from data in your DacEasy Accounting files. These graphs can be displayed on the screen and printed.

To create a graph, select Graphics from the Report menu. You will see the Graphics screen, on which you define the graph's name, data file, layout, and headings.

Follow these steps to complete the fields on the Graphics screen:

1. In the Name Field, enter a name to identify the graph. This does not appear on the graph. You enter the title of the graph in the Title field.
2. A list of files from which you select data to graph is displayed when your cursor moves to the Data File field. Enter the number of the file you want to use.
3. Enter the number of the type of graph you want from the list that displays when the cursor moves to the Type field.
4. In the Format field, select to display your data in currency, percents, fractions, or general format.
5. To print the graph, as well as display it on screen, select Yes in the Print field. You will be asked to select the Printer Name and the Rotation, which is either Portrait (vertical) or Landscape (horizontal) and Print Size, which is either Small (condensed) or large (standard).
6. In the Border field, highlight Yes if you want to place a border around the graph.
7. Select Yes in the Display Values field, if, in addition to the graphic, you want the actual value in the file printed.

8. The Orientation field refers to the x and y axes and their placement on the graph. Vertical orientation places the y axis vertically on the graph. You can place grid lines across the graph horizontally, vertically, or both to make it more readable.
9. In the Headings portion of the screen, enter the Title, and if appropriate, a Subtitle to print at the top of the graph.
10. In the Footer field, you can enter text to be printed to the lower left of the graph.
11. In the X-Axis and Y-Axis fields, you can enter a label for the vertical and horizontal (x and y) axes to identify the parameters used in the graph.
12. Each heading can be printed in one of four type sizes. Use the F9 key to toggle between the choices: X-Large, Large, Medium, and Small.
13. Press F10 to save the format. Figure 15.11 shows an example of a completed Graphics screen for a sales analysis bar chart.

Once you define the layout and heading for a graph, you can use the format to graph various data. You can use the quick graph option

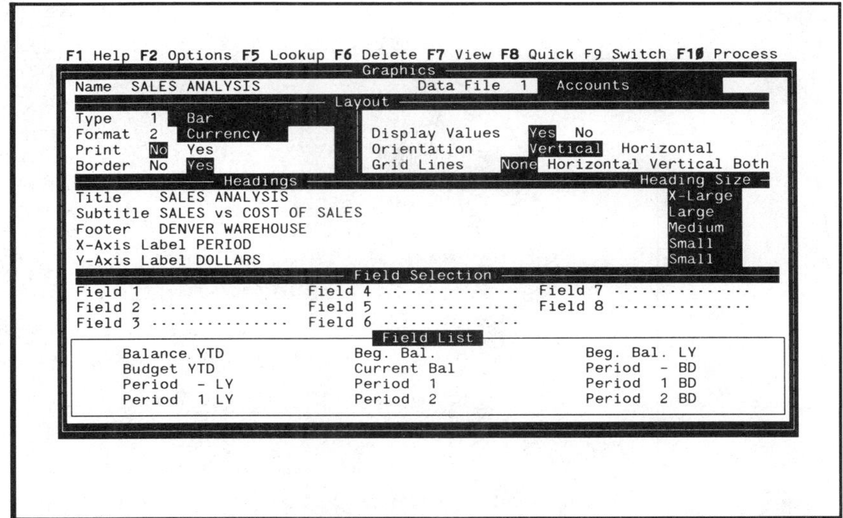

Figure 15.11: Defining the layout of a graph

to graph actual or year-to-date balances and budgets for this year and last year. The field selection window provides a greater selection of data. The steps below use the quick graph option.

1. Press F7 to display the Graph screen, on which you define the data you want on the graph.
2. In the Format field, select Actual to include actual activity for the periods you select, or Accumulating to graph the balances.
3. Use the F9 key to toggle between Yes and No to select the periods you want on the graph.
4. In the Account field, enter the number of each account you want on the graph. The account name appears in the Description field.
5. Use the F9 key to toggle between Yes and No in the This Year, Budget, and Last Year fields to identify the data you want to graph.
6. Press F7 to process the graph. It will appear on screen and should print if you selected Yes in the Print field.

The Graph screen for the sample chart is shown in Figure 15.12. Only period 12 and data from this year are selected. The screen display of the sample graph is shown in Figure 15.13.

To save your field selections, after defining the layout instead of using Quick Graph, continue to the Field Selection window. To define the fields you want in the graph, place the cursor in Field 1, press F5 to move to the Field List, highlight the type of data you want to graph, and press ↵ to select it. The completed graph definition appears as in Figure 15.14.

After you select the types of data, press F7 to display the Graphics Selection window. Place the cursor on each account you want to include and press F8 to set the notation in the Graph column to Yes as shown in Figure 15.15. Use F8 again if you want to remove the account from your selections.

After marking all accounts, press ↵ in the Graphics Record Selection window to display the graph. Each field you select will show

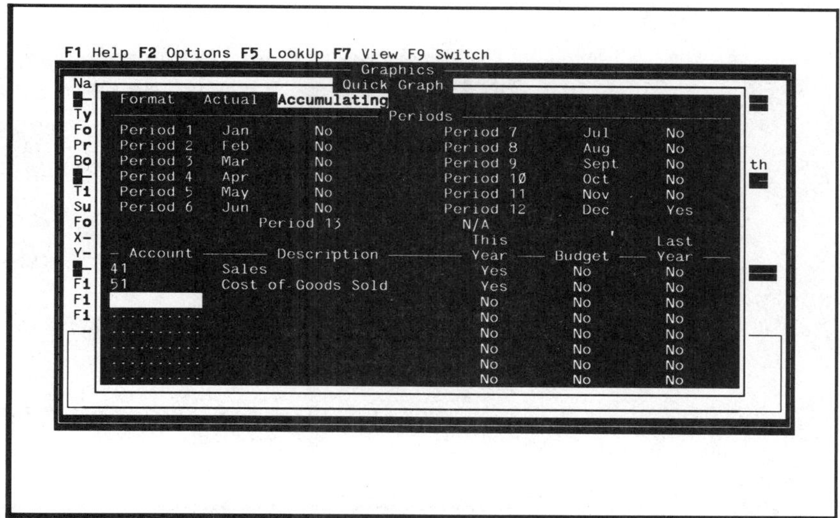

Figure 15.12: Selecting data for a quick graph

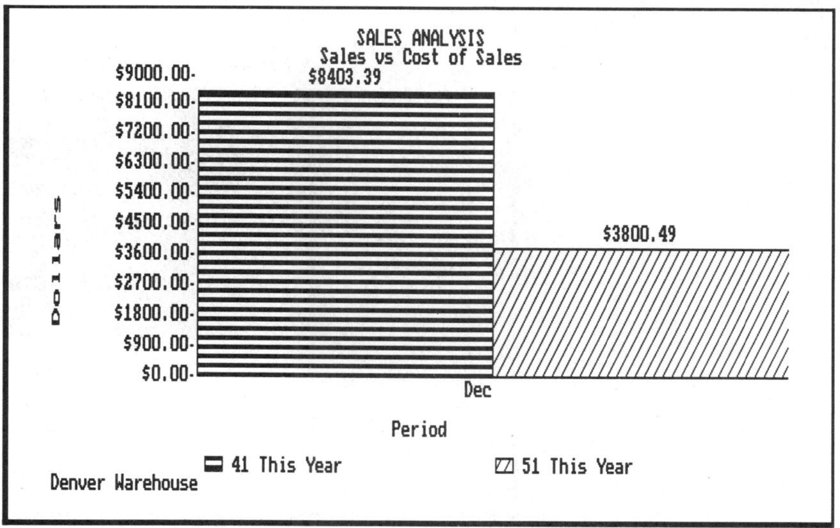

Figure 15.13: Displaying a bar graph of general ledger balances

on the graph for every account you select. In Figure 15.16, you see the activity for the last three periods of the year for both the telephone and postage accounts.

The graph will also print if the Print field is set to Yes. Press F10 to save the format and the field selections. Your account selections are

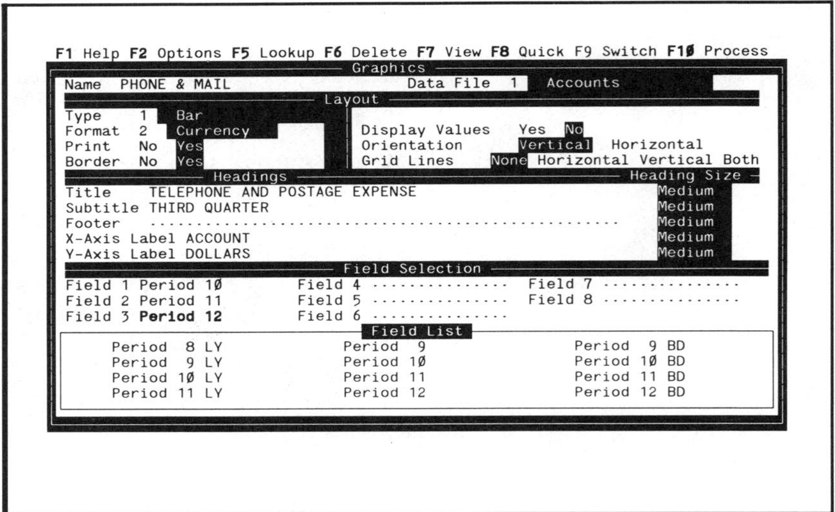

Figure 15.14: Selecting fields for a graph

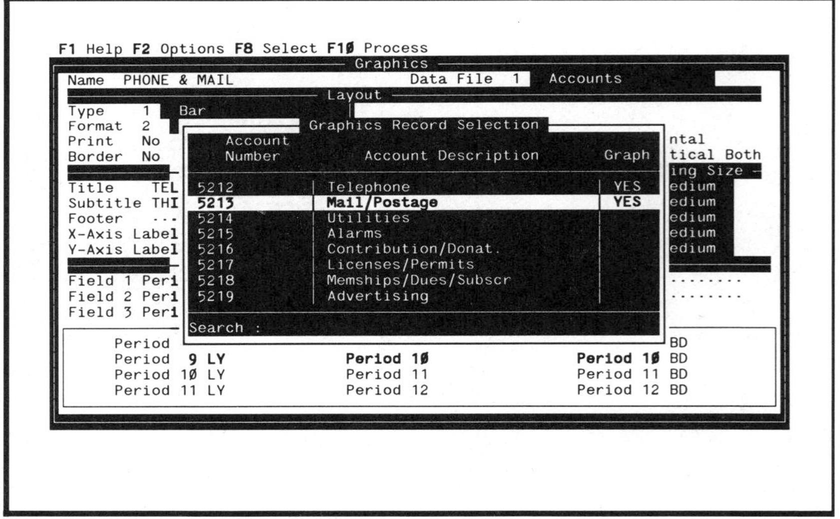

Figure 15.15: Selecting accounts for the graph

not saved. You must reselect them each time you process the graph.

This concludes the chapters on DacEasy Accounting. Next we'll discuss DacEasy Payroll, which manages payments to employees and personnel information.

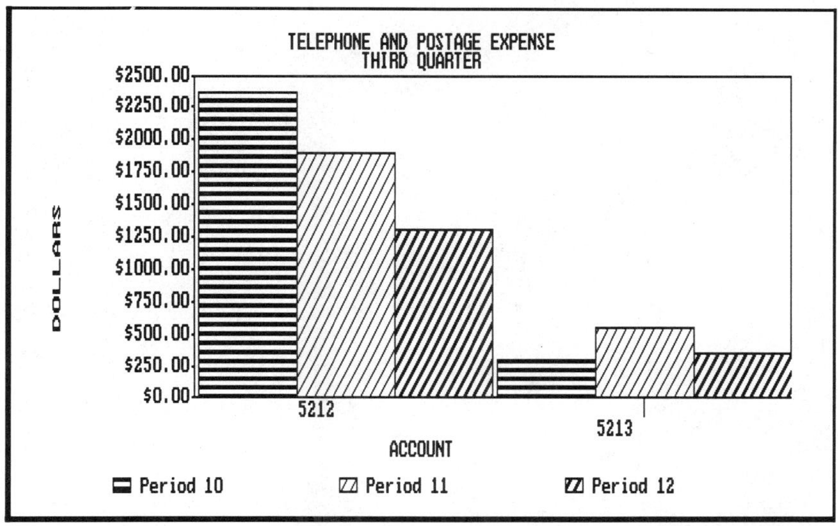

Figure 15.16: Period activity for two accounts

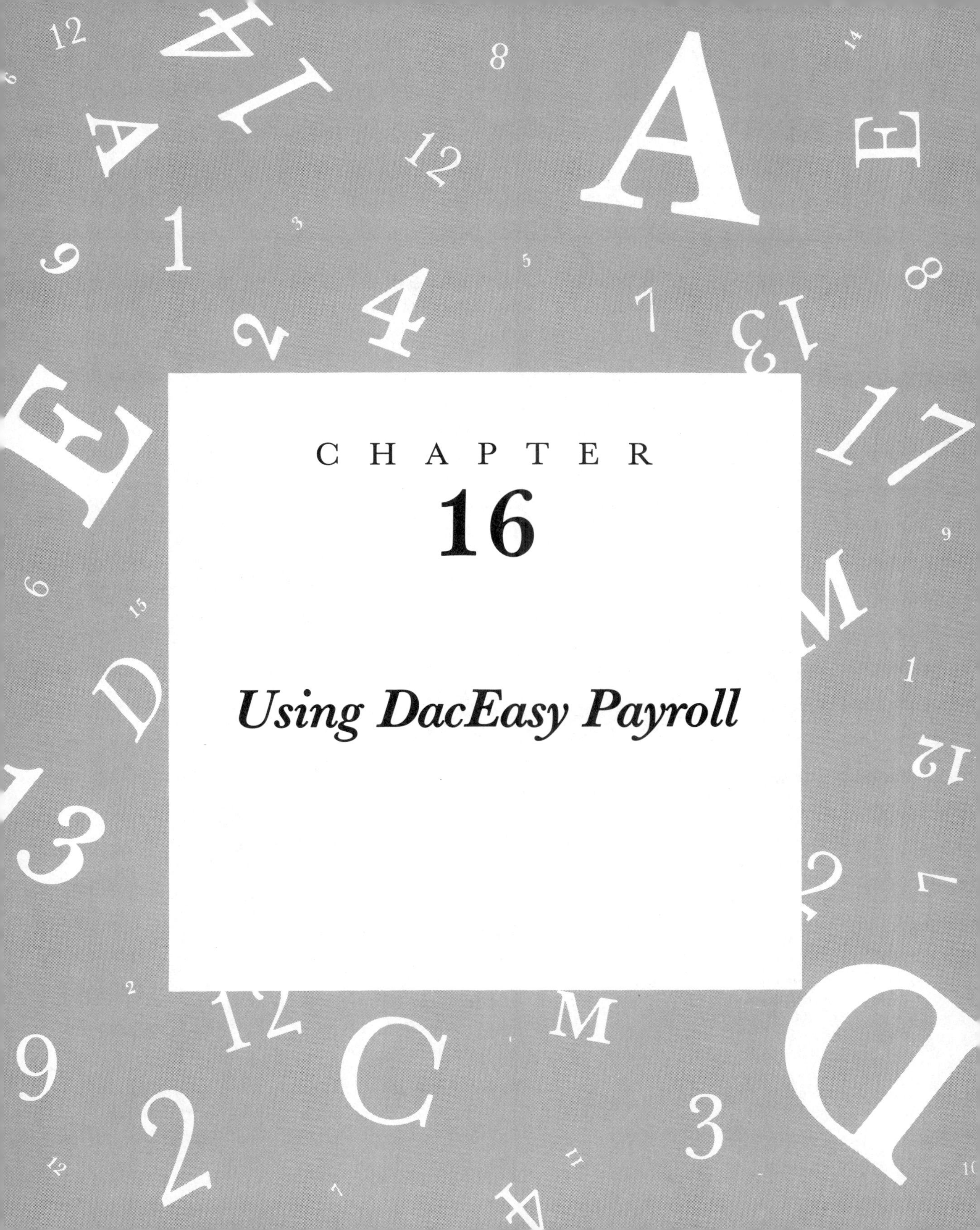

CHAPTER

16

Using DacEasy Payroll

THIS CHAPTER DESCRIBES DACEASY PAYROLL, VERsions 4.1 and 3.1. Both versions can be used alone or integrated with DacEasy Accounting. The information presented here is a brief overview of the payroll process, and it is specific to the DacEasy program. Not only do payroll regulations change, they vary from state to state. You should obtain a copy of labor and payroll regulations from both federal government and state agencies and adhere to those regulations. Also, have your accountant review your setup and reporting practices.

The optimum time to start a new payroll system is at the beginning of a calendar year. At any other time, you must enter data from your old system into the new system. Each employee's year-to-date wages and the total taxes withheld in each tax category, for example, must be included in records begun midyear.

SETTING UP DACEASY PAYROLL

After you install DacEasy Payroll, as explained in Appendix A, you are ready to initialize the program. Then you need to define system parameters.

INITIALIZING THE PROGRAM

3.1 Change to the subdirectory DEP3, and then begin the program by typing **dep3**. The instructions in this chapter assume your computer has a hard disk.

3.1 During initialization, you must also designate whether or not you have a color monitor and enter company information, which is explained later in this chapter. You also must switch disks to copy files from the Tax File disk.

Initializing DacEasy Payroll is similar to initializing DacEasy Accounting. Follow the steps below:

1. Turn on the computer. At the C: prompt, enter **cd\dep4** to change to the Payroll program subdirectory.
2. Enter **dep4** to initialize the program.
3. Press ↵ when asked if you are a new user.
4. Press ↵ to select Open from the File pull-down menu.
5. At the Identification Name and Directory Name/Path prompts, enter your company name and the path and subdirectory for your data files.
6. Press F10 to record the information. A message appears telling you the files are being created. When the initialization

process is completed, you will see the DacEasy Payroll Main menu, as shown in Figure 16.1.

DEFINING YOUR COMPANY

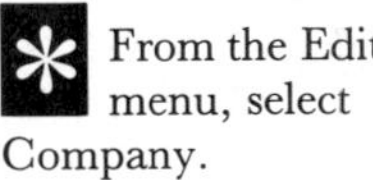
From the Edit menu, select Company.

Your next step after initializing the program is to define your company. You enter the name and address that will be used as headings on your reports, your company work hours, and file information.

To define your company, select the Company option from the Edit menu. You will see the Edit Company screen. Table 16.1 describes the fields on this screen, and Figure 16.2 shows a completed example.

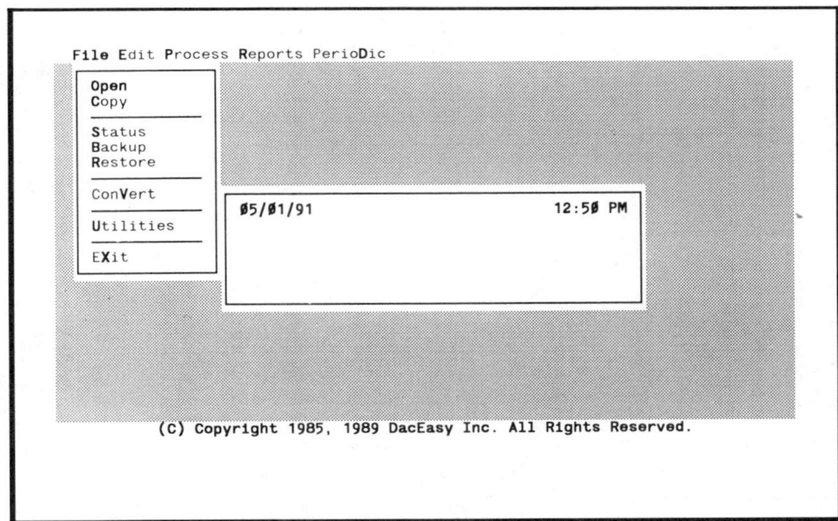

Figure 16.1: The DacEasy Payroll Main menu

Table 16.1: Fields on the Edit Company Screen

Field	Definition
Employer Id	The federally assigned employer number your company uses to report wages and taxes to the IRS.
Name	The name of your company.
Address 1	Your mailing address.
Address 2	Your street address.

Table 16.1: Fields on the Edit Company Screen (continued)

Field	Definition
City	The city where your company is located.
State and Zip	The abbreviation for the state your company is located in and the zip code.
Phone and Fax	Your area code, phone number, and fax number.
Days Year	The standard number of days an employee works in a year in your company.
Hrs. Day	The standard number of hours an employee works in a day.
Week	The standard number of hours an employee works in a week.
SemiMonth	The standard number of hours an employee works in a semimonthly payroll period.
FICA	The percent your company is assessed currently on employee wages for FICA (Federal Insurance Contribution Act) taxes. Use the *NN.NNNN* format; for example, enter 7.5100 for slightly over 7½%.
Limit	The maximum earnings per employee on which FICA taxes are assessed.
FUTA	The percent your company is assessed currently on employee wages for FUTA (Federal Unemployment Tax Act) wages.
Limit	The maximum earnings per employee on which FUTA taxes are assessed.
Erase check file after Post Process	Select No if you want to maintain a register of the payroll checks you issue. Otherwise, select Yes to have the file deleted after you post payroll.
Create Monthly file when Posting	Select Yes if you want to create a file which allows you to print the monthly report. Otherwise, select No.
Interface with DacEasy Accounting 4.1	Select Yes if you want to interface the Payroll program with DacEasy Accounting. Payroll transactions will be accumulated automatically into a journal labeled PY to be posted to the general ledger. If you are not using DacEasy Accounting or want to enter payroll information manually in your general ledger, select No.
DacEasy Accounting 4.1 Path	If you selected to interface with DacEasy Accounting, designate the path (drive, directory, and subdirectory) to the accounting files. If you used the default settings when installing the accounting program, the suggested c:\dea4\files is correct.

Enter your employer identification number, company address, and telephone and fax numbers on the top portion of the screen. In the Yearly Information section, indicate the standard number of work days per year and hours worked per day, week, and semi-monthly. The most common responses are shown in Figure 16.2.

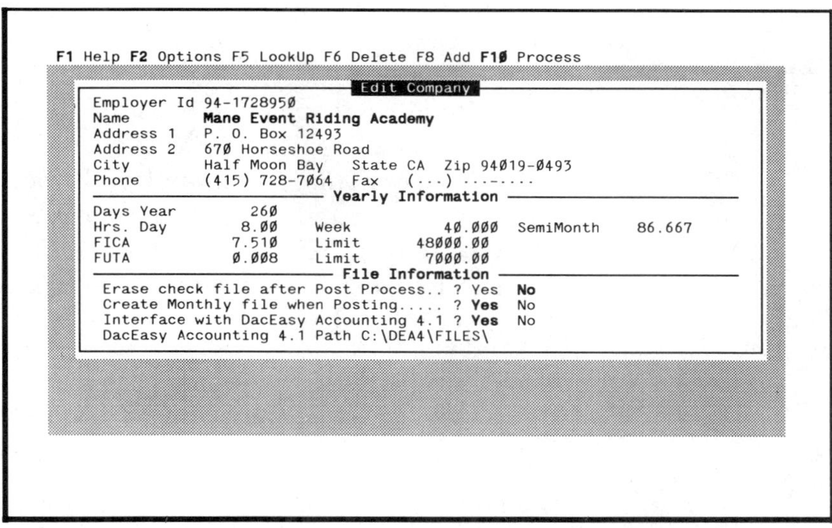

Figure 16.2: A completed company definition

The workday and hour calculations are all based on a full-time employee.

To calculate the entries for your company, base your figures on 52 weeks in a year. For example, if employees work 5 days a week, there are 260 days in your year. If employees normally work only 4 days a week, there are 156 days in your work year (4 work days × 52 weeks). Some companies routinely schedule employees to work 10 hours a day, 4 days a week, for a total of 40 hours a week. Other companies work a 7-hour day for a total of 35 hours a week. To determine the number of hours in your semimonth, multiply the number of hours per week times 52 weeks, and then divide the result by 24 (two pay periods a month).

In the File Information section, select whether or not to erase your check file after posting and whether or not to create a file for a monthly report. Also indicate if you are interfacing with DacEasy Accounting and the path to those files.

SETTING MONITOR AND PRINTER PARAMETERS

From the Edit menu, select Monitor Colors or Printers.

To set screen colors, select the Monitor Colors option from the Edit menu. See Chapter 3 for instructions for selecting how you want various areas of the screen to look. Areas on Payroll screens are the same as those in the Accounting program, except that the Accounting names Main Menu, Submenu, and Process are replaced by Horizontal, Vertical, and Background respectively.

3.1 From the Options menu, select Colors or Printer.

To set printer parameters, select the Printers option from the Edit menu. Move to the Printer Name field, press F5, and select your printer from the lookup window. If your printer is not listed, use its manual to determine the codes to enter for normal and condensed type. Payroll reports, like those in DacEasy Accounting, print in either 10- or 17-character-per-inch type. Printer codes are discussed in more detail in Chapter 3.

CREATING PAYROLL PASSWORDS

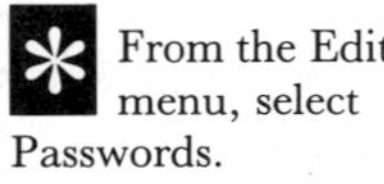

From the Edit menu, select Passwords.

You can restrict access to DacEasy by establishing passwords. The program will require the user to enter the correct password for the selected option. You can control access to levels 1 through 5 plus Controller, which are described in Table 16.2.

Table 16.2: Payroll Password Levels

Password Level	**Access**
Level 1	This lowest level gives users access to check printing and to check reconciliation.
Level 2	Allows users into level 1, as well as payroll generation and cancellation, payroll register, check register, department report, directory and labels, and purging.
Level 3	Allows users into levels 1 and 2 and report generation, the employee and tax files, and all periodic routines.
Level 4	Allows users into all options except posting, the password file, the File menu, and monitor and printer setup.
Level 5	Allows users into all options except the password file.
Controller	This top level allows the user into the entire program.

Version 3.1: Level 1 allows access to check printing and the Options menu (except Password option). Level 2 is the same as in 4.1, with the addition of check reconciliation and posting. Level 3 gives access to all options and files but the department, control, and password files. Level 4 excludes only the password file, and level 5 allows access to the whole program. The Controller level does not exist.

3.1 From the Options menu, select Password.

To enter passwords, select the Passwords option from the Edit menu. Then move the cursor to each level in turn and enter a password (up to eight characters) for that level. Press F10 to process your entries.

When you exit DacEasy and restart the Payroll program, you will be prompted to enter your password. As a safeguard, the characters you type will not appear on the screen. Chapter 3 discusses passwords in more detail.

CHECKING FILE STATUS

* From the File menu, select Status.

To check your file usage, select the Status option from the File menu. DacEasy alters the number of existing records during normal payroll processing. The Transaction file is cleared when you post. The Check Register file is reduced when you purge checks. The Employee Master file is cleared when you select to delete an employee record. You can only delete employee records after year-end processing, when no period-to-date totals exist in the record.

3.1 From the Options menu, select Status or Rehash.

CHECKING YOUR FILE STATUS AND REHASHING FILES IN VERSION 3.1 The File Status and File Rehash screens look identical, but you can only change file sizes through the rehash function. The default sizes created during initialization are based on the number of employees you say you have. If you need to enlarge or decrease the size reserved for your files, select the Rehash option from the Options menu.

Before running the rehash routine, back up your files. To change the size of your files, position the cursor on the file you want to edit and enter the new size. Press ↵ through any fields you don't want to change. The rehash process begins when you press ↵ at the Check Register file field.

MAINTAINING THE TAX TABLES

* From the Edit menu, select Tax Table.

Your tax files contain data from which payroll taxes are calculated. To define the federal and state taxes that apply to the payroll you issue, select the Tax Table option from the Edit menu. DacEasy displays the Edit Tax Table window.

3.1 From the File menu, select Tax Table. Press F7 and F8 to scroll through the list of states, then enter the number of the state in the No. field.

It is your responsibility to validate the state tax rates currently in effect. Most states require tax deductions for monies earned in the state; others require tax deductions from employees who live in the state, regardless of where the money was earned. Check your state regulations.

To find the number of the table you want to use, press F5, then PgUp and PgDn to scroll through the list of states, and then position the cursor and press ↵ to insert the number assigned to the state in the Table field. The description and default tax information appears, as shown in Figure 16.3 for employees working in Arkansas. The date in the State Id Number field in table #1 indicates how current the default tax information is. If the taxation figures have changed, enter the new data on the Edit Tax Table screen. The fields on this screen are described in Table 16.3.

```
F1 Help F2 Options F5 LookUp F6 Delete F8 Add F10 Process
                         Edit Tax Table
Table 07
------------------------- State Information ---------------------------
Description ARKANSAS               Id ..........          Code AR
Supplemental Earnings %     0.000
SUTA                  %     0.0000  Limit           0.000
SDIF                  %     0.000   Limit           0.000
------------------- Allowances/Credits/Exemptions ----------------------
Field1          0.000     Field2         0.100     Field3      500.000
Field4         17.500     Field5      6.000000     Field6        0.000
--------------------------- Tax Brackets -------------------------------
   Earnings      %       Base        Earnings      %          Base
       0.01    1.00       0.00           0.00    0.00          0.00
    3000.00    2.50      30.00           0.00    0.00          0.00
    6000.00    3.50     105.00           0.00    0.00          0.00
    9000.00    4.50     210.00           0.00    0.00          0.00
   15000.00    6.00     480.00           0.00    0.00          0.00
   25000.00    7.00    1080.00           0.00    0.00          0.00
       0.00    0.00       0.00           0.00    0.00          0.00
       0.00    0.00       0.00           0.00    0.00          0.00
       0.00    0.00       0.00
```

Figure 16.3: Tax table with default information for Arkansas

Table 16.3: Fields on the Edit Tax Table Screen

Field	Description
Table	The number of the tax table you want to edit. Table 1 is Federal-Single, table 2 is Federal-Married, and tables 3 through 77 are state tables (selected from the State Tax Table window).
Description	The program displays the description for the table number entered.
Id	Your state employer number in tables 3 through 69 or federal employer number in table 1 or 2.
Code	The state abbreviation.

Table 16.3: Fields on the Edit Tax Table Screen (continued)

Field	Description
Supplemental Earnings %	The percentage assessed by the taxing entity on irregular earnings, such as tips or prizes.
SUTA %	The SUTA (State Unemployment Tax Act) percentage.
Limit	The maximum earnings per employee on which SUTA tax is calculated.
SDIF	The SDIF (State Disability Insurance Fund) percentage.
Limit	The maximum earnings per employee on which SDIF taxes are calculated.
Field 1 through 6	These fields are used to define allowances, credits, and exemptions. The definition in each field varies according to the taxing entity you are maintaining the tax table for, as defined in the DacEasy Payroll manual. The contents of the fields vary from state to state.
Earnings	The annual earnings level to which the tax applies.
%	The tax percent that is assessed on the amount over the earnings in the Earnings field for this tax bracket.
Base	The flat amount that is assessed if the amount exceeds the minimum earnings in this tax bracket. This is in addition to the percent assessed on the amount over the minimum.

* From the Edit menu, select Department.

3.1 From the File menu, select Department.

An *employer contribution* is a company-paid amount that is calculated on the employee's wages, but does not affect those wages (such as federal unemployment tax). It is an expense and also a liability until the amount is paid to the taxing entity. An *employee deduction* is an amount subtracted from the employee's gross wages (such as withholding taxes or union dues).

MAINTAINING DEPARTMENTS

Payroll departments are a means of defining the rate structure, contributions, earnings, and deductions that are common to a group of employees. They can also act as a cost center, helping you determine your payroll costs for different areas in your company. Rather than segregating data into numerous, department-related accounts in the general ledger, you can use the Payroll department report to break the figures down for analysis.

If you do not have a standard chart of accounts already set up, you must create a numbering scheme to identify these various liabilities, contributions, deductions, and earnings.

A department code, with associated earnings and deductions, must be defined before it can be used in an employee file. Each employee must be assigned to a department.

You maintain departments through a series of three screens. Table 16.4 describes the fields on these screens. Select the Department option from the Edit menu, and you will see the first Edit Department screen. Figure 16.4 shows a completed example.

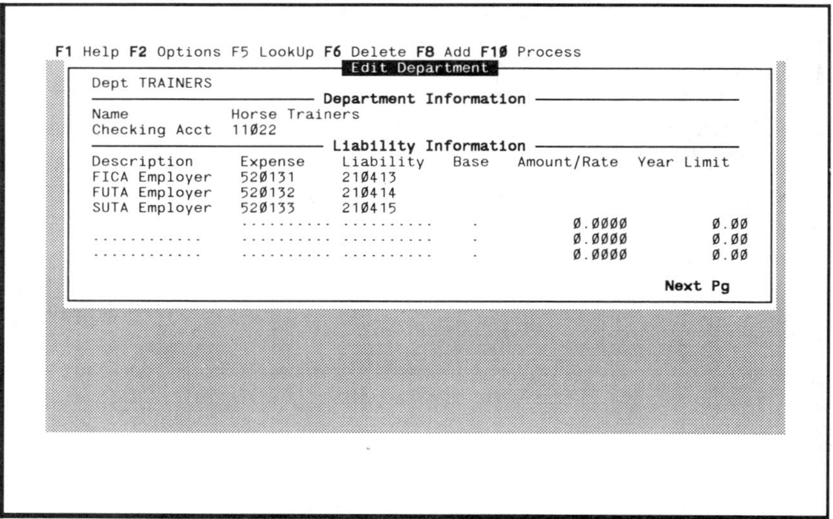

Figure 16.4: Defining employer expense and liability accounts

Table 16.4: Fields on the Edit Department Screens

Field	Description
Dept	Enter a new department code (10 alphanumeric characters maximum) or enter the number of an existing department you want to edit.
Name	The name of the department.
Checking Acct	The number of the general ledger cash account for the checking account from which you pay employees assigned to this department. Although it is better practice to have a separate checking and general ledger account for payroll checks, you can use the same account that you defined for payments on payables.
Liability Information	
Description	The description of the contribution. The program lists FICA Employer, for the FICA taxes paid by the employer on gross wages for social security; FUTA Employer, for the FUTA taxes paid by the employer on gross wages; and SUTA Employer, for the SUTA taxes paid by the employer on gross wages.
Expense	The number of the general ledger account where you track the payroll expense for this department. If you are interfacing with DacEasy Accounting, the account must be designated as a detail account in your chart of accounts.
Liability	The number of the general ledger account where you track the payroll liability for this department. It must be a detail account if you are interfacing with DacEasy Accounting.

Table 16.4: Fields on the Edit Department Screens (continued)

Field	Description
Liability Information (continued)	
Base	The basis used to calculate the tax. A *$* represents a flat amount. The other codes are for a percentage of an amount, as follows: *G* for net gross (earnings after nontaxable deductions have been subtracted), *T* for total gross (all earnings, codes 1 through 15) before deductions, *W* for federal withholding taxes, *F* for FICA withholding taxes, or *S* for state withholding taxes.
Amount/Rate	The percentage or the flat amount used in the calculation.
Year Limit	The maximum earnings amount on which the expense and/or liability applies. You must enter an amount. If no limit exists, enter an amount higher than any earnings an employee will have in one year so the contribution will be assessed on all earnings.
Earnings Information	
Code	Assigned by the system.
Description	Available after code 8 to describe a user- defined earnings code.
Account	The general ledger account that tracks the expense for these earnings.
Type	Only available for user-defined earnings. Enter one of the following codes: *1* for flat amount, *2* for percent of gross earnings for standard codes 1 through 8, *3* for unit (piece) rate or commission, *4* for a flat amount based on each hour worked in earnings code 2 category (hourly earnings), or *5* for a percent of gross earnings based on all earnings from codes 1 through 15 (Payroll 3.1 uses only codes 1 through 8). Unit rate earnings (type 3) are calculated by multiplying the number of units (determined by the number of hours paid on hourly employees or the number of days paid on salaried employees) by the special earnings rate. Flat amount earnings (type 4) are not available for salaried employees.
Amount/Rate	The amount or percent used to calculate the earnings. All tips, vacation and sick leave, and EIC earnings must be recorded through the Entry option during payroll processing.
Base	Indicates if earnings are subject to withholding taxes by the federal government (first column) or state government (second column) according to the following codes: *N* for nontaxable, *T* for taxable according to the regular tax tables, or *S* for taxable according to the supplemental tax rate.
Deduction Information	
Code	Assigned by the program. Codes 16 through 20 are predefined and cannot be changed.
Description	Available after code 20 for user-defined deductions. These might be for employee-paid insurance premiums, union dues, or other monies withheld from net earnings and administered by the employer codes.

Table 16.4: Fields on the Edit Department Screens (continued)

Field	Description
Deduction Information (continued)	
Account	The general ledger account to track the liability for the amount deducted from the employee's wages.
Type	Only available for user-defined deductions. Designate the deduction type from the following standard codes: *1* for flat amount, *2* for percent of gross earnings from codes 1 through 8, *3* for per unit, *4* for hourly rate, or *5* for percent of gross earnings from codes 1 through 15. For cafeteria plan deductions, use the following types: *A* for flat amount, *B* for a percentage of regular earnings codes 1 through 8, and *C* for percentage of all earnings codes 1 through 15 if the deduction is exempt from SUTA. If the cafeteria plan is SUTA taxable, use the following types: *D* for flat amount, *E* for earnings 1 through 8, and *F* for all earnings 1 through 15.
Amount/Rate	Only available for user-defined deductions. Enter the amount or percentage upon which the calculation for the deduction is based.
Base	Indicate whether the deduction is subtracted from gross earnings before calculating federal withholding taxes (column 1) or state withholding taxes (column 2) according to the following codes: *N* for not deductible from gross earnings, *T* for deductible before withholding calculations, or *S* for treated as supplemental earnings for withholding calculations and deductible from gross earnings (for example, for reported tips).

Enter the department number, name, and checking account information. Even if you are not interfacing with DacEasy Accounting, you must enter the general ledger account numbers to track totals for each payroll expense and liability.

3.1 You can add an expense account to your DacEasy Accounting chart of accounts during department entry. After you enter the new account number, DacEasy asks if you want to create it. Respond Yes and then enter the account name and general account number it is subsidiary to.

You can define three additional employer contributions per department. The liabilities and expenses will be generated on every payroll you process for employees in the department. You must complete the Expense and Liability fields for the three standard tax categories (FICA, FUTA, and SUTA) and any employer contributions you add. If you are using the chart of accounts supplied with DacEasy Accounting, the correct accounts for the standard payroll expenses and liabilities are shown in Figure 16.4. The Base, Amount/Rate, and Year Limit fields are only available for user-defined liabilities. The calculations for FICA, FUTA, and SUTA are determined from information in the tax tables.

After you have defined the last employer expense, or if you press PgDn, the screen for defining earnings codes appears. Figure 16.5 shows a completed example, which includes hourly and overtime rates.

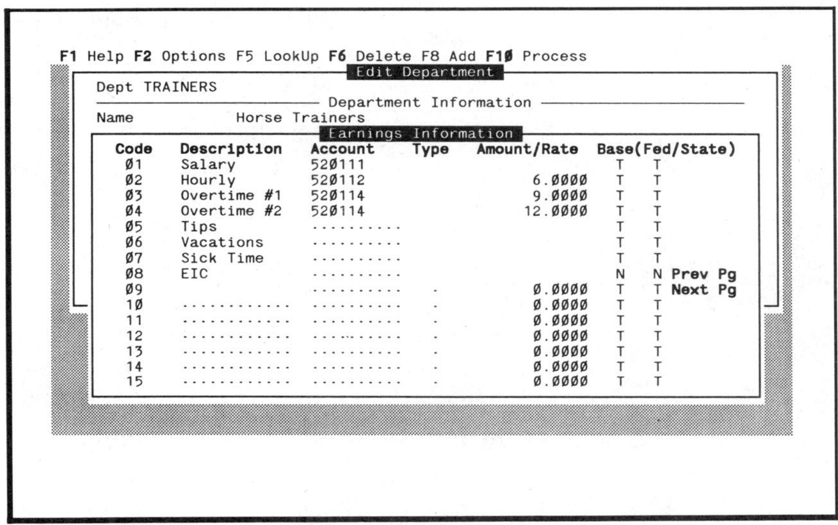

F1 Help **F2** Options F5 LookUp **F6** Delete F8 Add **F1Ø** Process

Edit Department

Dept TRAINERS

Department Information

Name Horse Trainers

Earnings Information

Code	Description	Account	Type	Amount/Rate	Base(Fed/State)		
Ø1	Salary	52Ø111			T	T	
Ø2	Hourly	52Ø112		6.ØØØØ	T	T	
Ø3	Overtime #1	52Ø114		9.ØØØØ	T	T	
Ø4	Overtime #2	52Ø114		12.ØØØØ	T	T	
Ø5	Tips	....			T	T	
Ø6	Vacations	....			T	T	
Ø7	Sick Time	....			T	T	
Ø8	EIC	....			N	N	**Prev Pg**
Ø9		....	.	Ø.ØØØØ	T	T	**Next Pg**
1Ø	....	....	.	Ø.ØØØØ	T	T	
11	....	....	.	Ø.ØØØØ	T	T	
12	....	....	.	Ø.ØØØØ	T	T	
13	....	....	.	Ø.ØØØØ	T	T	
14	....	....	.	Ø.ØØØØ	T	T	
15	....	....	.	Ø.ØØØØ	T	T	

Figure 16.5: Defining earnings codes

Earnings are monies paid to an employee or independent contractor for work performed.

Earnings codes define the categories of earnings possible in a given department. DacEasy supplies standard earnings categories for codes 1 through 8, as follows:

- Code 1, Salary, is for monies paid as a flat amount each pay period. The amount must be defined in the employee record.
- Code 2, Hourly, is for monies paid at the regular rate for the standard number of working hours.
- Code 3, Overtime #1, is for monies paid at a special rate for hours worked beyond the standard number in a pay period, for example, hours over eight a day at the regular hourly rate.
- Code 4, Overtime #2, is for monies paid at a premium rate for hours worked under special circumstances, for example, holidays at double the regular hourly rate.
- Code 5, Tips, is for tips paid to an employee through the company.
- Code 6, Vacations, is for monies paid when an employee is on vacation.

- Code 7, Sick Time, is for monies paid when an employee is ill.
- Code 8, EIC, is for monies paid that qualify for earned income credit (applicable to low-income, working parents). Wages that qualify are not taxed.

You can define seven additional earnings per department. You might want to include categories such as sales commissions, employee bonuses, shift differential, travel allowances, and payments for contract labor. Additional earnings are only calculated for employees you designate, either by entering the related code in the employee record or through the Entry option on the Process menu (described later in the chapter).

You must complete the Account, Type, Amount/Rate, and Base fields for each category of earnings applicable in this department. If you are using the chart of accounts supplied with DacEasy Accounting, the correct accounts for basic earnings are shown in Figure 16.5. If you want to track company-paid tips, vacation and sick pay, and EIC payments separately, you can edit the remaining accounts, titled Compensations (520115), Bonuses (520116), and Other Wages (520117), to suit these earnings or create new accounts.

After you enter the earnings code information, press PgDn to scroll to the screen devoted to deduction codes. A completed example is shown in Figure 16.6.

Some deductions might not be classified as a liability, such as payments on a loan the employee received from the employer. These would be credited to accounts receivable rather than to a payroll account.

DacEasy supplies five standard deduction categories:

- Code 16, FWH Tax, is for federal withholding tax.
- Code 17, FICA, is for the employee's portion of taxes assessed for social security.
- Code 18, SWH Tax, is for state withholding tax.
- Code 19, CWH Tax, is for city or county withholding tax, if applicable.
- Code 20, SDIF, is for the tax paid by the employee into the state disability insurance fund, if applicable.

```
F1 Help F2 Options F5 LookUp F6 Delete F8 Add F10 Process
                         Edit Department
 Dept TRAINERS
               ----------- Department Information ----------
 Name          Horse Trainers
                        Deduction Information
  Code  Description   Account    Type  Amount/Rate  Base(Fed/State)
   16   FWH Tax       210411                          N   N
   17   FICA          210412                          N   N
   18   SWH Tax       210416                          N   N
   19   CWH Tax       210417                          N   N
   20   SDIF          210418                          N   N
   21                 ..........  .        0.0000     N   N
   22   ............  ..........  .        0.0000     N   N
   23   ............  ..........  .        0.0000     N   N Prev Pg
   24   ............  ..........  .        0.0000     N   N
   25   ............  ..........  .        0.0000     N   N
   26   ............  ..........  .        0.0000     N   N
   27   ............  ..........  .        0.0000     N   N
   28   ............  ..........  .        0.0000     N   N
   29   ............  ..........  .        0.0000     N   N
   30   ............  ..........  .        0.0000     N   N
```

Figure 16.6: Deduction codes screen

The government strictly regulates Cafeteria plans (125P) and 401K retirement plans. Get professional advice before implementing either.

If you change the amount for a special earnings or deduction code in the department record, the amount for that code in the employee record does not change. This is because the amount in the employee record is meant to override the department record figure. If you want to use the new department amount, you must change each affected employee record.

3.1 At the Duplicate from Dept # prompt, enter the number of the existing department.

You can define ten additional deductions per department. A 401K tax-deferred retirement deduction must have *401K* in the Description column for the system to process the deduction properly. Cafeteria plans must use types A through F to be properly handled. Additional deductions are only calculated for employees you designate, either by entering the related code in the employee record or through the Entry option on the Process menu.

You must complete the Account, Type, Amount/Rate, and Base fields for the standard and user-defined deductions applicable to this department. If you are using the chart of accounts supplied with DacEasy Accounting, the correct accounts for the standard payroll liabilities are shown in Figure 16.6.

When you have completed all the fields, press F10 to record the department with its contribution, earnings, and deduction codes. The screen clears, and you can proceed to add another department.

Adding a new department is easier if you duplicate the parameters of a previously defined department. Enter the number of the existing department that has parameters closest to the new one. Press F8 to duplicate it. Type the new department name over the name and make any changes, deletions, or additions to the parameters. Before you use a code, you can alter its definition by typing over the description, account number, and calculation method.

DELETING LIABILITY, EARNINGS, OR DEDUCTIONS CODES You cannot truly delete a code from a department after it is set up. However, you can change the amount or rate used to calculate the contribution, earnings, or deduction to zero. This prevents an amount from being included during payroll generation. Still, the description, general ledger account, and calculation method continue to display and take up space in the department record.

You can write over the description, account number, and calculation method to use the code for another purpose, but it's not a good idea. It will not alter the description or amount existing in an employee's record. Any transactions involving the code will be posted to the new general ledger account, but the amounts in the employee record will continue to accumulate under the original period-to-date category for the code number.

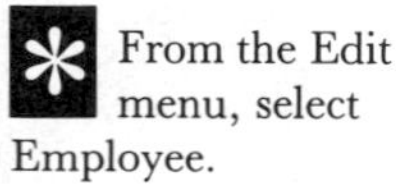
From the Edit menu, select Employee.

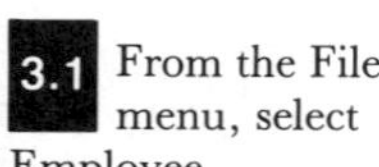
From the File menu, select Employee.

MAINTAINING EMPLOYEE RECORDS

After you have set up your department file, you can create employee records. Employee records are maintained through a series of six screens. The fields on the screens are described in Table 16.5.

Table 16.5: Fields on the Edit Employee Screens

Field	Definition
Code	The employee number or code (10 characters maximum).
Account Information	
Name	The name of the employee. Enter last name, first name, and middle initial.
Address	The employee's mailing address.
City, State, Zip	The employee's city, state, and zip code.
Phone	The employee's area code and telephone number.
Social Security	The employee's social security number for reporting earnings and withholding taxes.

Table 16.5: Fields on the Edit Employee Screens

Field	Definition
Account Information (continued)	
Sex	Select Male or Female.
Marital Status	Select Married or Single.
Origin	A user-defined code to identify ethnic origin for equal employment opportunity reporting requirements (4 characters maximum).
Memo	Any comment about the employee.
Dates	
Birth	The employee's date of birth in MMDDYY format.
Hire	The employee's date of hire.
Raise	The date for the employee's raise. This, and the next three date fields, can be defined as a past or future date, according to your company's practice. You can record when the event happened or when it is scheduled to occur.
Review	The date for the employee's review.
Promotion	The date for the employee's promotion.
Termination	The date the employee was terminated.
Payment Information	
Dept	The department the employee is assigned to. The department determines what standard earnings and deductions are included when generating payroll.
Title	The employee's job title.
Pay Type	The code designating the employee type. Select Hourly, Salaried, or Contractor.
Pay Suspended	Select Yes if the employee is still on staff but ineligible to receive pay at this time, for example, if he or she is on leave of absence.
Frequency	Designate how often the employee is paid: Weekly, Biweekly, Semimonthly, or Monthly. These pay cycles control all payroll processing. Only employees sharing the same cycle can be processed at the same time.
Amount	If salaried, the employee's annual salary. If hourly, the employee's hourly rate.
Overtime 1	The hourly rate of pay for overtime work in category 1. Not available for salaried employees. Salaried employees are not eligible for overtime payments in DacEasy. Instead, you must manually enter earnings that exceed the employee's standard salary through the Entry option.

Table 16.5: Fields on the Edit Employee Screens (continued)

Field	Definition
Payment Information (continued)	
Overtime 2	The hourly rate of pay for overtime work in category 2. Not available for salaried employees.
Vacation: Date	The date accrued vacation time begins to accrue.
Frequency	How often accrued vacation time is calculated. Enter *W* for weekly, *B* for biweekly, *S* for semimonthly, or *M* for monthly.
Hrs	The number of vacation hours accrued each time vacation is calculated.
Acrd	The number of vacation hours the employee has accrued.
Paid	The number of vacation hours the employee has been paid for.
Max	The maximum hours the employee can accrue.
Sick Time: Date	The date the sick time begins to accrue.
Frequency	How often accrued sick time is calculated.
Hrs	The number of sick hours accrued each time sick leave is calculated.
Acrd	The number of sick hours the employee has accrued.
Paid	The number of sick hours already paid to the employee.
Max	The maximum hours the employee can accrue.
Tax Information	
Codes	For Marital, indicate the employee's marital status for taxation purposes: 1 for single, 2 for married filing separately, 3 for married filing jointly, or 4 for head of household. For EIC, indicate the employee's earned income credit status: 0 for none, 1 for employee only, or 2 for both employee and spouse.
Exemptions	Select Yes if the employee's wages are exempt from FICA, FUTA, or SUTA taxes. Otherwise, press ↵ to accept the default No.
Allowances	For Federal and State, the number of allowances the employee claims on the W-4 form.
State Tax Table	The number representing the state tax table applicable to the employee's earnings.
Modifications and Amount	Only entered if applicable in the state tax table in the DacEasy manual.
City Tax Base	Indicate if local taxes are None or a percent of Gross pay, Federal withholding, or State withholding.
Tax %	The percentage of the local tax. For example, 3¼% would be entered 3.250.

Table 16.5: Fields on the Edit Employee Screens (continued)

Field	**Definition**
	Tax Information (continued)
Added Amounts	The additional dollar amount the employee wants withheld for Federal, State, or City tax per pay period.
	Earnings and Deduction Information
Earnings Code	The earnings code (must be previously defined in the department the employee is assigned to).
Description	The program displays the description from the department record.
Frq	How often the extra earnings are paid. Enter *W* for weekly, *B* for biweekly, *S* for semimonthly, or *M* for monthly.
Amount/Rate	The program supplies the amount or percentage in the department record. You can enter an override.
Deduction Code	The deduction code (must be previously defined in the employee's department).
Description	The program displays the description from the department record.
Frq	How often the deduction is taken. Enter *W* for weekly, *B* for biweekly, *S* for semimonthly, or *M* for monthly.
Amount/Rate	The program supplies the amount or percentage in the department record. You can enter an override.
	Earnings and User Defined Earnings Totals
Earnings Totals	The gross earnings paid subject to federal withholding FICA, FUTA, and SUTA taxes.
Tips	The total tips.
EIC	The total wages subject to earned income credits.
User-Defined Earnings	The total wages paid in any user-defined earnings categories assigned to this employee.
	Deduction and User Defined Deduction Totals
Deduction Totals	The amount of federal income, FICA, state, city income, and SDIF tax withheld from the employee's wages.
User-Defined Deductions	The amount withheld from the employee's wages for each user-defined deduction.

Table 16.5: Fields on the Edit Employee Screens (continued)

Field	Definition
Liability, User Defined Liability, and Payment Totals	
Liability Totals	The FICA, FUTA, and SUTA taxes to be paid by the employer resulting from wages paid to this employee.
User-Defined Liability Totals	The liability incurred by the employer for each user-defined deduction from the employee's pay.
Payment Totals	The net amount paid to the employee after taxes and deductions, the number of regular days paid to a salaried employee, the number of regular hours paid to an hourly employee, and the number of overtime hours paid to an hourly employee. Vacation and sick pay are not included in the days and hours paid totals.

To begin, select the Employee option from the Edit menu. You will see the first Edit Employee screen, as shown in Figure 16.7. Here you supply basic information about the employee and his or her employment status. This includes the pay cycle, employee type, and vacation and sick time data. Enter the information, and then press PgDn to advance to the second screen, which is for tax information. Here you supply data that determines how taxes will be calculated.

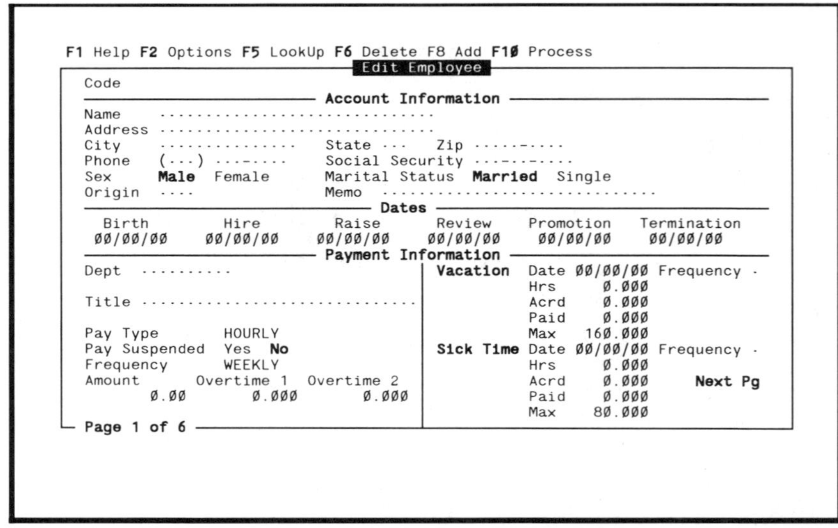

Figure 16.7: First employee maintenance screen

3.1 An employee record consists of only three screens in contrast to the six in version 4.1, however the fields are similar. Only three additional earnings and seven additional deduction codes are possible.

Press PgDn to display the next screen, which is for earnings and deductions information. You can enter up to eight earnings codes per employee in addition to the regular salary or hourly rate and eight deduction codes in addition to the standard deductions. Earnings codes 9 through 15 and deduction codes 21 through 30 must be entered in an employee record before the related earnings or deductions will be generated for the employee during payroll generation. Special earnings or deductions beyond the eight allowed here can be entered through the Entry option during payroll processing. However, the accumulated totals for any additional earnings or deductions won't be tracked in the employee record.

To delete a special earnings or deduction code, press Shift-F6, and then press ↵ to verify that you want to delete the code. You cannot delete a code if period-to-date totals exist for it. You cannot define more than eight additional earnings or deduction codes, even if one or more of the codes in the employee record has become inactive prior to year-end processing.

Use caution when entering amounts. You can override or delete the period-to-date amounts calculated by the program. If you do so in error, employee reports, including W-2's, could be inaccurate.

Press PgDn to advance to the fourth employee maintenance screen, which is for earnings totals. If you are starting payroll midyear, enter the quarter-to-date and year-to-date amounts in the categories on this screen. When you begin payroll processing, the program updates these fields automatically.

Press PgDn to advance to the fifth employee maintenance screen, which is for deduction totals. Enter the quarter-to-date and year-to-date amounts, and then press PgDn to advance to the final Edit Employee screen, which is for liability and payment totals. Enter the amounts and press F10 to record the employee data. This concludes the process of setting up your files. Now you can process your employees' earnings using DacEasy Payroll.

PROCESSING PAYROLL

Processing payroll entails several steps:

1. Update employee and department files.
2. Enter any nonstandard amounts, and then let the program calculate the standard payroll amounts automatically.

3. Print the payroll register to verify the calculations before you print checks.
4. Print the checks.
5. Print a check register for a permanent copy of your checks.
6. Print a department report for a record of the payroll amount totals by department.
7. Post Payroll to update the employee records and provide totals for your general ledger.

The following sections explain how to complete these steps.

ENTERING IRREGULAR PAYROLL DATA

* From the Process menu, select Entry.

3.1 From the Process menu, select Data Entry.

To record an irregular payroll amount for an individual, select the Entry option from the Process menu. You use this option only for nonstandard payments, such as the following:

- Less or more than normal pay for the pay period of a salaried employee
- Less or more than the standard hours in the pay period of a full-time, hourly employee
- Part-time employees
- Overtime
- Vacation or sick leave
- Commissions or bonuses
- Piece rate
- Tips
- Special earnings you want to enter manually
- Earnings from a department other than the one in the employee record
- Other special earnings or deductions that are not recorded in the employee record
- Contract labor

Salary and regular hours, standard withholding, as well as extra earnings and deductions in the employee record, are processed automatically. You must use the Entry option under the following circumstances:

- If you are withholding deductions that are calculated per unit or that you want to enter manually
- If you are running DacEasy parallel to your manual system
- If you are recording a payroll check written manually

Figure 16.8 shows an example of the entries for a payment to an employee who is being paid for a job that he does not normally perform and that is not in his employee record.

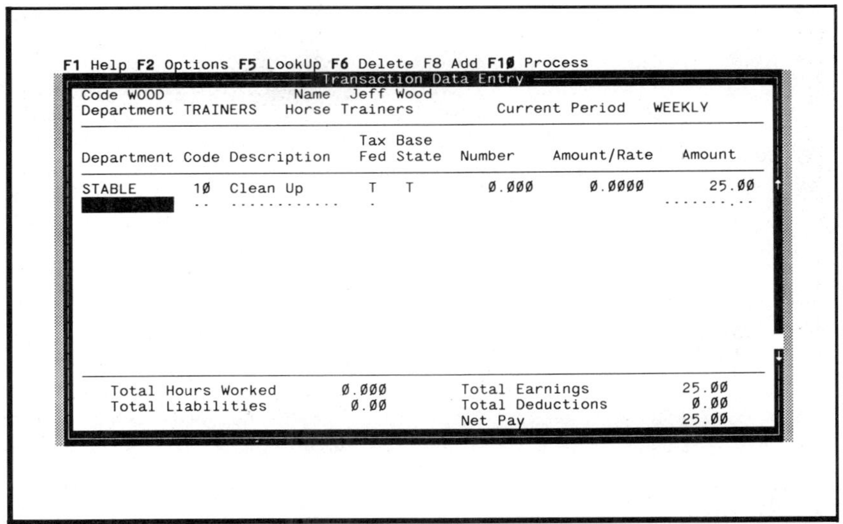

Figure 16.8: Entering irregular earnings

3.1 The prompt is Enter Payroll Period to be Processed? (W-B-S-M). Throughout the program, rather than highlight an option to select it, you must enter the letter designating your choice.

When you select Entry, DacEasy displays the prompt

Which pay frequency would you like to set up?
Weekly, Biweekly, Semimonthly, Monthly

Select the payroll period you want to process. This corresponds to the frequency defined in the payment information area of the employee record. Next complete the fields on the Transaction Data Entry screen, which are described in Table 16.6.

Table 16.6: Fields on the Transaction Data Entry Screen

Field	Definition
Code	The number of the employee who has an irregular transaction.
Name	The program displays the employee name from the employee record.
Department	The program displays the department the employee is assigned to.
Current Period	The program displays the current pay period.
Department	In the data-entry portion of the screen, enter the department where the work occurred.
Code	The code for the earnings, deduction, or company liability. Enter the following codes for earnings: *01* for salary, *02* for hourly, *03* for overtime rate 1, *04* for overtime rate 2, *05* for tips (company-paid tips are treated like other regular earnings for tax purposes and are included in net wages), *06* for vacation time (vacation and sick time are paid by the hour, regardless if the employee is hourly or salaried), *07* for sick time, or *08* for EIC. You can enter user-defined earnings for codes *09* through *15*. Enter the following codes for deductions: *16* for federal withholding, *17* for FICA withholding, *18* for state withholding, *19* for city withholding, or *20* for state disability insurance. You can define deductions for codes *21* through *30*. Enter the following codes for liabilities: *31* for FICA employer, *32* for FUTA, *33* for SUTA, or *40* for reported tips (tips reported by an employee are added to gross earnings for tax calculation for employee deductions and employer liabilities, but they are not included in the calculation of net wages). You can enter user-defined liabilities for codes *34* through *36*.
Description	The program displays the description for the code entered.
Tax Base	The program supplies the tax base from the department file. You can override the tax base for earnings by entering the following codes: *N* for nontaxable earnings, *T* for earnings taxed at regular rate, or *S* for earnings taxed at supplemental rate. The following codes apply to deductions: *N* for deduction not deductible from gross earnings, *T* for deduction before withholding is calculated on gross earnings, or *S* for deduction from gross earnings to be treated as supplemental earnings for withholding.
Number	Depending on the code entered, enter the number related to the type of earnings or deductions, such as the number of days worked for salaried employees, the number of hours worked for hourly employees, the number of hours used of vacation or sick leave, or the flat amount or number of pieces.
Amount/Rate	When you use earnings codes 2 through 5, you must enter the rate or percent to be used to calculate the earnings based on the number entered in the previous field. The default rate or percent for the earnings code appears, but you can enter an override.
Amount	Depending on the code and number entered, the calculated amount appears, except for codes 2 through 5, which are calculated during payroll generation.
Total Hours Worked	The program calculates the total hours worked.

Table 16.6: Fields on the Transaction Data Entry Screen (continued)

Field	Definition
Total Earnings	The program calculates the total earnings.
Total Liabilities	The program calculates the total liabilities.
Total Deductions	The program calculates the total deductions.
Net Pay	The program calculates the net pay.

When an employee does not work the standard number of regular hours, enter the number of regular hours the employee worked (code 2 earnings) through the Entry option. If you don't, the program will calculate the regular number of hours at the regular rate during payroll generation.

Be sure you have made all your irregular payment entries before proceeding to payroll generation. Taxes are not computed on transactions entered or changed through the Entry option after payroll generation has been processed.

When you have entered all the irregular pay, deductions, or liabilities for the employee, press F10 to record the data.

ENTERING MANUAL CHECKS When you record manual checks through the Entry option, remember to include special earnings and deductions. Be careful to enter the exact amount of deductions taken and be sure to include the employer's contributions.

Figure 16.9 illustrates an example of the entries for a check written manually. The salary rate in the employee record appears when you enter the code. You must enter the number of days or hours worked in the pay period, and the program calculates the total. When you enter the code for a 401K (employer-sponsored, tax-deferred retirement plan) deduction, the program calculates and displays the standard wages used in the calculation, the rate, and the total. You should change the number, rate, or total of any line to match the check that was written.

In Figure 16.9, notice the codes 17 for FICA, the employee's portion, and 31 for FICA, the employer's portion. The entries described as FICA LIAB and FUTA LIAB are employer contributions that do not affect the employee's wages, but must be included to ensure accurate payroll records.

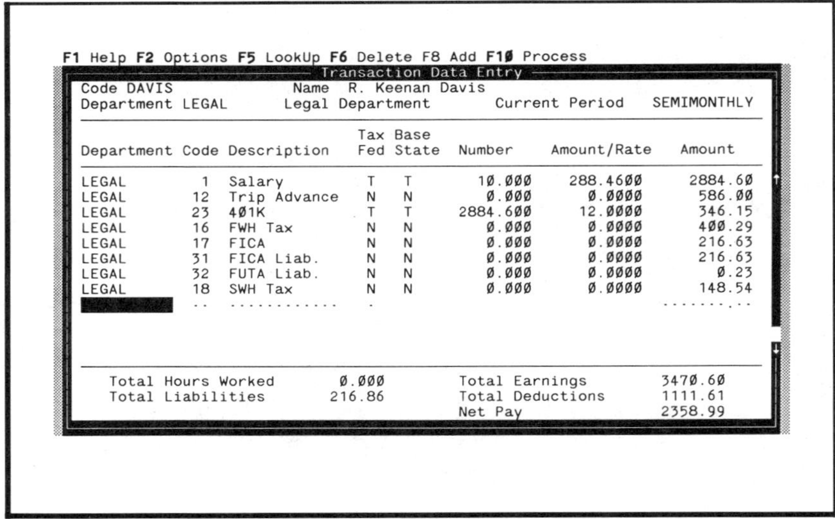

Figure 16.9: Entering a manual check

GENERATING AUTOMATIC PAYROLL DATA

* From the Process menu, select Generation.

3.1 From the Process menu, select Automatic Generation.

If an employee worked more or less than the standard days or hours or had another type of irregular payment, enter that information through the Entry option on the Process menu before proceeding.

During payroll generation, DacEasy calculates the standard payroll for each individual assigned to the specified pay cycle. DacEasy processes standard contributions, earnings, and deductions defined in the department the employee is assigned to, along with extra earnings and deductions in the employee record.

Always back up your files immediately before payroll generation. If a file becomes corrupted because of an error, you can restore data from your latest backup copy to remedy the situation.

To generate payroll data, select the Generation option from the Process menu. You will see the Automatic Generation screen, shown in Figure 16.10.

If you entered any transactions through the Entry option, the pay cycle you selected then appears in the Current Period field. You cannot define another period until the current one is processed.

If you printed and posted checks for the previous payroll and have not used the Entry option, you will see the prompt

Which pay frequency would you like to set up?
Weekly, Biweekly, Semimonthly, Monthly

Select the pay cycle you want to generate.

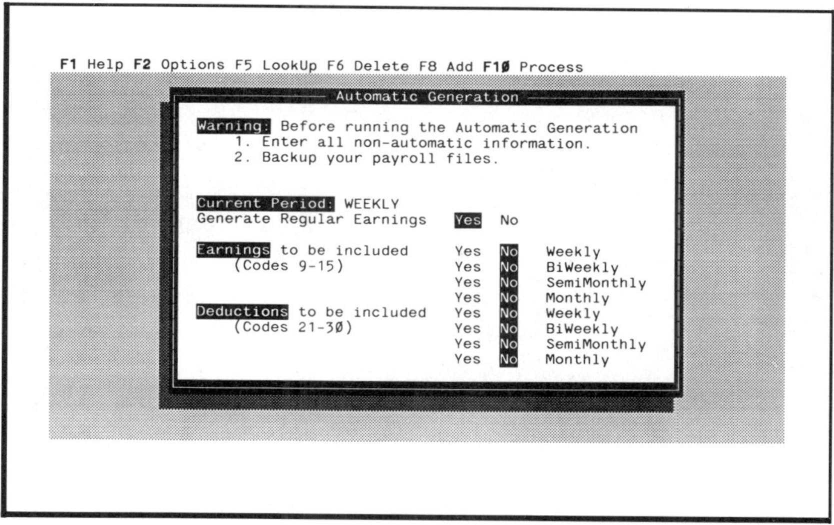

Figure 16.10: Generating payroll data

An example of a reason not to generate regular earnings is when you are just printing vacation checks. You would enter vacation hours through the Entry option, and then select Generation only to calculate taxes on the vacation pay, without also generating regular earnings.

3.1 Press ↵ at the final prompt to begin payroll generation.

In the Generate Regular Earnings field, press ↵ to accept the default Yes to generate regular payroll amounts. Any earnings for codes entered through the Entry option will not be calculated during automatic generation (preventing duplication). If you do not want to generate regular earnings, select No.

The next two fields allow you to include earnings and deductions with a specific frequency. If you do not want to designate special frequencies, press ↵ to accept the default No, and then press F10 to begin generation. If you do want to use frequencies to calculate user-defined earnings and deductions, select Yes beside each frequency you want to process. The earnings and deductions to be calculated do not have to be of the same frequency as the pay period. For example, you might deduct union dues once a month when you calculate the first weekly payroll of the month. All special earnings and deductions in the employee record with the frequencies you select will be included in or deducted from the employee's earnings. You can press F10 at any frequency to accept the default No for the remaining earnings or deductions frequencies and begin generation.

If the data entries and automatic payroll calculations result in a negative check for any employee, DacEasy will cancel the payroll generation process. You must restore your latest backup to return your Payroll records to the status they had before the process began. Adjust the data on the erroneous check, and then run the process again.

DacEasy notifies you when the process is complete. Press ↵ to exit the option.

PRINTING THE PAYROLL REGISTER

* From the Process menu, select Payroll Register.

The payroll register is one of your most important reports. It is the only record you have of each individual transaction involved in creating payroll checks. You should review the payroll calculations shown in the register before printing checks. If you need to void a posted check, you must refer to the payroll register.

The register lists the normal and irregular earnings, the deductions and liabilities, and corresponding codes for the payroll you have processed. Totals are printed for each employee within the department, for each department, and for the company. This data is deleted from the register when you post.

3.1 Some selections, such as employee type, are made by pressing the spacebar until the appropriate option appears. The report is sent to the printer; you cannot select a report disposition.

To print the payroll register, select the Payroll Register option from the Process menu. In the Employee type field, select Hourly, Salary, Contract Labor, or All. In the Departments From and To fields, enter the first and last departments to be included, or press ↵ to begin with the first department in the file and end with the last one. Enter the code for the first and last employees to be included on the register (or press ↵) in the Employees From and To fields. Press F10 and select the report disposition.

Verify the data generated. Are all appropriate earnings paid and deductions made for this pay cycle? Were all new employees included and terminated employees excluded? If necessary, cancel the automatic generation and recalculate it or make corrections to the data-entry transactions, as described in the following sections. Then reprint the register. When the payroll data is correct, print the checks, as explained shortly.

CANCELING AUTOMATIC PAYROLL

* From the Process menu, select Cancel Generation.

If you review the payroll register and find you neglected to include or exclude an item affecting several employees, you can void the calculations made during payroll generation. This voids the entire run.

3.1 From the Process menu, select Cancel Automatic Generation. Press ↵ to accept the default Y at the prompt to continue and the prompt to start.

Note that selecting to cancel automatic generation does not cancel the entries you keyed in through the Entry option.

If there are payroll errors for only one or two employees, you can correct them individually through the Entry option, as explained in the next section.

To void the payroll run, select the Cancel Generation option from the Process menu. The program will ask if you want to cancel automatic generation. Select Yes to delete the payroll generation, or No to cancel the cancellation. DacEasy notifies you when the process is complete. Press ↵ to exit the option.

CORRECTING OR DELETING A PAYROLL TRANSACTION

* From the Process menu, select Entry.

3.1 From the Process menu, select Data Entry. Press Alt-D to delete a line.

If you discover an error in an employee's payroll when reviewing the payroll register, you can correct it. This procedure can be used to edit data created through payroll generation or data entered directly.

To correct a payroll transaction prior to posting, select the Entry option from the Process menu. Enter the employee code to display the transaction. You can add a new line or press Shift-F6 to delete a line. Remember to calculate and adjust tax amounts or other transactions related to a new or deleted line.

To delete the entire transaction for this employee, press F6 and respond Yes when the program asks if you want to delete employees from the transaction file. Be aware, if you already ran automatic generation, this also deletes all the data created during payroll generation.

PRINTING CHECKS

* From the Process menu, select Checks.

When the payroll data is complete and accurate, you are ready to print the payroll checks. Load the payroll check forms (available from Dac Software, Inc.) into the printer before you proceed. Choose the Checks option from the Process menu, and you will see the Check Generation screen, shown in Figure 16.11.

In the Employee type field, select the appropriate type; then select to sort the checks by employee or department. Enter the first and last departments to be included in the check run (or press ↵) in the Departments From and To fields. Enter the codes for the first and

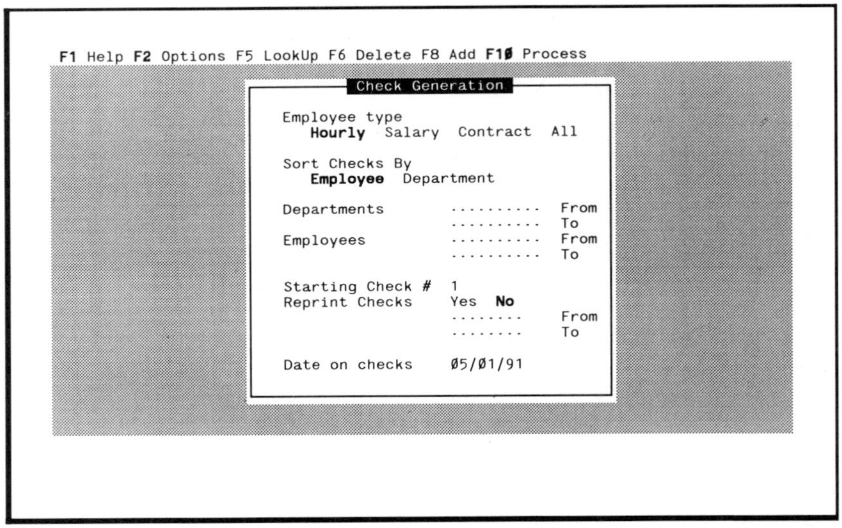

```
F1 Help F2 Options F5 LookUp F6 Delete F8 Add F1Ø Process

                    Check Generation
Employee type
   Hourly  Salary  Contract  All

Sort Checks By
   Employee  Department

Departments          ..........  From
                     ..........  To
Employees            ..........  From
                     ..........  To

Starting Check #     1
Reprint Checks       Yes  No
                     ........    From
                     ........    To

Date on checks       Ø5/Ø1/91
```

Figure 16.11: Selecting payroll checks to print

last employees to be included in the check run (or press ↵) in the Employees From and To fields.

In the Starting Check # field, enter the number of the first check loaded in your printer. For Reprint Checks, press ↵ to accept the default No if this is the first printing of the checks. Select Yes if you need to reprint checks that were damaged in the printer, and then enter the number of the first and last checks to be reprinted in the From and To fields.

Press ↵ to accept the default of the system date in the Date on checks field, or enter the date you want to print on the checks. Press F10 and select Printer as the Report Disposition. Then press ↵ to print an alignment test. The test characters should print on pin-feed checks at the perforation line between the check stub and the check. When the checks are properly aligned and ready for printing, press ↵ at the final alignment prompt.

Examine the checks thoroughly before posting. The entries for voiding a posted check are complex.

DacEasy will void the first check and then print the payroll checks for the payroll period you are processing. If you are reprinting checks, the program marks the originals *Void* in the check register.

PRINTING THE CHECK REGISTER

* From the Process menu, select Check Register.

If, in the company file, you selected to erase the check file after posting, you cannot print a check register.

The check register includes the check number, date, employee code and name, gross earnings, total deductions, and net pay. It also has a column indicating if the check is paid or not (checks are marked paid in the check reconciliation process discussed later).

To print the register, select the Check Register option from the Process menu. In the Sorted by field, select to sort by either check number or employee. Enter the first and last numbers or codes you want included on the register (or press ↵) in the From and To fields. In the Include field, select the check type: Paid, Unpaid, or Both. Press F10 and select the report disposition.

PRINTING THE DEPARTMENT REPORT

* From the Process menu, select Department Report.

The department report lists the department, payroll type, employee number and name, number of hours/days/units paid, earnings and deductions codes, description, account number, and the debit or credit amount.

To print the report, select the Department Report option from the Process menu. In the Report type field, select Detail or Summary. Enter the first and last departments to be included on the report (or press ↵) in the Departments From and To fields. Enter the codes for the first and last employees to be included (or press ↵) in the Employees From and To fields. Press F10 and select the report disposition.

POSTING PAYROLL TRANSACTIONS

* From the Process menu, select Posting.

Posting updates employee records. It also creates payroll totals to be posted to your general ledger either by hand or through the interface to DacEasy Accounting, depending on the parameters in your control file.

Before posting Payroll, it is critical that you print the payroll register, print the checks, review the checks for accuracy, correct incorrect checks, and back up your files.

Use extreme caution when selecting to post. You can post a calculated payroll without printing a payroll register or the related checks,

Print the payroll register and checks before posting. Also, take the precaution of backing up your payroll files. If, in the Payroll control file, you indicated you wanted to interface with DacEasy Accounting, back up those files also.

which is what you would do if you entered checks written manually. However, if your intent is to generate checks through DacEasy, you must do so before posting. If you post before printing checks, your employee and account records will be updated, but each check will have to be prepared by hand. Without a payroll register to guide you, it may be impossible to duplicate the data generated by DacEasy.

To interface with DacEasy Accounting, you must have entered valid account numbers in the Payroll department file and a correct path for the accounting files in the control file. Otherwise, DacEasy will cancel the payroll posting process. When this happens, you must restore the Payroll files from your most recent backup copy, correct the account or path name, and post again.

The posted transaction will have the posting date, rather than the date the transactions were created. To change the date before posting, press F4 and enter the date in MMDDYY format at the prompt.

When you are ready to post, load plain paper in the printer in preparation for the report that prints automatically when the posting process is completed. Then select the Posting option from the Process menu. In the Vacation and Sick time to be accrued fields, select the desired calculation frequency.

3.1 Press ↵ at the prompt to accept the default Y to start posting now, or enter N to cancel the process.

Press F10 to begin posting and select the report disposition for the posting report. When DacEasy completes the posting process, it notifies you and prints a listing of total debits and credits to be posted to each general ledger account. Press any key to exit the option.

The employee records are updated with the posted amounts, but if you are not interfacing with DacEasy Accounting, you must enter and post the amounts to your general ledger. If you are using DacEasy Accounting, verify that the payroll amounts were transferred to the general ledger transaction file by printing the General Ledger journal identified as PY in the Accounting program. When you post the general ledger for the date you posted Payroll, the payroll amounts will be posted along with the transactions in the journals from the other modules.

The transaction file is cleared of records when you post. Posting finalizes the payroll process.

VOIDING A POSTED CHECK

To void a check, you must adjust data in both the general ledger and the employee record.

After posting a check, you can void it only by reversing it in the general ledger and adjusting the figures in the employee record. You cannot create a reversing entry through the Payroll program; it will not allow you to generate a transaction that results in a negative payment.

In the general ledger, you must duplicate every line of the original transaction, posting a debit where a credit was originally posted and vice versa. You will need a copy of the payroll register, which lists every code and amount from the original transaction. Then you must refer to the department records to determine which accounts would have been affected by the posted check.

A sample general ledger transaction to reverse entries from an original check is shown in Figure 16.12. The value of taking time to verify payroll transactions before posting cannot be overstressed. By studying the illustration, you will see how complex correcting a posted check can be. It should also make you appreciate the work DacEasy Payroll does automatically for you during normal payroll processing.

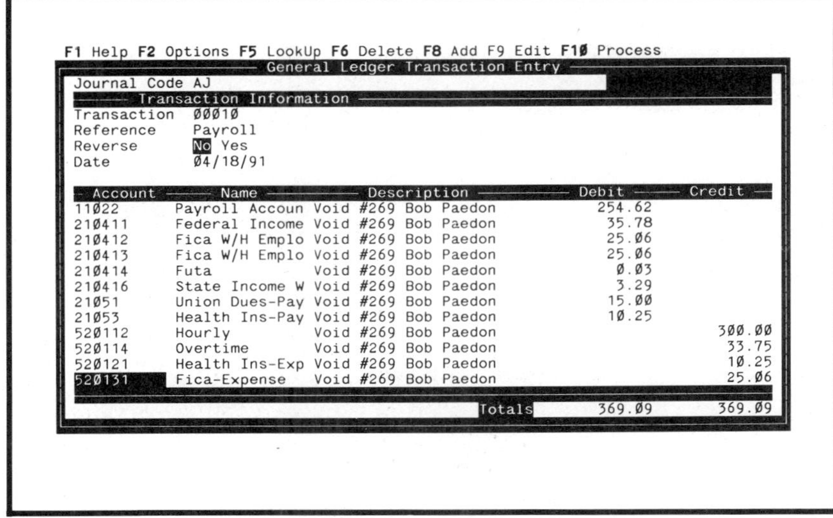

Figure 16.12: Voiding a posted check

It is critical that the data in the employee record is accurately updated for tax reporting. In the employee record, you must subtract the check amounts from the quarter-to-date and year-to-date totals for all earnings, deductions, and liabilities categories, including the number of regular and overtime hours or days paid. If the employee is not entitled to vacation or sick time that was accrued with the payroll, those fields must also be corrected. Remember to use the Check Reconciliation option to mark the check void in your check register, as discussed later in the chapter.

REPORTING

DacEasy Payroll provides several standard reports: an employee directory, employee labels, monthly and quarterly reports, and W-2 and 1099 form data. Additionally, the program has an option that allows you to generate custom reports.

PRINTING AN EMPLOYEE DIRECTORY, HISTORY REPORT, AND LABELS

* From the Reports menu, select Directory, Employment History, or Labels.

3.1 The default N excludes terminated employees.

Unlike the vendor and customer directories produced by DacEasy Accounting, the Payroll employee directory prints all the information contained on the six employee maintenance screens. You might want to create a listing that prints only name, code, address, phone, date of hire, department, title, and pay rate. You can do so through the Report Generator option, described later in the chapter.

To print the employee directory, select the Directory option from the Reports menu. In the Sorted by field, select All or Department. Press ↵ to accept the default Yes at the prompt to include terminated employees, or select No to exclude them. In the Departments From and To fields, enter the first and last departments to be included in the directory (or press ↵). Enter the code for the first and last employees to be included in the directory (or press ↵) in the Employees From and To fields.

The employee history report lists the original entries in the employee record and changes in status for items such as pay rate, marital code, department, and title. To print the report, select

Employment History from the Reports menu. When prompted, select Yes or No to include or exclude terminated employees in the list. Enter the code of the first and last employee you want on the report, press F10, and then select the report disposition.

You can print employee mailing labels, which contain selected names and addresses, or labels for attendance cards, which include the name, employee number, title, and department.

To print labels, select the Labels option from the Reports menu. In the Sorted by field, select the sorting method: All or Department. Next, press ↵ to accept the default Yes to print labels for terminated employees, or select No.

Enter the codes of the first and last departments to be included in the Departments From and To fields. Enter the codes for the first and last employees to print a label for in the Employees From and To fields. In the Pay type field, select from Weekly, Bi-Weekly, Semi-Monthly, Monthly, or All. In the Employee type field, select from Hourly, Salary, Contract, or All.

Next, select the Label type: Mailing or Attendance Card. Enter the number of lines on the entire label or attendance card in the Line per Label lines field. The default is 7 lines for a 1-inch label. Test to determine the number of lines to use for other sizes. Finally, press F10 and select Printer as the Report Disposition.

PRINTING THE MONTHLY AND QUARTERLY REPORTS

From the Periodic menu, select Monthly Report or Quarterly Report.

If, in the company file, you did not select to create a monthly file when posting, you cannot print a Monthly Report.

The monthly report lists activity for the month. It includes regular, overtime, and other earnings; federal withholding, social security, and other deductions; the employer FICA, FUTA, and SUTA contributions; and other liabilities for each employee.

To print the report, select the Monthly Report option from the Periodic menu. Respond to the prompts for dates by pressing ↵ to begin and end with the first and last dates in the month, or enter the dates to begin and end with. Press F10 and select the report disposition.

The quarterly report prints each employee's social security number, name, taxable FICA wages, taxable gross wages, and state unemployment wages, along with the state code and total by state. It is not in a format that you can print directly on government preprinted forms. You must transfer the data on this listing to the proper forms for reporting wages to state and federal tax-collecting agencies. Remember to print the quarterly report *before* you close the quarter.

To print the report, select the Quarterly Report option from the Periodic menu. Respond to the prompts for states by pressing ↵ to start and end with the first and last states in the file, or enter the codes of the first and last states to include in the report. Press F10 and select the report disposition.

PRINTING W-2 AND 1099 FORMS

From the Periodic menu, select W-2's/1099's.

You must report taxable wages and taxes withheld to both the government and your employees on a W-2 form. The federal government requires you to submit W-2 information on magnetic tape or disk if you have more than a specified number of employees. The file also must be in the government-specified format.

You should use 1099 forms to report contract labor payments to the government and to the independent contractors who work for you if you paid more than a specified amount to any one individual. Obtain current specifications for W-2 and 1099 reporting from the IRS and your state taxing agency.

Print W-2 and 1099 forms *before* you close the year. Also, be sure you have posted the last payroll paid in the year. As always, back up your files.

To print W-2 or 1099 forms, load the forms in the printer and select the W-2's/1099's option from the Periodic menu. In the Report Format field, select the appropriate form: W-2 forms, 1099 forms, or Magnetic Media. Enter the four digits of the year you are closing in the Print for year field.

3.1 The default subdirectory is DEP3/FILES.

If you are creating magnetic media, enter your state identification number for submitting payroll information on disk in the State Id No. field. The information is immediately written to file. The W-2 information is placed in the payroll data subdirectory in a file named W2REPORT. If you accepted the default settings when installing the program, this subdirectory is DEP4\FILES. You must copy the file onto a disk for transmission to the IRS.

If you are printing forms, you will see the prompt

```
Custom Design  Yes No
```

Press ↵ to accept the default No if you do not have custom-designed forms. Press F10, select the report disposition, and then respond to the alignment test prompts. The test characters should print on the line above the perforation line.

If you are printing custom W-2 forms, you must complete Box 16 and 16a and Boxes 17 through 22, to report 401K information, for example. You can enter your own description or select from a list. To choose from a list, press ↵ in the box to display the choices, use the arrow keys to select an entry, and then press ↵ again. Press an arrow key to leave a box blank. If you are printing custom 1099 forms, use the same procedure to complete Boxes 1 through 7, to report royalties, for example. Then proceed with the alignment test.

CREATING CUSTOM PAYROLL REPORTS

* From the Reports menu, select Report Generator.

You can design your own formats for payroll data reports. Select the Report Generator option from the Reports menu to display the Report Generation screen (see Figure 15.1).

Enter the new report name in the Name field, and then select the file you want to use in the Data File field: Employee, Department, Transaction (only after checks are generated and before they are posted), Check Register (if you do not erase the file after posting), or Monthly (if you create the monthly file when posting).

To design a report, follow the steps in Chapter 15 (the procedure is the same as in DacEasy Accounting). To print or display a report, enter the name of the report on the Report Generation screen, move the cursor to Column 1, and press F7. When the Data Selection window appears, select to print all records or to enter criteria. Selecting criteria is discussed in Chapter 15 in the section about creating custom listings.

CREATING PAYROLL REPORTS IN VERSION 3.1 The first time you select the Report Generator option from the Reports menu, a blank screen appears. The names of reports you create will display there. You can delete, duplicate, edit, or print those reports. To do so, place the cursor on the report name and press the appropriate function key listed in the prompt at the bottom of the screen.

To add a report, press F3. You will see the screen for designing reports. The fields on this screen are shown in Table 16.7.

Table 16.7: Fields on the Report Formatting Screen in Version 3.1

Field	Definition
Name	An abbreviated name to identify the report (10 characters maximum).
Head 1	The first line of the title that is to appear on the printed report (40 characters maximum).
Head 2	The second line of the title that is to appear on the printed report.
Col 1	The first column that prints on the report. It defaults to the employee name which, along with the code, prints on all reports. You can also place the address and memo lines here.
Col 2, 3, 4	The second, third, and fourth columns in which you can place data to print on the report.
Col 5, 6, 7	Three more columns that can hold data for the printed report. They display when you move the cursor past column 4.
Line 1, 2, 3	Three lines that print on the report under the columns. You can have three stacked lines for each column.

Follow these steps to design a report:

1. Enter a name and a one- or two-line title. The program centers the title lines when the report prints.
2. Use the arrow keys to position the cursor on the line and column where you want to place data. To display columns 5, 6, and 7, place the cursor in column 4 and press the right-arrow key.
3. Press ↵ when the cursor is in position. The cursor moves to the data-field window.
4. Press PgDn or PgUp to scroll through all the fields in the employee record.
5. Use the arrow keys to move to the type of data you want and press ↵ to place it in the report. The cursor returns to the formatting window.
6. Press F10 to save the format.

3.1 To return the cursor to the formatting window without selecting a data field, press Esc. To delete a field from the format, place the cursor on it in the formatting window and press Alt-D.

To print or display a report, on the report generator screen, place the cursor on the report name, and then press F10.

In the Sort by field, press the spacebar to select All (to include all departments) or Department (to limit the number of departments included in the report). Enter the code of the first and last departments, or employees if you selected All, to include (or press ↵) in the Sort by From and To fields.

In the Sort field, press ↵ to move the cursor to the data-field window. Use the arrow keys to position the cursor on the data you want to sort the report by, and then press ↵ to select the field. Enter the first and last records to include in the ranking (or press ↵) in the From and To fields.

Press the spacebar in the Print to field to select from Paper (to print hard copy on a printer) or Screen (to display the report results on the monitor). When prompted, select whether or not to include terminated employees in the report.

PERFORMING PERIODIC PROCESSES

Periodic processes include reconciling the payroll checks to your bank statement; purging the payroll checks from your files; and closing a month, a quarter, and the year. Note that if, in the company file, you selected to erase the check file after posting, you cannot reconcile checks through the program and you do not have to purge checks. You must reconcile the statement to copies of the check registers that you printed before posting. If you selected not to create a monthly file, you do not have to close the month.

RECONCILING PAYROLL CHECKS

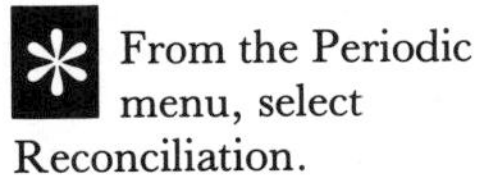
From the Periodic menu, select Reconciliation.

3.1 From the Periodic menu, select Check Reconciliation.

You should reconcile your bank statement to your check file monthly. The checks you mark as paid by the bank or voided can later be purged from the file.

To reconcile checks, select the Reconciliation option from the Periodic menu. The unpaid checks are listed on the screen. In the Chk Flag field, enter a V for a voided check, Y for a check that has cleared the bank, or an N for a check that has not yet cleared the bank. When you have flagged each check, press F10 to process your entries. Note that marking a check void in check reconciliation does not alter the data in the employee record or the general ledger. You must make adjusting entries to both records.

PURGING PAYROLL CHECKS

* From the Periodic menu, select Purge.

3.1 From the Periodic menu, select Purge Checks.

Purging checks deletes from the check register file checks that are dated on or prior to the date you enter, and which have been marked as void or cleared during check reconciliation. This process keeps the check register file from becoming large.

To remove checks from the file, select the Purge option from the Periodic menu. At the prompt

Delete all paid and void checks before 00/00/00

press ↵ to accept the default of the system date, or enter the date you want to use for purging. Press ↵ to exit the option. DacEasy notifies you when the process is completed.

CLOSING THE MONTH, QUARTER, AND YEAR

* From the Periodic menu, select Close Month, Close Quarter, or Close Year.

The only effect closing the month has in DacEasy Payroll is to delete the data held in the file that enables you to print the monthly report. Before you close the month, print the monthly report and back up your files. Then select the Close Month option from the Periodic menu and choose Yes to continue the process or No to cancel.

Quarter-end processing clears the quarter-to-date fields in the employee file in preparation for the next quarter's transactions. Before closing the quarter, print the quarterly report for each state and back up your files. Then select the Close Quarter option from the Periodic menu. Press ↵ to proceed, or select No to cancel.

When you close the year, the year-to-date amounts in the employee file are deleted. This is why it is critical that you print your 1099 and W-2 forms *before* closing the year. You should also print all the yearly payroll reports and back up your files. Then select the Close Year option from the Periodic menu. At the prompt

Net vacation and sick time Yes No

press ↵ to accept the default Yes to subtract the amount of vacation and sick leave taken from the total amounts accrued this year. Select No if you do not want to calculate net time (you may prefer to leave accrued time intact and keep a running total of time taken). Then press ↵ to start closing or choose No to cancel. Press ↵ when the process is completed to exit the option.

PROCESSING MULTIPLE PAYROLL COMPANIES

The procedure for setting up multiple companies in Payroll is similar to the procedure for setting them up in DacEasy Accounting. You can copy an existing company structure by selecting the Copy option on the Payroll File menu.

When you have more than one payroll company defined, you can choose the company you want to work in by selecting Open from the File menu. Select a company from the list displayed. Refer to the section about creating multiple companies in Chapter 4 for details.

CONVERTING AND MANAGING FILES

DacEasy provides an option to convert earlier versions of DacEasy Payroll to version 4.1. The software also includes an option to review and update the status of your files.

CONVERTING FILES

If you have been using DacEasy Payroll, you must convert your existing files to DacEasy Payroll 4.1. Before you run the conversion supplied with your 4.1 software, be sure you have posted all your transactions in the earlier version. The File Status option in the earlier version should show zero transactions, indicating that everything has been posted. If you are using version 1.0, contact DacEasy; you must upgrade to either 2.0 or 3.0 before you can convert to 4.1.

To convert your files to DacEasy Payroll 4.1, select Convert from the 4.1 File menu. Highlight the version you are currently using, 2.0

or 3.0. Enter the drive, directory and file where your previous files reside. For example, if you have used the defaults for version 3.0, your path would be: C:\DEP3\FILES.

Enter the path where you have installed your new 4.1 version. If you accepted the default during installation, the path would be: C:\DEP4\FILES. Your old files will be copied into the new files. After the conversion, you must define SUTA, SDIF, and printer codes since the conversion does not address these three items.

MANAGING YOUR FILES

From time to time, you should check the status of your files. You may need to correct the indexes or you may want to compress your files to gain more disk space. Using these utilities is a simple bit of housekeeping that leaves your data intact.

Select Utilities from the File menu. Press F5 at the File Number field to display the list of files, highlight the file you want to review, and then press ↵ to select it. The first utility you want to use is the Status option.

On the Status screen, if the Supplemental Indexes is anything other than zero, exit the status screen, then select to Drop Indexes for the file. If the File Access Status field contains the message

```
Run File Recovery
```

exit the status screen. To rebuild and compress the file, select the Recovery option for the file.

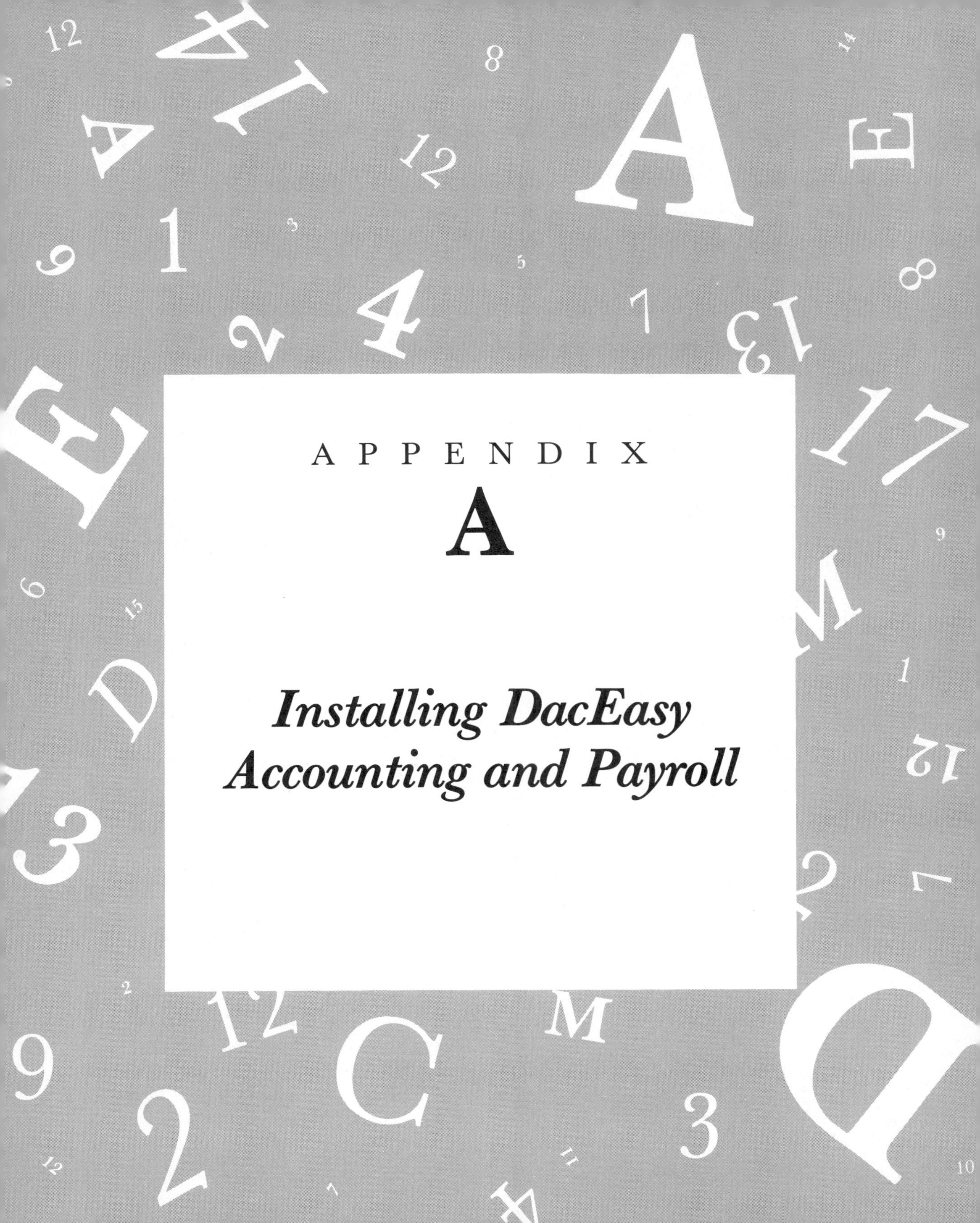

APPENDIX

A

Installing DacEasy Accounting and Payroll

Handle your computer disks with care. You can damage the data on a disk by getting fingerprints on the exposed portion, so always handle a disk by its jacket. Keep disks away from dust, smoke, heat, liquids, and magnets. Write on the label *before* sticking it on the disk.

BEFORE YOU INSTALL A PROGRAM, YOU SHOULD make working copies of the original disks. To do so, format as many blank disks as you have originals. Label them to match the labels on the originals. Place write-protect tabs over the notch on the original disks.

Copy the contents of each original disk onto a blank disk with a matching label. To do so, load DOS, and then place the original disk in drive A and the blank disk in drive B. At the A: prompt, type **copy *.* b:** and press ↵. If your computer has only one floppy disk drive, you will have to swap disks to make the copies. Follow the instructions on the screen. When the copy operation is complete, store the originals in a safe place and use the working copies for installation.

INSTALLING DACEASY ACCOUNTING VERSION 4.1

Follow these steps to install DacEasy Accounting version 4.1. In the instructions, *enter* means to type the characters indicated, and then press ↵ to record the input.

Do not create a directory for DacEasy. One will be created during installation. If you have partitioned your hard disk, change to the drive where you want DacEasy installed. Substitute its letter for C: in the text, and enter it as part of the path name when prompted.

If your computer uses 3½-inch disks, disk swapping is not required.

1. Turn the computer, monitor, and printer on.
2. Place the disk labeled Install/Program Disk #1 into drive A.
3. At the C: prompt, enter **a:** to change from drive C to drive A, where the DacEasy Accounting disk is currently located.
4. At the A: prompt, enter **install**. When the Welcome to DacEasy Accounting Version 4.1 screen appears, press ↵.
5. At the next prompt, which asks if DacEasy Accounting version 4.1 is to be installed for the first time, enter **Y**, or **N** if converting from 4.0.
6. When you are prompted to enter the disk drive letter from which you are installing, enter **A**.
7. Then enter the path name. The suggested path is C:\DEA4, which means the program files will be copied to drive C into a directory named DEA4 created by the installation program. To give the directory another name, type over the DEA4. Be sure to leave the drive letter, colon, and backslash (\). Press ↵ to continue. The files on Disk 1 are copied into the DEA4

directory. Wait until the process is complete. A Search/Explode processing notice will flash on the screen as the files are decompressed and placed in usable form on your system.

8. When you are prompted to, remove Disk #1 from drive A and insert Disk #2. Press ↵ to continue.
9. You will be prompted to replace the second disk with the third one. Remove Disk #2 from drive A, insert Disk #3, and press ↵ to continue.
10. Replace Disk #3 with Disk #4 when prompted to and press ↵ to continue.
11. The next screen refers to the CONFIG.SYS file on your hard disk. Press ↵ to continue. When the process is complete, a message will inform you that the program is installed.
12. Remove Disk #4 from drive A. Press the Ctrl, Alt, and Del keys simultaneously to reboot the computer.
13. When the C: prompt appears, type **cd\dea4**, and press ↵ to change to the newly created DEA4 directory, where your DacEasy files are located.
14. You can enter **dir/p** to display the DEA4 directory contents. The file names and sizes are displayed.

The CONFIG.SYS file tells the computer how your system is configured. DacEasy will either create or edit an existing CONFIG.SYS file to meet its minimum requirements of Files = 20 and Buffers = 16. The Files indicator shows how many files can be open at one time, and the Buffers indicator shows how many buffers you have available to store directory and file allocation table (FAT) information. If your CONFIG.SYS file is set higher, DacEasy will not disturb your settings.

You are now ready to initialize your program, as described in Chapter 2.

INSTALLING DACEASY ACCOUNTING VERSION 3.1

DacEasy Accounting version 3.1 can be installed on a hard disk or a floppy disk computer system, as described in the following sections. In the instructions, *enter* means to type the characters indicated, and then press ↵ to record the input.

HARD DISK INSTALLATION

Follow these steps to install DacEasy Accounting version 3.1 on a hard disk system:

Do not create a directory for DacEasy. One will be created during installation. If you have partitioned your hard disk, change to the drive where you want DacEasy installed. Substitute its letter for C: in the text, and enter it as part of the path name when prompted.

If your computer uses 3½-inch disks, disk swapping is not requested.

1. Turn the computer, monitor, and printer on.
2. Place the disk labeled DacEasy Accounting Disk #1 into drive A.
3. At the C: prompt, enter **a:** to change from drive C to drive A.
4. At the A: prompt, enter **install**.
5. When asked if you want to install DacEasy Graph+Mate, press ↵ to accept the default, Y, or enter **N** if you do not want to install the graphics program.
6. When asked if you are installing DacEasy on a floppy or hard disk, press ↵ to accept the default, H.
7. The next screen requests the path name, followed by C:\DEA3, which means the program files will be copied to drive C into a directory created by the installation program and named DEA3. You can name the directory something other than DEA3 by typing over it. Be sure to leave the drive letter, colon, and backslash (\). Press ↵ to continue. The installation program creates a directory, names it, and copies files from Disk #1 into the directory. Wait until the process is complete.
8. When prompted to, replace the disk in drive A with Disk #2 and press ↵ to copy its files into the DEA3 directory.
9. The next screen refers to the CONFIG.SYS file on your hard disk. DacEasy will either create a new or edit an existing CONFIG.SYS file to meet its minimum requirements. Press ↵ to continue. A message tells you when the installation process is complete. You should verify that all went well.
10. Remove Disk #2 from drive A. Press the Ctrl, Alt, and Del keys simultaneously to reboot the computer.
11. When the C: prompt appears, type **cd\dea3** and press ↵ to change to the newly created DEA3 directory, where your DacEasy files are located.

If you put DacEasy on a drive other than C, when the C: prompt appears, change to the correct drive and continue.

12. Enter **dir/p** to display the DEA3 directory contents. The file names and sizes are displayed. There should be 18 files in the directory; the first two are a single and double dot, respectively.
13. Compare your screen with Figure A.1 to verify that all the files were copied in total. If the files or their sizes listed on your screen do not match those in the figure, carefully repeat the entire installation procedure.

```
                                                                   2Ø:3Ø:31
 Volume in drive D is 4-Ø7-89                                      Tue  3-19-1991
 Directory of  D:\DEA3

.            <DIR>      3-19-91   8:22p
..           <DIR>      3-19-91   8:22p
DEA3     EXE   229862   4-3Ø-89   3:1Øa
DA3-HLP1 DAT    18278   4-3Ø-89   3:1Øa
DA3-HLP1 KEY      14Ø   4-3Ø-89   3:1Øa
DA3-ØØ   EXE   287946   4-3Ø-89   3:1Øa
DA3-HLP2 KEY      136   4-3Ø-89   3:1Øa
DA3-HLP2 DAT    29554   4-3Ø-89   3:1Øa
GM       EXE    87853   4-3Ø-89   3:1Øa
GMREPORT EXE    72791   4-3Ø-89   3:1Øa
GMEXPORT EXE    65891   4-3Ø-89   3:1Øa
GMGRAPHS EXE   121661   4-3Ø-89   3:1Øa
GRAPHICS PRN      335   4-3Ø-89   3:1Øa
INSTALL  EXE    75299   4-3Ø-89   3:1Øa
GRAFMATE DD     2Ø938   4-3Ø-89   3:1Øa
GRAFMATE HLP    14863   4-3Ø-89   3:1Øa
READ     ME      9Ø97   4-3Ø-89   3:1Øa
GMDRIVER COM     6749   4-3Ø-89   3:1Øa
       18 File(s)   94Ø2368 bytes free

D:\DEA3
```

Figure A.1: DEA3 directory contents

After you have verified that the program installation was successful, you are ready to initialize your program, as described in Chapter 2.

FLOPPY DISK INSTALLATION

During floppy disk installation, the program makes copies of your original disks. Therefore, it is not necessary to make working copies before beginning the installation process, but you must have two blank, formatted disks labeled Disk 1 and Disk 2. (DacEasy refers to them as Program 1 and Program 2 on the screen.) You also need a third blank, formatted disk labeled Data Disk. If you plan to install Graph+Mate, then format two more blank disks and label them Graph+Mate Disk #1 and Graph+Mate Disk #2.

To install DacEasy Accounting version 3.1 onto floppy disks, follow these steps:

1. Place your DOS disk in drive A and turn on the computer and monitor. Remember to close the drive door.
2. When DOS is loaded, remove the DOS disk and insert DacEasy Accounting Disk #1.
3. At the A: prompt, enter **install**.
4. When asked if you want to install DacEasy Graph+Mate, press ↵ to accept the default, Y, or enter **N** if you do not want to install the graphics program.
5. When asked if DacEasy is to be installed on a floppy or hard disk, type **F** and press ↵.
6. With Disk #1 in drive A, place the blank, formatted working Disk #1 you prepared in drive B.
7. Press ↵ to continue. DacEasy copies the data from the original disk onto the working copy.
8. When prompted, remove working Disk #1 from drive B and insert the blank, formatted working Disk #2. Press ↵ to continue.
9. When prompted, place the DacEasy Accounting Disk #2 in drive A. Press ↵ to continue.
10. When prompted, place the blank Graph+Mate Disk #1 in drive B and press ↵.
11. Then replace the Graph+Mate Disk #1 with the blank Graph+Mate Disk #2 in drive B, when prompted, and press ↵ to continue.
12. At the prompt

    Do you want DacEasy to check, and if necessary, modify CONFIG.SYS?

    press ↵ to accept the default, Y. A final message notifies you of the completion of the installation.

13. Remove both disks. Store the originals and use the working copies from now on.
14. Place the DOS disk into drive A and reboot the system (press the Ctrl, Alt, and Del keys simultaneously) to reinitiate it using the new CONFIG.SYS parameters.

This completes the installation of a floppy disk system. Read the next section regarding initialization of the program.

INITIALIZING A FLOPPY DISK SYSTEM

The instructions for initializing DacEasy Accounting (in Chapter 2) are written for a hard disk computer system. Floppy disk users should place Disk #1 (working copy) in drive A, type **dea3**, and press ↵. Follow the instructions, but the sequence will differ slightly and you will be prompted to swap disks occasionally. When you arrive at the screen that asks you to enter the directory name for your data files, first place the third blank, formatted disk labeled Data Disk in the available disk drive (usually drive B). Then press ↵ to accept the default to use drive B, or enter the letter of the drive where DacEasy will find your data disk.

When you maintain your files for accounts, customers, vendors, and products (see Chapter 3), DacEasy will prompt you to swap back and forth between Disk #1 and Disk #2 (because specific programs are stored on each disk). These program disks should always reside in drive A; your data disk should remain in a secondary drive. Follow the instructions that appear on the screen.

INSTALLING DACEASY PAYROLL VERSION 4.1

DacEasy Payroll can be used alone or with DacEasy Accounting. After installation, you indicate in the company record if you want to interface with the accounting program or not. To install DacEasy Payroll version 4.1, follow the steps below:

1. Turn on the computer and monitor.
2. Place Payroll Program Disk #1 in drive A.

3. At the C: prompt, enter **a:** to change to drive A.
4. At the A: prompt, enter **install**.
5. Press ↵ at the Welcome screen.
6. When asked if you are installing DacEasy Payroll for the first time, press ↵ to accept the default, Y.
7. When prompted, enter the disk drive letter from which you are installing DacEasy Payroll. Press ↵ to accept the default A, or enter the letter for the floppy drive from which you are installing the disks to your hard drive.
8. The next screen requests the path name for the directory where you want to store your Payroll program, followed by C:\DEP4. Press ↵ to accept the suggested name, or enter the drive and directory you want to use. A Search/Explode processing notice will flash on the screen as the files are decompressed and placed in usable form on your system.
9. When prompted, remove Disk #1 and insert Disk #2, and then press ↵ to copy the remaining files onto your hard disk.
10. When the CONFIG.SYS notice appears, press ↵ to continue. DacEasy will either create a new or edit an existing CONFIG.SYS file to meet its minimum requirements.
11. Press ↵ when asked if you want to print the READ.ME files. Be sure your printer is ready.
12. Place Disk #1 in drive A and press ↵ to begin printing.
13. When the copying is complete, remove the program disk from drive A.

This completes the installation of DacEasy Payroll version 4.1. Instructions for initializing and using the program are in Chapter 16.

INSTALLING DACEASY PAYROLL VERSION 3.1

The following instructions for installing DacEasy Payroll version 3.1 assume you are using a hard disk computer and DOS is

3.1 To install the program on a floppy disk computer, load DOS, place the Payroll Disk in drive A, enter **install**, and follow the instructions on the screen.

loaded. Remember to protect your original disks and use working copies for installation.

1. Turn on the computer and monitor.
2. Place the Payroll Disk #1 in drive A.
3. At the C: prompt, enter **a:** to change to drive A.
4. At the A: prompt, enter **install**.
5. When prompted to, place the Tax File Disk in drive A and press ↵.
6. When asked, enter **H** to indicate you are installing DacEasy Payroll on a hard disk computer.
7. Then, when the CONFIG.SYS notice appears, press ↵ to continue.
8. The next screen requests the path name for the directory where you want to store your Payroll program, followed by C:\DEP3. Press ↵ to accept the suggested name, or enter the drive and directory you want to use.
9. The next prompt asks if you want to create the directory. Enter **Y**. The directory for your Payroll program is created.
10. At the next prompt, remove the Tax File Disk from drive A, insert the Payroll Disk, and then press ↵. DacEasy asks you to wait while all the program files are copied onto the hard disk into the directory.
11. Replace the program disk with the Tax File Disk once more and press ↵.
12. When the copying is complete, remove the program disk from drive A.

This completes the installation of DacEasy Payroll version 3.1. Instructions for initializing and using the program are in Chapter 16.

APPENDIX

B

Upgrading DacEasy Accounting

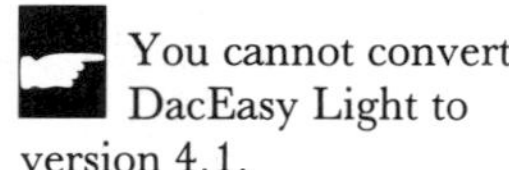

You cannot convert DacEasy Light to version 4.1.

DACEASY PROVIDES PROGRAMS THAT ALLOW YOU to upgrade your current files to versions 4.1. You must install and initialize the new version of the DacEasy Accounting program before you can convert your current files (see Appendix A and Chapters 1 and 2).

PREPARING FOR CONVERSION

Save yourself time and frustration and protect your data by backing up your current files before proceeding. Although the process is simple, the conversion might be interrupted by a power failure or by insufficient disk space.

To prepare your current files for conversion, enter and post all activity for the month in your old program, including general ledger activity, and then close the month in every module. Print reports showing the status of your current files before the conversion to compare them with the converted files.

Print the following reports before converting your files:

- The customer directory to review customer definitions
- The vendor directory to review vendor definitions
- The Accounts Receivable and Accounts Payable aging reports (detail) to list outstanding invoices
- The product activity report to list stock on hand
- The service report to list all services
- The trial balance, including level 9 (general accounts) and inactive accounts to list every account and its balance
- Statistical year-to-date reports for Accounts Payable, Accounts Receivable, Inventory/Service, and General Ledger to print historical and forecast data

CONVERTING TO VERSION 4.1

You can upgrade all earlier versions directly to 4.1 without upgrading to 3.1 first. After you install and initialize 4.1, define your general ledger accounts and accounting periods. The accounts must be identical to those in your previous version. All balances will be placed in the current period, which is then marked closed. To convert your data, follow the steps below:

1. Select Convert from the File menu of version 4.1. The File Convert screen, shown in Figure B.1, appears. In the example, we have already entered the default file locations.

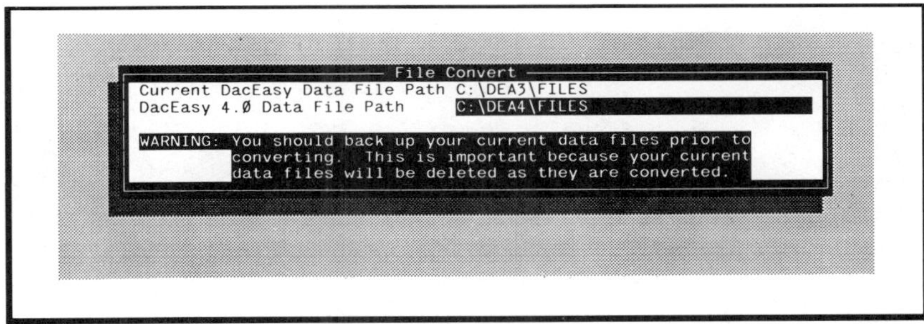

Figure B.1: File conversion in version 4.1

To print aging reports and directories, select Reports from the Main menu, then Receivables, then Aging or Directory. Do the same for Accounts Payable and Inventory/ Service reports. To print the trial balance, select General Ledger from the Reports menu, then Trial Balance. To print the statistical reports, select Periodic from the Main menu, then Receivables, Payables, or Inventory, and then Print Statistical YTD.

2. In the field next to the first prompt, enter the name of the drive, directory, and subdirectory where your current data files are located, using the following format: drive letter, colon, backslash (\), DacEasy Accounting directory name, backslash, DacEasy Accounting data file subdirectory name.
3. When prompted for the DacEasy 4.1 data file path, enter the drive, directory, and subdirectory where you want to store the data in the new 4.1 version.
4. Verify your entries. The data in your current files will be deleted as it is copied into the new subdirectory. Press F10 to begin the conversion process.
5. When the process is complete, at the C: prompt, enter **cd\dea4** (or the name of the directory where you placed your 4.1 program).
6. Print the reports listed at the beginning of the appendix and compare them with the reports from your old system.

If your new files agree with the old ones, you can remove the old DacEasy directory (DEA or DEA3) and subdirectory (DEA\FILES) from your hard disk. Refer to your DOS manual for instructions on deleting files and directories. Always do so with caution. If there are discrepancies, you should restore the backup copy of your old system and repeat the conversion process.

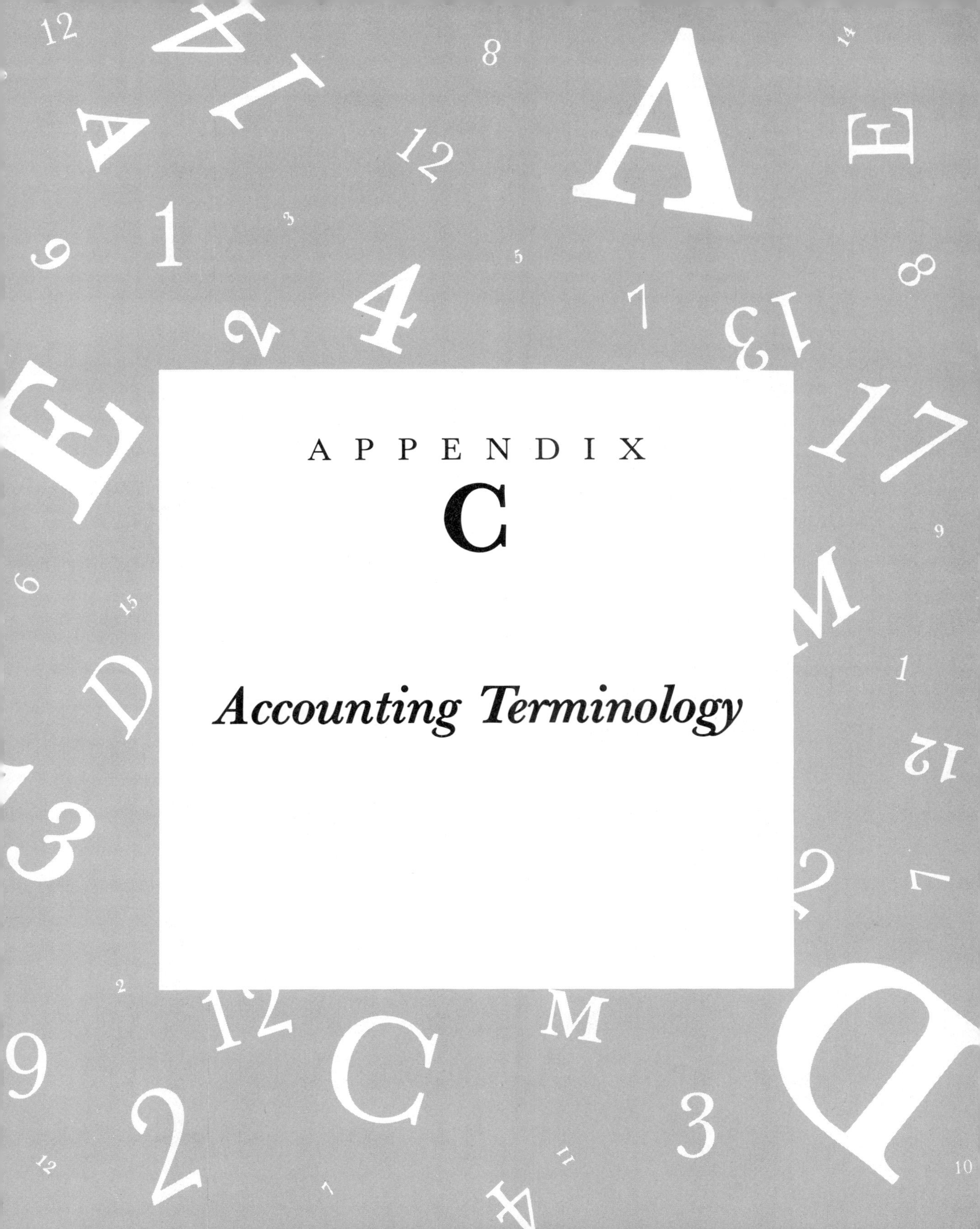

APPENDIX

C

Accounting Terminology

THIS APPENDIX DEFINES COMMON ACCOUNTING terms and provides a quick lesson in debits and credits:

- To increase an asset account, enter a debit. Asset accounts include cash, accounts receivable, fixed assets, inventory, prepaid insurance, and utility deposits.
- To increase a liability account, enter a credit. Liability accounts include accounts payable, sales tax payable, and notes payable.
- To increase an equity account, enter a credit. Equity accounts include current earnings, stock, and retained earnings.
- To increase an income account, enter a credit. Income accounts include sales, customer finance charges, and dividends.
- To increase an expense account, enter a debit. Expense accounts include cost of goods, rent, maintenance, insurance, travel, and cash shortages.

ACCOUNTING TERMS

Abnormal balance: Each account type normally carries either a debit or a credit balance. When the balance is the opposite of what that type should be, it is called an abnormal balance. This usually applies to contra accounts.

Account: A unit used to store the accounting data of a business.

Account type: A category to classify general ledger accounts. Account types are asset, liability, equity, revenue, income, and expense.

Accounts payable: Debts owed for purchases of goods or services.

Accounts receivable: Monies owed to a company by its customers.

Accumulated depreciation: A contra asset account that records the depreciation claimed on the related asset.

Accrual basis: An accounting method in which income is recorded when goods or services are delivered, and expenses are recorded when they are incurred.

Accrued assets or liabilities: Unrecorded assets or liabilities that exist at the end of an accounting period.

Acid test: The ratio of current assets to current liabilities.

Adjusting entries: Journal entries that update accounts for activity that is not reflected in routine transactions.

Aging period: A time frame that determines the age of an invoice based on its due date.

Aging report: A listing of invoices, their balances, and the age of the balance (determined by how many days from the current date the due date falls).

Applied: Payments or adjustments made against a specific invoice.

Asset: Property or anything of value owned by a company.

Asset, current: An asset readily convertible to cash (usually within one year) in the normal course of business.

Asset, fixed: An asset not readily convertible to cash nor acquired for resale, such as property or machinery that is used in the operation of the business.

Average cost: A method of valuing resale merchandise in which the cost for all items purchased is divided by the number of units purchased.

Bad debt: An amount due to a company that is not collectable.

Balance, account: The net result of all transactions, debits, and credits affecting a general ledger account.

Balance, customer: The net result of all charges and payments in a customer's record.

Balance forward: A statement type that shows only the current period in detail and carries forward amounts due from previous periods in the form of an accumulated balance.

Balance sheet: The company's assets, liabilities, and owner's equity presented in a formal report.

Balance, vendor: The net result of all charges and payments in a vendor's record.

Book inventory: The units of resale merchandise on hand according to records of purchases and sales without regard to breakage or loss.

Budget: An estimate of revenues and expenses in a specific period.

Capital account: A general ledger account in which an owner's investment in the business and percent of the company's earnings are recorded.

Cash basis: An accounting method in which income is recorded when payment is received, and expenses are recorded when they are paid for.

Cash disbursement: Payments made to a vendor.

Changes in financial position: A statement showing the money that came into a business and what it was spent for.

Chart of accounts: A listing, usually numeric, of all accounts in the general ledger.

Closing the books: Transferring the balances from all income and expense accounts into the retained earnings account. In DacEasy, this occurs when you close the year (not when you close the period).

Contra account: An account whose balance is subtracted from an associated account on the balance sheet.

Contractor: Someone who agrees to do work for a company under contract, usually with no income taxes or other items deducted from the payment.

Contributions: Payroll-related amounts paid solely by the company, such as federal unemployment taxes.

Cost: The amount paid to obtain assets or resale merchandise.

Cost center, customer: A method of allocating costs and revenue based on customer.

Cost center, product: A method of allocating costs and revenue based on product.

Cost of goods sold: An expense denoting the cost of goods purchased then resold to customers.

Count sheets: Listings of every inventory item on the books, used to take a physical count of all merchandise actually on hand.

Credit: An entry to a general ledger account that decreases an asset or expense account and increases a liability, equity, or income account.

Credit memo: A form issued by a company to reduce the liability of a customer.

Current assets: Cash and other assets that can be converted to cash quickly.

Current liabilities: Debts that are due within a year or less.

Customer: A person, company, or organization who purchases merchandise or services from a business.

Debit: An entry to a general ledger account that increases an asset or expense account and decreases a liability, equity, or income account.

Debit memo: A form issued by a company to increase the liability of a customer.

Deductions: Amounts taken out of an employee's gross wages, such as income taxes or union dues.

Depreciation: A portion of the cost of an asset posted periodically to an expense account that represents a reduction in the value of an asset.

Detail account: A subaccount in the general ledger that can accept direct entries in DacEasy.

Discount: An amount deducted from the invoice amount if the invoice is paid within a specified time period.

Discount date: The last day on which a company or customer can take a discount on what is owed on an invoice.

Discount percent: The percentage a company or customer is allowed to deduct from an invoice when taking a discount.

Drawing account: An account to track withdrawals by a partner or proprietor in a business.

Effective date: The date transactions are reflected in the general ledger or on a customer or vendor record.

Equity: The combination of capital invested in a company and earnings retained in the company.

Expense: A cost related to conducting business, such as postage expense.

Finance charges: A penalty assessed for not making payment in the specified time period.

Financial statements: Records of the financial status of a business, including a balance sheet and income statement and, often, a statement of changes in financial condition.

Fiscal year: A company's normal business cycle. It may or may not coincide with a calendar year, but is of the same duration.

Forecast: A prediction or estimate of future business transactions.

General account: An account in DacEasy that accumulates the total of all transactions posted to lower level detail accounts.

General ledger: A ledger containing the financial statement accounts of your business.

Income: Money or value received as a result of doing business.

Income statement: A financial statement showing the net profit or loss in a business for a specific time period.

Inventory, physical: The count of merchandise actually on hand and available for sale.

Inventory, value: The value placed on merchandise held for resale, in DacEasy standard cost, average cost, or last purchase price is used to arrive at inventory value.

Invoice: An itemization of goods or services purchased and the amount charged for them (a bill).

Journal: Where you originally record a transaction. Journals are identified by abbreviations such as AJ for adjustments. Similar transactions are recorded in the same journal type. Typical journals are cash receipts, cash disbursements, purchases, sales, and payroll.

Last purchase price: A method of valuing all the units of an inventory item at the last price paid for the item.

Late charge: An amount added to a past due invoice as a penalty for nonpayment.

Liability: A debt owed by the company.

Merchandise return: Merchandise returned to a vendor by the company (see *purchase return*).

Net profit: The amount by which income exceeds expenses.

Net sales: The amount of sales after deducting sales returns, freight charges, and discounts allowed.

Normal balance: The typical balance (debit or credit) of a given type of account. For example, asset accounts typically have a debit balance.

Notes payable or receivable: Long-term debts or receivables evidenced by a note that are tracked separately from ongoing accounts payable or receivable.

Offsetting entry: An entry that counterbalances (equals) another in a transaction.

Open item: A statement type that includes all open transactions, regardless of the period they occurred in.

Open payables or receivables: Invoices from vendors or on customer accounts that have not yet been paid.

Open period: A period into which you can still post transactions; one that has not been closed.

Packing slip: A copy of information on an invoice, without the prices or amount due, that usually is enclosed with the merchandise.

Period: A division of an accounting year. You can define up to 13 periods in DacEasy.

Perpetual inventory: An inventory tracking method in which book inventory is adjusted to match physical inventory.

Posting: Applying transactions to customer, vendor, and general ledger accounts.

Prepaid expense: Expenses that have been paid for in advance; they are recorded as an asset and reduced as the actual expense is incurred.

Product costing: The means of valuing inventory: by average cost, standard cost, or last purchase price.

Purchase discount: The discount a company takes when paying a vendor early for goods or services purchased.

Purchase order: A form used to place an order with a vendor.

Purchase return: Merchandise returned to a vendor for credit.

Purchase tax: A tax the company pays when making a purchase, usually of a non-resale item.

Quarter-end: In payroll processing, the end of a 3-month period when wages and taxes must be reported to the IRS on a 941 form.

Resale item: An item purchased (usually without paying sales tax) for resale to a customer.

Retained earnings: The accumulated net earnings of a company less distributions to owners or stockholders.

Revenue: An amount earned, for example, interest or money from a sale.

Reversing entry: A journal entry on the first of the month to reverse adjusting entries made at the end of the preceding month, for example, for accrued salary expense.

Sales discount: The discount a customer is allowed to take when paying a bill early.

Sales return: Merchandise returned by a customer for a refund or credit.

Sales tax: The tax a customer pays when purchasing from a company.

Standard cost: A nonfluctuating estimate of what an item will cost. In DacEasy, one method of valuing inventory.

Subaccount: An account subordinate to a general account.

Subsidiary ledger/journal: A ledger or journal subordinate to the general ledger that contains detail supporting the amount in the general ledger, for example, an accounts payable ledger or a purchases journal.

Taxes payable: Income taxes withheld from an employee's gross wages and the employer's related liability, or sales tax collected, that must be paid by the company to the appropriate taxing agency.

Terms: Conditions under which a sale is made or a debt incurred outlining how and when payment is expected.

Transaction: Recordable events that affect the general ledger accounts of a company.

Trial balance: A complete listing of the accounts in the general ledger, with the debit and credit balances totaled to determine if they are equal. It is used to verify the accuracy of posted transactions.

Turnover: The number of times an asset is replaced within a specific period, normally a year. Turnover is usually calculated for accounts receivable, inventory, and other assets.

Vendor: A person or company who sells goods or services.

Year-end: The end of a fiscal or calendar year when the business closes the income and expense accounts and calculates its retained earnings.

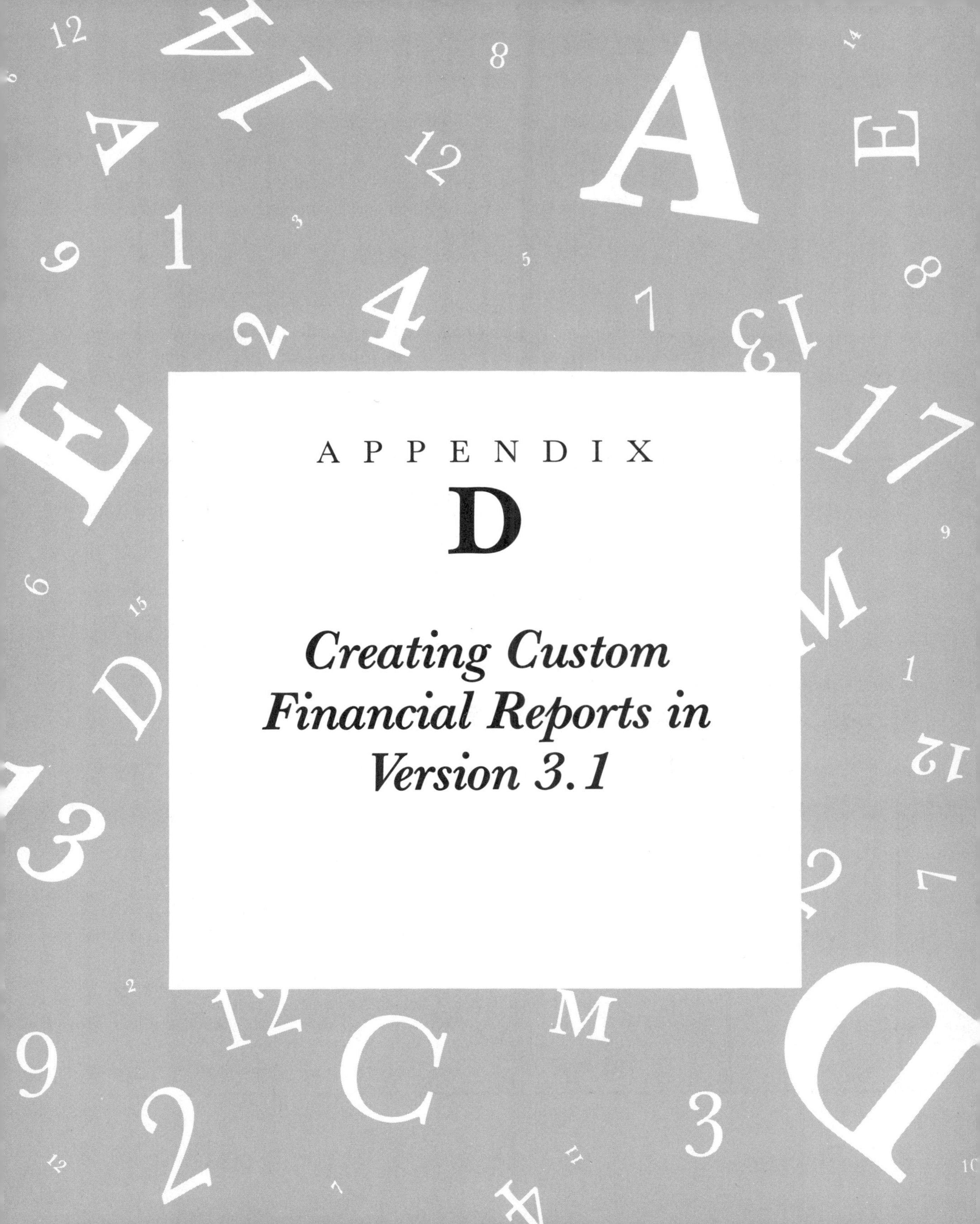

APPENDIX D

Creating Custom Financial Reports in Version 3.1

IF YOU USE DACEASY'S SAMPLE CHART OF ACCOUNTS, a comparative balance sheet and income statement and two ratio reports are supplied with the Financial Statements Generator in version 3.1. If you altered or did not use the sample chart of accounts, you must edit these reports or create others.

This chapter explains the procedures for adding, editing, and printing financial reports, which are based on the balances in your general ledger. To create reports from other information in your database, you must use DacEasy Graph+Mate.

ADDING A FINANCIAL REPORT

To add a financial report, select the Financial Statements Generator option from the Financials menu, and then select Edit Financial Reports. You will see the Financial Statements Maintenance screen, which lists the names of the reports supplied by DacEasy (described in Chapter 13). From this screen, press F3, and you will see the report-generator screen. The fields on this screen are described in Table D.1.

Table D.1: Fields on the Report-Generator Screen

Field	Description
Enter Report Name	Enter an abbreviated name to identify the report (four characters maximum).
Print (Y/N)	Enter Y to print the line on the report or N to suppress it from printing. You can use unprinted lines (marked N) to total preceding information and move the total elsewhere, to clear accumulations, or to enter or accumulate an amount to be used in percentage calculations.
Acct. #	The number of the account whose balance you want to use in the report.
Description	The description of the line. If you entered an account number, the description from the general ledger record appears. You can edit it for this report only. The description will only print on the report if you designated the line as a printed line.
Amount From	Indicate which column to total: 1, 2, or 3. Other possible symbols are *0* to enter a description only (no total), *99* to draw the amount from the account balance in the general ledger, and / (slash) to calculate a ratio based on the totals of two columns designated in the Amount To fields.

Table D.1: Fields on the Report-Generator Screen (continued)

Field	Description
Amount To 1, 2, 3	Indicate where the amount or total should be placed for further accumulation or use. The possible symbols are + to add the amount on the line to the column total, – to subtract the amount on the line from the column total, *N* to use the column total as the numerator (top of the fraction) in a ratio calculation, *D* to use the column total as the denominator (bottom of the fraction) in a ratio calculation, and *0* to clear the column total.
%	A plus sign (+) in the % field indicates the amount on the line is the basis for percentage calculations. Only one line per report can be designated as the comparison amount.
Lines 99 = pg.	Indicate printing format instructions. The possible symbols are *99* to start a new page, *C* to center the description on the report, - (hyphen) to print a single underline in all amount columns, = to print a double underline in all amount columns, *1* to skip one line before printing the next line, and *2* to skip two lines before printing the next line.

For the report name, enter an abbreviation of up to four characters to identify the report. This is the name DacEasy displays on Financial Statement Maintenance screen. You enter the title that actually appears on the printed report as a description of the line.

On the first line, press ↵ in the Print (Y/N) field to print the line, press ↵ again to move to the Description field, and type the title to be printed on the report. DacEasy will insert a 0 in the Amount From column; it assumes that the line does not involve amounts because you did not enter an account number. Press ↵ six times to accept the 0 and move past the Amount To and % fields to the Lines field. Enter a C to center the title. You can use this procedure to enter any text-only lines.

You can suppress printing of a line in the report by entering an N in the Print (Y/N) field. Unprinted lines are useful for accumulating data to be used in other calculations.

Enter the number of the general ledger account whose balance you want to use on this line of the report in the Acct. # field, and DacEasy will display the title from the record. This is the description that will be printed on the report. You can type over the description to use another one for the report without affecting the name in the record. When you enter an account number, DacEasy inserts a 99 in the

Amount From field. This means that the amount for the line is the balance in this general ledger account. You can enter a 1, 2, or 3 to tell the program which column total to print on the report. To calculate a ratio based on the immediate total of two columns, enter a slash (/). For descriptions only (text lines), enter a zero.

The Amount To 1, 2, and 3 fields indicate where to place the amount—in column 1, 2, or 3—and how to use it. You press the spacebar in the appropriate Amount To column to display a + (add the amount to the column total), – (subtract the amount), N (use the column total as the numerator for a ratio), D (use the total as the denominator for a ratio), or 0 (clear the column total).

Although the report-generator screen allows you to work with three columns to accumulate separate totals, the results print on the report in only one column. The three on-screen Amount To columns simply tell the program which amounts to accumulate into a given total. You cannot print the amounts in separate columns. You can indicate a subordinate amount on the printed report by indenting its description. Press the Insert key, and then press the spacebar to add one (or more spaces) before the text in the Description field.

Only one comparison amount can be used in a report. For example, you cannot calculate each asset as a percent of total assets and calculate each liability as a percent of total liabilities on the same report. The liabilities will also be shown as a percent of total assets.

You can make only one entry in the % (percent) field for the entire report. On the line whose amount you want to base all the percentage calculations on, press the spacebar to display a + (plus sign) in the % field. Every amount line in the report will be shown as a percentage of the one amount you choose.

The Lines field allows you to format your report. Along with a C for centering, you can enter 99 to start a new page, - (hyphen) to print a single underline in all amount columns, = (equal sign) to print a double underline, 1 to skip one line, or 2 to skip two lines.

After you enter the information for all the lines in the report, press Alt-P to print a copy of the report format. Then press F10 to record the new format.

For your financial reports, DacEasy can use information from three statistical areas of your account records: year-to-date balance, last year's balance, and forecast. However, you do not designate the type of balance to use when you create the report; you just supply the line sequence and mathematics to perform. You choose the statistical area the information should be drawn from for a particular report when you request to print it.

Dealing with contra accounts can be tricky. Contra accounts are those that are related to, and deducted from, another account. For example, Accumulated Depreciation is a contra account that reduces its associated account, Fixed Assets. You must remember that all accounts are of a specific type in DacEasy, and each account type has a normal balance:

- Debit for asset accounts
- Credit for liability accounts
- Credit for equity accounts
- Credit for revenue accounts
- Debit for expense accounts

If you are dealing with a contra account, the balance is preceded by a minus sign to indicate that it is abnormal (the opposite of what that account type should be), regardless if it is normally a debit or credit balance. Unfortunately, these amounts will also appear on the report preceded by a minus sign, whether or not you are subtracting them in the report. Also, if you want to accumulate the balance of a contra account in a column in your report, you must enter the opposite parameter of what you intend to do; to add the contra account amount, place a minus sign in the Amount To field, and to subtract the amount, put a plus sign in the column.

The format for a simple sales analysis report, which uses accounts from the sample chart of accounts, is shown in Figure D.1. The report shows sales activity, cost of sales, and sales income as a percentage of gross sales. Its design illustrates most of the entries you can use to create reports. Figure D.2 shows an example of a printed report in this format.

In the first Acct. # field of the sample format is the number of the general ledger account for total sales (41). The name from the account record was replaced with the description Gross Sales. In the Amount To 1 field, the + indicates that the amount on this line is to be added to column 1. The + in the % field indicates that the amount on this line is the one all percentage calculations are based

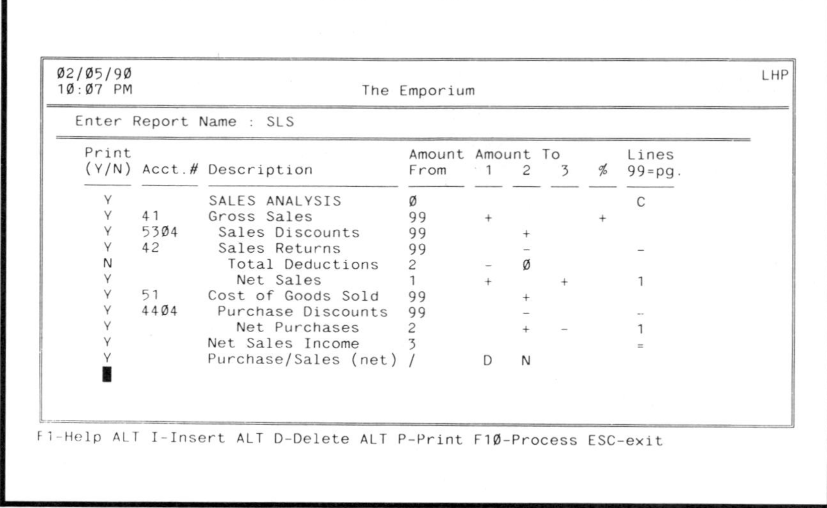

02/05/90 LHP
10:07 PM The Emporium

Enter Report Name : SLS

Print (Y/N)	Acct.#	Description	Amount From	Amount To 1	2	3	%	Lines 99=pg.
Y		SALES ANALYSIS	Ø					C
Y	41	Gross Sales	99	+			+	
Y	5304	Sales Discounts	99		+			
Y	42	Sales Returns	99		-			-
N		Total Deductions	2	-	Ø			
Y		Net Sales	1	+		+		1
Y	51	Cost of Goods Sold	99		+			
Y	4404	Purchase Discounts	99		-			--
Y		Net Purchases	2		+	-		1
Y		Net Sales Income	3					=
Y		Purchase/Sales (net)	/	D	N			

F1-Help ALT I-Insert ALT D-Delete ALT P-Print F10-Process ESC-exit

Figure D.1: Sample design for a financial report

Date : 08/30/89 The Emporium Page no. 1
Time : 07:26 PM 123 Main Street
Yourtown, USA

FINANCIAL STATEMENTS

Acct #	Description	Year to Date	%
	SALES ANALYSIS		
41	Gross Sales	7,343.63	
5304	Sales Discounts	130.00	1.8
42	Sales Returns	-520.63	-7.1
	Net Sales	6,693.00	91.1
51	Cost of Goods Sold	3,560.49	48.5
4404	Purchase Discounts	79.46	1.1
	Net Purchases	3,481.03	47.4
	Net Sales Income	3,211.97	43.7
	Purchase/Sales (net)	0.52	

Figure D.2: Report created from sample format

upon. So, for the sample report, all amounts will be shown as a percent of total sales.

The next Acct. # field contains the account number for Sales Discounts (5304). The description is indented one space so the account name will be indented on the printed report. In the Amount To 2 field is a +, which indicates this amount is to be added to column 2.

The next Acct. # field contains the number for the Sales Returns account, whose description is also indented one space. In the Amount To 2 field, a - appears to indicate this amount is to be included in the total for column 2. In the example, Sales Returns is a contra account to Sales. It should be used to reduce the amount in the Sales account to present a more accurate picture of sales income. Both accounts are designated as revenue accounts. The Sales Returns account carries a minus sign, however, indicating it has an abnormal (debit) balance for a revenue account.

In order to add the Sales Returns amount to the Sales Discounts amount, the entry for the Sales Returns amount is a minus (two negatives make a positive). The account balance we are adding the Sales Returns amount to, Sales Discounts, has a normal balance (debit) for its designation as an expense account. Therefore, we used the normal entry, a plus sign, to add it to the column.

On the same line, the - in the Lines field causes a single underline to print in each amount column after the sales return figures.

On the next line, an N is entered to suppress printing, and the description, Total Deductions, is indented two spaces. This memo field allows us to total the sales discounts and sales returns and use that total to calculate an amount that will be printed on the report. You can accumulate this data and move it to another column without having to print it. The 2 in the Amount From column totals the amounts in column 2. In the Amount To 1 field, the - indicates that the total from column 2 is to be subtracted from the amounts in column 1. In the Amount To 2 field, the 0 clears the total from column 2 so we can use the column again to accumulate data for our next section. You see, it is possible to accomplish several functions on one line.

The description on the next line, Net Sales, is indented three spaces. In the Amount From field is a 1 to total the amounts in column 1, which will be the difference between gross sales and total deductions. The Amount To 1 and Amount To 2 fields both contain a + to place the net sales amount in both columns for further calculations. The Amount From field tells the program which column total—1, 2 or 3—to print on the report. The Amount To column indicates where to accumulate the same total for further use. The Lines field contains a 1 to skip one line before printing the next line.

On the next line is the account number and description for the Costs of Goods Sold account. The + in that Amount To 2 column indicates this amount is to be added to column 2.

On the next line, the number of the Purchase Discounts account is entered, and the description is indented one space. For this illustration, we are assuming that discounts for inventory item purchases only, not all purchase discounts, are tracked in this account. In the Amount To 2 field, the - subtracts the amount on this line from column 2. The - in the Lines field prints a single underline in the amount columns under the purchase discount figure.

The Description field on the next line, which is indented three spaces, says Net Purchases. The 2 in the Amount From field places the total from column 2 on this line. The amounts in column 2 now are the cost of goods sold and the purchase discounts taken when paying for the resale merchandise. In the Amount To 2 field, the + adds the net sales amount to column 2 for further calculations. In the Amount To 3 field, the - subtracts the net sales amount from column 3. In the Lines field, the 1 leaves a blank line after the net purchases figure before printing the next line.

The next line has Net Sales Income as the Description and a 3 in the Amount From field to place the total from column 3 on this line in the report. The = in the Lines field prints a double underline under the net sales figures.

On the last line, the Description field contains Purchase/Sales (net), which describes the ratio to be calculated and printed on this line. In the Amount From field, the / indicates this line contains a ratio calculation. The D in the Amount To 1 field indicates the total in this column, which is net sales, is to be used as the denominator in the equation. In the Amount To 2 field, the N indicates the total in this column, which is net purchases, is to be used as the numerator. Thus, net purchases will be divided by net sales to show the ratio of purchases to sales.

You can only compare the last total in a column to the last total in another column. For example, you cannot calculate the ratio of net sales income to gross sales if, as in our example, you have accumulated net sales in the same column as net purchases.

EDITING AND DELETING FINANCIAL REPORTS

You can edit any financial reports listed on the Financial Statements Maintenance screen. However, you should first make a copy of the original report format, and then edit the copy. Keep the original version until you are satisfied with the edited report.

To copy the format, on the Financial Statements Maintenance screen, place the cursor on the name of the report and press F8. Enter an abbreviated name for the new report. DacEasy copies the original report and displays the new name on the screen.

To edit the format, place the cursor on the new report name and press F2. The report format appears on the screen. Move the cursor to the line you want to edit. If you want to use another account, type its account number over the existing one. Press ↵, and the new account description will appear. To change any of the parameters, move the cursor to the column and press the spacebar until the parameter you want to use appears.

To delete the line entirely, press Alt-D. Use this command with caution as calculations on other lines might depend on the deleted line.

Use caution when deleting because you cannot retrieve a deleted report. Creating a report takes time, but deleting it takes only two keystrokes.

To add a new line, place the cursor on the line below where you want to insert the new line and press Alt-I. Then enter the data for the new line. Press F10 to record the changes.

When you are finished editing the report, print it (as described later) to verify the results, and edit it if necessary. When you are satisfied with the new report format, you can delete the original report if you won't be using it.

To delete a financial report, place the cursor on the name of the report on the Financial Statements Maintenance screen. Press F6 to delete it, and enter Y at the prompt.

PRINTING FINANCIAL REPORTS

You can print DacEasy financial reports in one of three formats: year to date only, year to date compared to last year, or year to date compared to forecast. The sample printed report is in the year-to-date only format.

To print reports, select the Financial Statements Generator option from the Financials menu, and then choose Print Financial Reports. On the Print Financial Reports screen, move the cursor to the name of each report you want to print and press F2. Press F10 to print those selected. At the Report Format prompt, press the spacebar to select the type of balances to be included: YTD Only, YTD/Last Year, or YTD/Budget (Forecast).

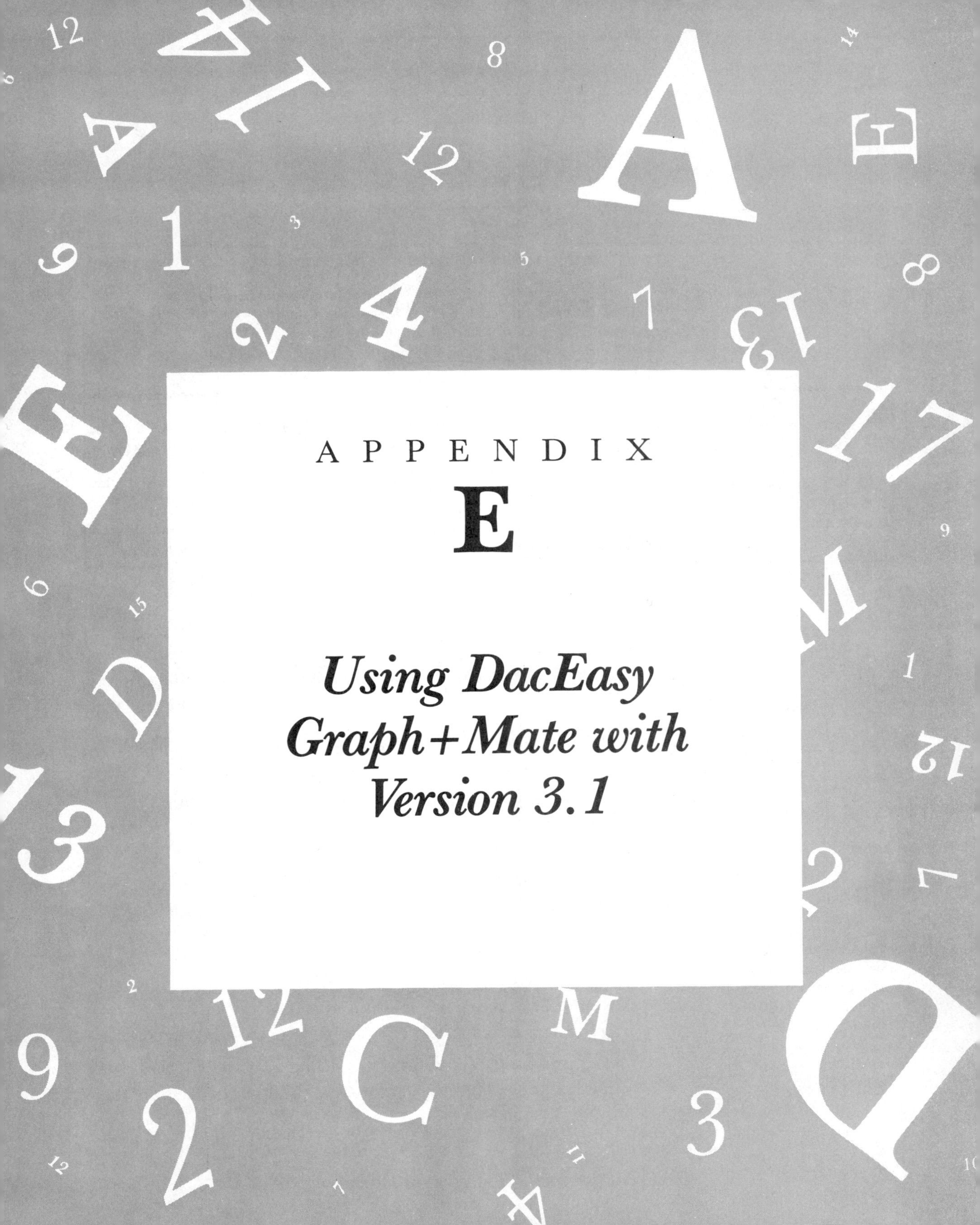

APPENDIX E

Using DacEasy Graph+Mate with Version 3.1

DACEASY GRAPH+MATE IS A COMPANION PROGRAM to version 3.1 of DacEasy Accounting and DacEasy Payroll. With it, you can view selected fields from your records on screen, create reports from data stored in the record fields, and create graphs from your DacEasy financial data. You are prompted to install Graph+Mate when you install DacEasy Accounting version 3.1.

INITIALIZING GRAPH+MATE

Information about Graph+Mate is available in the program. At the DacEasy directory prompt, enter **type read.me**. Press Ctrl-S to pause and resume scrolling or Ctrl-Break to cancel the display.

After installing DacEasy Graph+Mate, you must initialize the program. Graph+Mate contains several default definitions, which you can use or change. To initialize the program, at the C: prompt, enter **install**, and when asked if you have a color monitor, enter a **Y** or an **N** as appropriate to your computer system. Next, you'll see the Installation menu, which notes the memory available for running the DacEasy programs.

SETTING OPTIONS

To select a menu item, move the cursor to the option and press ↵, or press the first letter of the option name.

You can use the Options menu selections to define your company name, the directories where your DacEasy programs are located, the hot keys you want, and a password, as follows:

A hot key is actually a combination of two keys that you press simultaneously to access certain features of Graph+Mate while in another DacEasy application.

- To define the name and address you want printed as a heading on reports, select the Installation Name option. Type your company's information over the Dac Software name and address and press F10 to record it.
- If your directory paths for your DacEasy program files are not the default (C:\DEA3\FILES), select the Default Directories option. Enter the path to the subdirectory for the DacEasy Accounting files, and then the path for the Graph+Mate program and files. Press F10 to record the path designations.
- If you want to change the default hot keys (Alt-F10 for Graph+Mate, Alt-C for the Calculator, Alt-N for the Notepad, and Alt-M for Macros), select the appropriate 'Hot' key

option. Press the new key combination, and then press Esc to exit the hot key definition.

- If you want to use a Graph+Mate password, select the Password Editing option. Type up to an eight-character password at the prompt (the password characters will not appear on the screen), press ↵, and then enter the password again to validate it.

CHOOSING MONITOR COLORS

To define your monitor, select the option for each area of the screen you want to change from the Colors menu. You can set a color for four elements of each window type: N for normal, which is for text; I for inverse, which is highlighting; B for border, which is the lines around a window; and E for extra, which is for special characters.

Select one of the four designators (colors) and use the arrow keys to change the color. The up and down arrow keys control the foreground color, and the right and left arrow keys control the background color. The colors on your screen change as you move through the selections. Press ↵ when you like the choice (or Esc to abandon the changes). Monochrome screens offer bright or dim, and clear or solid boxes.

IDENTIFYING APPLICATIONS

You can view the default applications available, enter the paths, and add or remove applications from use with Graph+Mate. To see the list of default applications, select the List Applications option from the Applications menu. Figure E.1 shows the list.

To define the applications you are using and the path to locate them, select the Edit Applications option from the Applications menu. Then select the application you want to define and enter the name and path information.

You can determine the program name and extension. Access the directory, and list the contents using the DOS command **dir/p**. Look for the file with a .COM or .EXE extension.

To define a new program, enter an abbreviated name of the program and the program name and extension. In the Program Path field, enter the drive and name of the directory where the program files are located. In the Data Path field, enter the drive, directory, and subdirectory where the data files are located. Press F10 to record the definition.

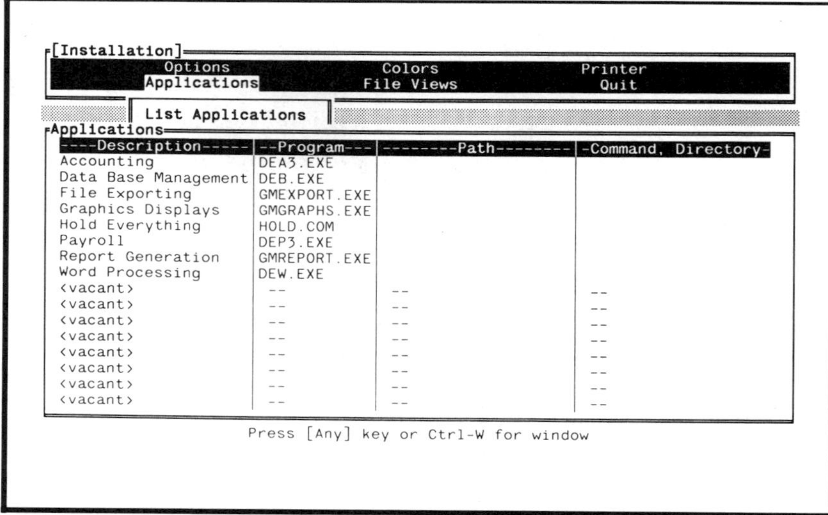

Figure E.1: Default applications available in Graph+Mate

ESTABLISHING FILE VIEWS

The File Views menu options allow you to designate how you want to view your accounting and payroll files. Again, DacEasy has provided default formats, but you can change them. Figure E.2 shows the default vendor record format. Other file views are provided for customer records, receivables invoices, payables invoices, and the employee file in payroll.

To change any of the default formats, select the file view you want to edit from the File Views menu. When you press F1 (Help), you'll see a window listing the keys to use in editing the format.

For example, suppose that you want to be able to view a customer's account while you are processing payroll. You could change the customer file view so you would be able to see the last payment, year-to-date sales, current balance, and the code for the salesperson who services the account. You would select the Customers (A/R) option from the File Views menu.

First, you must delete the fields you don't want to see, and then you add the ones you do want in your file view. Then move the cursor back to Customer Name and press Ctrl-S to make the customer name the sorting field. Now when you view the records, they will be

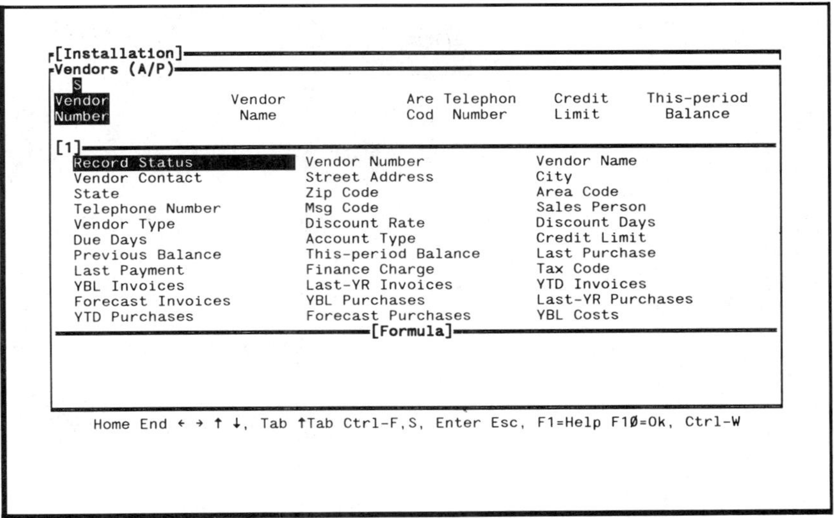

Figure E.2: Vendor record file format

in alphabetical order by customer name instead of appearing in customer number order.

ENTERING PRINTER PARAMETERS

Graph+Mate has predefined parameters for some printers. If your printer is listed, you simply select it from the Printer menu. Move the cursor to your printer's name in the list and press ↵.

If your printer is not listed, select the Edit Printer option from the Printer menu. Enter the parameters specified in your printer manual. At each field, DacEasy has provided help text to explain the parameters to enter. Press F1 and follow the instructions.

FINALIZING THE INSTALLATION DEFINITIONS

After you have defined the parameters for Graph+Mate, you can exit the initialization routine. You can alter any definition by accessing the Installation menu again (by entering **install** at the prompt for the Graph+Mate directory).

To finalize the installation definitions, select Quit from the Main menu. To quit the installation, enter Y. To save the configuration, again enter Y.

STARTING YOUR GRAPH+MATE PROGRAM

If you have a Hercules graphics adapter, before you load Graph+Mate, you must enter **gmdriver** at the directory prompt to load the Hercules video support routines first.

On a floppy system, place Graph+Mate Disk #1 in drive A and enter **GM** to load the program.

Graph+Mate is a utility that is loaded into the memory of your computer and can be accessed at any time from your Dac Software applications.

To load Graph+Mate, enter **GM** at the C: prompt. If you created a password, you must also enter it. The Graph+Mate Main menu appears, as shown in Figure E.3.

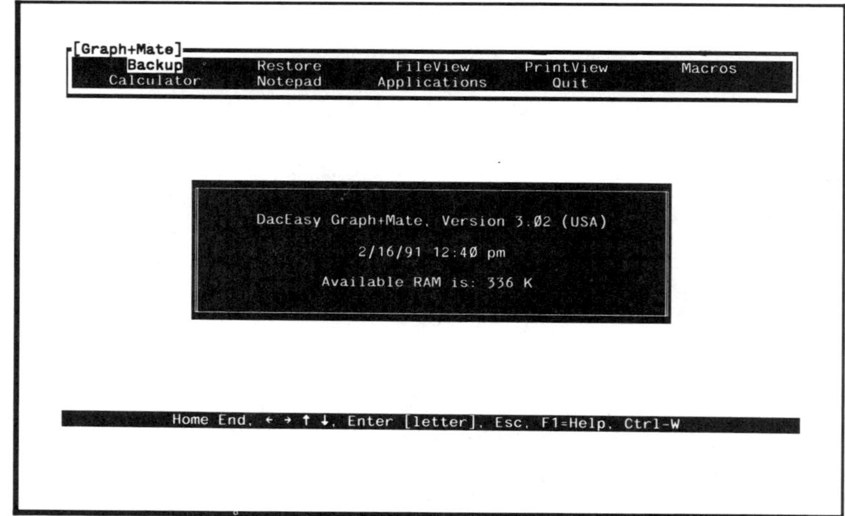

Figure E.3: The Graph+Mate Main menu

To use Graph+Mate while in a DacEasy application, you must load Graph+Mate first, then access the application by selecting it from the Applications menu.

For example, to enter DacEasy Payroll from Graph+Mate, you would select Payroll from the Applications menu. At the prompt

Program Parameters/data:

enter the drive, directory, and subdirectory where the Payroll files are located. If you accepted the default path when you installed DacEasy Payroll, your response would be C:\DEP3\FILES. The Payroll program would be loaded, and the Payroll Main menu would appear.

On a floppy system, you will be prompted to replace the Graph+Mate disk with the Application program disk. When you exit the application, place the Graph+Mate disk back in drive A when instructed to do so.

When you exit Payroll (or whatever application you selected), you will return to Graph+Mate. You can access the Graph+Mate Main menu without exiting Payroll by pressing Alt-F10 (or whatever hot key you designated for Graph+Mate). When you press Esc to exit Graph+Mate, you will return to the Payroll program.

While in a DacEasy application, you can also access the Graph+Mate notepad, calculator, or macro features directly by pressing the appropriate hot keys.

BACKING UP YOUR FILES

Graph+Mate provides a simple way to back up your files. Have several blank, formatted disks ready, then select either the Accounting Files or Payroll Files option from the Backup menu. Enter the drive and path for the files you want to back up in the Data Directory field. In the Backup Directory field, enter the drive and, if you are backing up to a hard disk, the directory and subdirectory name where you want to store the backup copy.

Place a blank, formatted disk in the floppy drive where you want to make the backup copy. If your files require more than one disk, DacEasy notifies you when you must replace a completed backup disk with a new blank, formatted disk. Label each disk with the program name, the date, and its sequence in the backup process. The sequence is important because you must restore the information in the same order it was copied.

RESTORING YOUR FILES

If your files are damaged, you can restore your latest backup copy to return your files to the condition they were in at the time of the backup operation. Then you can reenter and process data to bring your files up to date.

To restore your backup copy, select either Accounting Files or Payroll Files from the Restore menu. Enter the drive and path where the data files for the application you are restoring are located in the Data Directory field.

In the Backup Directory field, enter the drive and, if you are restoring from a hard disk, the directory and subdirectory name where the backup copy is located.

If you are restoring from floppy disks, place the backup disk labeled #1 in the drive you indicated in the Backup Directory field. If your files occupied more than one disk, DacEasy notifies you when you must place the next backup disk in the floppy drive. Remember to do so in the sequence in which the copies were made.

VIEWING FILES

Graph+Mate allows you to view your files during data entry, so you can look up the customer, vendor, or employee code. If you want to view files while you are in a DacEasy application, return to the Graph+Mate Main menu by pressing the hot key. From the File Views menu, select the records you want to view. Enter the drive and path for those records in the Data Directory field. For example, the entry C:\DEA3\FILES indicates the records are stored on drive C, in the accounting directory DEA3, and in the subdirectory FILES.

Enter the identification of the first record you want to view in the Low Range field. The identifier is the field you selected to sort the records by. If you chose customer name, enter the first name you want to review. If the sort field is vendor code, enter the code of the first vendor you want to review. In the High Range field, enter the identification of the last record you want to view. The program will compile and display the information. To exit the file view, press Esc.

CAPTURING OTHER DACEASY APPLICATION REPORTS

Reports you produce in other DacEasy products can be captured in Graph+Mate, and then viewed on the screen, printed, or stored on disk. However, you must first access the application through Graph+Mate.

From the application, press the hot key to access Graph+Mate. From the PrintView menu, select the Capture A Report option. At the prompt

Specify Capture Directory:

enter the drive, directory, and subdirectory where you want to hold the report results.

Select the report you want to process and respond to the prompts as if you were requesting to print the report normally. The program processes the report, but does not print it.

After the report is captured, press the Graph+Mate hot key again. To display the report on the screen, select the View a Captured Report option from the PrintView menu. To print it, select the Print A Captured Report option.

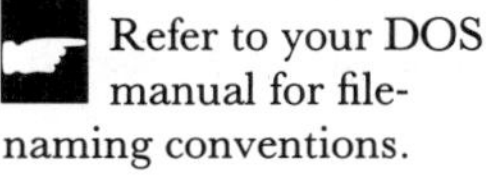
Refer to your DOS manual for file-naming conventions.

If you want to save the report results in a file on disk, select the Write/Append Report to File option from the PrintView menu. Then enter the drive, directory, and subdirectory where you want to store the report in the Output Directory field. For Output Filename, enter a name and three-character extension (usually PRN or TXT) for the report file. When asked if you want to append data, enter Y if you want to append the report results to an existing file; otherwise, enter N.

USING THE CALCULATOR AND NOTEPAD

To access the Graph+Mate Calculator from another application, press Alt-C (or your defined hot key). From within Graph+Mate, select the Calculator option from the Main menu. The calculator in Graph+Mate operates the same as the calculator feature in DacEasy Accounting version 4.1. Refer to the section about using the calculator in Chapter 5 for details.

The Graph+Mate Notepad is a limited word processor for making notes while you are working in a DacEasy application. Press Alt-N (or your defined hot key) to display the notepad area. From within Graph+Mate, select Notepad from the Main menu. In the notepad, type whatever information you want to save. Press F1 to see a list of editing keys. When you are ready to store the notes you have typed, press Esc.

CREATING AND PRODUCING REPORTS

In Graph+Mate, you can create reports that supplement the standard reports provided with DacEasy Accounting and Payroll. These Graph+Mate reports can be displayed on the screen, printed, or sent to a file on your computer disk.

CREATING GRAPH+MATE REPORTS

To create a report, select the Report Generation option from the Applications menu. At the prompt

```
Program Parameters/data:
```

enter the drive, directory, and subdirectory where the files you want to use in the report are stored. The Report Generation menu appears.

Select Edit Report from the menu, and complete the fields on the Graph+Mate report-generator screen, which are described in Table E.1.

The fields in the selected file that are available for reporting appear. Use the arrow keys to place the cursor on the first field you want on the report and press ↵ to place it in the heading. Repeat this until you have placed each field in turn. You can use as many fields as space permits. Each field requires a specific number of columns, which DacEasy determines for you. As you place a field, the cursor moves to the far right of it and indicates the column number where the next field will begin. In Figure E.4, we are creating a report to analyze the difference between the standard and average cost in the inventory record. Note the cursor position and the column indicator (48) after placing the Average Cost field.

To create a formula to use for a field, press Ctrl-F to display the formula window. Use the arrow keys to place the cursor on the fields

Table E.1: Fields on the Graph+Mate Report Generator Screen

Field	Description
Select	Select New Report to create a new report or select an existing report to edit.
Specify the REPORT name	Enter the name if you are creating a new report.
Print Title	The program supplies the name of the company as the title. Enter whatever you want to appear at the top of each report page.
Print Subtitle	The program supplies the name you gave to this report as the subtitle. Enter whatever you want printed under the first line of the title.
Page Width (cols).	Enter the maximum number of columns (characters) that will print horizontally on the page. The standard page width indicators are 80 or 132. Reports wider than 80 columns will be in compressed print.
Page Depth (lines)	Enter the maximum number of lines on your paper. The standard number of lines are 6 per inch, which results in 66 lines for 11-inch paper.
Vertical Margins	Enter the number of lines to leave blank at the top and bottom of the page as a margin.
Horizontal Margins	Enter the number of columns to leave blank at each side of the page as a margin.
DacEasy File	Select the accounting or payroll file to use in this report.

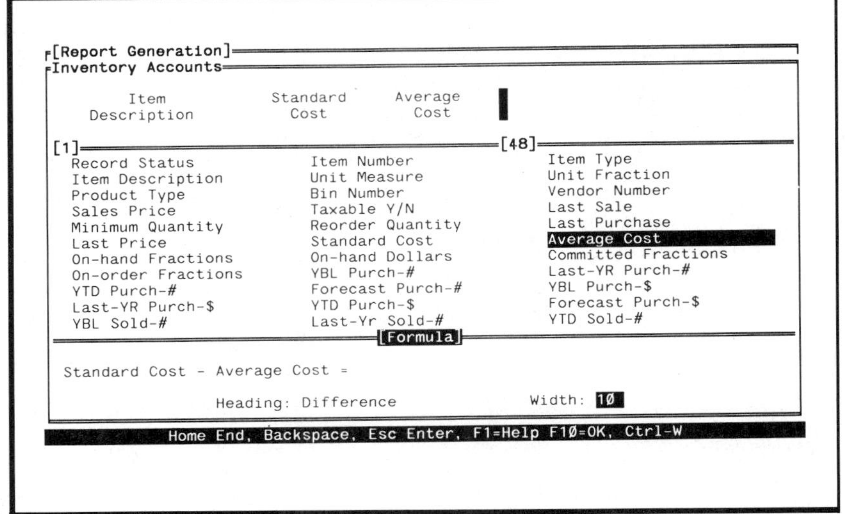

Figure E.4: Creating a report that uses a formula

you want to include and press ↵ to place them in the formula. Use the symbols to add (+), subtract (−), multiply (*), divide (/), or total (=) the data in the fields. Enter a title for the formula and the width of the field you just created (the largest number of characters that will result from your calculation).

You can subtotal or total a field in the report. Place the cursor on the report field in the heading and press Ctrl-B to subtotal the column or Ctrl-G for a grand total of the column.

Press F10 to save the report format. At the prompt

Update Report Name into Dictionary? Y

press ↵ to save the report format.

PRODUCING GRAPH+MATE REPORTS

To produce your report, select the Report Generation option from the Applications menu. Specify the drive, directory, and subdirectory where the files you want to use in the report are stored at the prompt for parameters, and select Produce Report from the Report Generation menu. Complete the fields on the report-production screen, which are described in Table E.2.

Press Esc to exit the screen display. When asked if you want to send the report to the printer, press ↵ if you want a printed copy;

Table E.2: Fields on the Graph+Mate Report Production Screen

Field	Description
Select	Select the name of the report you want to process.
Data Directory	The program supplies the directory you entered at the parameters prompt.
Low Range	Enter the first record you want on the report, or press ↵ to start with the first record in the file.
High Range	Enter the last record you want on the report, or press ↵ to print through the last record.
Show Totals?	Press ↵ to generate subtotal and total lines on the report.
Disposition	Use the arrow keys to select from Screen, Printer, Disk, or Route. If you select Route, choose which printer device the report results should be sent to: PRN, LPT1, LPT2, COM1, COM2, or NUL. These refer to printer or communication ports on your computer. Refer to your DOS manual for a definition of each device.

Table E.2: Fields on the Graph+Mate Report Production Screen (continued)

Field	Description
Output Directory	If you are sending the report to disk, enter the drive, directory, and subdirectory where you want to store the report results. The default is the Graph+Mate directory.
Output Filename	If you are sending the report to disk, enter a file name and extension to identify it. The default is REPORT.PRN.

otherwise, enter N. Note that when you select to use inventory files, the service records are also included. You cannot separate service records from product records in Graph+Mate reports.

CREATING GRAPHS

You can create graphs in several styles, including pie and bar charts, from data in your DacEasy Accounting and DacEasy Payroll files, totals generated in a Graph+Mate report, or external ASCII files.

SETTING UP A GRAPH FORMAT

To create a graph format for DacEasy data, select the Graphic Display option from the Applications menu. At the prompt for parameters, enter the drive, directory, and subdirectory where the data you want to graph is located. Select Edit Graph from the Graphics Display menu, and complete the fields on the formatting screen, which are described in Table E.3.

DISPLAYING OR PRINTING A GRAPH

The options on the Display Graph submenu allow you to create graphs from three sources. Primarily, you will display or print graphs in the formats you defined (through the Edit Graph option) by selecting the Defined Graph Specification option. However, you can also graph the most recent data captured as totals in a report-generator report, which is identified as GMREPORT.PRN, by selecting the Report Generator Totals option.

Table E.3: Fields on the Graph Formatting Screen

Field	Description
Select	Select New Graph to create a new graph or select an existing graph to edit.
Specify the GRAPH name	Enter the name if you are creating a new graph.
Chart Types	Select a type by highlighting it and pressing ↵. Types to choose from are pie (section), line bar, stacked-bar, perspective (3-D) bar, text-mode bar, and text-mode stacked-bar. Perspective bar charts are only available with EGA or VGA monitors.
Display Modes	Select the type of display from those listed.
Chart Title	The name of the default company defined for Graph+Mate reports appears. You can override it for this graph.
Chart Subtitle	The name you gave the graph appears. You can override it with the subtitle you want to appear on a printout.
Application File	Select the DacEasy records you want to use for the graph: G/L Accounts, Customers, Vendors, Inventory Accounts, or Employee Master File.
File Format	The graphic file format appears. Select the fields to graph in the same manner as you select them for file view. Press F10 to save the format.
Low Range	Enter the first record to include in the graph, or press ↵ for the first record.
High Range	Enter the last record to include in the graph, or press ↵ for the last record.
# X fields	Select from the record selection screen that appears. The range it displays is determined by your input in the Low and High Range fields. Use the arrow keys to move around the display, and press the spacebar to select the records to include in the graph. Limit your selection to 10 to 15 records for the best display. Press F10 to save your selections.
Update -Graph Name - into Dictionary ? Y	Press ↵ to record the graph definition. The graph is stored and ready to be displayed or printed.

Most ASCII files end with the extension .PRN.

You can graph data residing in an ASCII file by selecting the External ASCII PRN File option. Enter the directory and path where the file is located, and then enter the external file name.

To display or print a graph, select the Display Graph option from the Graphics Display menu, and then choose the source of the data from the three options on the submenu. Select the name of the graph you want to generate. When asked if there are any changes, either press

↵ to accept the default information for each field or override it. The fields on the graphics display screen are described in Table E.4.

Table E.4: Fields on the Graphics Display Screen

Field	Description
Graph Type	The chart types appear. Press ↵ to accept the default or make another selection.
Display Modes	The default definition appears. Press ↵ to accept it or make another selection.
Graph Printing	Select the printing style: None to display the graph on the screen, Portrait to print lengthwise, or Landscape to print widthwise.

EXPORTING DACEASY FILES TO OTHER SOFTWARE

Through Graph+Mate, you can take information from your DacEasy records, put it into a special file, and then import it into another software application. To export files, select the File Exporting option from the Applications menu. At the prompt for parameters, enter the drive, directory, and subdirectory where the files you want to export are located. The File Exporting menu appears.

To create an export file, select the Edit Export option from the File Exporting menu, and then complete the fields on the screen, which are described in Table E.5.

Table E.5: Fields on the Edit Export File Screen

Field	Description
Select	Select New Export to create a new export file or select an existing export format.
Specify the EXPORT name	Enter the name if you are creating a new export format.
Produce Headings?	Press ↵ to include the column headings in the export file, or enter N to exclude them.
Underline Headings?	If you include headings, press ↵ if you want an underline to follow them in the file. Otherwise, enter N.

Table E.5: Fields on the Edit Export File Screen (continued)

Field	**Description**
Field Delimiter	Use the arrow keys to select from Space, Comma, or Both to indicate how to separate fields in the output file.
Text Delimiter	Select from Double (quotation marks), Single, or None to indicate how to enclose text fields in the output file.
DacEasy File	Select the file you want to export data from: G/L Accounts, Customers, Vendors, Inventory Accounts, Receivables Invoices, Payables Invoices, or Employees.
File Export Format	The format for the export file appears. Select the fields you want to export, and then press F10.
Update - Export Name - into Dictionary ? Y	Press ⏎ to accept the default and record the export definition. The export format is stored and ready to be performed.

After an export file is defined, you can export the selected data. Select the Perform Export option from the File Exporting menu, and then complete the fields on the screen, which are described in Table E.6.

Graph+Mate displays a message when the file has been exported. It can be copied or moved from the export directory to another location or imported into other software programs that accept ASCII files.

Table E.6: Fields on the File Exporting Screen

Field	**Description**
Data Directory	Enter the drive, directory, and subdirectory of the data that you want to export.
Low Range	Enter the first record you want to export, or press ⏎ to start with the first record.
High Range	Enter the last record you want to export, or press ⏎ to end with the last record.
Export Directory	The program supplies the Graph+Mate directory. You can enter an override.
Export File Name	The program supplies EXPORT.PRN. You can use eight characters and a three-character extension to identify your exported file. The extension PRN is standard for ASCII data files.

Index

B

G

I

J

L

N

O

Q

R

S

T

U

V

FREE CATALOG!

Mail us this form today, and we'll send you a full-color catalog of Sybex books.

Name ______

Street ______

City/State/Zip ______

Phone ______

Please supply the name of the Sybex book purchased.

______

How would you rate it?

____ Excellent ____ Very Good ____ Average ____ Poor

Why did you select this particular book?

____ Recommended to me by a friend
____ Recommended to me by store personnel
____ Saw an advertisement in ______
____ Author's reputation
____ Saw in Sybex catalog
____ Required textbook
____ Sybex reputation
____ Read book review in ______
____ In-store display
____ Other ______

Where did you buy it?

____ Bookstore
____ Computer Store or Software Store
____ Catalog (name: ______)
____ Direct from Sybex
____ Other: ______

Did you buy this book with your personal funds?

____Yes ____No

About how many computer books do you buy each year?

____ 1-3 ____ 3-5 ____ 5-7 ____ 7-9 ____ 10+

About how many Sybex books do you own?

____ 1-3 ____ 3-5 ____ 5-7 ____ 7-9 ____ 10+

Please indicate your level of experience with the software covered in this book:

____ Beginner ____ Intermediate ____ Advanced

Which types of software packages do you use regularly?

____ Accounting	____ Databases	____ Networks
____ Amiga	____ Desktop Publishing	____ Operating Systems
____ Apple/Mac	____ File Utilities	____ Spreadsheets
____ CAD	____ Money Management	____ Word Processing
____ Communications	____ Languages	____ Other ________________ (please specify)

Which of the following best describes your job title?

____ Administrative/Secretarial	____ President/CEO
____ Director	____ Manager/Supervisor
____ Engineer/Technician	____ Other ________________ (please specify)

Comments on the weaknesses/strengths of this book: ____________________

____

____

____

____

PLEASE FOLD, SEAL, AND MAIL TO SYBEX

SYBEX, INC.
Department M
2021 CHALLENGER DR.
ALAMEDA, CALIFORNIA USA
94501

SEAL

DACEASY ACCOUNTING VERSION 4 .1 FIRST-LEVEL MENUS

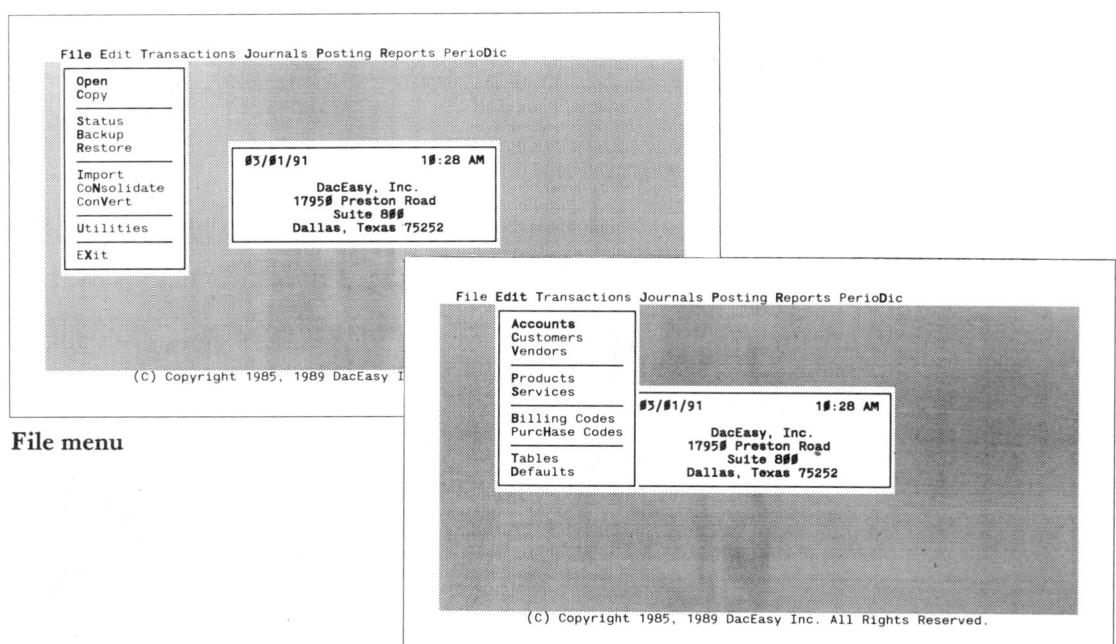

File menu

Edit menu

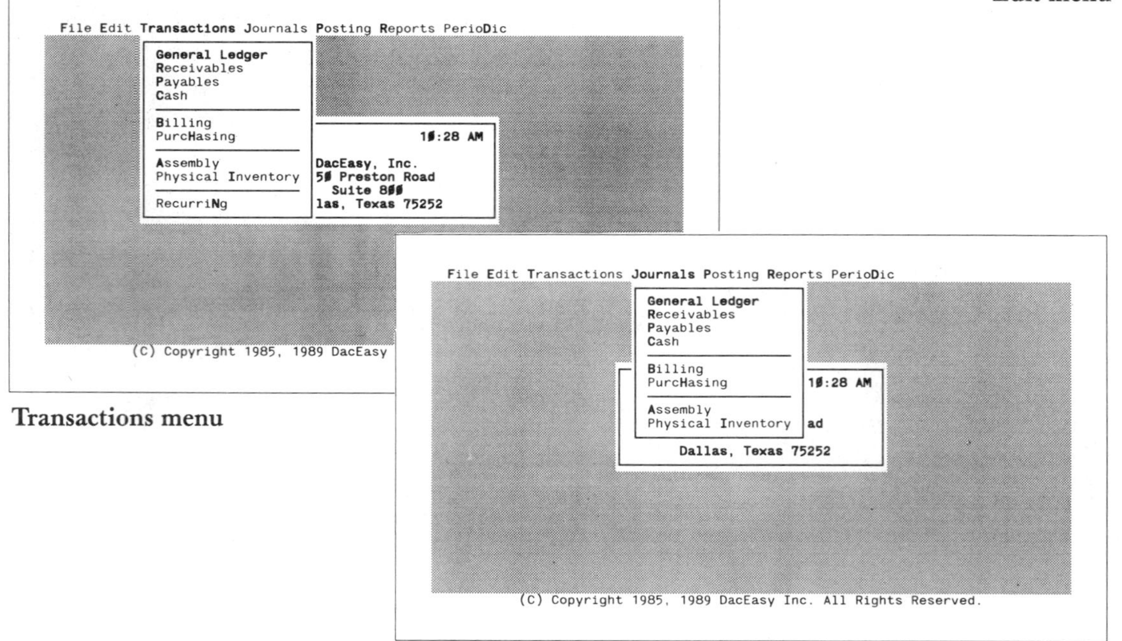

Transactions menu

Journals menu